Month-By-Month
GARDENING
IN
GEORGIA

Month-By-Month GARDENING *IN* GEORGIA

Walter Reeves and Erica Glasener

COOL SPRINGS PRESS

Nashville, Tennessee

A Division of Thomas Nelson, Inc.
www.ThomasNelson.com

Dedication

To my wife, Sandi, my gardening partner forever.
—W. R.

To my Nana, who loved nature and beauty, and whose art continues to inspire me.
—E. L. G.

Acknowledgements

We are grateful for the research and information provided by the dedicated county agents, specialists, and Master Gardeners who tirelessly serve the citizens of this state through The University of Georgia Cooperative Extension Service.

Erica especially thanks Daryl and her family for their loving support.

Erica Glasener
    Month-by-month gardening in Georgia / Erica Glasener, Walter Reeves
    p. cm.
    ISBN 1-888608-27-7 (pbk.: alk.paper)
    1. Gardening -- Georgia I. Reeves, Walter. II. Title.

SB453.2.G4 g3 2001
635'.09758--dc21   2001001049

Published by Cool Springs Press, a Division of Thomas Nelson, Inc., P.O. Box 141000, Nashville, Tennessee 37214.

First printing 2001

Printed in the United States of America
10 9 8

Visit the Thomas Nelson website at: www.thomasnelson.com

Contents

Contents

Basic Horticultural Practices for All Gardeners

Are you instantly skilled at whatever you try to do? Of course not! You practiced long and hard in your parents' car before you were ready to hit the highway. Professional athletes spend their youth mastering the basics of their sport in order to rise to the top of the sports world. Great cooks don't become so by making macaroni and cheese from a box.

Successful gardeners don't become so without experience. Maybe in the past they started a few annuals, planted some seeds, pruned a bush, or dug weeds from their lawn. Each completed task gave them confidence to try another. Many say that they learned the most from their failures, not from their achievements.

Some folks are convinced their thumbs can never be as green as their neighbors'. They look at a beautiful bed of flowers, a pristine lawn, or a neat landscape and persuade themselves that others have some secret they can never share.

In truth, all they lack is *experience*. A basketball player will practice his jumpshot thousands of times. Some shots will go in; some will bounce off the rim; some will fly over the backboard. Still the ballplayer practices, confident that eventually his successes will outnumber his failures.

To be a good gardener, you have to start somewhere. If you were lucky enough to have a parent or neighbor who taught you the basics, GREAT . . . but you still have lots to learn! If you grew up in a tenth-floor apartment and have never planted a plant, GREAT . . . you can learn the basics without having to get rid of any misconceptions.

One of Walter's acquaintances took great pains to have his photo taken while holding a rake in the front yard of his first home. He sent copies to all his friends in New York with the caption "I own a garden tool! I must be a grownup now!" He had never mown a lawn, pruned a shrub, or pulled a weed. Now, years later, his home is just as nice as everyone else's on his block. He bought a mower and some more tools. He learned quickly. He is not the greatest gardener in the world, but he is competent; he knows the basics.

Every gardener needs to know the basics. What follows are some of the skills and techniques you should know in order to grow as you garden.

Testing Your Soil

Plants need adequate nutrients in order to grow properly, and they receive the nutrients from the soil and from the fertilizer you add. In order to know how much fertilizer to add, your soil should be tested at least every two years.

Good gardeners notice when they have different soil types in different areas of their landscape. It is possible that you have the same soil throughout. It might be a dark brown, sandy loam; a gray, sticky clay; or common Georgia red clay. If earth grading was done before your home was built, perhaps the front yard is one soil type and the backyard is another.

Separate samples of soil should be collected from each of your soil types. After you have tested the soil, you can make decisions on how to fertilize each area properly.

Testing the Soil

1 Use a clean trowel and bucket. In each area with different soil, take ten plugs (deep hearty scoops) of soil. A plug should be four to six inches deep so

Basic Horticultural Practices

that soil from the plant root zone will be tested, not the soil on top of the ground. Place the plugs in the bucket.

2 When ten plugs have been collected from an area, mix them together in the bucket. Remove stones, grass, worms, and other materials. Scoop out approximately two 8-ounce cups of soil—this is a representative sample of all the soil in a particular area.

Repeat steps 1 and 2 for each different type of soil in your landscape.

3 Test the soil.

Using a Commercial Kit: Purchase a soil-testing kit from a garden center and read the directions carefully. If you do not understand them, ask a garden center employee or a gardening friend to explain them. Most kits require that you add chemicals to a small sample of soil and water, and wait for a color change. Once the color has developed, it can be compared to a color chart, giving you an estimate of the nutrients available for your plants. Commercial kits are generally easy to use, but the results might not be as accurate as you would like. It takes a sharp eye to compare colors, a

task that is made more difficult by the orange color of Georgia red clay.

Using a Laboratory: The most convenient soil-testing laboratory is usually the University of Georgia Soils Laboratory. Look in the phone book under the government listings for your county. Listed as "Cooperative Extension Service" or "University of Georgia," your county Extension office can give you details on how to bring a soil sample to them. There is a nominal charge, in the range of $4.00 to $8.00, for each sample. The University of Georgia Soils Laboratory will test your soil and send you a written report on the nutrients it contains. The acidity (pH) of the soil will be noted. Fertilizer recommendations are included, along with the amount of lime needed by your soil. A single composite sample of soil can be tested for five different plants that might be growing in that soil type in your landscape. In other words, if you are growing flowers, **Fescue, Azaleas,** and a **Maple** tree in your front yard, specify that your soil should be tested, and recommendations given, for each. The single laboratory charge includes up to five individual tests.

4 Interpret the results: The most important soil-test result is the acidity (pH) of the soil. Add the recommended amount of lime to your soil before worrying about fertilizers. The **commercial** kits will make general recommendations for the amount of fertilizer to use. The **laboratory** will recommend specific amounts of fertilizers. Don't worry if you cannot find the exact fertilizer analysis mentioned in a soil-test result. If 10-10-10 fertilizer is recommended, either 8-8-8 or 13-13-13 can be substituted as long as you use a bit more or a bit less, respectively, than the recommended amount of 10-10-10.

Organic Fertilizer Recommendations

Some gardeners prefer to use plant nutrients that come from natural sources: manure, compost, bloodmeal, fish emulsion, bonemeal, etc. A plant can't tell the difference between nutrients that come from a cow or those that come from a chemical plant—but organic gardeners believe in feeding the soil and allowing the soil to feed their plants. Good arguments can be raised on both sides of the question for the *best* fertilizer sources, but no one disagrees that all plants need nutrients to thrive.

Basic Horticultural Practices

If you receive a soil-test result that recommends synthetic fertilizers, there is no reason you can't convert it to an organic recommendation. The first step is to notice the synthetic fertilizer nutrient ratio. If a fertilizer like 16-4-8 is recommended, the ratio is 4-1-2. Knowing this ratio allows you to combine organic fertilizers to approximate what your plants need.

For example, let's say the soil-test recommendation is: *Use 16-4-8 fertilizer*. You see the nutrient ratio is 4-1-2. Add together the numbers of the organic fertilizers you have available—

Bloodmeal:	12-0-0
Cottonseed meal:	6-2-1
Wood ashes:	0-2-5
Added together:	18-4-6
Nutrient ratio:	4.5-1-1.5
(pretty close to 4-1-2)	

Practical application: Mix ten pounds each of bloodmeal, cottonseed meal, and wood ashes in a wheelbarrow. You now have thirty pounds of the *organic* equivalent of thirty pounds of 16-4-8 synthetic fertilizer.

Understanding the Numbers on a Fertilizer Bag

There are three major nutrients needed by a plant: Nitrogen (N), Phosphorus (P), and Potassium (K). The numbers on a container of fertilizer denote the percentage of N, P, and K inside. For example, a bag of 24-4-8 has 24 percent Nitrogen, 4 percent Phosphorus, and 8 percent Potassium. Thirty-six percent of the bag's content is plant food; the rest is an inert filler, like clay.

1 *What does nitrogen do?*
Nitrogen promotes the growth of roots, stems, and leaves. An appropriate supply of nitrogen gives plants healthy dark-green foliage. Too much nitrogen can cause growth to be too rapid, causing the plant to grow tall and fall over. Excess nitrogen can also delay or prevent flower and fruit formation or make plants more susceptible to disease.

2 *What does phosphorus do?*
Plants store energy in their seeds, roots, and bark, and they need adequate phosphorus in order to flower. Phosphorus is essential for flower, fruit, and seed production. Plants lacking sufficient phosphorus usually have purplish leaves, petioles, and stems. They grow slowly and mature very late.

3 *What does potassium do?*
Potassium is important for the manufacturing of carbohydrates (sugar and starch) by plants. When sufficient potassium is available, plants produce stiff, erect stems, and the plants are more disease-resistant. When insufficient or excess potassium is in the soil, plants contain too much water, are susceptible to cold injury, and growth is reduced.

4 *What do micronutrients do?*
Nitrogen, phosphorus, and potassium are called *macronutrients* because plants need them in significant amounts. Plants also need other chemicals in order to grow and remain healthy. Because smaller amounts of these nutrients are needed, they are called *micronutrients*. Calcium (Ca), magnesium (Mg), iron (Fe), sulfur (S), and many other chemicals are needed in small amounts. A lack of calcium in tomatoes causes the condition known as *blossom end rot*. A lack of iron can cause leaves to turn yellow. Most Georgia soils have enough micronutrients to keep plants healthy. If your soil is very sandy or is all clay, additional micronutrients may be needed. The best way to supply micronutrients is by mixing composted manure, home-made compost, or "enriched" fertilizer with your soil.

Basic Horticultural Practices

5 *What does garden lime do?*
Garden lime raises the pH of soil. Georgia soils tend to be acidic by nature, and regular applications of fertilizer tend to acidify the soil even further. Acid soil ties up many nutrients. They are less *available* to your plants even though they may be physically present in the soil. For this reason, lime is regularly applied to soil to counteract the soil's acidity and raise its pH.

6 *What is pH?*
pH is a numerical measurement of a soil's acidity. The pH number scale ranges from 0 to 14. A number from 0 to 7 indicates acid conditions. A number from 7 to 14 indicates an alkaline soil. Most plants grow best when the soil pH is between 5.5 and 6.5. Some plants, like **Azaleas, Blueberries,** and **Centipede Grass,** tolerate more acidic soil than other plants and usually do not need to be limed.

Preparing a Bed

One of Walter's sharpest memories is the occasion when he presented a newly married couple with a bag of **Daffodil** bulbs.

"What should we do with them?" they asked, wide-eyed.

"Oh, just prepare a bed and plant them!" was Walter's airy reply.

In unison, the two cried out, "Surely we don't have to keep them under our sheets?!"

Just as newlyweds select a cozy bed to share each night, plants must be given a comfortable bed (of a completely different nature) in which to grow. Preparing the bed is a simple but vital job. If you plant bulbs in hard clay, they will never look like the picture on the garden magazine cover. If you install a **Hosta** in full sunshine and sandy soil in south Georgia, you'll have nothing but bleached leaves by July.

Preparing a bed requires a bit of work, but it is a chore that will reward you and your plants for years to come. Plant roots need three things: oxygen, moisture, and nutrients. The magic ingredient that provides these three things is organic matter. Whether you use composted pine bark, animal manure, or compost that you make yourself, it is almost always a good idea to mix organic matter into your existing soil before you plant.

Adding the right amount is important, too. A dusting of rotten leaves added to a bed does no good. Your goal should be to have a bed that is one-third organic matter and two-thirds existing soil.

Preparing a Cozy Bed

1 Use a shovel or rented rototiller to dig up the soil in the location you've chosen. The soil should be loosened to a depth of ten inches.

2 Thoroughly break up the big clods of earth. All clumps should be less than one inch in diameter.

3 Add a layer of organic matter two inches thick to the area you tilled. Mix it deeply and completely with the existing soil.

There is an alternative to adding *only* organic matter to the soil. Expanded shale (PermaTill, see Chemicals, p. 327) can be added to the soil to keep it loose on a long-term basis. Expanded shale does not hold moisture or nutrients very well, but unlike organic matter, it does not disappear from your soil. Mix a two-inch layer of expanded shale plus a one-inch layer of organic matter into your bed if you use this product.

Replacing Organic Matter

Summer heat and Georgia rainfall will slowly cook away the organic matter in your garden soil. A few years after you worked so hard to make good planting beds, they will need another infusion of rich organic matter. This presents a problem if you have a bed of perennials or shrubs that you don't intend to move. The best way to replenish organic matter is to add a one-inch layer of composted manure on top of the soil each January. First rake away any mulch around your plants, add the manure, then cover with fresh mulch. When the soil warms, earthworms will go to work tilling the soil—without any more work on your part!

Composting

The best source of organic matter for your garden is homemade compost. Why is it better than the store-bought stuff? Because it's alive!

Compost is full of tiny fungi, bacteria, and other creatures. These organisms can digest leaves, grass clippings, lettuce leaves, and wood chips. Euphemistically, we say they "break down" these items. In fact, they *eat* and then *excrete* organic materials. As anyone who has changed a baby diaper knows, poop is *sticky*. The sticky excreta of fungi and bacteria is made that way by a substance called *glomalin*. This glomalin glues together the tiny particles of clay in your soil. When tiny grains of soil become big soil granules, the soil becomes soft and loose. Sterilized cow manure can't

do that. Composted wood fiber can't do that. Both are valuable soil amendments . . . but compost is best.

Composting is not rocket science! If you have a corner where two fences meet, pile your fall leaves there. In six months, you'll have compost. In fact, there are just two steps to making compost:

1 PILE IT UP. Compost bins can be purchased, or you can simply make one out of stiff welded-wire fencing. Join the ends of a piece of fencing that is four feet high and ten feet long. The hollow barrel you create is a perfect compost bin. Pile leaves and grass clippings in it during the year. Next spring, lift the bin off the pile and scoop out the rich compost underneath the top layer.

2 LET IT ROT. There is no need for "compost helper" products; Mother Nature will make compost without your help. Experienced composters turn their piles a few times a year to make the process go faster. However, organic matter will decompose whether the pile is turned or not. A good spraying with the garden hose while the leaves are being piled will help keep the pile moist. A shovelful of soil sprinkled over each successive bag of leaves will

introduce all the fungi needed to make perfect compost by next summer.

You can also add grass clippings, raw kitchen vegetables, raked leaves, coffee grounds, and many other things. Eventually compost will happen!

Sunshine *vs.* Shade

Jekyll Island is a great place to sit on a sunny beach during the hot summer. Even the hardiest beach bums, though, know to apply lots of sunscreen before they sit down for a noontime picnic. Brasstown Bald is a magnificent mountain, but even locals don't climb it in January without dressing in their warmest clothing. The point is, people can adapt to their surroundings. In general, plants can't. The location you choose for your plants must match their tolerance for sunshine and other weather conditions.

This is not as hard as it seems. Nurseries do a good job labeling the conditions their plants prefer. Study the plant label before you purchase a plant to make sure it will be happy where you site it.

That said, sometimes nursery labels are less informative than you'd like. What does a sunshine icon on a label mean when it is half darkened? Does it mean the plant prefers con-

Basic Horticultural Practices

stant partial shade or a half-day of full sunshine? Is the label truly accurate for Georgia's intense sunshine conditions? Would the plant be happy in full Ohio sunshine but scorched after a day's worth of Georgia's July heat?

Judging Light Conditions

We realize that sunshine intensity differs across Georgia. Compare the noon sunshine in Savannah to noon sunshine in Blairsville: they're radically different! This is how we define sunshine conditions in Georgia:

Full sunshine in south Georgia is unfiltered sunshine for more than eight hours per day; in north Georgia, it is unfiltered sunshine from morning to night.

Partial shade (moderate shade) in south Georgia is all-day sunshine filtered through high **Pine** or hardwood (**Oak, Maple, Poplar,** etc.) foliage OR three hours of direct sunshine between sunrise and noon followed by shade; in north Georgia, it is sunshine filtered through high **Pine** foliage OR four hours of direct sunshine between sunrise and noon.

Shade in south Georgia is all-day sunshine filtered through dense hardwood foliage OR direct sunshine that hits the plant less than two hours per day; in north Georgia, it is all-day sunshine filtered through scattered hardwoods OR direct sunshine that hits the plant less than three hours per day.

Dense shade means that no direct sunshine hits the plant all day; this might be the shade under a **Southern Magnolia,** or the shade between two houses whose shadows prevent sunshine from hitting the earth at all.

And What About Those Tongue-Twisting Latin Plant Names?

Latin plant names help gardeners know *exactly* which plant they have or want, regardless of the plant's physical appearance. A plant's common name is usually unique, but not always. The plant your neighbor calls **Wild Honeysuckle** is likely not the pestiferous vine—it is probably a native **Azalea.** Neither **Rose of Sharon** nor **Moss Rose** are true roses. Someone just thought they looked like a rose, and the names have been commonly used through the years.

When we want you to know about a specific plant in this book, we use the scientific name so you'll know exactly which one we are describing. You don't have to know or use Latin plant names, but it does help to know that there is a big difference between the magnificent **Dogwood** *Cornus florida* '**Cherokee Princess**' and the sparsely flowering *Cornus florida* 'Transplanted It Out of the Woods Years Ago'!

Summary

Gardening success can be summarized in just three rules:

1 Know your plants.

2 Know your site.

3 Even if you ignore the first two rules, *plant anyway!*

You might have success in spite of yourself or you might suffer failure. Either way, you'll learn and have fun and you will have started down the road to being

A GARDENER IN GEORGIA!

Introduction

Gardening in Georgia is a year-round affair. Gardeners in the northern United States have a long rest each year during their severe winters. Not us! Even in winter there is a day or two each week when something productive can be accomplished in your garden. Our growing season is such that many different plants can be grown in Georgia, from tropical fruit in Hahira to alpine evergreens in Hiawassee.

A beautiful landscape can enhance your home in many ways. Not only does your property value increase when you landscape your home, your house has more curb appeal. Your landscape garden can serve as a retreat from the hectic pace of everyday life or an extension of the indoors, providing a place to entertain friends or dine outdoors. Like any other art form, gardening gives you an opportunity to be creative, whether you simply plant a few pots of brightly colored annuals or develop an elaborate landscape with shrubs, trees, annuals, and perennials, offering something of interest for every season. Gardening is also a stress reliever. Plants don't talk back, and many reward us with fragrant flowers, colorful foliage, and striking bark.

With all the gardening opportunities we enjoy, it is natural to feel a bit overwhelmed. There are weeks in April when it seems that *everything* must be done *now*! That's why we decided to write this book: to help guide you through your garden tasks all year long.

We have divided the book into ten chapters, each devoted to a group of plants we think is important. Each chapter follows the calendar year (January through December) with suggested tasks for each month, such as planning, planting, watering, fertilizing, pest control, and pruning. When possible, we have included lists of plant combinations or plants for special areas, such as ground covers for shade or annual vines with colorful flowers.

In addition to the calendars in each chapter, we provide charts of plants recommended for our region. Our soil, heat, and humidity dictate what can be grown and require that you prepare the soil before you plant. Knowing which plants will thrive, and what they need, is half the battle. We also provide information about using (or not using) pesticides. The section on garden chemicals attempts to give you the information you need when you are deciding whether or not to use a pesticide.

Gardening in Georgia is, above all, a humbling experience. No one can know *everything* about every plant. Rosarians might not know **Rutabagas;** fruit growers might not know a **Ficus** from a **Fothergilla.** Each of us will be an amateur at one thing and an expert at something else. Gardeners who have just begun to learn can be discouraged by failure. Every leafless plant or fruitless **Tomato** seems to signify that the gardener did something *wrong*. Gardeners who have traveled farther down the path, though, think of failure as just one more way to make good compost.

We hope this book helps you find an area in your garden in which you can excel. There is no shame in trying small bits at a time, and there is great enjoyment when your efforts succeed. Read closely, work hard, look for miracles . . . and have a great time gardening in Georgia!

Introduction

Georgia's Gardening Regions

The United States Department of Agriculture has divided the country into hardiness zones based on the lowest temperatures expected in the region. Georgia spreads across two hardiness zones. The area below a line drawn between Columbus and Augusta is zone 8. The area above that line is zone 7. Colder parts of the country have zones with lower numbers. When purchasing a perennial plant or shrub, you will find its care tag often specifies the hardiness zone for which it is best suited.

Always consult plant tags to determine if plants are suited for your weather. If a plant is listed as "Hardy to zone 6," it is assumed that it can withstand any cold temperatures that zone 7 might present. On the other hand, a plant listed for zones 8 to 9 cannot be expected to survive a winter in the mountains without extremely good care!

Garden Tools

Gardening is not a mental exercise. It requires tools to help you accomplish a task quickly or properly. While we occasionally recommend motorized tools such as lawn mowers, aerators, and rototillers, the following list of basic tools should be adequate for you to start gardening with.

Basic tools for the garden or landscape:

1 **Long-handled, round-blade shovel.** The rounded point allows you to push it deeper into the soil than a flat-blade shovel. The long handle gives the leverage needed to lift and turn over the soil.

2 **Handpruners.** The kind with bypass blades usually lasts longer than the type with a blade and anvil, and also makes cleaner cuts on hollow or more herbaceous stems.

3 **Spading fork.** It looks like a pitchfork, but the tines are shorter and wider. Great for digging bulbs or potatoes, a spading fork also penetrates clay soil better than a shovel.

4 **Bow rake (also called an iron rake).** It has short tines on one side attached to a steel frame (the bow). Useful for raking soil smooth.

5 **Hand trowel.** Solid, one-piece models like Corona™ and others last much longer than those with flimsy handles, which are only slightly less expensive.

6 **Leaf rake.** Plastic or metal, they are more useful and quieter than a leaf blower.

7 **Wheelbarrow.** Every time you have to carry a heavy bag of lime from your car or transport a pile of leaves to your compost pile, you'll be glad you have this handy tool.

As your interest in gardening increases, you will probably want to purchase additional tools, depending on the type of gardening you do. To save money, keep an eye out for tools at flea markets or yard sales.

USDA Hardiness Zone Map

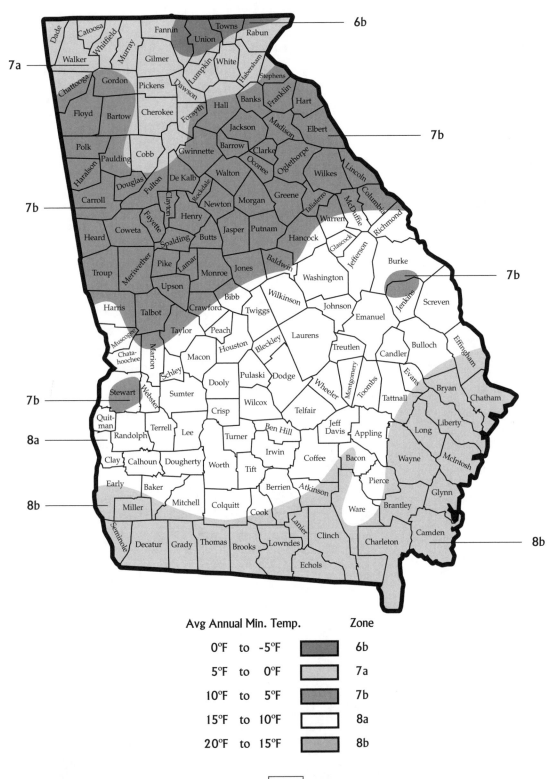

Avg Annual Min. Temp.		Zone
0°F to -5°F		6b
5°F to 0°F		7a
10°F to 5°F		7b
15°F to 10°F		8a
20°F to 15°F		8b

Annuals

Annual flowers are the workhorses of a summer garden. Many perennials bloom for only a few weeks, but annuals can provide colorful flowers for months at a time. As their name implies, annual plants live for only one growing season, although some seem to be perennial because they self-seed each year. Summer annuals, like **Impatiens,** are planted in spring and die with the first frost. Winter annuals, like **Pansies,** are planted in fall and bloom through spring until summer heat sets in.

Most landscapes include both annual and perennial plants, drawing on the strengths of each. While perennials set up housekeeping in one spot for the long haul and may not achieve blooming maturity before a year has passed, annuals have a "live fast, die young" attitude.

There is another class of flowering garden plants that take *two* years to reach maturity. These plants are known as *biennials* because they require a season of growth, followed by a period of rest, in order to produce their blooms. **Foxglove** is an example of a biennial. Seedlings should be planted in early fall in order to accomplish good growth before winter. After a rest during the cold months, the **Foxglove** plant will grow even more before producing its spire of tubular blooms the following spring.

Though they may live in your garden for less than a year, annuals require the same attention to soil preparation as do other plants. See Horticultural Practices, p. 7, to find out how to make the soil ready for planting.

Designing with Annuals

Because annuals are usually inexpensive to purchase or to grow from seed, they are excellent candidates for installation as a broad sweep or drift of color. They can also be used to define the edge of a specific area. If your landscape color seems to be mostly shades of green, annuals break up the color monotony of shrubs, evergreens, trees, and lawns.

Annuals are also excellent for use in patio containers and as temporary cover for an area where you'll later plant perennials or shrubs. Because they bloom for a long period, annuals give you the opportunity to cultivate a long-lasting personal garden spot just for your sentimental favorites or for cut flowers you can bring indoors or share with neighbors.

Purchasing

Flats of annuals can be purchased at garden centers every spring. If you have a large area to plant, it is very easy to grow annuals from seed yourself. You'll find instructions in February, as well as plans for a simple light stand to get the seedlings off to a good start.

Fertilizing

The main purpose of growing annual flowers is to have a long season of bloom. They will need regular feeding. The April calendar details a simple fertilizing schedule to follow. Though they are a bit more expensive, slow-release long-lasting fertilizers really do free you from remembering when to fertilize your beds. Note the October tips on fertilizing winter annuals. Cold soil slows root growth, and using the kinds of fertilizer recommended in the October calendar will make a lot of difference in your winter beds.

Watering

Watering during the year is obviously important, but it can be tricky when watering restrictions are mandated. The Xeriscaping tips in May will help you plan your landscape to accommodate dry weather. Keep in mind that annuals do not need watering every day. If your soil contains plenty of organic matter, a deep irrigation once or twice a week will keep your plants happy.

Removing Flowers: Deadheading

Never forget that flowering plants are not blooming solely for your pleasure. Their purpose is to attract pollinators so the flowers can make seed and reproduce. Once pollinated, a flower sends hormonal signals to the rest of the plant, telling it to quit flowering. You might think that feeding and watering a plant are most important in determining flower quality, but regularly removing faded blooms is almost as important if you want flower-filled beds.

Planning

The lists of annuals at the end of this introduction can be helpful when trying to decide what to plant. We have also collected lists of our favorite annuals for certain situations.

Once you have chosen your annuals, how close to each other should you plant them? In general, annuals should be spaced at the distance of their mature width, which can be determined from the chart at the end of this introduction. In other

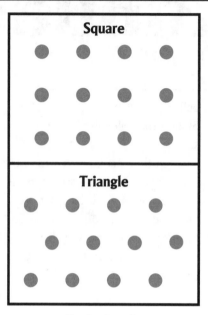

Spacing Annuals

words, if a **Begonia's** mature size is 12 inches, the **Begonias** in a bed should be spaced 12 inches apart, center to center. To achieve a fuller look more quickly, the distance can be reduced a few inches. Ground cover **Petunias** such as **'Purple Wave'** may spread 2 to 3 feet in a season, but they are usually planted 12 to 18 inches apart so the bed will be covered in a short time.

You'll find that planting annuals, and most other plants, in staggered rows will look better to the eye than planting them in rigid ranks. One of the *rules of landscaping* is that an odd number of plants in a grouping looks better than an even number.

Annuals That Plant Themselves

Certain annuals and biennials are known for their ability to self-seed without your help. Often these "volunteers" will appear in your garden year after year for generations. Because they are annuals, most are easy to control and can be easily pulled out if they threaten to take over an area. To take full advantage of these self-seeders, don't be too quick to remove seedlings you don't recognize. Good self-seeders include the following plants:

- **Borage** (*Borago officinalis*) has starry blue flowers and soft gray-green foliage.

- **Bronze Fennel** (*Foeniculum vulgare*) **'Purpureum'** has feathery anise-scented foliage.

- **Common Sunflower** (*Helianthus annuus*) is quite versatile in a landscape, coming in 3-foot and 10-foot selections.

- **Cosmos** (*Cosmos bipinnatus*) comes in many colors and forms. It is used extensively in highway wildflower medians.

- **Impatiens** (*Impatiens wallerana*) are excellent for shady spots that receive little maintenance except a bit of water in summer.

- **Johnny-jump-up** (*Viola tricolor*) has purple-and-yellow spring flowers that look like **Pansy** blooms.

- **Larkspur** (*Consolida ambigua*) is a good substitute for **Delphinium,** and is much easier to grow in Georgia.

- *Lobularia maritima* is a ground-hugger with tiny honey-scented white flowers.

- **Love-in-a-mist** (*Nigella damascena*) blooms quickly in spring, but plants dry up in summer.

- **Melampodium** (*Melampodium paludosum*) is an attractive annual covered by yellow flowers throughout the summer.

- **Mexican Heather** (*Cuphea hyssopifolia*) has tiny purple or white flowers scattered along slightly arching stems.

- **Perilla** (*Perilla frutescens*) has purple foliage that stands out against green backgrounds; it can be invasive.

- **Shirley Poppy** (*Papaver rhoeas*) has red, pink, or white flowers on 2- to 5-foot stems. Excess seedlings can be removed once recognized.

- **Spider Flower** (*Cleome hasslerana*) has spiky pink/purple flowers that sit atop wiry 3- to 5-foot-tall stems.

- **Wheat Celosia** (*Celosia spicata*) is almost grasslike in appearance—**'Flamingo Feather'** and **'Flamingo Purple'** are excellent passalong plants.

Annuals for Cut Flowers

One of the pleasures of growing flowers is having some to bring indoors or to share with neighbors. Some gardeners maintain showy beds of landscape annuals and a private, separate bed of flowers for cutting, so that landscape color will not be reduced when blooms are removed from the cutting garden. The following annuals produce wonderful flowers that you can enjoy in arrangements indoors:

Ageratum	Marigold
Bachelor's Buttons	Phlox
	Salvia
Calendula	Scabiosa
Celosia	Snapdragon
Cleome	Stock
Cosmos	Strawflower
Dianthus	Sweetpea
Gomphrena	Zinnia

Planting for Pollinators

An environmental tragedy has quietly occurred in Georgia in the last decade: the wild honeybee population has been decimated due to mite pests. Many flowers and vegetables depend on bees and other insects to move pollen from flower to flower. The insects don't realize they are pollinating the plants they visit—they're just looking for food in the flowers. You can help the fruit, vegetable, and flowering plants in your neighborhood by planting a pollinator-friendly flower garden. Bumblebees, solitary bees, pollinating wasps, and other insects will try to fill in for honeybees. It is important to have something blooming almost year-round in order to attract these beneficial insects. The following list of plants that attract pollinators includes both woody and herbaceous plants and their monthly bloom times:

February: **Redbud**

March: **Carolina Jessamine**

April: **Ajuga, Crimson Clover**

May: **Schip Laurel, Otto Luyken Laurel**

June: **Nandina**

July: **Beebalm, Chaste Tree, Sunflower**

August: *Verbena bonariensis*, **Butterfly Bush, Glossy Abelia**

September: **Butterfly Weed**

October: **Mexican Sage, Pineapple Sage**

November: **Aster**

Annuals Good for Drying

Some annuals are known for their good looks as dried flowers in winter as well as for their blooms in summer. Drying is easy—just cut the blooms after they dry in the morning, and hang them upside

Annuals

down in a warm, dark place for a few weeks. The following annuals have attractive dried flowers:

Celosia	Money Plant
Chinese Lantern	Statice
Globe Amaranth	Strawflower

Annuals for the Coast

Coastal gardens require annuals that are sun-tolerant, wind-tolerant, and sometimes salt spray–tolerant. The following plants are good for seaside conditions:

- **Cape Plumbago** *Plumbago auriculata*

- **Common Lantana** *Lantana camara*

- **Creeping Zinnia** *Santivalia procumbens*

- **Dusty Miller** *Senecio cineraria*

- **Hibiscus** *Hibiscus rosa-sinensis*

- **Lily-of-the-Nile** *Agapanthus africanus*

- **Moss Rose** *Portulaca grandiflora*

Annuals Satisfactory for Most Areas of Georgia

The following is a list of annuals that are satisfactory for most areas of Georgia. The information was taken with permission from "Flowering Annuals for Georgia Gardens," a publication of The University of Georgia College of Agricultural and Environmental Sciences compiled by Dr. Paul Thomas, Extension Horticulturist. It is by no means complete, as many lesser-known annuals also grow well in Georgia. The plants are listed alphabetically by common name with additional common name(s) in parentheses.

Ageratum *Ageratum houstonianum* (Floss Flower). Most varieties now offered in the trade are compact and range in height from 6 to 12 inches. Blues predominate, but white and magenta varieties are available. Tall cutting varieties are also available.

Alyssum *Lobularia maritima* (Sweet Alyssum). A low-growing (4 to 8 inches), spreading plant, **Alyssum** blooms from late spring until frost. Colors range from white to rose to purple. **Alyssum** may decline in midsummer due to extreme heat.

Amaranth *Amaranthus caudatus* (Love-lies-bleeding, Purple-tassel Flower, Summer Poinsettia). *A. tricolor* (Joseph's Coat). **Amaranth** is grown for its highly colored foliage. *A. caudatus* varieties range in height from 3 to 5 feet, terminating in vividly colored foliage and long tassels. *A. tricolor* varieties are more highly branched and range in height from 1 to 4 feet.

Aster *Callistephus chinensis* (China Aster, Annual Aster). Plants range in height from 6 inches to 3 feet. Taller varieties require staking. It is an excellent cut flower, available in almost all colors. **Aster** is subject to many insect and disease problems. Do not confuse **Callistephus** with the true **Asters** (many of which are dependable perennials).

Baby's Breath *Gypsophilia elegans*. White, rose, and purple varieties are available. Plants form round clumps 1 to 2 feet high. They bloom only about six weeks; successive plantings are necessary to ensure season-long flowers. Do not confuse with *G. paniculata* (Perennial Baby's Breath).

Annuals

Balloon Vine *Cardiospermum halicacabum.* **Balloon Vine** is a woody perennial vine usually grown as an annual for its showy fruit. It is useful for quick cover on fences and trellises.

Balsam Apple *Momordica balsamina.* A member of the **Cucumber** family, **Balsam Apple** is a fast-growing vine. The orange fruit, up to 3 inches long, is edible.

Balsam. See **Impatiens.**

Basil *Ocimum basilicum* (Sweet Basil, Common Basil). Grown principally as a culinary herb, several varieties have been developed for ornamental use. Most produce plants 1 to 2 feet high, and some have purple foliage.

Begonia *Begonia* Semperflorens Group (Wax Begonia, Fibrous-rooted Begonia). One of the most popular bedding plants, **Begonias** flower from spring until frost. Colors range from white to pink to vivid red. Some varieties have bronze foliage and some green leaves variegated with white. Some varieties are more sun-tolerant than others. *B.* × *tuberhybrida* (Tuberous Begonia) is also grown, but is not as well suited for landscape use in the South.

Bells of Ireland *Moluccella laevis.* This plant is grown for its shell-like green calyx; the true flower is actually rather inconspicuous. Erect plants are 2 to 3 feet high. The plant is grown primarily as a cut flower for fresh or dried use, but is also used in mixed borders.

Browallia *Browallia speciosa* (Amethyst Flower, Sapphire Flower). Plants range in height from about 6 to 18 inches, depending on variety. Colors range from white through a variety of pale to dark blues. **Browallia** grows best in partial shade.

Calendula *Calendula officinalis* (Pot Marigold). Varieties range in height from 1 to 2 feet. Yellow and gold predominate in the color range. A half-hardy annual, **Calendula** performs poorly under hot conditions, but is good for early- and late-season color.

Calliopsis *Coreopsis basalis.* **Calliopsis** is an easy-to-grow annual about 18 inches high with numerous yellow flowers. This species is not as commonly grown as are the perennials *Coreopsis lanceolata* and *C. verticillata.*

Canary Bird Vine. See **Nasturtium.**

Candytuft *Iberis umbellata.* Several colors are available in addition to the familiar white. Plants have a mat-like habit. **Annual Candytuft** is not as commonly used as *I. sempervirens* (Perennial Candytuft).

Celosia *Celosia cristata* (Cockscomb). Many new varieties of **Celosia** have been developed in recent years. Heights range from $1/2$ to $2^{1}/_{2}$ feet. Colors range from cream to yellow, gold, pink, and red. Flower types vary from convoluted combs to feathery spikes. Some varieties have bronze foliage.

Chinese Lantern *Physalis alkekengi* (Japanese Lantern). **Chinese Lantern** is grown primarily for its 2-inch orange-red calyx, which is useful in dried arrangements.

Annuals

Chrysanthemum *Chrysanthemum* × *morifolium*. **Chrysanthemum** is usually thought of as a perennial and is often grown for fall color; all colors except blue are available. Many varieties, however, are not reliably winter hardy and are treated as annuals. Some seed-propagated varieties flower the first year.

Cleome *Cleome hasslerana* (Spider Plant). The plant is useful for background and screening. Varieties range in height from 3 to 5 feet, and in color from white to pink to lilac. Plants grow under poor conditions, but require ample moisture and fertilizing for vigorous growth. **Cleome** reseeds prolifically.

Coleus *Coleus* × *hybridus*. An excellent choice for shady locations, although some varieties are sun-tolerant. Heights range from 1 to 3 feet, depending on variety and conditions. **Coleus** is grown for its colorful foliage; many varieties also have deeply lobed or cut margins. Flower spikes should be removed as they appear.

Cornflower *Centaurea cyanus* (Bachelor's Buttons). The species is naturalized in much of Georgia and is considered a weed by farmers. Because of its short bloom season, it should probably be relegated to the cut-flower garden or naturalized areas. Several varieties are available in addition to the common blue. *C. montana* (Perennial Bachelor's Buttons) may be more useful in the landscape.

Cosmos *Cosmos sulphureus. C. bipinnatus*. Ranging in height from 1 to 4 feet, **Cosmos** plants are among the easiest annuals to grow. Taller varieties have a tendency to fall over and may require staking. *C. sulphureus* varieties are predominantly yellow and gold; *C. bipinnatus* varieties are white to pink to crimson.

Cup-and-Saucer Vine *Cobaea scandens*. A strong climbing vine, it flowers on 10-inch-long peduncles; the flowers are violet to greenish-purple. A white variety is also available.

Cypress Vine. See **Morning Glory.**

Dahlia *Dahlia pinnata*. Most seed-grown varieties for landscape use are dwarf types ranging in height from $1^1/_2$ to 2 feet. The taller, exhibition types are usually grown from tubers, require staking, and should generally be relegated to the cut-flower garden. Although often listed as *D. pinnata*, many of the available varieties are actually hybrids.

Dianthus *Dianthus chinensis* (Pinks). *D. chinensis* is a half-hardy annual which will sometimes overwinter. Most varieties range in height from 6 to 12 inches. They grow best under cool conditions and may slump in midsummer. White, pink, and red predominate in the color range. Do not confuse this species with *D. caryophyllus* (Carnation), *D. barbatus* (Sweet William), or *D. plumarius*, all of which are perennials.

Dusty Miller *Senecio cineraria*. **Dusty Miller** is grown principally for its whitish-silver, woolly leaves. Varieties range in height from 6 to 12 inches. Daisy-like cream or yellow flowers are produced in late summer.

Annuals

Forget-me-not *Myosotis sylvatica. Cynoglossum amabile* (Chinese Forget-me-not). The familiar tiny sky-blue flowers combine nicely with a variety of other plants, particularly spring bulbs. More correctly termed a biennial, it seeds freely. White and rose-colored varieties are also available.

Four-o'-clock *Mirabilis jalapa*. Plants form a bushy, shrublike mass 1½ to 3 feet high. The fragrant flowers, which open in late afternoon, are white, red, yellow, pink, or striped.

Foxglove *Digitalis purpurea*. Most **Digitalis** are biennials, and a few are true perennials. Some varieties will flower the first year from seed. Height ranges from 2 to 5 feet depending on variety. A wide variety of colors are available, mostly pastel shades.

Gaillardia *Gaillardia pulchella* (Blanket Flower). **Gaillardia** is considerably more heat- and drought-tolerant than most annuals. A number of varieties are available, ranging in color from yellow to red. Height ranges from 1 to 2½ feet.

Gazania *Gazania rigens*. A perennial often treated as an annual, **Gazania** is a good choice for hot, dry locations. Plants range from 6 to 12 inches in height with daisylike yellow, gold, orange, pink, or red flowers. It is not very tolerant of wet soils.

Geranium *Pelargonium* × *hortorum. Pelargonium peltatum* (Ivy-leaved Geranium). Geraniums have become very popular bedding plants, particularly now that many seed-propagated varieties are available. Colors range from white to pink, salmon, and red. **Ivy-leaved Geraniums** are popular for hanging baskets and windowboxes. Do not confuse **Pelargonium** with the true perennial **Geraniums,** many of which are cultivated.

Gomphrena *Gomphrena globosa* (Globe Amaranth). **Gomphrena** is a little-used annual that deserves more widespread use. It is drought- and weather-resistant. Plants range in height from 8 to 24 inches. Colors range from white to rose to purple.

Hibiscus *Hibiscus moscheutos* (Rose Mallow, Mallow Rose, Swamp Mallow). Grown primarily for its large flowers (6 to 12 inches wide), the plant forms a large (3- to 8-foot) shrub. White, pink, and red **Hibiscus** are available. The plant is actually a herbaceous perennial and will overwinter in Georgia. Do not confuse this **Hibiscus** with *H. syriacus* (Althea), a woody deciduous shrub common in the landscape, or with *H. rosa-sinensis* (Chinese Hibiscus), a tropical **Hibiscus** that is not hardy in Georgia winters.

Hollyhock *Alcea rosea*. Most **Hollyhocks** are biennials useful in the background or border where a tall, upright habit is desired. Nearly all colors are available. Several varieties flower the first year from seed.

Impatiens *Impatiens wallerana* (Sultana). *Impatiens balsamina* (Balsam, Touch-me-not). **Impatiens** are one of the most popular bedding plants in America, providing continuous flowering from spring until fall. Almost all colors except blue are available in varieties ranging in height from 6 inches to 2 or 3 feet. Impatiens generally do

Annuals

best in shade, but many varieties are sun-tolerant if given adequate moisture. **Balsam** is erect in growth habit, ranging in height from 1 to 3 feet. When ripe, the seedpods burst upon touching, hence the common name **Touch-me-not.**

Kochia *Kochia scoparia trichophylla* (Summer Cypress, Burning Bush, Firebush). **Kochia** is grown for its fine-textured foliage which turns red in fall. Plants grow to a height of 2 to 3 feet and are useful for low, temporary hedges. It has potential for weed problems.

Larkspur *Delphinium* and *Consolida* species and hybrids. **Larkspur** is an old garden favorite for providing tall, spiky effects in the garden, and is frequently used as cut flowers. The tall hybrid perennial **Delphiniums** usually perform poorly in the Southeast, but the **Larkspur** types do well.

Lobelia *Lobelia erinus*. Many **Lobelias** are cultivated, including many perennial species. The most popular annual **Lobelia** is *L. erinus*. In sunny locations, it is dense and compact; in shady locations it tends to spread. Available in a variety of blues and purple-reds, annual **Lobelia** flowers best under cooler conditions.

Marigold *Tagetes erecta* (African Marigold). *T. patula* (French Marigold). *T.* species and hybrids. **Marigolds** are a staple annual in Georgia gardens. Many varieties are available, primarily in shades of yellow, gold, orange, and mahogany red. The **African Marigolds** have larger flowers than do the **French Marigolds**. Triploid Marigolds are hybrids of the two species. Heights range from 6 to 36 inches.

Melampodium *Melampodium paludosum*. This is a wonderfully easy annual to grow from seed. It is tough, one of the most drought-resistant and disease-free annuals for poor-soil locations. One plant can form a 3-foot mound of dime-sized yellow flowers. It blooms from spring through summer, and on until frost. It is also a rampant reseeder, so do not put this plant in your best garden areas.

Money Plant *Lunaria annua* (Dollar Plant). Actually a biennial, **Money Plant** is grown primarily for use in dried floral arrangements. It also provides early-spring color—white, pink, and purple. It reseeds readily and can become weedy.

Monkey Flower *Mimulus* × *hybridus*. **Monkey Flower** is a less common half-hardy annual that probably deserves more widespread use. Its cultural requirements are similar to those of the **Pansy.** It is not heat-tolerant and may not survive the summer but is valuable for early-season color.

Moonflower. See **Morning Glory.**

Morning Glory *Ipomoea purpurea. I. quamoclit* (Cypress Vine, Cardinal Climber). *I. alba* (Moon Vine). All are vigorous vines useful for fast coverage. **Morning Glory** is often considered a weed, but many cultivated varieties are available. **Cypress Vine** has delicate fernlike foliage and small red flowers. **Moon Vine** is grown for its large, fragrant nocturnal flowers.

Nasturtium *Tropaeolum majus. T. peregrium* (Canary Bird Vine). **Nasturtium** is an old garden favorite with a reputation for thriving in poor sites where other annuals fail. Bush and trailing types

Annuals

are available, ranging in height from 1 to 6 feet. Colors range from white to yellow, orange, and red. The flowers and leaves are edible. **Canary Bird Vine** is a fast-growing vine suitable for fast coverage.

Nicotiana *Nicotiana alata* **(Flowering Tobacco, Ornamental Tobacco).** In addition to coming in a rich variety of colors–white, lavender, crimson, maroon, green, pink, lime, and yellow–the flowers are fragrant. Varieties range in height from 1 to 3 feet.

Ornamental Kale (Cabbage) *Brassica oleracea.* Plants form nearly perfect circular rosettes of leaves with centers tinged with pink, red, or purple. It is grown for its foliage. Plants are usually set in fall but are not reliably winter hardy in all parts of the state.

Ornamental Pepper *Capsicum annuum. Solanum pseudocapsicum* **(Jerusalem Cherry). Ornamental Peppers** are grown for their highly colored elongated fruit (pods), which range in color from yellow, orange, red, and purple to near-black. Multiple colors are often present on the same plant. The fruits are extremely hot to the tongue and should be used with caution around children. **Jerusalem Cherry** is similar in appearance except that the fruit is round and poisonous if eaten.

Pansy *Viola × wittrockiana.* **Pansies** are the most popular hardy annual grown in Georgia. Most are planted in the fall and produce some flowers in fall and winter followed by peak flowering in spring; established plants can be planted in early spring. Nearly all colors are available. The smaller-flowered multiflora types are generally more satisfactory for landscape use than the giant-flowered types.

Petunia *Petunia × hybrida.* **Petunias** remain a popular flowering annual. They are heat-tolerant, but require ample moisture and fertility to thrive. Virtually all colors are available. Several flower forms are also available, including fully double types. The single multiflora varieties are generally best for landscape use. It is a half-hardy annual that performs particularly well along the coast.

Phlox *Phlox drummondii* **(Annual Phlox, Drummond Phlox).** Many species of **Phlox** are cultivated, and many are perennials. **Annual Phlox** is a half-hardy annual useful for early-season color. It typically slumps in midsummer, but may reflower strongly in fall. Many colors are available.

Polka-dot Plant *Hypoestes phyllostachya* **(Pink Polka-dot Plant, Freckle Face). Polka-dot Plant** is grown principally for its unique speckled foliage.

Poppy *Eschscholzia californica* **(California Poppy).** *Papaver nudicale* **(Iceland Poppy).** *P. rhoeas* **(Shirley Poppy).** These poppies are excellent annuals for naturalizing. Seeds are usually sown in late fall or early spring for early blooms. Many colors are available.

Portulaca *Portulaca grandiflora* **(Moss Rose, Rose Moss).** Few annuals can match the performance of this low-growing, spreading plant in hot, dry locations. A wide variety of colors is available in single and double flowers. *P. oleracea,* a close relative, is often grown in hanging baskets.

Annuals

Purple Fountain Grass *Pennisetum setaceum* is a striking ornamental grass that does well in Georgia landscapes. The plant's foliage is tinted with a rose to purple-bronze cast when grown in full sun and provides wonderful fall and winter color to otherwise barren landscapes. Commonly propagated by division or seed, this grass will not overwinter when soil temperatures reach freezing.

Salvia *Salvia splendens* (Scarlet Sage, Red Salvia). *S. farinacea* (Blue Salvia, Mealy-cup Salvia). **Salvia** is a garden staple, ranging in height from 10 to 30 inches. In addition to the familiar red, numerous other colors, including cream, pink, and violet-purple, are available. **Blue Salvia,** a perennial, is often used as an annual.

Scaevola *Scaevola aemula*. **Scaveola** is a blue-flowering, semi-succulent leafed plant that does well in hanging baskets or as a fast-growing ground cover. The blue-and-white flowers are prolific from spring until frost. The cultivar **'Blue Wonder'** is patented and can be found at better garden centers. The species is well adapted to Georgia and has very few pest or disease problems.

Scarlet Runner Bean *Phaseolus coccineus*. **Scarlet Runner Bean** is an edible bean also grown as an ornamental for its bright-red flowers.

Snapdragon *Anthirrhinum majus*. Many varieties and colors are available, ranging in height from 6 to 36 inches. The taller varieties require staking and are grown principally as cut flowers.

Snow On The Mountain *Euphorbia marginata* (Ghostweed). **Snow On The Mountain** is an erect annual ranging in height from 2 to 4 feet. It is tolerant of hot, dry locations. The milky sap may cause dermatitis.

Statice *Limonium sinuatum*. **Annual Statice** is grown primarily as a cut flower. The flowers dry easily, and many colors are available. Several perennial **Statice** species are cultivated.

Stock *Matthiola incana*. Widely grown as a cut flower and for early color, a wide range of colors is available. Varieties range in height from 1 to $2^1/_2$ feet. Stock is not particularly heat-tolerant.

Strawflower *Helichrysum bracteatum*. **Strawflower** is grown primarily as a fresh-cut or dried flower. Flowers dry easily by hanging upside down in a dry, shady place. Varieties range in height from 1 to 3 feet, with flowers 1 to 2 inches in diameter.

Sunflower *Helianthus annuus*. Dwarf varieties of **Sunflower** are available, but the taller (up to 10 feet) varieties are more common. Blossoms and seedheads may be more than a foot across. Soils must drain well and must be moist and rich for maximum growth. **Sunflower** is an important commercial seed and oil crop.

Sweetpea *Lathyrus odoratus*. **Sweetpea** is grown primarily for its fragrant colorful flowers, which make good cut flowers. Bush and climbing types are available. The climbing types can be used on fences and trellises. **Sweetpea** grows best under cool conditions.

Annuals

Thunbergia *Thunbergia alata* (Black-eyed Susan Vine). **Thunbergia** is a vigorous climbing vine suitable for fast coverage. Flower color ranges from white to yellow and orange.

Tithonia *Tithonia rotundifolia* (Mexican Sunflower). Tithonia is a rugged annual suitable for hot and sunny locations. Ranging in height from 4 to 6 feet, it is used principally for backgrounds and screens. The flowers, orange-red in color, are **Zinnia**-like in appearance. It attracts swallowtail butterflies.

Torenia *Torenia fournieri* (Wishbone Flower, Bluewings). **Torenia** grows best in light shade but will tolerate sun and higher temperatures if given adequate moisture. It is a compact plant 6 to 12 inches high, and its flower color ranges from white to blue.

Verbena *Verbena × hybrida*. **Verbena** is a dependable summer annual available in a wide variety of colors, as bush and spreading types. Flowering may cease under hot, dry conditions but continues when conditions moderate. Some perennial species are also cultivated.

Vinca *Catharanthus roseus* (Madagascar Periwinkle). With improved varieties and additional colors, **Vinca** has become a popular annual in the South. It is heat- and drought-tolerant, and grows well on poor soils. Do not confuse **Catharanthus** with the true **Vincas, *V. minor*** and ***V. major***, which are evergreen perennial ground cover vines.

Wallflower *Erysimum asperum* (Cheiranthus). Colors range from cream to yellow, and pink to maroon. **Wallflower** is usually planted in the fall for spring flowering. Technically a perennial, modern strains are short-lived under Southern conditions and are usually treated as biennials or hardy annuals.

Zinnia *Zinnia elegans.* Zinnia is a versatile annual. The plants grow well under hot, sunny conditions but need ample moisture to thrive. They range in height from 6 to 36 inches and are available in many different colors and flowers. **Creeping Zinnia** is a reliable annual for hot, dry areas, with yellow flowers that resemble small **Zinnias.** The plants have a spreading habit and are useful annual ground covers.

Quick Reference to Common Annuals

Name	Height[1] (in.)	Spacing[2] (in.)	Color[3]	Exposure[4] SU	S-S	SH
Ageratum	6–24	12	WB	*	*	
Alyssum	4–8	12	WPL	*	*	
Amaranth	12–60	12–24	F	*	*	
Aster	6–36	12–18	All	*		
Baby's Breath	12–24	12–24	WPL	*	*	
Balloon Vine	Vine	——	F	*	*	
Balsam	12–36	12	—B		*	*
Balsam Apple	Vine	——	F	*	*	
Basil	12–24	12–24	F	*		
Begonia	6–12	12	WPR	*	*	*
Bells of Ireland	24–36	12–18	F	*	*	*
Browallia	6–18	12	WB		*	*
Calendula	12–24	12	YGO	*		
Calliopsis	18	12	Y	*		
Canary Bird Vine	Vine	——	Y	*		
Candytuft	8–12	12	WPRL	*	*	*
Castor Bean	60–120	24–36	F	*		
Celosia	6–30	12	—B	*		
Chinese Lantern	18–24	12	F	*		
Chrysanthemum	12–24	12–24	—B	*		
Cleome	36–60	12–24	WPL	*		
Coleus	12–36	12	F		*	*
Cornflower	12–36	12	WPRBL	*		
Cosmos	12–48	12	YGP	*		
Cup-and-saucer Vine	Vine	——	LW	*	*	
Cypress Vine	Vine	——	R	*		
Dahlia	18–72	12–36	All	*		
Dianthus	6–12	12	—B	*		
Dusty Miller	6–12	12	F	*		
Forget-me-not	6–12	12	BWP	*	*	
Four-o'-clock	18–36	12–24	WRYP	*		
Foxglove	24–60	12–24	—B	*	*	
Gaillardia	12–30	12	YGR	*		
Gazania	6–12	12	YGPRO	*		
Geranium	12–24	12	—B —Y	*	*	
Gomphrena	8–24	12	WPL	*		
Hibiscus	36–96	24–36	—B —Y	*		
Hollyhock	12–72	12–24	All	*		
Impatiens	6–36	12	—B	*	*	*
Kochia	24–36	12–24	F	*		
Larkspur	24–36	6–12	BPWL	*		

Quick Reference to Common Annuals

Name	Height[1] (in.)	Spacing[2] (in.)	Color[3]	Exposure[4] SU	S-S	SH
Lobelia	3–6	6–12	BLR	*	*	*
Marigold	6–36	12–24	YGRO	*		
Melampodium	12–24	12–18	Y	*		
Money Plant	12–36	12	F	*	*	
Monkey Flower	6	6–12	YR		*	*
Moon Vine	Vine	——	W	*	*	
Morning Glory	Vine	——	—Y—G	*		
Nasturtium	12–72	12–24	YORW	*	*	
Nicotiana	12–36	12–24	—B	*	*	
Ornamental Kale	6–12	18–24	F	*		
Ornamental Pepper	6–12	6–18	F	*		
Pansy	6	6–10	All	*	*	
Petunia	6–12	12–18	All	*		
Phlox	6–12	12	All	*	*	
Polka-dot Plant	12–18	12	F	*	*	
Poppy	12–24	6–12	All	*	*	
Portulaca	1–3	12	—B	*		
Purple Fountain Grass	30–48	12–24	F	*		
Salvia	10–30	12–18	RWBPL	*	*	
Scaevola	4–8	10–20	B	*		
Scarlet Runner Bean	Vine	——	R	*		
Snapdragon	6–36	12	—B	*	*	
Snow On The Mountain	24–48	12–24	F	*		
Statice	18–24	12–24	—R	*		
Stock	12–30	12–24	All	*		
Strawflower	12–36	12–24	YG	*		
Sunflower	24–120	24–36	YG	*		
Sweetpea	12–96	6–12	All	*		
Thunbergia	Vine	——	WYGO	*	*	
Tithonia	48–72	24–36	R	*		
Torenia	6–12	6–12	WB		*	*
Verbena	6–12	12	All	*	S-S	
Vinca	6–18	12	WPL	*	*	
Wallflower	6–12	12	WPRY	*		
Zinnia	6–36	12–24	—B	*		
Zinnia linearis	12–18	12–18	O	*		

[1] Height may vary considerably among varieties.
[2] Spacing depends on ultimate size of plant and effect desired.
[3] G = gold, W = white, P = pink, Y = yellow, R = red, B = blue, L = lavender, O = orange, A = all colors,
   — = one or two colors are absent, all others represented, F = grown for foliage or fruit.
[4] SU = full sun, S-S = semi-shade (filtered light or protection from midday and afternoon sun), SH = shade.

Planning

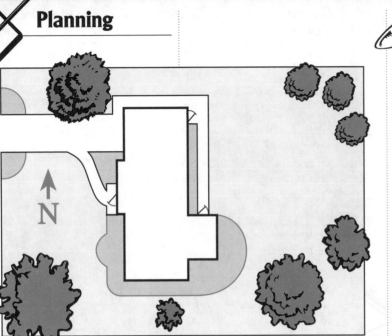

Although the weather is a mixture of chilly and cold now, this is an excellent time to plan how you will use annuals in your landscape this year.

1 *Sketch* a rough map of your property. Include your home plus existing large trees, shrubs, and flower beds. Make several copies of the sketch at a copy center.

2 Use colored pencils to shade the areas where you want annual flowers to provide landscape color. Remember that a mass of color in one spot is much more effective than a mixed "polka-dot" planting of several flower colors.

3 Indicate sunny and shady areas—this knowledge will dictate which annuals you can plant in those spots.

A word about color combinations: Professional garden designers spend hours looking for just the right flower color or hue to match a home's paint, or its shutters, or an adjoining bed of perennial blooms. While a carefully planned color combination can be a visual knockout, don't spend too much time aiming for perfection. Nature has designed flowers to look pleasant in combination with almost any other color. Until you have mastered the skills of raising healthy plants almost without fail, concentrate on the simple design ideas mentioned above, and leave the agonizing to those who are paid for their expertise.

Planting

In south Georgia, colorful annuals can be planted even when the weather is cold. Flowering cool-season plants make an immediate impact in a bare landscape.

In north Georgia, winter annuals can be planted as long as daytime temperatures for the next few days are predicted to be above 40 degrees Fahrenheit accompanied by bright sunshine.

- *Plant* **Dianthus, Pansy, Viola, Snapdragon, English Daisy, Ornamental Kale,** and **Parsley.** All prefer a sunny spot. (See Annuals, October, for special planting directions.)

- *Plant* on sunny days, when the soil is more likely to be warm, and *water* the plants immediately.

- Purchase plants in **3-inch** or larger pots so blooms will continue to appear (plants in smaller containers will stop blooming as they try to establish roots).

- *Do not* install "six-pack" plants now. They are too small to survive the cold temperatures and wind that surely will occur between now and spring.

Care for Your Annuals

Don't worry if **Pansy** leaves look pitiful in the morning; they will recuperate by noon as moisture fills the leaves. **Pansies** protect themselves during cold weather by wilting their leaves. Other plants use a variety of coping mechanisms.

Scatter pine straw loosely over flower beds if cold, windy weather is predicted. When daytime temperatures are above 40 degrees Fahrenheit, lift the straw off the plants and use it for mulch around nearby shrubs.

Watering

If the soil is frozen or dry, the roots of winter annuals cannot absorb the moisture they need. *Test* soil moisture weekly by digging 4 inches into the ground and squeezing a lump of soil in your palm. If it is dry and crumbly, water is needed.

Water your flower beds as needed so moisture is available when plant roots require it after cold nights.

Fertilizing

Fertilize **Pansies** and other cool-season annuals with a product containing nitrate nitrogen (see Annuals, October).

Pest Control

Visit your flower beds each week to look for weeds such as chickweed, bittercress, and henbit. Pull weeds by hand, put them into a container, and *remove* them from the garden. This will eliminate the possibility of weed seeds being dropped onto the soil. Suppress further weed development by mulching with pine straw or pine bark mini-nuggets.

See Annuals, September, for information about preventing weeds with a pre-emergent herbicide.

Grooming

Remove faded blooms from plants as you notice them. This procedure (*deadheading*) is particularly important for **Pansies**—these plants produce many more flowers if deadheaded regularly. Hold the plant stems with one hand while tugging on individual flowers with thumb and fingers. Garden scissors can also be used to remove flowers. Snip the blooms with one hand while gathering them with the other.

Planning

Many annual flowers can be easily grown from seed. This month is a good time to purchase seed and to assemble materials needed for seed-starting.

Most homes do not have enough natural light in an appropriate spot to make seedlings prosper. Purchase or build a *light stand*, which uses fluorescent bulbs above the seed flats. PVC pipe is easily available at home improvement centers and is quite easy to work with. The pipe fittings allow sturdy connections at the corners of the structure. Special "plant light" fluorescent tubes are not necessary; two cool white 40-watt tubes will be sufficient.

Here is a simple light stand described by Bob Polomski in *Month-by-Month Gardening in the Carolinas*. He attributes the design to Master Gardener Joe Maple. The dimensions shown are only suggested—you can lengthen or shorten the pipes to fit your own situation. One-half inch PVC pipe can be used, but ³/₄-inch pipe will make a sturdier stand. Not all joints need to be glued. With a little planning, the light stand can be made so it can be disassembled after use and stored in an attic or closet.

Planting

Since individual plants at a garden center cost between $.20 and $2.00, raising annuals from seed can save a lot of money!

1 Fill a plastic nursery flat (or an aluminum pan in which drainholes have been poked) with sterile seed-starting mixture.

2 Make several "furrows," 2 inches apart and ¹/₂ inch deep, across the surface of the growing medium with the point of a pencil.

Some seed, like **Impatiens** *and* **Poppy,** *need light in order to germinate. They should simply be scattered onto the soil surface. Pat the soil with your hand to press them into good soil contact. Read seed packets carefully.*

3 For tiny seed, *mix* ¹/₄ teaspoonful of seed with a tablespoon of dry sand. Fold an index card in half, and pour the seed/sand mixture in the center. Gently tap the card to direct the seeds and sand to drop in the furrows in the growing medium. Large seed can be placed by hand in the furrows. *Cover* the seed with a thin layer of vermiculite

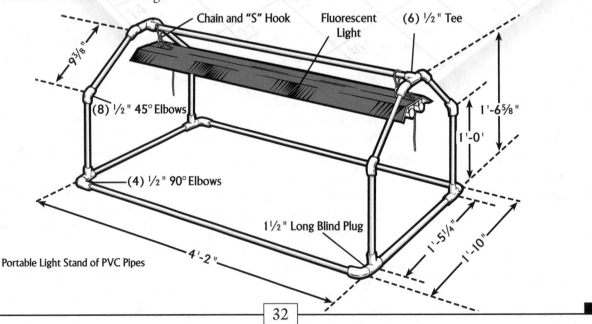

Chain and "S" Hook Fluorescent Light (6) ¹/₂ " Tee

9³/₈ "

(8) ¹/₂ " 45° Elbows

1'-6⁵/₈ "

1'-0'

(4) ¹/₂ " 90° Elbows

1¹/₂ " Long Blind Plug

1'-5¹/₄ "

1'-10"

4'-2 "

Portable Light Stand of PVC Pipes

FEBRUARY

unless directed on the seed pack to expose the seed to light.

4 *Spray-mist* the medium with water to moisten the soil. It should be just slightly moist, not soggy.

5 *Cover* the tray or pan with clear kitchen plastic wrap. Affix masking tape to the end of the container, and note the name of the seed, the date planted, and the date the seed should germinate.

6 Place the seed-starting trays in bright but indirect sunlight (a south- or west-facing window is ideal), or under the light stand described earlier (the fluorescent tubes should hang just a few inches above the plastic covering).

7 *Remove* the plastic when most of the seeds in a tray have sprouted. Raise the fluorescent tubes as the plants grow. If the plants become crowded, use a spoon to scoop individuals out of the tray, to be planted in separate plastic pots.

In south Georgia, you can lightly scratch the soil and *scatter* **Poppy** seed in your flower beds. Since they need light in order to germinate, do not cover with soil. **California, Iceland,** and **Corn Poppies** will sprout when the ground warms up.

Care for Your Annuals

The fragrant flowers of **Sweetpea** are a sure harbinger of spring. Most **Sweetpea** varieties are climbing vines. Now is the best time to plant the seed. You can make an informal trellis with three slender pruned branches from your **Crapemyrtle, Apple,** or **Flowering Cherry** tree. Lean or tie the branches together at the top to make a 4- to 6-foot-high teepee form for the vines to ascend. Make a rich planting soil by mixing bagged manure, sand, and soil in a 1:1:1 ratio. When the seeds sprout, train them up your trellis. *Flowers will appear March through May.*

Watering

Windowboxes and other outside containers need watering more often than in-ground flower beds. *Dig* 2 inches into the soil with your fingers. If the soil at that depth is dry, add enough water to the container until water runs out the bottom. Inspect and *water* flower beds as needed (see Annuals, January).

Fertilizing

Fertilize **Pansies** (see Annuals, October).

Pest Control

It is quite disappointing to observe seedlings suddenly fall over, as if broken at the soil level. The disease *damping off* causes this problem—it is caused by overwatering, crowding, or poor ventilation of the young plants. To prevent damping off: Use fresh, sterile seed-starting medium each time you raise seedlings. Keep the medium moist but never soggy. Increase light and ventilation as soon as symptoms are noticed.

Grooming

Remove faded blooms from plants as they occur (see January).

Helpful Hint

Seed packets note how long it should take from planting the seed to having plants big enough to place outdoors (generally six to ten weeks). The last frost will usually occur between April 1 and April 15 in the northern half of our state, and two weeks earlier than that in the southern half. This means that north Georgia gardeners should start their annual seeds indoors between February 15 and March 1. South Georgia gardeners can plant indoors in early February.

Planning

It is easy to get caught up in planting fever when you visit a garden center full of spring flowers. Before you visit, make an index card for each bed you'll be planting: *Sketch* the bed's shape on the card, particularly if it is irregular instead of rectangular. Write down the approximate square footage of the bed. Write down how much sunshine it receives and if parts of the bed are more shady than others. Jot down the flowers you intend to plant and the number you need to buy.

Design ideas for annuals:

- Choose a spot you want to highlight. Plant enough annuals of one color to draw the eye to that spot. White flowers can lighten a shady spot, but in bright sunshine brilliant red, orange, or yellow flowers are needed to compete with the existing light.

- Don't repeat the same mass of a single color throughout your landscape. One bed of Begonias is fine—but six identical beds is as boring as hearing the same piano note repeated endlessly.

- Use backyard beds to intrigue viewers from the street. You can enjoy your private view from your kitchen window, but allow

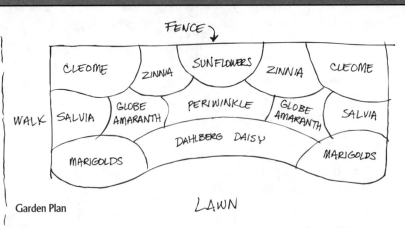

Garden Plan

part of the bed to be seen through a side gate or around a corner of the house.

- A long bed edged in a single color tires the eyes. Try to make oval or irregular, rounded beds of distinct, single-color annuals that adjoin each other.

- *Combine* annuals and perennials to have a progression of blooms from spring to fall.

A spot planned to attract butterflies can be the most interesting area of your garden. The butterfly life cycle requires different plants for the different life stages of the insect—the garden should have plants that feed caterpillars as well as plants whose flowers attract butterflies. *Caterpillar-feeding plants* include **Parsley, Dill, Fennel, Milkweed, Clover, Aster, Snapdragon**, and **Sunflower**. *Butterfly-attracting plants* include **Lantana, Butterfly Weed, Pentas, Impatiens, Cosmos, Salvia, Petunia, Core-opsis, Snapdragon, Marigold, Tithonia, Aster**, and **Black-eyed Susan**. Another ingredient for attracting butterflies is a *source of water*. Butterflies will not drink from large, open water areas. Wet sand or mud provides excellent watering holes. A saucer designed to fit under a clay or plastic pot makes a good container:

- Fill it completely with sand, and add water up to the rim. Make a few shallow depressions with your fingers where water can accumulate.

- A rock in the center of the saucer provides a resting spot for the butterfly.

Planting

There's still time to start seeds of annual flowers indoors (see February).

MARCH

If you like fragrant flowers, several "old-fashioned" varieties add spicy scents to your garden. Try planting **Stock, Sweet Alyssum, Sweetpea, Nicotiana,** and **Annual Phlox** *Phlox drummondi.*

In south Georgia, *plant* cool-season annuals from six-packs as they become available at garden centers: **Viola, Snapdragon, Pansy, Sweet William,** and **English Daisy** will bloom in your landscape for the next six weeks or longer.

In north Georgia, you can't expect every plant you installed last fall to make it through the winter. Fill holes in your flower beds with new plants. Purchase 3-inch or larger pots; smaller plants will bloom for only a few days.

Care for Your Annuals

Check for the seedlings of annuals you planted last fall. You should be able to see **Poppy** and **Larkspur** seedlings easily. Plants should be 6 to 12 inches apart. Gently *transplant* to an empty spot any seedlings that are too close. If you have more seedlings than space, *remove* some of the crowded seedlings by pinching them off at ground level.

Watering

Check the plastic covering on flats of seeds you are starting indoors. If a slight haze of condensed moisture isn't present, *remove* the plastic, and *mist* the soil until damp.

Fertilizing

Fertilize flowering annual plants (see October).

Fertilize the seedlings you have grown indoors with water-soluble houseplant food once the true leaves have appeared (true leaves are the leaves that emerge after the rounded first leaves unfold from the soil). Once plants are a few inches tall, fertilize them every two weeks until they are ready to be planted outdoors.

Pest Control

Seedlings grown indoors may become infested with whiteflies if your houseplants have them. *Spray* with insecticidal soap, and use a yellow sticky trap (see Edibles, August).

Grooming

Remove faded flowers from **Pansies.**

Helpful Hint

If you can't find the seed of annuals you prefer at a local garden center, consider buying from a seed catalog.

Park Seed
1 Parkton Avenue
Greenwood, SC 29647-0001
Phone: (800) 845-3369

Seeds of Change®
P.O. Box 15700
Santa Fe, NM 87506
Phone: (888) 762-7333

Johnny's Selected Seeds
RR 1 Box 2580
Albion, ME 04910-9731
Phone: (207) 437-4301

Planning

One of the hottest landscaping trends in the last few years has been the "Tropical Look." While a year-round tropical landscape might be possible in Brunswick or Savannah, gardeners in other parts of the state usually settle for a tropical corner in the yard.

Two of the most popular plants for the Tropical Look are **Elephant's Ear** and **Banana.** Common **Elephant's Ear** produces green leaves that gently sway in the breeze; **'Jet Black Wonder'** has dusky black leaves; **'Frydek'** sports velvety green leaves with white veins. **Fiber Banana** (*Musa basjoo*) is reputed to withstand winter temperatures down to 10 degrees Fahrenheit; **'Rojo'** displays green leaves with a red stripe. See October for tips on storing **Elephant's Ear** corms and **Banana** trees for the winter. Other annuals with that Tropical Look include **Amaranth, Chenille Plant, Coleus, Dusty Miller, Perilla Mint, Polkadot Plant,** and **Purple Basil.**

Planting

Soil temperatures determine when you can plant seeds outdoors. When the weather for several days in a row is warm enough to work outside wearing shorts and a T-shirt, *it's time to plant!* Annuals that are easy to grow from seed outdoors in spring include **Marigold, Cosmos, Zinnia, Celosia, Cleome, Sunflower,** and **Nasturtium.**

Care for Your Annuals

Though it may be warm during the day, nights are still chilly. The annual plants you have raised from seed for the past weeks can't tolerate cool temperatures. To accustom them to growing outdoors, they should be *hardened off*.

- If daytime temperatures are above 60 degrees Fahrenheit, take the plants outdoors and place them in a shady spot, for seven days in a row, bringing them indoors at night.

- When nighttime temperatures are 50 degrees or above, you can leave the plants outside both day and night. Bring indoors if temperatures fall below 50 degrees.

- *Examine* your plants daily to make sure they do not wilt.

- After two weeks outdoors, they are ready to be transplanted into your garden.

Less care will be needed if you select the healthiest plants when purchasing annuals. Be wary of buying a plant fully in flower— nursery techniques that force a plant to flower all at once can leave it weakened and bare in just a few weeks. Choose plants that have just one or two flowers and plenty of unopened flower buds. Gently pull one or two plants from the pot to examine their roots. Soggy soil and brown, jelly-like roots can indicate root rot problems. Evaluate the nursery as a whole. Are most plants in good health, or do they seem to be underwatered or overgrown and floppy? Consider buying plants in 4-inch pots rather than in six-packs. Though they are more expensive, larger plants have more complete root systems and are likely to bloom earlier.

Watering

April is likely to have several days with temperatures in the eighties. Newly planted annuals can quickly dry out, especially on windy days. *Water* each plant immediately after planting.

1 Water again twenty-four to forty-eight hours later.

2 Water again four days after the initial planting.

3 Begin weekly watering for all your annuals once they seem adapted to their new homes.

Fertilizing

Nutrients are needed to get annuals off to a good start. Water-soluble fertilizers (Peters®, Miracle-Gro®, Watch Us Grow®, etc.) provide the quickest way to feed plants immediately. Slow-release fertilizers (Osmocote®, Dyna-mite®, etc.) provide nutrients for the entire growing season.

- Use water-soluble fertilizer for the first watering, following label directions.

- Consider placing slow-release fertilizer granules in the bottom of each hole in which you plant an annual, following label directions.

- If you choose not to use slow-release fertilizer, you'll need to feed your plants every six weeks with one pound of 10-10-10 for every 100 square feet of flower bed. Alternatively, use one of the water-soluble products according to label directions.

Helpful Hint

"Flowering Annuals for Georgia Gardens" is a free booklet available at your local Extension office (see Resources, p. 353), or download it from the Web at www.ces.uga.edu/pubcd/b954-w.html. You can also refer to the **Georgia Gardener's Guide** for more information about great annuals for Georgia.

Pest Control

Aphids love the lush tips of fast-growing plants. They can suck plant sap easily from stems or leaves and can disfigure the growing tip. Suspect aphids if you see many ants on a particular plant. Examine the undersides of leaves at the branch tips. Aphids may be green, yellow, or black, and they are visible with the naked eye.

If you find aphids, blast them off the plant with a strong stream of water.

Grooming

Although it may seem harsh, the best way to help a plant establish a good root system is to *remove* blooms at planting—blooms take the energy needed for root growth and focus it on seed formation. Bloom removal is particularly important for plants purchased in "six-packs;" their root systems are small compared to their foliage. Plants purchased in 4-inch or larger pots do not require this clipping.

Planning

Plant labels are quite useful in a garden. They help you remember the names of particular flowers, and they can remind you of a plant's source and special care. If you include a plant's scientific name, you can teach yourself the rudiments of botanical Latin! Labels can be made from plastic picnic knives, medical tongue depressors, aluminum window blind slats, strips of plastic cut from recycled non-dairy topping containers, or strips of aluminum cut from recycled aluminum pie pans. Most garden centers sell more attractive and permanent labels: fired clay markers for herbs, rectangular metal tags attached to steel hairpin legs, and copper tags that attach loosely to woody plant stems with wire.

Planting

Good gardeners use planting tricks to avoid later chores. Here is the technique Dr. Gary Wade, Extension Horticulturist, uses to combat weeds, conserve water, and get rid of old newspapers:

- Thoroughly *till* the soil for your bed of annuals. You should have soft soil 6 inches deep.

- Unfold the Sunday newspaper, making a stack of all the sheets. Place near your planting spot.

- Fill a 5-gallon bucket with water; station it near your bed.

- Soak a group of three sheets of newspaper momentarily in the water. Spread them in a single stack over your tilled soil.

- Repeat this process, laying each group adjacent to the previous one, until the entire bed is covered with newspaper.

- Pour mini–pine bark chips in a layer 1 inch thick over the newspapers.

- Use a sharp trowel to stab through the mulch and wet paper, making a planting hole for each of your plants.

- Continue planting until the bed is completed.

Caution: Do not use the comics for this process. If you do, your plants will grow funny!

Care for Your Annuals

Annual vines give lots of vertical interest and beautiful blooms to a flower garden, but they must be supported on a trellis, fence, or wall. Good annual vines include **Moon Vine, Morning Glory, Purple Hyacinth Bean, Scarlet RunnerBean, Cypress Vine, Sweetpea,** and **Thunbergia.** A few trellis possibilities are bamboo canes; long, limber branches pruned from your **Crapemyrtle, Flowering Cherry, Pear,** or **Apple** tree; *tuteurs* (ornamental towers made from metal or wood, purchased at a garden center); and wire or strings attached to a wooden fence.

Watering

Nearly every year brings a drought to part or all of Georgia. You can prepare for water shortages by adhering to the principles of xeriscaping (dry-weather landscaping).

1 **Planning and Design:** Establish low-, moderate-, and high-water-use zones. Group plants with similar water needs in the same zone.

2 **Soil Analysis:** Have your soil tested by your local Extension office (see Horticultural Practices, p. 7) to determine what is needed for your plants to develop drought-tolerant root systems.

3 **Appropriate Plant Selection:** Choose plants that thrive naturally in your local environment.

4 **Practical Turf Areas:** Plan to have turf only in small areas near your home's entrance, in recreation areas, or on gentle

slopes where other plants would be impractical.

5 **Efficient Irrigation:** Zone your irrigation system to water plants with different needs separately.

6 **Use of Mulches:** Use mulch to prevent evaporation and to maintain even soil moisture.

7 **Appropriate Maintenance:** Water after midnight and before noon. Less water will be lost to evaporation, and it will have more time to soak into cool soil.

Fertilizing

One of the advantages of feeding annuals with slow-release fertilizer at planting (see Annuals, April) is that you don't have to rack your brain to remember if you fertilized recently. If you didn't use a slow-release fertilizer, you have two choices for applying nutrients: balanced, granular fertilizers (10-10-10, 8-8-8, Nursery Special™, etc.) and water-soluble products (Peter's®, Miracle-Gro®, Watch Us Grow®, etc.). If you use a granular product:

- Note how often the product must be applied—usually every four to six weeks.

- Note, and follow, the application rate recommended on the bag.

- Determine how you will spread the granules evenly. Garden centers sell small "whirly bird" spreaders for just this purpose.

If you use a water-soluble fertilizer:

- Note how often the product must be applied—usually every two weeks.

- Mix at the recommended rate for the plants (annuals, perennials, shrubs, etc.) you're tending.

- Since these nutrients can be absorbed by plant leaves as well as roots, use a sprinkling can to get the best coverage. Otherwise, use a bucket and a comfortable dipper to pour the recommended amount beside each plant.

If you have a large area to fertilize, a special device called a *siphoning mixer* is very useful. This brass gadget attaches to your hose and injects concentrated liquid fertilizer into the water flowing through the hose. A water wand screwed onto the end of the hose allows you to sprinkle the enriched water quickly onto dozens of plants.

Pest Control

Spider mites attack many plants and are common pests of **Foxglove, Verbena,** and **Butterfly Bush.** Symptoms include yellow-speckled leaves and wilted foliage (see Roses, July, for more information). The key to their control is regular inspection of your plants and sprays with horticultural oil (see Chemicals, p. 327) if warranted. *Prune* nearby **Butterfly Bushes** down to 12 inches tall in March. *Be vigilant about pulling weeds whenever you see them. If you can remove them before they drop seed, you'll save many headaches during the summer.*

Grooming

As temperatures warm up, **Pansies** look like nothing more than green flowering spaghetti now. *Pull them out*, and replace with **Petunias, Marigolds, Coleus, Geraniums,** or other colorful summer annuals.

Planning

Gardeners know they can get just as much exercise from their activities as their neighbors who jog or visit a gym. Physical activity researchers have compiled the METs (metabolic equivalents) for hundreds of activities. A MET of 1 is the amount of energy you expend at rest. For an activity to help your body's circulation or strength, it should have a MET between 3 and 6.

Weeding or planting	4.5 MET
Digging or pushing a	
lawn mower	5 MET
Riding a mower	2.5 MET
Watering the lawn	1.5 MET

Doctors recommend that adults accumulate 30 minutes of physical activity above 3 MET each day. A gardener who weeds for 15 minutes in the morning and pushes a mower for 20 minutes in the evening has met his or her needs for daily physical activity.

Planting

There's still lots of time to set out annual flowers for summer color. Try **'Wave' Petunias**, *Zinnia linearis*, **Mexican Heather,** and **Portulaca** in sunny spots.

Care for Your Annuals

When planting transplants, don't just dig a small hole and shove the root system into it. Try to gently *untangle* some of the roots so they will quickly explore the soil around them. *Firm* the soil around each plant with your fingers to eliminate air pockets in the soil. Once a bed is finished, *water* each plant thoroughly (see below). *Do not* allow transplants to dry out.

Watering

Now that your plants are well along, it's time to think about how to water them, with the least effort, for the rest of the summer.

1 Black soaker hoses can be laid in a bed or down a row of flowers, and later covered with pine straw.

2 Drip irrigation systems are available at large garden centers. Though they are a bit more complicated to set up, you can be assured that plants will get the exact amount of water they need.

3 Some lawn and landscape irrigation systems can be adapted to water flower beds. The beds should always be on a different zone from the lawn—the water demands of flowers are completely different from those of lawn grass.

4 A water wand is indispensable for watering garden plants. The stream from a hose blasts plant leaves and scatters soil, but the gentle waterfall from the nozzle of a wand soaks the ground around a plant without disturbing it. Both metal and plastic wands work well.

An easy-to-operate valve is essential. Spend the money to buy a wand that has a valve with a long handle. Your fingers will thank you every time you turn the water on and off.

Fertilizing

If you use a ground pine bark soil amendment to prepare your beds (see Horticultural Practices, p. 7), the soil may be deficient in nitrogen for a month afterwards, and plant growth may be slow. Apply an extra dose of water-soluble fertilizer early this month to counteract this phenomenon. As the summer passes, nutrients from the breakdown of the woody materials will slowly be released for your plants to enjoy.

Continue to fertilize at two- to six-week intervals as discussed in Annuals, May. When using granular products, be sure to *water* afterwards to carry the nutrients down to plant roots.

Nasturtium is one flower that actually prefers a sunny location with poor soil. *Plant* seeds now. *Fertilize* very lightly when sprouts are 6 inches tall. *Do not* fertilize again. Flowers will appear in fifty days.

Pest Control

A great advantage of soaker hose and drip systems is that water is applied only to the roots of plants. By keeping the foliage dry, leaf diseases are reduced.

Deadheading

Helpful Hint

If you do not recognize an insect pest or disease symptom, you won't know how to deal with it. No one is an expert on all plant problems, but you do have local resources which can help:

- Local University of Georgia Extension Service offices (see Resources, p. 353)–if you can't take a pest sample to them, take a photograph of the damage or pest, and mail it to their office. All offices have e-mail addresses to which digital photos can be sent.

- Experienced garden center personnel–call your local nursery, and ask who is their best pest identifier. Make an appointment to meet that person when it is mutually convenient.

- Long-time gardeners–if the pest is bothering you, it is probably bothering other folks as well. Ask neighbors and friends for their advice and expertise.

- Mass media–read the garden section of your local paper and listen to the local gardening radio show. Search the Internet for "garden problems."

Grooming

Annuals produce flowers not for our enjoyment but to make seed to ensure their reproduction. On many plants, the flowering process stops if the flowers are allowed to fade as the seeds are maturing. It is therefore important to regularly *remove* withered flowers from your annuals. *Deadhead* Ageratum, Calendula, Cosmos, Marigold, Pansy, Rudbeckia, Scabiosa, Verbena, and Zinnia each week. *Remove* the yellow flowers from **Dusty Miller** as they are produced in late June.

Planning

Beds of annual flowers should be planned not only for beauty but also for ease of maintenance. A garden designed for a young or vigorous gardener should be different from a garden designed for a less vigorous gardener. Easy access gardens should have:

- narrow beds that are more easily reached from the lawn or a solid path.

- raised beds that demand less bending.

- flat, wide paths in the garden that allow wheelchairs or walkers to maneuver easily.

- tools designed for easy grasping (see Helpful Hint).

All gardeners should pay attention to these body-saving ideas:

- Alternate between movements. If you swap between digging, raking, weeding, and pruning, you can avoid repetitive motion injuries.

- Bend from the knees, not from the back. Lift large pots and sacks of fertilizer by first bending your knees, then grasping the object and straightening your knees. *Avoid* bending over to lift even light items—the lower back is prone to injury and should be spared whenever possible.

Planting

Choose plants carefully. Avoid floppy or stretched-out plants. Ask your garden center manager when the next fresh shipment will arrive. Inspect plants for insects, like whiteflies or spider mites, before purchasing.

Plant **Zinnia** seed. They will sprout in six days and bloom in just a few weeks. *Plant* dwarf **Sunflower** seed now. Varieties like **'Teddy Bear'**, **'Sunspot'**, **'Pacino'**, and **'Prado Red'** take up little space but delight the eyes of humans and birds alike. *Plant* more **Caladiums** and **Coleus.** They'll look better in fall than the early-bird plants you put out in May.

Care for Your Annuals

When planting a large pot with summer annuals, there is no need to fill the entire pot with potting soil. After all, the roots of annual flowers rarely penetrate more than 10 inches into the soil. Fill the pot partially with empty plastic soft drink bottles. Add potting soil, and *shake* the pot vigorously to settle it around the bottles. When the soil no longer recedes below the bottles, fill the pot completely, and plant your annual flowers.

Watering

Watering restrictions and, sometimes, outright bans have become a way of life in the metropolitan areas of Georgia. When municipal water is in short supply, there are other sources of water for your plants.

- Water from a dehumidifier or from an air conditioner condensate drain is perfectly safe to use on plants. This water has been condensed from the ambient air—just like rainwater!

- Bathwater can be used to water most plants. The soap, shampoo, and conditioner are so diluted that they will not harm leaves or roots. Avoid using *only* bath water on **Azaleas** and **Rhododendrons;** these shrubs like acid soil, and soapy water is slightly alkaline.

- If you are lucky enough to live on a lake, it is theoretically possible to pump water from it for your landscape. Before you attempt this, consider: 1) An electrician will be needed to install a 220 volt power line for an electric pump (gasoline pumps are rarely adequate). 2) Irrigation sprinklers demand moderately clean water. How will the lake water be filtered and how often must the filter be cleaned? 3) The initial cost of an irrigation system is not insubstantial. Wouldn't it be cheaper to design a landscape that did not demand so much water? (See Annuals, May).

Avoid pumping water from a nearby creek without considering the effect the lower water level downstream will have. Small fish, frogs, and invertebrates depend on water for their lives. Birds and other predators depend on smaller animals for their food.

Fertilizing

Continue to fertilize at two- to six-week intervals as discussed in Annuals, May. When using granular products, be sure to *water* afterwards to carry the nutrients down to plant roots.

Some gardeners prefer to use "organic" fertilizers like manure, blood meal, and fish emulsion. These products are slightly more expensive but have the advantage of adding plenty of *micronutrients* to the soil. Research by Dr. Tim Smalley, horticulture professor at the University of Georgia, has shown that composted hen litter continues to release plant food for four years after a 2-inch layer is rototilled into flower beds.

Apply an organic fertilizer at the rate recommended on the container.

Pest Control

It may seem contradictory, but the highest incidence of garden root rot problems seems to occur when summer watering restrictions are imposed. Perhaps gardeners fear that since water is limited, they should water all the more! Root rot is caused by soggy soil, which leads to weak root growth and an increase in soil fungi. Symptoms include yellow leaves, wilting, and plant stems that break at ground level.

Prevent root rot by watering annuals deeply once per week and mixing plenty of organic amendments into the soil before planting.

Continue checking for insect damage to your plants. The key to insect control is to identify the insect or other pest responsible. Many can be identified by their characteristic damage, like the lace doily effect of Japanese beetle feeding and the round leaf notches of leaf-cutter bees.

Helpful Hint

Here are some sources of tools for physically challenged gardeners:

Walt Nicke Co.
P.O. Box 433
Topsfield, MA 01983
(800) 822-4114

Not Stooped Garden Tools, LLC
P.O. Box 40185
Denver, CO 80204-0185
(303) 837-8490

The Calais Co., Inc.
P.O. Box 355
Mendham, NJ 07945-0355
(973) 543-5665

Grooming

Continue deadheading annual flowers, as described in June.

Planning

Concentrate on maintaining one or two blooming "oases" in your landscape—even if you have to allow the rest of the yard to dry out. Scavenge water from your bathtub or sink to keep your oases beautiful (see July, Watering, and Annuals, May).

Planting

Few Georgia gardeners manage to keep *every* plant alive over a hot summer. *Remove* annuals that have died or become unattractive. *Replace* plants whose removal leaves holes in a bed of flowers. Purchase mature plants of the same size as those in your bed.

Care for Your Annuals

Mulches such as pine straw or shredded wood chips help conserve moisture by preventing evaporation. About 3 inches of mulch placed 2 to 3 inches back from the base of a tree or shrub is ideal for maintaining even moisture under even the driest conditions. Fine-textured mulches hold moisture better than coarse-textured mulches. Good mulches are pine straw, pine bark mini-nuggets, and shredded hardwood mulch or chips. *Avoid* large-nugget pine bark, rock, gravel, and marble.

Watering

Water restrictions or bans make the task of scheduling irrigation in your garden a bit more difficult. Don't make the mistake of watering heavily every time watering is allowed. Many annuals can go for several days between waterings if they are irrigated heavily (by rain or your hose) once per week.

A heavy irrigation is 1 inch or more of rainfall or irrigation or 1 gallon of water per foot of plant height.

Examine plants for signs of water stress (wilting, blue/gray leaves) before you water.

When watering by hand, apply 5 gallons of water per 10 square feet. This is approximately the amount of water delivered by a garden hose operating for 1 minute at medium pressure.

A soaker hose can effectively water a swath 1 foot wide on either side of the hose. A 50-foot-long hose can water 100 square feet of landscape bed.

Apply 50 gallons of water per 100 square feet when plants show water stress.

Newly purchased soaker hoses are unwieldy at first as you stretch them among plants.

Use soil anchor pins made from surplus clothes hangers (see Annuals, December) to hold the hose in place.

Several granular products designed to conserve water have appeared in the last few years. The small granules look like grains of salt when dry; when mixed with water, they absorb the moisture and swell to many times their previous size. Manufacturers claim that by mixing the granules with the soil in a hot, dry flower bed, water can be stored and then released when plants need it. Research has shown these products hold some promise but are not "miracle" substances.

The best way to mix them with your soil is to sprinkle a few tablespoons of crystals in a wheelbarrow and add water. Follow the manufacturer's recommended rate. Once the crystals have become like jelly, slowly add garden soil to the wheelbarrow and mix thoroughly. Use the soil to fill your flower bed.

Some water-conserving products are diminished by fertilizer; others are consumed by soil organisms. In a few years you'll have to add more of the granules to your soil in order to continue reaping the benefits.

Fertilizing

Continue to fertilize at two- to six-week intervals as discussed in Annuals, May. When using granular products, be sure to *water* afterwards to carry the nutrients down to plant roots.

Pest Control

The slug and snail population builds and wanes during the year, depending on the weather. The numbers can grow to such heights that most of an annual or perennial plant can be consumed overnight. Symptoms include large, irregular holes chewed in leaves, and silvery slime trails that can be seen on nearby leaves and mulch. There are several environmental controls you may wish to try:

- Press a saucer into the ground near affected plants, and fill with stale beer. Slugs and snails will fall into the beer and drown.

- Support a 10x10-inch board slightly above the ground on small stones. *Check* it in the afternoon, and swipe the creatures into a pail of soapy water.

- Scatter inverted plastic plant "six-packs" or hollowed-out cantaloupe halves around affected plants. Check these slug and snail refuges every day, and *discard* those filled with the pests.

- Copper repels mollusks. Place a 1-inch-wide strip of copper screen around the top edge of the clay pot in which affected plants grow.

Some prefer chemical controls:

- Apply a band of iron phosphate paste (see Chemicals, p. 327) around plants.

- Place metaldehyde pellets (see Chemicals, p. 327) in an empty small plastic soft drink bottle. Lay the bottle on its side. Use a rock, soil, or a twig to make a bridge from the soil level up to the neck of the bottle. Slugs and snails will feed on the pellets, but the poison will be inaccessible to pets and children.

Grooming

Cut back faded but healthy annual flowers by half, then water, and fertilize lightly with a water-soluble fertilizer. A second season of blooms will begin to appear in two weeks.

Helpful Hint

Intense sunshine may be beneficial to some plants, but it is no friend to a gardener's skin.

- Keep containers of sunscreen in places convenient to the garden so you won't forget to apply it before working in the sun. If you dislike the greasy feel on your fingers, purchase the spray-bottle kind. Products with an SPF greater than 15 are best.

- It might be a good idea to anoint the skin under your shirt as well. A T-shirt has an SPF of only 5.

- Wear a hat to protect your face and neck.

- Long-sleeved, specially made sun-protective clothing is available at camping/hunting/outdoor equipment stores.

Regularly examine your skin for changes in moles and skin pigmentation. A yearly appointment with a dermatologist is a good idea if you work in the sun constantly.

Planning

Most large flower beds contain several kinds of flowers—some may be perennial, some annual, some brightly colored, and so on. When you plan the layout of the flowers in the bed, a paper sketch might not be as helpful as physically marking where the groups of different flowers will be placed. Use a sharpened stake to draw onto the soil the outline of the different flower groups. When you are satisfied, sprinkle kitchen flour into the lines the stake has made. The white flour contrasts nicely with the soil. If you need to make a change, "erase" the flour with new soil, and draw a new line with flour.

Planting

Though garden centers often have **Pansies** and spring bulbs on hand in September, it is too early to plant them. If a bed of summer annuals is on its last legs, pull out the plants, and begin preparing the soil for the cool-season planting that will begin in October. See Horticultural Practices, p. 7, for the steps in preparing a bed.

Care for Your Annuals

Though the weather is still hot, it's time to plan for saving the seed of some plants and rooting others to hold indoors during the winter.

Saving Seed

1 As the seedpods on **Impatiens, Cleome, Hollyhock, Foxglove,** and **Moon Vine** dry out, collect them, and place each in a separate labeled envelope. In a week or so, the pods will split and release the seeds.

2 Seedheads from perennials like **Purple Coneflower, Shasta Daisy, Black-eyed Susan,** and others can be collected when dry and gently crumbled above a sheet of paper. *Separate* the seeds from the pods, petals, and chaff as best you can. One way is to purse your lips and blow gently on a mound of seed. Place the cleaned seed in a small envelope, and label it clearly.

3 Insert several envelopes of seed into a pint jar. Enclose 2 tablespoons of dry milk powder in tissue paper, then wrap with a rubber band. Slip this into the jar with the seed.

4 Tighten the jar lid securely, and place it on a back shelf of your refrigerator. A storage temperature between 35 and 45 degrees Fahrenheit plus the drying action of the milk powder makes for an excellent environment to keep the seed viable until next spring.

Taking Cuttings

1 Several plants, including **Coleus, Pentas, Begonia,** and **Geranium,** can be propagated in fall and grown indoors until spring. Use a sharp knife to take 3- to 4-inch cuttings from the ends of vigorous, unflowering branches. *Remove* all lower leaves; allow just two or three leaves to remain on the cutting tip.

2 *Dip* the cut end into a rooting hormone such as Rootone™.

3 Fill several small pots with a 50:50 mixture of perlite and peat moss. Make a 2-inch-deep hole in the center of the rooting medium. *Insert* a single cutting 2 inches into a hole. *Firm* the medium around the cutting. Repeat until all holes are filled. Water the pots, and let drain.

4 Put the pots into clear plastic bags, and seal. Set the pots in a bright east- or north-facing window (not in direct sunlight).

5 Open the bags in three weeks. *Remove* the plants, and care for each as a houseplant until the

weather is warm enough to set them out in April.

Watering

Watch "indicator plants" like **Impatiens** and **Pentas** for signs of drought stress. When these plants are drooping, it's time to *water* your flower beds.

Fertilizing

Continue to fertilize at two- to six-week intervals as discussed in Annuals, May. When using granular products, be sure to *water* afterwards to carry the nutrients down to plant roots.

Pest Control

The seeds of winter annual weeds such as chickweed, henbit, and annual bluegrass begin sprouting later this month. You can prevent them in your beds of winter flowers by applying a weed-preventer by mid-month. Read the label on any product you are considering to make sure it can be used on flowers. Be sure to *irrigate thoroughly* after applying the weed-preventer, to dissolve the chemical into the soil.

Helpful Hint

Take care when weeding your landscape by hand this month. There are several stinging caterpillars that feed on plant leaves; they can make a nasty welt on your skin accompanied by an intense burning sensation.

- The bright-green saddleback caterpillar, $3/4$ to 1 inch long, has a large brown "saddle" in its back and white poisonous bristles at each end of its body.

- The puss caterpillar, 1 to $1^1/2$ inches long, has a flattened shape and is covered with brown hair that conceals stinging spines.

Control stinging caterpillars, if you choose to, with a contact insecticide or with a *B.t.* product (see Chemicals, p. 327).

Other caterpillars are dangerous-looking but harmless. Let them go about their business, and you might be rewarded later with a glimpse of a moth or butterfly.

- A hickory horned devil, 4 to 5 inches long and blue-green with orange horns on its head, becomes a regal moth after it pupates.

- A hornworm (which comes in several varieties) has a characteristic horn on one end of its body; it will become a sphinx moth if allowed to mature.

- Fall webworms form large colonies protected by a large web at the end of tree branches; these caterpillars are covered with white hair but are harmless.

- The spicebush caterpillar has fearsome black eyes at one end of its body; it will become a beautiful spicebush swallowtail butterfly after pupation.

Grooming

Reserve a day this month to tidy up plants that have tattered leaves, dead stems, and faded flowers. Even tired plants look better when they are neat.

Planning

This is **Pansy**-*planting month throughout the state.* Follow these tips in order to have color from their blooms in your landscape in winter.

Timing: In north Georgia, begin planting in early October as daytime temperatures fall into the seventies. In south Georgia, begin planting mid-October or later. Ideal conditions are when the weather is predicted to be cool for the next several days.

Bed preparation: Pansies have fine roots and need very soft soil in order to grow well. They cannot tolerate soggy soil. *Rototill* a 2-inch layer of organic material into prospective **Pansy** beds.

Spacing: Pansies can be planted at a 6-, 8-, or 10-inch spacing between plants. The smaller spacing results in a fuller appearing bed but may make **Pansies** more susceptible to disease due to crowding next spring. Use a 10-inch spacing when planting 3- or 4-inch-size potted plants.

Planting

In north Georgia, *plant* **Poppy, Larkspur,** and **Sweet Alyssum**

seeds now. Lightly scratch the ground around fading perennial flowers using an iron rake. Scatter seeds lightly. Press into place in the soil with the palm of your hand. ***Do not*** cover with earth, since these seeds need light to germinate. ***Do not*** water; allow nature to nurture the seeds. Little seedlings will germinate by November, and they can be thinned. The seedlings will survive the winter without harm and will grow into larger plants next spring.

Pansies are not the only sources of flowers for fall through spring— **Dianthus, Snapdragon, Stock,** and **Viola** easily withstand winter weather conditions. **Ornamental Kale** and **Cabbage** as well as **Lettuce** and **Parsley** can lend their colorful foliage to your winter landscape.

Care for Your Annuals

The magnificent leaves of **Banana** trees and **Elephant Ear** tubers will not survive a freeze. Though it is a bit of work, they can be stored and planted outside once again in late spring.

To store **Banana:** *Cut off* all leaves close to the main trunk. Use shovels to excavate a rootball approximately 24 inches in diame-

ter. Wrap the rootball tightly with burlap or sheet plastic. Invite friends to help you move the leafless trunk and its rootball to your basement or to a place where temperatures will not go much below freezing.

To store **Elephant's Ear:** Allow frost to kill the leaves. (Use caution when chopping green stems: the sap can damage your eyes.) In the northern third of the state, dig the tubers, and allow them to dry in a covered spot. Store in a place where temperatures are between 50 and 70 degrees Fahrenheit. A cool basement is actually not as good as a closet upstairs. In the lower two-thirds of Georgia, **Elephant's Ear** tubers will usually survive the winter when left in the ground.

Watering

Plants dry out rapidly on sunny days, even when temperatures begin to cool off. ***Don't wait*** for plants to wilt; check soil moisture regularly with your fingers.

Fertilizing

Pansies and other cool-season plants bloom wonderfully during the winter as long as they

receive proper nutrients. Fertilizing cool-season plants is different from fertilizing summertime annuals because the soil is cold while they are growing and blooming—soil organisms that help release fertilizer nutrients in warm soil are not very active in chilly soil.

- Immediately after planting, *fertilize* with a water-soluble, quickly available fertilizer such as Miracle-Gro®, Watch Us Grow®, or Peter's®.

- Repeat two weeks later if day-time temperatures are still in the seventies.

- Every four weeks thereafter, while the soil is cold, fertilize with a product such as Pansy Booster™, which contains a high percentage of nitrate nitrogen. Nitrate nitrogen does not rely on soil organisms to convert it to a form the plant can use. (Fertilizer products that do not contain nitrate nitrogen do very little for **Pansies** that are growing in cold soil.) Continue to fertilize according to label directions until March 15.

- Resume fertilizing, with a water-soluble fertilizer, in late March. Fertilize every two weeks until you replace cool-season plants with summer annuals.

Overwintering Geraniums

Geraniums with an attractive flower color can be removed from the ground and kept indoors for the winter. Although keeping the plants in a sunny window will allow you to observe them daily, a **Geranium's** fleshy stem and roots allow it to survive a few months in darkness.

- Water plants thoroughly a week before frost is predicted.

- Dig individual plants and place in separate paper bags. Medium-sized grocery bags are ideal.

- Place several of the bags in a cardboard box. Put the box in a cool place, such as an unheated basement or a crawl space.

- Check on the plants at Christmas; moisten the soil with a spray bottle; remove yellow leaves. Repeat in mid-February.

- In late March, bring the plants into a moderately shady, protected spot, and water thoroughly.

- In a week or so, sprouts will emerge from the stems, and the plant can be planted in its spring/summer home (remember to protect from freezing with a covering of pine straw if a late frost threatens).

Pest Control

Before the first frost, newly planted **Pansies** are sometimes devoured by caterpillars of the fritillary butterfly. Symptoms include leaves that have been consumed back to the mid-vein. Look for small black droppings on the soil under the plant. *Spray* affected plants immediately with **B.t.** (see Chemicals, p. 327).

If you plant in early October, or if you've had caterpillar prob- *lems before, consider applying a preventative spray of* B.t. *or a contact insecticide (see Chemicals, p. 327) just after planting.*

Grooming

Remove summer annuals as they deteriorate. It is usually easier to remove everything all at once from a bed, even though some annuals are still blooming. Rototill the soil, and add organic amendments (see Horticultural Practices, p. 7) before planting any winter annuals.

Planning

Many gardeners dream of having a greenhouse in which they can putter with their plants throughout the weekend. Greenhouse kits can be purchased from home improvement centers or through specialized garden catalogs. Before you invest a great deal of money, consider the following questions:

Do I have a proper site and enough room?

The greenhouse should be in full sun to avoid high winter heating bills. Placing it near trees invites frequent damage to the glazing. Municipal building codes often limit how close you can build next to a property line. Check with your local zoning office.

How will I provide heat to the greenhouse?

Solar heating will not keep it warm on cold winter days. A natural gas or electric heater will be required.

How will I provide electricity?

The cost of running an electric line from your home to the greenhouse can be substantial. Installation should only be performed by a licensed electrician.

How will I provide water?

Extending a water line can be accomplished by a handy gardener, but a trench must be dug at least 12 inches deep in which to place the pipe.

Would a cold frame serve some of my needs just as well?

See Care for Your Annuals in this month.

Local offices of the University of Georgia Cooperative Extension Service (see Resources, p. 353) have a free publication, *Managing the Hobby Greenhouse.* Other sources of greenhouse information and supplies are:

Charley's Greenhouse Supply
17979 State Route 536
Mt. Vernon, WA 98273
(800) 322-4707

ACF Greenhouses
380 Greenhouse Drive
Buffalo Junction, VA 24529
(800) 487-8502

Planting

Winter annuals, especially **Pansies,** that are not growing vigorously by this time will not survive a severe winter. *Replace* weak plants with large ones. *Examine* the root systems of the replacements to make sure they are healthy. Roots should be white and numerous, and spread uniformly in the potting soil.

In north Georgia, look for already-sprouted seedlings of **Foxglove, Hollyhock, Money Plant,** and **Flowering Tobacco;** they should be no closer than 6 inches apart. Unless they are already in a favorable place, move the small plants to a "nurse bed" where they can grow for the winter. Next spring you can move them from the nursery to their appointed spots.

Plant **Poppy, Larkspur,** and **Sweet Alyssum** seed now (see Annuals, October).

Care for Your Annuals

On a warm weekend, make a final cleanup of your landscape:

1 Clip the dried stalks of annuals and perennials close to the ground.

2 Tuck pine straw around newly planted annuals.

3 Gently brush fallen tree leaves off flower beds. Use them for mulch under trees and shrubs.

A cold frame is a smaller, unheated version of a greenhouse. In it you can protect half-hardy annuals from brief freezes and can toughen annual seedlings before planting in beds next spring. Many cold frame designs have been tried. Here is one you can make yourself from a double-hung storm window and some 2×6 lumber:

1 Purchase the storm window first. A large one (approx. 36 by 75 inches) is best. Make sure both sashes can be slid easily.

2 Using the storm window dimensions and the 2x6 lumber, construct a bottom-less and topless box onto which the storm window can be mounted. Attach the storm window to the box frame with screws.

3 Using the same dimensions as the first one, construct two or three more bottomless/topless boxes.

4 Place a bottomless/topless box on the ground in a sunny, sheltered spot. Stack one or two boxes on top—use two if you need the additional height. (Whether you use two or three boxes in the stack, the one to which the storm window is mounted should be the very top one.)

5 Seal the joints between the boxes with duct tape on the inside and outside.

6 Open one of the storm window sashes, and place your plants inside. Leave it open on sunny days (so it does not overheat), and close it at night. Your plants will enjoy the mini-greenhouse in fall and spring even though you can't be in there with them!

Watering

Water **Pansies** and other flowers that you have recently planted if no rainfall occurs. All these plants need to be growing vigorously as colder weather approaches; make sure the soil is moist to 6 inches deep.

Fertilizing

Fertilize cool-season flowers (see Annuals, October).

Pest Control

Pull weeds like chickweed and hen-bit now, before they have time to

Helpful Hint

Collect the bags of leaves (especially pine straw) that your neighbors stack so helpfully at the curb. Use the leaves to build several compost piles (see Horticultural Practices, p. 7). Use the pine straw immediately for mulch, or pile it under a plastic tarp to use later in the winter.

mature and drop seed. *Dig out* the roots of wild violet, wild onion, and dandelion; simply pulling off the leaves will not control these perennial weeds.

Grooming

Spend a warm afternoon clipping and removing the brown stems of annuals killed by frost. Accumulate your clippings in one spot and transport them to the compost pile when finished. Vacant beds can be covered with pine straw and left for the winter, or you can plant winter annuals (see Annuals, October). *Remove* faded flowers from the **Pansies** you planted in October.

Planning

December is a time for slow walks through your landscape, coffee in hand, to reflect on what has pleased you in the last year and what can be improved. If you have taken photographs regularly, you can spread them on the kitchen table to follow the progress of your flowers during the growing season.

Were there times when nothing was blooming?

Research the peak bloom time for different annuals. Make notes in your garden journal on what to plant in the bare spots next year. Don't forget that some selections of the same annual plant bloom before or after the plant you commonly use. If you're always successful with a particular annual, look for other selections that bloom at the time you need flowers.

Did some plants grow larger than expected?

Make notes of where to plant or move them next spring so they won't overshadow their neighbors.

Was the backdrop for your flowers always effective?

Refer to the lists of good trees, shrubs, and grasses in other chapters of this book for ideas. Consult the Georgia Gardener's Guide *for our recommendations of the best plants for Georgia conditions.*

Planting

Cool-season annuals make great companions in a pot. Find a decorative container (or several!), and plant arrangements of **Pansies, Parsley,** and **Snapdragons.** Keep the pots outdoors (by your front door, on your deck, etc.) for most of the winter, but bring them indoors for a few days at a time to decorate during the holiday season.

Care for Your Annuals

Overenthusiastic gardeners may find there is not enough room in their home to carry-over the plants that would normally reside outdoors. Rooted cuttings on windowsills, patio plants stacked by the sliding glass door, and houseplants may all vie for space.

Refer to the plans for a PVC light stand (Annuals, February) or an A-frame stand (Houseplants, February) for supplemental lighting options. Consider "lending" your plants to a school lobby or a personal care home. Both plants and people will benefit from the change of scenery.

Hoes, rakes, and shovels are expensive. It is easy to prolong their life by following a few good garden habits:

1 Rinse tools with fresh water as soon as you are finished using them to remove dirt. Soil left on wooden handles causes them to deteriorate quickly.

2 Paint boiled (not raw) linseed oil on wooden handles three times a year. Let it soak in overnight, then wipe off with a rag.

3 Use sandpaper on wooden handles that have become rough. They will feel much better to your touch. After sanding, give the handle a linseed oil treatment.

4 Spray a lubricant like WD-40 on the blades to protect them.

5 See Edibles, December, to learn how to sharpen tools.

A product called "floating row cover" is underappreciated for its usefulness in the garden. Made of very lightweight, translucent, woven plastic, a sheet of row cover can be spread over newly planted annuals to protect them from frost. Since the row cover is not opaque, it can be left on the plants for a few days until they are hardened off. Row cover is also useful for protecting annuals from unexpected frost in the spring. You can make soil anchors for the row cover from surplus clothes hangers.

Use tin snips to make three cuts: in the center of the long, straight part and on both sides of the hook, under the twisted wire. Pliers may be needed to straighten the wire slightly so it slides into the soil easily.

Watering

Water winter annuals if rain has not fallen in the last seven days. *Do not* allow their roots to become dry.

An overlooked benefit of winter mulch is that it retains soil heat. Pine straw, in particular, traps an insulating layer of air close to the earth.

Keep an extra couple of bales of pine straw in a sheltered spot so straw will be handy if needed.

Fertilizing

Fertilize cool-season flowers again (see Annuals, October).

Pest Control

Rabbits are often unfairly accused of eating the leaves of annuals in winter. It is more likely that the leaves wither due to insufficient roots during windy, cold days or to root rot. Visit your beds after a rain and note if water stands there for more than a few minutes. If so, the bed is not well drained.

Consider redirecting the source of the water (moving gutter drains, trenching around the bed, etc.).

Helpful Hint

Good stocking stuffers are a water timer, solid aluminum trowel, indoor-outdoor thermometer, handpruners, indoor plant food, rain gauge, a garden book (see Bibliography, p. 351), or a garden magazine subscription.

Examine the roots of plants whose leaves have disappeared. If they are almost nonexistent, re-dig the bed, and add more soil amendments to raise it farther above the surrounding soil.

Plant large-sized replacements in the bed.

Grooming

Remove faded flowers from **Pansies**, **Dianthus**, and **Snapdragons**.

Helpful Hint

If you don't have a garden journal, now is the time to ask for one, along with a digital camera to chronicle your garden on the computer. Happy Holidays!

Bulbs

Bulbs are amazing. A bulb in its dormant stage, whether a true bulb, corm, tuber, or rhizome, gives no hint of the beauty that lies within. Bulbs are all different, yet they possess similar characteristics in the way they store energy, actively grow, then go through a dormant period. During dormancy, growth is slowed to a minimum, roots die away, and new ones replace them. Portions of the underground plant contain stored food, leaves, flowers, and seeds. The dormant stage can be extended if bulbs are dug up when they are leafless and rootless. This means that unlike most other plants, bulbs can be shipped in their dormant state all over the country and world with relative ease, provided they are kept cool and dry.

There are types that bloom in spring, summer, and fall, and there are even a few that bloom in late winter, like **Snowdrops** *Galanthus nivalis.* We in Georgia are fortunate. In most parts of the state, there is enough cold in winter to meet the chilling requirements that many bulbs have before they will bloom in spring, yet it is also mild enough that we can grow some of the tropical-type bulbs such as **Tuberose** and **Alstroemeria.** In coastal areas where temperatures are warmer than in other parts of the state, bulbs may need to be prechilled before they are planted to ensure good blooms (see October for details).

Some bulbs are swollen and fat and others are small and shriveled, but such characteristics do not determine the beauty of the flowers that individual bulbs produce. For example, the **Windflower** *Anemone blanda* has a tuberous root that looks like a dried-up raisin, but the flowers, 1 to 1$^1/_2$ inches across, are delicate and beautiful, sky-blue daisies that appear on stems 3 to 4 inches above soft ferny foliage.

Colchicums bloom even before you plant them, while other bulbs bloom five to six months after planting. **Narcissus** bulbs have been known to persist, blooming each spring in the same site for over one hundred years, surviving long after the generation of gardeners that planted them.

By selecting the right bulbs (see March for sun and shade preferences) for the right location, you can have large areas of bulbs that naturalize in a short period of time. With a well-thought-out plan, your garden can feature bulbs for every season.

Types of Bulbs

A **true bulb** may be considered a bud. An onion (a true bulb) sliced lengthwise shows the budlike structure. Pale-green leaves in the center are protected by concentric layers of fleshy tissue called scales. The scales contain stored food and energy for the plant when it is actively growing, and the future flower is protected by the scales and the leaves. At the base of the bulb is a stem to which the scales and small leaves are joined; at the bottom of this is the *basal plate*, where roots emerge when the bulb is planted. If the basal plate is damaged, there may be fewer and smaller roots. It is for this reason that a healthy basal plate is important. The outer layer on a bulb is dry and papery and keeps the bulb from drying out. This layer is called a *tunic*. **Daffodils, Tulips,** and **Hyacinths** all have tunics; a **Lily** bulb has scales that are short and fleshy, and there is

Bulbs

no tunic or outer layer to protect them. A bulb is usually underground, but small bulbs called *bulbils* may appear in leaf axils of a plant like the **Blackberry Lily,** or in flowers and on stems of certain bulbous plants.

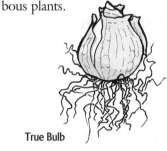

True Bulb

A **corm** is a short, enlarged, fleshy underground stem. Like a bulb, it is usually surrounded by a tunic, but the inside is solid. One or more buds give rise to leaves, stems, and flowers above ground; it roots from the base. Examples of corms are **Colchicum, Crocus,** and **Gladiolus.**

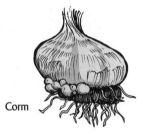

Corm

A **rhizome** is a thickened stem that grows completely or partially underground, like rhizomatous **Iris,** which should be planted so the rhizome is barely covered. Growing points initiate at the tip or along the length of the rhizome, and roots develop from the underside. Rhizomes include **Calla Lilies** and **Bearded Iris.** (**Dutch Iris** grow from bulbs.)

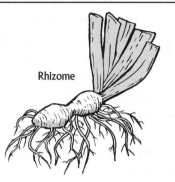

Rhizome

A **tuber** is a swollen underground branch or rootstock that contains a supply of stored food. It has "eyes" or buds from which stems are produced. **Cyclamens,** some of the **Anemones,** and **Caladiums** are examples of tubers. When you divide tubers, make sure each section has a growth bud. While **Cyclamen** tubers continue to get larger over time, they never produce offsets as do **Caladiums.** (**Caladiums'** offsets can be removed and planted.)

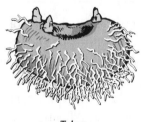

Tuber

Tuberous roots store nutrients. **Daylilies** and **Dahlias** are examples of tuberous roots. Their growth is such that the roots grow in clusters, radiating out from a center point, and buds are produced at the bases of old stems. When you divide tuberous-rooted plants, make sure each section has roots and shoots.

Planting and Care for Your Bulbs

When you purchase bulbs, select those that are firm and have the smallest number of nicks or bruises. If they are soft and mushy, they will probably die. If you buy your bulbs from a mail-order source, order from a company that grades its bulbs or specifies a size so you will have a better idea of their quality. You will save money in the long run if you start with bulbs that are healthy. Open boxes or bags of bulbs as soon as you receive them, and keep them in a cool (60 degrees Fahrenheit or cooler), dry, airy place until you can plant them.

Most bulbs will grow in an average garden soil, provided it is well drained. Adding 2 to 3 inches of organic material, like compost or shredded pine bark, will help improve drainage if there is a problem. Mix in the organic material to a depth of 10 to 12 inches.

Take a soil test (see Horticultural Practices, p. 7) before you plant your bulbs, and the results will tell you what you need to add in the way of nutrients and lime. The pH for most bulbs should be between

Bulbs

6 and 7. As with all plants, the better the soil and the more vigorous the bulbs, the bigger the blooms will be. Prepare your planting area ahead of time. The sooner you get bulbs in the ground, the better.

Wait to plant spring-flowering bulbs when the soil temperatures are at 60 degrees Fahrenheit or cooler in the fall. Depending on where you live in the state, this varies from October to early January (see Lawns, Introduction to learn how to measure soil temperature).

There are several methods of planting bulbs. You can dig holes and plant individual bulbs, or you can dig out a large area (a circle, a square, or an irregular shape) and space bulbs out in the area, in a random pattern. The second technique is especially effective for naturalistic plantings that use large drifts of one type of bulb like **Daffodils** or **Crocus.**

As a rule of thumb, most bulbs should be planted at a depth that is three to four times the width of the bulb you are planting. There are exceptions, like the **Bearded Iris,** which should be planted shallowly (see January for details about planting depths).

Water deeply after planting, **and** apply a good layer of mulch. If you get 1 to 2 inches of rainfall per week, that should be adequate. Use small cans like tuna fish or cat food cans to measure rainfall. Once there is $3/4$ to 1 inch of water in the can, the bulbs have received enough moisture.

If watering by hand, apply 5 gallons of water per 10 square feet. This is approximately the amount of water delivered by a garden hose operating one minute at medium pressure, and it should be enough water to penetrate at least 6 inches into a soil with a good percentage of clay. Repeat this step if bulbs are planted deeper than 6 inches.

Fertilizing Bulbs

Spring-blooming bulbs should be fertilized in the fall and then again in spring when you see shoots emerging. Do not put fertilizer directly in the hole when planting bulbs, for it could burn tender new roots as it dissolves. Instead, topdress with a complete fertilizer. Use 1 to 2 pounds of 10-10-10 per 100 square feet. For topdressing in the spring, use a water-soluble formula (like 10-10-10) that will get to the roots quickly while the bulb is actively growing and before it blooms.

Do not fertilize spring-blooming bulbs while they are blooming or just after they finish blooming. See November for more information on fertilizing bulbs.

Pest Control

Bulbs are not bothered by many pest or disease problems, and good cultural practices can greatly reduce or eliminate most of the problems they do have. Most bulbs need plenty of moisture while they are actively growing, but during the dormant season, too much water can cause root rot. Make sure that you plant bulbs in a well-drained soil.

Aphids, thrips, and mites can attack the foliage and flowers of bulbs. Leaves and buds may be distorted, and leaves may be speckled. Inspect on a regular basis, and, whenever possible, use an insecticidal soap for pest problems before resorting to stronger pesticides (see Chemicals, p. 327).

Bulbs for Georgia

Botanical Name (Common Name)	Size	Season of Bloom	Culture	Remarks
Allium christophii **Ornamental Onion**	12 to 20 inches tall.	Blooms in early summer. Clusters of silvery amethyst flowers form a large head.	Sunny locations and well-drained soils.	Combine with other perennials like **Hostas** and **Daylilies.**
Allium giganteum **Giant Ornamental Onion**	Softball-sized heads of lilac flowers on stems 40 to 48 inches tall.	Blooms in late spring.	Plant in full sun in a well-drained soil.	Combine with other bulbs and perennials like **Hardy Geraniums, Siberian Iris,** and **Peonies.**
Allium spaerocephalon **Drumstick Allium**	Quarter-sized flowers on stems 18 to 30 inches high.	Maroon-colored flowers in midsummer.	Plant in full sun in a well-drained soil.	A great bulb to perennialize. Combine with **Crinums, Daylilies,** and **Asiatic Lilies.**
Alocasia cvs. **Elephant's Ear**	5 to 10 feet or taller, and equal in width.	Grown for its handsome foliage, summer until frost.	Grows in full sun or shade. Prefers a moist soil.	Great for containers, in ponds, or in the ground. A dramatic plant that gives a tropical flair.
Alstroemeria psittacina **Parrot Lily**	Flowers occur on stems 24 to 30 inches tall.	Midsummer blooms in shades of marigold-orange with violet splotches. There are also pastel selections.	Plant in light shade in a well-drained soil. Keep roots cool.	This plant makes a great cut flower. Look for hardy types **'Freedom'** and **'Redcoat'.**
Anemone blanda **Windflower**	3 to 4 inches tall.	Small daisylike flowers with fernlike foliage in early spring.	Plant in full sun or part shade in a moist soil.	Soak tubers overnight before planting. Great for naturalizing.
Caladium cvs. **Caladium**	Range in size from 8 to 40 inches tall.	Colorful foliage all summer until frost. Variegated green-and-white, red-and-green, pink, and spotted leaf types.	Wait until the soil is 60 degrees F. or warmer. Plant tubers 6 inches deep.	**Caladiums** are great for the shade garden. They are happy in containers or in the ground.
Canna cvs. **Canna**	Ranging in size from 2 to 8 feet tall, these lush perennials start as tuberous rootstock.	Lance-shaped leaves come in green, burgundy, variegated, and striped. Colorful flowers in summer to fall are a bonus.	Plant in containers, along the edge of a pond, or in the perennial garden.	Great in the garden for a dramatic tropical flair.

Bulbs for Georgia

Botanical Name (Common Name)	Size	Season of Bloom	Culture	Remarks
Colocasia esculenta Elephant's Ear	Leaves may be up to 2 feet wide and plants 4 feet or taller.	Grown for its colorful foliage, 'Black Magic' has dark purple-black leaves.	Part sun or shade is ideal. Prefers a soil that is rich in organic matter.	A great plant to use for adding colorful foliage to the shade garden.
Crinum spp. and cvs. Crinum	Large sword-shaped leaves form large clumps, up to 3 or more feet across.	Lily-shaped fragrant flowers 4 to 6 inches long appear on tall stalks in mid- to late summer.	Full sun or partial shade. The bulbs resent being disturbed. Provide plenty of moisture.	Rodents won't disturb this bulb. A good companion for perennials.
Crocosmia × *crocosmiiflora* Crocosmia	Swordlike foliage. Graceful 24- to 36-inch-tall stems, covered with flowers.	Flowers in shades of orange to orange-red appear in late summer.	Plant in full sun in a soil that is moist but well drained.	Long-lasting as a cut flower. 'Lucifer' is a robust selection.
Crocus sp. and cvs. Crocus	**Crocus** range in size from 3 to 6 inches tall.	There are both fall- and spring-blooming types.	Plant corms 2 to 3 inches deep in a well-drained soil. **Crocus** prefer full sun or partial shade.	Be warned, **Crocus** is a favorite of chipmunks, who will dig up and eat the flowers and the bulbs.
Dahlia cvs. Dahlia	The size of individual plants and flowers of this tuber ranges greatly from 12 to 80 inches high.	Flowers vary from the tiny pom-pom to the large dinner-plate type. Blooms summer through fall.	These showy flowers grow happily in full sun but will tolerate partial shade. A well-drained soil is best.	Pest-resistant, **Dahlias** come in a wide range of colors.
Galanthus nivalis Snowdrop	One-inch-wide, white, three-lobed, nodding, bell-shaped flowers on 6- to 9-inch stems.	Flowers appear as early as January and may continue on and off through March.	Plant these bulbs in full sun or partial shade in a moist, well-drained soil.	Because the bulbs are so tiny and dry out easily, the best time to divide them is right after they finish flowering.
Gladiolus spp. and cvs. Gladiolus	Depending on the particular type, **Gladiolus** range 1 to 5 feet tall with blooms 1 to 8 inches across.	If you plant a diversity of types, you can have **Gladiolus** blooms from spring to fall.	Plant in a rich sandy soil. A corm should be planted at a depth that is four times the height of the corm.	For a succession of bloom, plant in spring, after the soil has warmed, at one- to two-week intervals.

Bulbs for Georgia

Hemerocallis spp. and hybrids **Daylily**	Lilylike flowers range from 2 to 8 inches across and appear in clusters on plants that are 1 to 6 feet tall.	Depending on the the type, blooms occur from spring through fall.	Plant in full sun or light shade. **Daylilies** tolerate most types of soil.	**Daylilies** can be grown in containers, as a ground cover, or in a mass on a bank to control erosion.
Hyacinthus orientalis **Hyacinth**	Grows to 1 foot tall with fragrant, bell-shaped flowers in shades of white, pink, blue, and purple. Narrow, bright-green leaves.	Blooms in early to mid-spring.	Plant in full sun or partial shade in a soil that is moist but well drained.	This is an easy bulb to force to bloom out of season in winter. Extremely fragrant flowers.
Iris spp. and cvs. **Iris**	There are many different types and sizes of **Iris,** ranging from those that grow only 4 to 8 inches tall to those that grow 20 inches tall.	Dwarf species Iris bloom in late winter to early spring. **Dutch Iris** bloom in May or later.	Plant in full sun in a well-drained soil. Provide plenty of moisture fall through spring. Keep bulbs dry during summer when they are dormant.	**Dwarf Iris** make good rock garden plants. Both **Dwarf** and **Dutch Iris** make good container plants.
Leucojum aestivum **Summer Snowflake**	Pendulous white bells with tips that look as if they've been dipped in green paint appear on stems 12 to 18 inches tall.	Blooms occur in mid- to late spring.	Plant in most soils in full sun or partial shade. Great for naturalizing near streams or or under trees and shrubs.	Blooms in south Georgia occur November through winter. In other parts of the state they bloom in late winter and early spring.
Lilium spp. and hybrids **Lily**	Many different sizes, types and bloom times. Flowers can be trumpet- or funnel-shaped or have recurved petals.	Depending on the type, blooms occur spring through summer.	Plant in a loose, deep, well-drained soil that is rich in organic material. Keep roots cool and tops in full sun or light shade.	Viral or mosaic infection can cause problems. Purchase healthy bulbs from companies that specialize in bulbs.

Bulbs for Georgia

Lycoris spp. **Spider Lily and Naked Lady**	Flower stems range from 12 to 24 inches tall. Spider Lily foliage is straplike and dark green with a silver-white vein. **Naked Lady** leaves are wide, gray-green, strap-like.	**Naked Ladies** bloom in mid- to late summer, and **Spider Lilies** bloom in early fall.	Plant both types in a moist but well-drained soil. They grow in full sun or partial shade.	Plant these fall-blooming bulbs July to August for best results.
Narcissus spp. and cvs. **Daffodil**	**Daffodils** range in height from 3 to 20 inches tall. They are divided into thirteen different divisions according to flower shape.	There are early, mid-season, and late-blooming varieties of these spring bulbs.	**Daffodils** prefer a soil that is moist but well drained. They need a minimum of six hours of direct sunlight to thrive.	**Daffodils** are poisonous, and rodents will not disturb them. They are long-lived in the garden and require a minimum of maintenance.
Polianthes tuberosa **Tuberose**	Flowers shoot up 18 to 36 inches above foliage that is 1 foot high.	Twenty or more fragrant flowers on a stem; both single and double types bloom early to late summer.	Plant in a sunny site in a soil that in moist but well drained.	Start bulbs indoors for earlier bloom.
Tulipa spp. and cvs. **Tulip**	Vary greatly in size depending on type, from species only 3 inches tall to Darwin hybrids that reach 28 inches tall.	Flowers occur from early to late spring in a range of colors and shapes.	In coastal areas, **Tulips** need prechilling at 40 degrees F. for 2 to 3 months and should be planted December to mid-January. Plant in full sun in a well-drained soil.	Many of the species **Tulips** bloom early. They are well adapted to the summer heat and will usually perennialize.
Zephyranthes spp. and hybrids **Rain Lily**	Grassy foliage 1 to 2 feet long.	Depending on the variety, flowers occur in spring, summer, and fall in shades of pink, white, and yellow.	Plant bulbs 1 to 2 inches deep in full sun. They tolerate periods of wet and dry. Flowers appear after a rain.	Plant among ground covers for a good show.

Tools for Planting Bulbs

Bulb Trowels

Designed especially for planting blubs, these trowels have long handles and a narrow sharp pointed stainless steel blade, so they won't rust. They come in different sizes, and unlike traditional trowels which are designed to scoop out the soil, you simply stab the soil and pull the trowel toward yourself to create a planting hole. The 9- or 12-inch trowel is perfect for planting smaller bulbs like **Crocus** or **Anemones.** The 22-inch trowel has a blade that is 2 inches wide, making it suitable for planting larger bulbs whether in the lawn or the flower bed.

Bulb Planter

There are different versions of this tool, but the basic construction is a planter that is 40 inches high from the tip of the stainless steel blade to the handle which is on a steel frame. These heavy duty tools can weigh 61 pounds or more. The blade is a cylinder. Using your feet, push the blade into the soil and then pull out a large plug of soil. Place the bulb in the hole and replace the cylinder of soil on top of the bulbs.

Bulb Planter for Naturalizing or for Soil that is Unprepared

A heavy–duty steel tool, 38 inches tall, it can weigh as much as 81 pounds. Like the Bulb Planter, you operate this planter by standing on the foot bar. The notched 2$\frac{1}{2}$-inch-wide blade is heavy enough that it is easy to push into the ground, whether it's the lawn, a border, or a meadow.

Planning

If you live in a coastal area, there is still time to plant spring-flowering bulbs, provided they have been prechilled (see October for more information). Plan for a sequence of bloom in the spring by planting bulbs that will bloom early, mid-season, and later, beginning with **Snowdrops** and **Crocus,** then species **Tulips** and early **Daffodils.**

Sometimes spring bulbs will begin to emerge (2 inches or so), and **Snowdrops** may be blooming now in the northern parts of the state. Gardeners worry that these flowers might be damaged by the cold. Just *cover* them with some pine straw, and they should be fine.

Planting

Once your **Snowdrops** finish blooming, you can *divide* them. Because these bulbs are so tiny and dry out easily, the best time to divide is while they are still bloom-ing or as soon as the blooms fade. Dig up a clump you want to divide, and gently tease apart the bulbs, making sure each division has bulbs with roots, shoots, and foliage. *Replant* them as soon as possible in their new location, leav-ing the foliage intact. Water them in, and next year you should have blooms again.

Name	Planting Depth	Number of Bulbs or Spacing
Anemone blanda	2 to 3 in.	10 to 15 sq. ft. (soak overnight before planting)
Allium Giant	3 to 4 times the depth of the bulb measured from the base	large, 5 sq. ft.; small, 10 sq. ft.
Alstroemeria	9 to 12 in.	1 sq. ft.
Caladium	6 in.	1 sq. ft. (soil should be 60 degrees F. or warmer)
Canna	5 in.	10 to 18 in. apart (tuberous rootstock with 3 to 5 eyes)
Colocasia	3 x the width of bulb	18 in. on center
Crinum	plant so neck protrudes	1 sq. ft.
Dahlia	12 in.	1 sq. ft.
Galanthus	1½ to 2 in.	10 sq. ft.
Hyacinthus	4 to 6 in.	5 sq. ft.
Iris reticulata	4 in.	10 to 12 sq. ft.
Leucojum	3 in.	5 to 6 sq. ft.
Lilium	small, 2 to 3 in.; medium, 3 to 4 in.; large, 4 to 6 in. exception **Madonna Lilies** - 1 in. deep	smaller bulbs 2 to 3 sq.ft; larger bulbs, 1 to 2 sq. ft.
Narcissus	larger bulbs (2 to 3 in. in diameter) 6 to 8 in. deep; medium-sized bulbs (1 to 2 in. in diameter) 3 to 6 in. deep; small or miniature bulbs (1½ to 1 inch in diameter) 2 to 3 in. deep	
Polianthes tuberosa	2 in.	3 sq. ft.
Tulipa	regular-sized **Tulips,** 8 to 10 in. deep; small **Tulips,** 4 to 6 in. deep	
Zephyranthes	1 to 2 in.	8 to 10 sq. ft.

Different types of bulbs should be planted at different depths, depending on the size of the bulb. (See list on previous page.) Plant shallower in heavy clay soils and slightly deeper in light or sandy soils.

Watering

Water bulbs as soon as you plant them. Soak the planted area several times, once a week. Apply 2 inches of mulch (pine straw or pine bark) over the planted area.

Fertilizing

Wait until shoots emerge in spring, then apply a water-soluble fertilizer (10-10-10 is good) if you did not fertilize bulbs when you planted them in fall.

Pest Control

In South Georgia, check for aphids feeding on new foliage and buds of bulbs. Use a strong blast from the hose to try to eradicate these hungry pests.

Helpful Hints

Gardeners with sandy soils, beware: Voles love such an environment, and if you grow **Crocus** or **Tulips,** these animals can be a challenge. To discourage voles, don't apply a layer of mulch that is too thick (2 to 3 inches is plenty), or the soil will become warmer and more inviting to the pests.

To avoid problems with voles, grow different types of **Narcissus** and other members of the Amaryllidaceae family (including **Leucojum** and × **Amarcrinum**), which are resistant to rodents and deer. **Narcissus** bulbs contain a poisonous alkaloid that acts as a natural pest-repellent.

Professional bulb growers Brent and Becky Heath of Gloucester, Virginia, have had success in controlling voles using two products, **Mole-Med®** and **Ro-pel®.** To discourage deer they recommend **Deer-Off®.** Look for all of these products at your local garden center.

One of the frustrating things for gardeners who want to grow bulbs is that they have to deal with animals digging them up and eating them. One technique to discourage this is to plant the bulbs and then *cover* them with wire mesh. The holes in the mesh should be large enough (1 inch or so) so that the foliage and blooms can fit through. Cover the mesh with a layer of mulch. Squirrels and chipmunks like to dig up **Crocus** and **Tulip** bulbs for a tasty treat. They often dig them up before or while they are in bloom. *Replant* them quickly if you notice they have been pulled out of the ground.

Pruning

No pruning is needed at this time of year.

Planning

Record in your garden journal what's blooming or what bulbs are coming up in the garden. Depending on where you live in the state, early spring bulbs like **Snowdrops** or **Glory of the Snow** (*Chionodoxa luciliae*) are beginning to bloom or are still blooming. Other early bloomers include *Narcissus* **'Rijnveld's Early Sensation'**, a classic **Daffodil** with a yellow trumpet and petals; and the reliable heirloom **Daffodil** *N.* **'February Gold'**, which is excellent for forcing and perennializing.

At the end of the month in the coastal part of the state, expect the old-fashioned *Narcissus jonquilla* to be in bloom. This species of **Daffodil** (called "Sweeties" for its sweet perfume), which has rush-like foliage and extremely fragrant flowers, has naturalized throughout the Southeast.

While most gardeners are familiar with **Daffodils** and **Tulips,** there are a host of other bulbs that bloom in early spring. Below is a list of small flowering bulbs known to be among the earliest of the spring bloomers. Many of these same bulbs are also good candidates for naturalizing in lawns. Because they bloom early, the foliage has time to ripen before the first mowing of the lawn.

- *Chionodoxa luciliae* **'Alba' Glory of the Snow** produces five to ten starry flowers in a spray per stem.

- *Crocus* **spp. and cvs. Crocus** is an easy-to-grow bulb with cup-shaped flowers and foliage only 3 to 6 inches tall. It can be tucked in pockets between tree roots, naturalized in the lawn, or featured in the rock garden.

- *Galanthus nivalis* **Snowdrops** have white, nodding, bell-shaped flowers that appear as early as January. This woodland wonder grows anywhere from 4 to 10 inches tall, depending on the selection.

- *Ipheion uniflorum* **Star Flower** is a small bulb that has star-shaped flowers with six petals. The fragrant blooms range in color from almost white to soft violet. Be warned, though, the grasslike foliage smells like garlic when crushed.

- *Iris reticulata* **Dwarf Iris** offers little flowers (4 to 8 inches tall with leaves) that glisten like jewels when they bloom in shades of purple, blue, and lavender.

- *Puschkinia scilloides* **var. *libanotica* Puschkinia** is an undemanding bulb that grows in sun or shade and produces many starry pale-blue to white flowers with dark-blue stripes. Growing only 4 to 6 inches tall,

it is ideal for combining with other bulbs or planting in masses in the lawn.

- *Scilla siberica* **'Spring Beauty'** has clusters of dark-blue, loosely formed bells on 6- to 8-inch stems.

Planting

If you have **Daffodils** or other bulbs that you didn't plant in the fall and the bulbs are still firm, go ahead and plant them. You may not get any blooms this spring, or if you do, they may be shorter than normal, but don't worry! These bulbs should catch up with the rest of your bulbs in a few years. If you don't get your bulbs planted now, they will dry out completely by next fall and there will be nothing to plant.

Watering

Water bulbs immediately after you plant them, soaking the area thoroughly. Don't water bulbs that you planted last fall until they begin actively growing (the leaves and stems should be several inches high). Once they start growing, they will need to be watered only if you don't get any rain (at least 1 inch per week). If you have a small area of bulbs (several square feet), you can use a watering can to water. Apply water to the spot, let it soak in, and repeat. You will want to make sure that water gets to the bulb roots. If you apply 1 inch of water, it should reach roots at a depth of 6 inches in a soil with a moderate amount of clay (30 to 40 percent). Applying double this amount should be enough for bulbs that are planted as deep as 9 to 10 inches.

Fertilizing

In the southern parts of the state, if your bulbs are actively growing and 2 or more inches of foliage has emerged, you can top-dress with a water-soluble formula like 10-10-10. It will get to the roots quickly while the bulb is growing and before it blooms. For **Daffodils,** look for a formula such as "Peters Hydro-Sol®" (5-11-26).

Pest Control

If you have problems with voles or chipmunks digging up your bulbs and you neglected to put down wire mesh when you planted, try this remedy: Mix some liquid dish detergent (a few teaspoons) and water in a quart spray bottle. Add some red

Helpful Hints

- A slow-release fertilizer releases nutrients gradually over time at a rate at which bulbs can use them. A special "Daffodil Fertilizer" is recommended by Brent Heath, a third-generation nurseryman in the **Daffodil** industry. A six-month slow-release, the 5-10-20 formula also contains trace amounts of manganese, iron, copper, sulphur, boron, and zinc. It is available from Brent and Becky's Bulbs (see Bulbs, August). Apply this fertilizer in the fall, $\frac{1}{2}$ pound (1/2 cup) per 10 square feet.

- Other products known as bulb fertilizers can be used in sequential doses (refer to product label for detailed directions) with the addition of extra potash, which will fulfill the potassium requirements of **Daffodils.**

- "Holland Bulb Booster" is a choice slow-release fertilizer for **Tulips** and members of the **Lily** family including **Alliums** and **Hyacinths.** If you use this fertilizer for **Daffodils,** be sure to add extra potash. A good source of potash is wood ash, which also contains trace elements bulbs need. Apply wood ash once per season (1 pound per 100 square feet). Wood ash also helps neutralize acidic soils because of its alkaline pH (be sure to keep it away from woody evergreens that prefer an acid soil; too much potash can cause evergreens to turn yellow and sickly).

pepper powder or hot sauce (a few teaspoons). *Spray* this around the area where the bulbs are coming up—this should discourage critters from digging up your treasures.

Another approach is to sprinkle red pepper directly on the soil where the bulbs are planted. Keep in mind that rain or dew will make these treatments lose their effectiveness.

Pruning

Remove faded blooms as they occur. Leave the foliage until it turns yellow and collapses.

Planning

Now that spring bulbs are beginning to bloom, plan ahead for the bulbs you would like to have blooming in summer and fall. Keep in mind that even if summer bulbs like **Caladiums** are available for sale in stores now, you *should not* plant them until the soil temperature is at least 60 degrees Fahrenheit or warmer and the fear of frost is past. **Caladiums** require warm soil and air temperatures of 70 degrees or above during the day and, ideally, not below 60 degrees at night. Depending on where you live in the state, these temperatures could occur in April or May. Purchase a soil thermometer or refer to the Lawns, Introduction for information on how to measure soil temperature. Certain perennial summer-blooming bulbs like *Alstroemeria* should be planted in the fall.

Below is a list of summer-blooming bulbs (including rhizomes, tubers, and tuberous roots) with brief descriptions, including whether they prefer sun or shade. While some begin blooming in late spring and continue through summer, others start in summer and continue until frost. There are a number of plants that have striking foliage and insignificant flowers, such as **Elephant's Ear** and **Caladium.** There are also some types of **Canna** that have fantastic foliage, colorful flowers, or both.

- *Alocasia* species and hybrids, including **Upright Elephant's Ear,** prefer partial shade to shade. There are many different selections, with large colorful leaves ranging in size from less than 1 foot to 2 feet across or longer and wider.

- *Bletilla striata* (**Chinese Ground Orchid**) prefers filtered shade. Plant in early spring. Lavender to magenta miniature orchid-like flowers occur May to June.

- *Caladium* hybrids (**Caladium**) prefer filtered shade to shade. Although some varieties that take sun have been bred, this tropical is indispensable when color is needed in the shade garden. Large (to 1½-foot-long) heart- and arrow-shaped leaves on plants growing 2 to 4 feet tall (depending on the selection) come in a range of colors from almost pure white to dark green. They may be striped, banded, or blotched with rose, pink, silver, green, or bronze.

- *Canna* species and hybrids (**Canna**) prefer full sun to filtered shade. Their dramatic foliage, from dark red to variegated and all the variations, gives your garden a tropical flair. They range in size from 2 to 6 feet tall and can be left in the ground year-round in coastal areas. Plant 5 inches deep and 10 inches apart.

- *Colocasia esculenta* (**Taro** or **Elephant's Ear**) prefers filtered shade to shade. This tuberous herb is edible as well as ornamental; in lowland tropical areas, the starchy roots are a staple food. Selections of this plant can grow to 6 feet tall in the garden. Some produce huge leaves, 2 feet long and even broader, in one growing season.

- *Dahlia* hybrids (**Dahlia**) prefer full sun. These summer bloomers, usually started from tubers, range from 15 inches to over 6 feet tall. The flowers come in almost every color and form imaginable.

- *Gladiolus* (**Gladiolus**) prefer full sun and bloom from spring until fall, depending on when you plant. The dwarf species *Gladiolus byzantinum* has maroon flowers, 1 to 3 inches, in clusters of six to twelve on 2- to 3-foot stems. Smaller and more refined than some of the larger types of **Gladiolus,** this heirloom is also winter hardy.

- *Gloriosa superba* '**Rothschildiana**' (**Climbing Lily**) prefers sun to filtered shade. Flowers are made up of six bright red segments banded with yellow. Grow in pots. Start tubers indoors in February.

MARCH

Planting

You can start **Caladium** tubers in pots indoors. Start **Tuberose** indoors and plant outside when soil temperatures warm up. Plant the rhizomes 2 inches deep and 4 to 6 inches apart. In coastal areas, they can be left in the ground year-round.

Watering

Keep spring bulbs that are actively growing and blooming well watered. If you don't get at least an inch of rain per week in your garden, *water.* Apply 5 gallons of water to a 10-square-foot area.

Fertilizing

Fertilize spring bulbs after they emerge, before flowering. *Top-dress* with a water-soluble formula like 10-10-10 that will get to the roots quickly while the bulb is growing and before it blooms. For **Daffodils,** look for a formula such as "Peters Hydro-Sol®" (5-11-26).

Pest Control

You may notice that your early-blooming varieties of **Daffodils** have

Starting Caladiums

If you want to get a jump on the summer season, you can start **Caladium** tubers indoors in March. If you use bottom heat when you start them, their growth will be accelerated (look for a heat mat designed for seedlings). Move them outside in late April or early May once soil temperatures are 60 degrees Fahrenheit or warmer. Use a mix that is equal parts coarse sand, compost, and ground pine bark or peat moss. For tubers that are $2\frac{1}{2}$ inches long or smaller, use a pot that is 5 inches wide and deep. For larger tubers, use a pot that is at least 7 inches wide. You will encourage lots of side shoots if you scoop out the center growing tip. You can plant the tubers directly in a pot with the recommended mix, or scoop out the center growing tips first and then plant them.

1. Fill the pot with 1 inch of potting mix. Place the tuber in the pot. Position the tuber so the roots are at the bottom of the tuber toward the soil.

2. Add 2 inches of potting mix to cover the tuber. Water well until water rushes out of the holes in the bottom of the pot.

3. Keep the pot in bright light (a sunny window). Water when the soil feels dry to the touch.

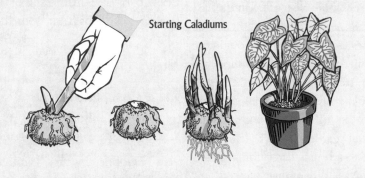

Starting Caladiums

not yet come up and there is no indication that they will, even when you dig down several inches into the soil. They may have root rot. Dig up and discard bulbs. Don't replant without improving drainage.

Pruning

Remove faded blooms from flowering bulbs, but leave the foliage to ripen.

Planning

Photograph your garden as more spring bulbs come into bloom. Make notes in your garden journal about which varieties are fragrant and which make good cut flowers.

After your **Easter Lily** finishes blooming, you can plant it in the garden. Choose a site where the soil is well drained but rich in organic matter. Plant the bulb at the same depth it was in the pot. Let the stems ripen and die down before you remove them. *Water* the **Lily** after you plant it. Next spring, *fertilize* with a complete fertilizer like 10-10-10. It may take several years before your **Lily** blooms during its normal season, midsummer.

Tulips are a favorite of many gardeners, but not all **Tulips** are created equal, especially when it comes to surviving in our hot, humid climate. While **Tulips** are often treated as annuals in Georgia, there are a few that are good repeat bloomers. (This does not apply to coastal gardeners, whose **Tulips** need to be prechilled before they are planted.) While their flowers are not as large and showy as those of the hybrids, most of the species **Tulips** tolerate the heat better and bloom year after year in the garden. Many of these have graceful, delicate flowers. Low growing and early blooming, species **Tulips** are

perfect for the rock garden or for growing in pots. If you're not already growing these **Tulips,** think of adding some to your garden next year. Here is a list of some species **Tulips** with brief descriptions.

- *Tulipa bakeri* **'Lilac Wonder',** with a sunny yellow heart and lilac-pink petals, grows to 6 to 8 inches at maturity.

- *T. clusiana* var. *chrysantha* has 9-inch stems that produce flowers that are crimson when they're closed. When they open, the inside is bright yellow.

- *T. greigii* has scarlet flowers that measure 6 inches across, on 10-inch stems. The foliage is striped or mottled with brown.

- *T. kaufmanniana* is called the **Waterlily Tulip** for the flowers that occur on 6-inch stems. They are creamy yellow marked with red on the outside, and yellow in the center.

- *T. tarda* offers bunches of star-shaped **Tulip** flowers of white and yellow, appearing on 6- to 8-inch stems in early spring.

- *T. turkestanica*, 6 to 8 inches tall, has white flowers with orange centers that perfume the air in early spring.

Planting

Plant **Dutch Iris** now for late-summer blooms. Check with your local Extension Service about the last frost date in your area. By mid-April in all but the most northern part of the state, it should be safe to plant many summer-blooming bulbs like **Canna, Elephant's Ear, Dahlia,** or **Gladiolus** outside—especially if you are planting them in containers. Before you plant, be sure soil temperatures are 60 degrees Fahrenheit or warmer.

Watering

Now that spring bulbs are actively growing and blooming, make sure they get plenty of water. *Water* your bulbs once a week unless you get a good rain, 1 inch or more per week.

Fertilizing

Remember, the ideal time to fertilize bulbs is in the fall when they produce roots that absorb nutrients, but you might choose to fertilize now, too, when spring bulbs are growing and about to bloom. Use a water-soluble fertilizer (10-10-10) that will get to the roots quickly while the bulb is actively growing and before it blooms.

Pest Control

Pull weeds that appear in your plantings of bulbs. Apply a weed-preventer in your established bulb beds (see Chemicals, p. 327). Read the label carefully before applying any pesticide.

One of the more perplexing problems observed by **Canna** growers is leaves that refuse to unfurl in spring. On closer examination, they find that the edges of the **Canna** leaves have been "stitched" together by silver webbing. Upon manually unrolling the leaf, a white grublike creature is found inhabiting the interior: the canna leaf roller. This grub is the larva of a moth that laid its eggs on the leaves as they emerged from the soil. *Examine* your **Cannas** each week, and *unroll* any leaves that seem to be developing abnormally.

Make a note in your garden calendar to remove and destroy all Canna *stalks and foliage next November. The moth overwinters in the dead leaves, but not if you disrupt the life cycle.*

Pruning

Remove faded blooms of **Daffodils** before they set seed. Remove the flowers, and leave the stems to help with photosynthesis.

Helpful Hints

If you love bulbs but are concerned about the awkward stage they go through when the foliage ripens, try companion planting. Plant your bulbs with companion plants and you can extend the blooming season and provide cover foliage to hide ripening bulb foliage. You can also layer your bulbs so that when one type finishes blooming, another begins. For example, you can plant **Tulips** 10 inches deep, **Daffodils** at 6 inches, and then **Crocus** and **Dwarf Iris** on top at 3 inches deep. With this method you will have a long season of spring bloom from your bulbs. Here are some planting combinations:

- **Crocus** with **Pansies** or lawn grasses
- **Daffodils** with **Hellebores** and **Hosta**
- **Daffodils** or **Surprise Lilies** with **English Ivy** (use larger-type **Daffodils,** not dwarf varieties, so they are robust enough to compete with the **Ivy**)
- **Daffodils** with ferns like **Japanese Painted Fern**
- **Dwarf Iris** with **Ajuga** or **Periwinkle**
- **Daffodils** with **Daylilies** in a sunny border (this way you will have blooms in spring and summer in the same spot)

In a shady woodland composed of deciduous trees, bulbs get enough light in the fall, winter, and early spring to ensure good blooms; and when summer arrives, they are protected from the hot afternoon sun.

Once the **Daffodils** finish blooming, some gardeners like to tie up their foliage with rubber bands or bunch them up. Not only is this practice unattractive, it prevents sunlight from getting to all the leaves, cuts off air circulation, and increases the chances of fungal problems.

It is important to let bulb foliage ripen. As leaves go through the process of photosynthesis, they store food for next year's blooms. The time to cut off the foliage is when it turns yellow and falls over. **Daffodil** expert Brent Heath recommends that you wait at least eight to ten weeks after bloom before cutting off bulb foliage.

Planning

Spring bulbs are finished, and summer will soon be here. Plan on adding at least a few summer bloomers to brighten the garden scene. You can easily grow summer bulbs in pots or in the ground. Think about combinations of different bulbs or bulbs and perennials. *Stake* Lilies before they get too tall and the task becomes more difficult (see Perennials, April for more information on staking).

One **Canna** with dark or variegated foliage can make a dramatic statement in the perennial border. A combination that promises to light up the shade garden is made of **Caladiums, Cannas, Elephant's Ears,** and **Impatiens.** For sun, try combining **Dahlias** with ornamental grasses, **Butterfly Ginger,** and one large **Elephant's Ear.**

Planting

Plant **Cannas, Caladiums, Dahlias, Elephant's Ear,** and **Gladiolus.** Transplant **Tuberose** that you started indoors to the garden. **Dahlias** are usually planted as tubers but can also be grown from seed; they range in size from only 15 inches to over 6 feet tall. For dwarf types, sow the seed directly in the spot where the **Dahlias** will grow. Start seed for taller varieties indoors in February or March.

Before you plant **Dahlia** tubers, make sure the soil has been amended with organic materials like compost or ground bark. Here are a few tips for planting the tubers:

- Space the largest types 4 to 5 feet apart, and make sure the hole is 1 foot deep.

- Space medium-sized tubers 3 feet apart and 1 foot deep.

- Space small tubers 1 to 2 feet apart and 1 foot deep.

- If you use fertilizer, use a complete fertilizer like 10-10-10. Mix in 1/4 cup thoroughly with the soil in the planting hole, then add another 4 inches of soil over this before you plant.

- With large tubers, it is a good idea to put the stake in the hole when you are planting. This way you won't risk damaging the tuber later with the stake. After you place the tuber horizontally, position the stake a few inches from the eye (growing point). Fill in and *cover* the tuber with 3 inches of soil. *Water* thoroughly. Gradually fill the hole with soil as the shoots grow.

Plant summer-flowering **Garden Gladiolus** at one- to two-week intervals, and this will give you a long season of bloom, up to six weeks. Before planting, treat them with bulb dust, an insecticide-fungicide. Some of the hybrids grow 5 feet high and don't require staking. They offer spikes of flowers with twelve to fourteen blooms at one time. For the most productive corms, select those that are $1^{1}/_{2}$ to 2 inches wide.

Watering

Keep bulbs watered while they are growing and blooming. One inch per week should keep them happy.

Fertilizing

Keep fertilizer out of direct contact with **Gladiolus** corms. Instead, mix a complete fertilizer into the soil thoroughly before planting, or use superphosphate 0-46-0 (4 pounds per 100 square feet).

Pest Control

Look for aphids on **Lilies, Dahlias,** and **Gladiolus.** *Spray* them with insecticidal soap or a synthetic pesticide (see Chemicals, p. 327). Sunspray® or other refined horticultural oils are also good. Aphids spread mosaic virus, which attacks **Lily** foliage and for which there is no cure. If any of your **Lilies** exhibit mottled leaves or stunted growth, they may have mosaic. *Dig and destroy* the bulbs. The best way to avoid this infection is to buy only healthy bulbs and remove injured portions before planting.

You may notice that your **Bearded Iris** have notches in the leaf margins, about 1/8 inch wide, and there is also a dark trail in the leaves. This means leaf borers. While you can use an insecticide like Cygon (see Chemicals, p. 327) to control these pests, you can also kill the borers by squeezing the infested leaves between your thumb and forefinger in the areas where you notice them feeding (the dark, water-soaked areas).

Helpful Hints

Dahlias are great for growing in the border, for cut flowers, or in containers. With pinching and thinning you can increase the number or size of the flowers. For tall varieties, remove all but one or two of the strongest shoots. When the shoots develop three sets of leaves, pinch off tips just above the top set. This should lead to the development of two side shoots from each pair of leaves, and more flowers. If you want to have large flowers, remove all but the terminal flower buds on the side shoots. This will encourage the plant to put its energy into making fewer but larger flowers.

When cutting **Dahlias** from the garden, cut them in early morning or evening. Remove any leaves below the top 2 inches of the stem. Place the base of the cut stems in 2 to 3 inches of hot water. Let the water cool for several hours or overnight. Once the water has cooled, fill the remainder of the container with water up to where the leaves begin on the stem.

Keeping Cut Flowers Fresh: Cut flowers will last longer if you use a container that is clean and free of dirt and bacteria. Changing the water daily will also help keep flowers fresh.

Pruning

Keep plants groomed. You can prevent diseases from spreading by removing dead or diseased leaves as soon as you notice them.

Planning

Gardeners agree that there is really no such thing as "low-maintenance gardening," but there are some bulbs that are proven winners in the low-maintenance quest. **Daylilies** are at the top of the list for choice summer-blooming bulbs (although not true bulbs, these members of the **Lily** family have tuberous fleshy roots). **Lily**-like flowers appear above clumps of arching, sword-shaped leaves. One or two divisions (a division is also called a fan, as the foliage looks similar to a fan) can quickly multiply and fill an area of your garden. **Daylilies** come in a wide range of colors and shades of red, orange, yellow, pink, purple, and more.

With just a minimum of care, **Daylilies** reward you every year with a long season of bloom and lush healthy plants. Plant them in full sun or light shade in a soil that is well drained. There are numerous selections, including types that bloom only once a season and those that bloom for weeks, rest, and then produce more blooms. Combine **Daylilies** in the same planting bed with spring-blooming bulbs and you will have a succession of blooms. Plant them in masses, mix them in with other perennials, or use them as ground covers or in containers. Most types offered for sale are hybrids with improved flowers and foliage. The modern hybrids include deciduous, evergreen, and semi-evergreen types. Evergreen types are well suited for coastal gardens; the hardier deciduous types are better for gardens in the middle and northern parts of the state.

For maximum impact, plant early, midseason, and late-blooming varieties. Modern **Daylily** hybrids range in size from dwarf, 1 foot tall, to the giant at 6 feet tall with flowers 3 to 8 inches across. The flower types are diverse, too, from spidery to ruffled. Some of the species and older varieties have flowers that are not only colorful but fragrant as well. Below is a list of a few **Daylilies** to consider for your Georgia garden. For more information about **Daylilies,** contact The American Hemerocallis Society. The Web site (http://www.daylilies.org) lists **Daylily** groups and display gardens in Georgia under a link for regional activities (Georgia is Region 5).

- *Hemerocallis fulva* **Orange Daylily** is a deciduous species that is also called **Ditch Lily** because it is commonly seen in roadside ditches or old gardens. A tough plant, it grows to 6 feet high and has leaves that are 2 feet or longer. The orange-red flowers, 3 to 5 inches wide, appear in summer and look great in combination with the old-fashioned blue "mophead" **Hydrangeas.** Although it is not as refined as many of the hybrids offered for sale, this tough "doer" is still a good choice for a care-free perennial bulb.

- *H.* **'Happy Returns'**, a long-blooming **Daylily** hybrid, offers yellow flowers, at about 2 to 3 feet high, for months, beginning in May and continuing until frost. Its compact size, about 18 inches high by 18 inches wide, makes it ideal for small gardens, containers, or masses.

- *H. lilio-asphodelus* (*H. flava*) **Lemon Daylily** is a deciduous type, growing to 3 feet tall or taller. This old-fashioned favorite is grown for its fragrant yellow flowers that appear in late May or June.

Planting

Plant Caladiums, Dahlias, Daylilies, and Gladiolus.

Divide Daylilies (refer to illustration in Perennials, March).

Watering

Keep summer-blooming bulbs watered. Check containers daily; feel the top 1 to 2 inches of soil and if it is dry to the touch, water until the water runs out the bottom of the pot. Check bulbs planted in the ground weekly. If you haven't received at least 1 inch of rain per week, water well.

Mulching your bulb plantings not only helps conserve moisture but cuts down on weed infestations. Apply 1 to 2 inches of mulch on top of the soil in areas where you plant bulbs.

Fertilizing

Once they're planted, **Dahlias** don't need supplemental fertilizer unless they are growing in poor soil. If this is the case, you can sidedress (see Garden Words, p. 323) when first flowerbuds appear. Apply the fertilizer in rows between the plants with a fertilizer that is high in phosphates and potash, like 5-10-15.

Fertilize **Caladiums** with a complete water-soluble fertilizer like 20-20-20 once a month during the growing season.

Fertilize **Gladiolus** with a complete fertilizer like 8-8-8 or 10-10-10 once they have developed five or more leaves. Keep the fertilizer 6 inches from the main stem of the **Gladiolus.** *Water* well after you fertilize.

Pest Control

Check **Dahlias** for thrips (see Roses, May)—new growth and buds will look distorted and flowers will fail to open normally. Leaf surfaces may look silvery or bronze. Black specks on the leaves are another indication that thrips are present. *Use a strong blast from the hose, and wash them off.* If you have a severe infestation, you may have to use a systemic insecticide (see Chemicals, p. 327).

Your **Dahlia** leaves may have tiny dark specks and a silvery cast, and the undersides of the leaves may have a fine webbing. This means spider mites. *Spray* with horticultural oil, insecticidal soap, or a synthetic miticide (see Chemicals, p. 327).

Helpful Hint

Daylily blooms open for one day and then fade away. As a general practice, it is best to pinch off dead blooms as soon as you notice them. This way the plant will not only look better but will put its energy into making more flowerbuds instead of seeds.

Pruning

Cut off the yellowing foliage of **Daffodils** that bloomed in early spring. (If it is mostly yellow and lying on the ground, it is safe to cut it off.)

73

Planning

If you have large clumps of **Daffodils** *that are healthy but have produced very few blooms in the spring, it is time to divide them.* While **Daffodils** welcome the sun in winter and early spring, they benefit from some shade in the summer. If you need to divide them, the best time is after the foliage has turned yellow and fallen over. Late-blooming varieties may still have foliage that is visible in July.

If there is still a bit of foliage to mark where the **Daffodils** are growing, it makes it easier to divide them. When you dig up a clump, dig around and under it with a digging fork or spade. Use caution so as not to cut off roots or slice into the bulbs. Shake soil off the bulbs, and gently untangle the roots. Don't break apart bulbs that are firmly attached to one another or you may injure them, which makes them more susceptible to disease. They will split apart in their own time once they are replanted. If you are moving your bulbs, have the new planting site prepared ahead of time.

If you don't replant immediately and want to store your bulbs, make sure you dry them completely. Use mesh bags like those used to store fruit or onions to store your bulbs. Nylon stockings make a good substitute if you don't have a mesh bag.

Use a fan to provide good air circulation while you dry the bulbs. Keep them in a cool, dark, dry place until you replant them in fall.

There are a number of late-summer/fall bloomers that can be planted in the summer as soon as you receive them, including **Spider Lily** *Lycoris radiata,* **Surprise Lily** *L. squamigera*, and **Autumn Daffodil** *Sternbergia lutea*. These bulbs are normally dug and shipped any time between June and August. Order them now for planting. They may not bloom the first season, but once they are established, they will reward you every year with flowers at a time when few other bulbs are blooming.

Planting

Plant another crop of **Gladiolus** so that you will have blooms all summer and into fall.

If your **Daffodils** are in a spot that is hot and sunny all summer, plant a summer crop of annuals over the bulbs. This will provide them with some shade and the annuals will use up excess moisture, helping the bulbs stay dry.

Watering

Stop watering **Daffodils** and other spring-blooming bulbs once they are no longer blooming. **Daffodils,** especially, require well-drained soils when they are dormant or they will develop basal rot.

Fertilizing

Fertilize **Caladiums** with a complete water-soluble fertilizer like 20-20-20.

Pest Control

Pull weeds in your bulb beds when they are young and before they flower and set seed. This will prevent them from spreading freely by seed.

Your **Dahlias** may look wilted even after you water them; some plants may have stunted growth, others have died, and when you cut open a stem you see brown streaking on the inside. This means your **Dahlias** have a fungus called Verticillium wilt. This fungus destroys tissues responsible for transporting water throughout the plant. There is no chemical control. *Destroy* infected plants, and dispose of them in the garbage, *not the compost pile.*

Do not plant **Dahlias** *in the same area again or you may have the same problem.*

Some of your **Daylilies** may have yellow and brown streaks, others may have dark brown spots that are irregular in shape, and some of these leaves eventually die. All this means your **Daylilies** are probably suffering from a leaf spot caused by a fungus. *Remove and destroy* any infected leaves. During hot, humid weather, plants are more susceptible to attack by certain fungi. Use drip irrigation or other alternatives to overhead watering. The faster leaves dry, the less chance fungi will have to attack.

Select varieties of **Daylilies** *that are recommended for your region. Check with The American Hemerocallis Society (http://www.daylilies.org).*

Pruning

Remove dead flowers from **Daylilies** and **Dahlias.**

Helpful Hints

While many summer-blooming bulbs are great in the garden, there are a number of types that also make great cut flowers.

- *Alstroemeria* **(Peruvian Lilies)** hybrids produce clusters of orchid-like flowers on tall stems (24 to 36 inches high) that last for weeks.

- *Crocosmia* cultivars have graceful arching stems, 24 to 36 inches high, with tubular flowers in brilliant red, orange, or yellow.

- *Dahlia* hybrids offer many different colors, shapes, and sizes from 1 foot high to 6 feet or higher.

- **Dutch Iris** blooms in late spring to early summer, with tall slender stems and foliage. Flowers tend to be two-toned in shades like violet and blue, yellow and white, or silvery white and yellow.

- *Gladiolus* offers colorful blooms on 4- to 5-foot-tall stems.

- *Ixia* **(Cornflower)** cultivars produce 8- to 16-inch spikes with upfacing, six-petaled flowers on wiry stems. Flowers range from white to fuchsia pink and purple.

- *Liatris* species and cultivars have 2- to 3-foot spikes of bottlebrush-type flowers opening from top to bottom. Flowers are rosy-lavender or white.

- *Lilium* **Asiatic, Oriental,** and species **Lilies** have flowers that open from late spring until frost in a wide range of colors.

- *Polianthes tuberosa* **(Tuberose)** has fragrant white flowers with a waxy coating. One stem will perfume an entire room.

- *Tritonia* **(Blazing Star)** cultivars offer charming flowers that look like stars in the garden in shades of white, red, orange, and pink.

- *Zantedeschia* **(Calla Lilies)** hybrids and cultivars have white, yellow, and red flowers.

For more information about bulbs, check out http://www.bulb.com.

Planning

It's time to begin planning for this fall and next spring. Make a list of bulbs you would like to add to your garden. This is a good time to place your order for spring bulbs. They are usually shipped for fall planting beginning in August and continuing through November.

While there are many spring-blooming bulbs, there are also bulbs that bloom in late summer and fall. Some of these fall bloomers have foliage that appears in spring and then disappears. When the flowers appear in autumn, it's almost like magic. Plant fall-blooming bulbs in combination with ground covers like **English Ivy** or **Pachysandra**. The dark-green background will help mask the bulb foliage as it ripens and will show off the flowers when they appear in fall. Double your pleasure, and plant **Daffodils** in the same spot. This way you will have blooms in spring and fall. Fall-blooming bulbs also complement fall perennials like **Sedums, Asters,** and ornamental grasses. Here are some fall bloomers:

- *Colchicum* species and culti-vars—often called **Autumn Crocus** because they look like a giant Crocus, these tough bulbs are pest-proof. Flowers are up to 4 inches across in white, lavender, and rose. Plant these bulbs where they will get partial shade in a well-drained soil.

- *Crocus* species—there are a number of **Crocus** that bloom in autumn. They vary in color and size, from 3 to 6 inches, in shades of white, lilac, and blue. Plant in a sunny location in a well-drained soil.

- *Lycoris radiata* has bright-red spidery flowers on naked stems that stand out in the early fall garden. This bulb thrives in a shady garden with a well-drained soil.

- *Sternbergia lutea* is called the **Autumn Daffodil,** but the flowers of this small bulb look more like a yellow **Crocus** on 4- to 5-inch stems. This fall bloomer produces foliage and flowers at the same time. Plant these bulbs and be patient. Some may take two to three years before they bloom well. Once they are established, leave them alone for at least six to eight years before you divide them.

Mail-Order Sources of Bulbs:

Brent and Becky's Bulbs
Gloucester, VA 23061
877-661-2852
www.brentandbeckysbulbs.com

McClure & Zimmerman
Friesland, WI
800-883-6998
www.mzbulb.com

Old House Gardens—
   Heirloom Bulbs
Ann Arbor, MI
734-995-1486
www.oldhousegardens.com

Planting

Plant late-summer/fall-blooming bulbs like **Spider Lilies, Surprise Lilies,** and **Autumn Daffodil.**

Plant spring-blooming **Bearded Iris,** and *divide* those that are over-grown. By doing this now the rhizomes will have plenty of time to acclimate before cold weather sets in. When planting the rhizomes, space them 1 to 2 feet apart, and *cover* them lightly with soil so the rhizomes are just below the soil surface. Growth is initiated from the end of the rhizome with leaves; point this end in the direction you want the **Iris** to grow.

Iris Rhizome

If you are dividing a clump of **Iris** that is crowded and producing very few flowers, lift the entire clump, and break off the healthy rhizomes. *Discard* any that are shriveled or leafless. You can break apart rhizomes with your hands, or separate them with a sharp knife. Let the cut ends heal for at least a few hours or up to a day before you replant them. Trim the leaves back to a height of 2 to 3 inches, and *replant*. The best soil to plant in is one that has been amended with lots of organic material. After planting, water well. Continue watering (check the soil on a weekly basis until frost arrives) as the plant puts down roots.

Watering

Water summer bulbs that are actively growing or blooming. **Cannas, Elephant's Ear, Caladiums,** and **Ginger Lilies** should be putting on a show now. There's no need to water spring bulbs that are dormant. *Water* fall-blooming bulbs when you plant them.

Mulch any new bulb plantings with 1 to 2 inches of mulch. Use buckwheat hulls, cocoa hulls, pine straw, pea gravel, or other products.

Fertilizing

When you add bulbs to the garden, topdress with fertilizer such as Bulb Booster™. *Fertilize* **Caladiums** with a complete water-soluble fertilizer like 20-20-20.

Pest Control

Chipmunks and other rodents love to dig up your favorite **Crocus** while it's blooming. When you plant bulbs that critters like, *cover* the planted area with a wire mesh. The squares should be 1 inch wide so the bulbs have room to emerge but animals are discouraged from digging them up.

Handpull any weeds as soon as you notice them.

Helpful Hints

Rain Lilies belong to the genus *Zephyranthes.* There are both native and exotic types of this charming bulb. The autumnal flowers of *Z. candida* are triggered by rain at the end of the summer and continue through fall. The starry white blooms stand out against the dark-green rushlike foliage and pop into bloom as soon as it rains. Because the bulbs are so tiny and dry out easily, it is best to purchase them when they are actively growing.

Pruning

Cut fall-blooming bulbs and bring them into the house to enjoy.

Planning

There is still time to order your spring bulbs.

Take a soil test. Most bulbs will be happy with a pH that is slightly acid to neutral (a pH of 7 is neutral, and less than 7 is acid). If you're not sure about the specific requirements of a particular bulb you're growing, check with your local Extension Service (see Resources, p. 355).

Prepare the soil in areas where you will be planting bulbs. All bulbs will benefit from a soil that is rich in organic matter and well drained. To prepare the soil, spread 3 to 4 inches of organic material evenly over the area you plan to amend. Use composted horse or cow manure, leaf compost, or similar materials. You can also broadcast a complete fertilizer like 10-10-10 (follow the directions to determine the amount per square foot) evenly over the area, or you can *fertilize* at the time of planting. *Rototill* the soil to a depth of 1 foot or deeper. Bulbs need a good 6 to 8 inches of good soil underneath them for their roots. Soils that have a high percentage of organic matter make it easier for nutrients to get to your plants.

Make notes in your garden journal about what bulbs are blooming in your garden now and how your summer bulbs fared.

Planting

Continue planting fall-blooming bulbs like **Spider Lilies, Crocus,** and **Colchicums.**

Plant **Lily** bulbs as soon as you receive them, or keep them in a cool, dry place until you plant them. There are many different types of **Lilies,** differing in size, habit of growth, and time of bloom. Before you plant, treat **Lilies** with a fungicide (see Chemicals, p. 327). This usually comes in the form of a dust. **Lily** bulbs should be spaced 1 foot apart, but for a mass effect, you can plant them as close as 6 inches apart. Dig a hole to the required depth (see below), and place the bulb in the hole, spreading out the roots. Make sure it is firmly in place.

- Plant small bulbs (1 to 2 inches wide) 2 to 3 inches deep.

- Plant medium-sized bulbs (2 to 3 inches wide) 3 to 4 inches deep.

- Plant larger bulbs (3 inches or wider) 4 to 6 inches deep.

- One exception is **Madonna Lilies.** Never plant them deeper than 1 inch.

Don't worry if you plant your **Lily** bulbs too shallowly—they have special roots that will pull them down to the proper planting depth as long as the soil below is soft.

Watering

Continue to *water* Lily bulbs until the foliage turns yellow and begins to collapse. Adjust the watering to reflect the change in season. Don't let **Lily** bulbs dry out, but don't overwater either. Push your finger into the soil. When the top 2 inches is dry to the touch, water thoroughly. For one plant that is well established, use 1 gallon of water. Let it soak in, then apply another gallon.

Fertilizing

Fertilize bulbs when you plant them, using a complete fertilizer like Bulb Booster™. You may choose to use a special formula for **Daffodils** (see February, Helpful Hints).

To help improve drainage and make nutrients readily available, add lots of organic material and mix it in with the existing soil.

If you use a complete fertilizer, like 8-8-8 or 10-10-10, it is safer to topdress after you plant the bulbs. If you add it directly to the hole when you plant a bulb, there is the possibility of burning young, tender roots.

Pest Control

Your **Bearded Iris** leaves may have turned yellow and have dark streaks. If the leaves pull off easily and the plant dies, you probably have borers. Borers can hollow out the rhizomes, which then become infected with a bacterial rot. To prevent this problem, *pull off and destroy* old brown leaves in the fall and winter. Provide excellent drainage and, if necessary, spray new foliage in spring when it is 5 inches high. Use Cygon, and read the product label completely before spraying (see Chemicals, p. 327).

To prevent unwanted crops of chickweeds and other winter weeds in established beds, apply a granular weed preventer (see Chemicals, p. 327). NOTE: Read the label carefully before applying any pesticide. A pre-emergent weed control should be used only if bulbs are established (they have been growing and thriving in the same area for two or three years). Some bulbs may be sensitive to this type of chemical.

Pruning

If you still have **Daylilies** blooming, *pinch off* dead blossoms before they form seed unless you want to save the seed. *Cut off* and save any ripe seedpods from bulbs that you want to grow from seed next year. Once the pods turn from green to brown and they begin to dry out, the seeds inside should be ripe. Store the seed in a dry, cool place (see Annuals, September). If the foliage on your **Lilies** has turned yellow or brown, it is safe to cut them back now to a height of 2 to 3 inches.

Helpful Hints

The best time to fertilize your spring-blooming bulbs is in the fall. Often we forget where we planted bulbs until they come up in spring. Use golf tees to mark the location of your bulbs; place them in a circle around a clump of **Daffodils** or other bulbs. When fall arrives, you will know where to fertilize. You can also use plants to mark where you have bulbs planted. If you plant **Daffodils** in a bed of ground cover, fertilize the ground cover in autumn and the bulbs will be fertilized, too. Because **Grape Hyacinth** foliage comes up in the fall, you can plant it to mark where clumps of **Daffodils** are.

OCTOBER

Planning

Gardeners who live in the warmest parts of the state (coastal gardeners and those who live in zone 8 or 9) need to pre-chill some of the spring-flowering bulbs before they plant them. Although it is possible to purchase bulbs that have already had a prechilling treatment, it is easy to do yourself. When purchasing bulbs, be sure to read the fine print. If bulbs are prechilled, that should be stated on the package; otherwise, it is safe to assume they are not prechilled.

Many of the large **Tulips** require ten weeks of prechilling. Place them in a breathable bag in the refrigerator. Keep them away from any ripe fruit that releases ethylene gas, as ethylene gas can interfere with the production of flowers. After this prechilling they will be ready to plant in the garden once the soil temperatures are 60 degrees Fahrenheit or cooler.

Some **Daffodil** cultivars require a minimum of fourteen to sixteen weeks of constant cold before they will initiate flowerbuds. (Check with your local Extension Service about the best bulbs for your region. Bulb suppliers should provide specific information about cold requirements for specific bulbs.) Store them in a breathable bag in the refrigerator for six to eight weeks. They will be ready to plant

in the garden when the soil temperatures are 60 degrees Fahrenheit or cooler at a depth of 3 to 4 inches.

You can force bulbs to bloom early for blooms indoors, or you can bring them out to the garden and place the pots around for additional color in the spring.

If you want to force bulbs to bloom earlier than they normally would, you can pot them up and store them in the refrigerator or in a room where the temperature can be held below 60 degrees Fahrenheit while the bulbs are rooting for six to eight weeks. After this period, store them at a temperature of 35 to 45 degrees for another six to eight weeks. If it is cold enough outdoors (35 to 45 degrees), you can place the pots under a mulch pile. Daffodil expert Brent Heath recommends using a potting mix that is coarse so that roots will be able to penetrate easily and there will be good drainage. Mixes that contain peat moss, ground pine bark, perlite, and granite sand work well. Water the bulbs when you pot them up, and then only when the soil surface feels dry to the touch. When potting up the bulbs, they should just be touching one another, depending on the size of the pot—for example, five bulbs are good for a 6-inch pot.

Once roots begin to emerge from the bottom of the pot, bring it into the house or greenhouse. A temper-

ature of 70 degrees is ideal—the top of the refrigerator is usually this warm or warmer. Give your bulbs the maximum amount of daylight so that they develop strong stems; grow lights can be used to provide supplemental light in the evening.

Check pots regularly now to see if they need water. *Water* when the soil is dry to the touch, but don't overwater. There is no need to fertilize your bulbs unless you want to plant them in the garden after they finish blooming (be sure the threat of frost has passed). In this case, use a water-soluble fertilizer that is high in phosphorus, potash, and trace elements.

Planting

In the middle and northern parts of the state, you can plant spring bulbs provided the soil temperatures have cooled off to 60 degrees Fahrenheit. Use a soil thermometer to measure the temperature at 3 to 4 inches deep.

Start **Paper-whites** in pots so you will have blooms for Thanksgiving. By staggering the times you plant **Paper-whites,** you can have fragrant blooms indoors from Thanksgiving well into the New Year. **Paper-whites** do not require a chilling period before they grow and bloom, and some will be in bloom just three to four weeks after you pot them up. Keep them in a cool, dark place until they put on a good bit of growth (the foliage should be 3 or more inches tall). At this point, move them gradually into the light.

If you are potting up lots of bulbs for forcing (**Paper-whites** and other types, too), use a potting mix that is one part coarse builder's sand, one part perlite, two parts peat moss, and two parts ground pine bark. All pots must have drainage holes. You may place a pot with drainage holes in a decorative pot that doesn't have holes if you like.

Fill the pot 3/4 full with the soil mix. Place the bulbs in the pots, with the sides barely touching, then fill in with small gravel or pebbles to hold the bulbs in place. As the bulbs begin to grow and the stems stretch, *stake* them so they won't fall over once they begin to bloom. Try placing three attractive bamboo stakes in the pot, at equal distances from one another, and use a natural jute twine or raffia to form a ring around the stakes. Water the bulbs after you pot them up, and then only when the soil is dry to the touch.

See the Helpful Hints for the best varieties of **Daffodils** to force. These can be enjoyed indoors or brought out to the garden when they are ready to bloom.

Watering

Water your bulbs as soon as you plant them. Give them a good soaking. If you apply 1 inch of water, it should reach roots at a depth of 6 inches in a soil with a moderate amount of clay (30 to 40 percent). Applying double this amount should be enough for bulbs that are planted as deep as 9 to 10 inches.

Fertilizing

If you plant spring bulbs now, you can *topdress* with a complete fertilizer like 10-10-10 or Bulb Booster™. If you mixed fertilizer into the soil when you tilled it, there is no need to fertilize again.

Pest Control

Clean up any dead or diseased leaves on your summer bulbs. Dispose of these in the garbage. This will reduce the spread of potential insect or disease problems that might otherwise overwinter.

Pruning

There is no pruning required at this time.

Helpful Hints

Forcing **Daffodils** is fun and rewarding. Below is a list of the best varieties to force as recommended by Brent Heath.

- All **Paper-whites**
- *Narcissus* 'Abba'
- *N.* 'Bridal Crown'
- *N.* 'Cragford'
- *N.* 'Garden Princess'
- *N.* 'Ice Follies'
- *N.* 'Johann Strauss'
- *N.* 'Jumblie'
- *N.* 'Kassels Gold'
- *N.* 'Little Beauty'
- *N.* 'Little Gem'
- *Narcissus obvallaris*
- *Narcissus* 'Pipit'
- *N.* 'Rijnveld's Early Sensation'
- *N.* 'Tete-a-Tete'
- *N.* 'W.P. Milner'

Planning

If you don't have any **Daffodils** *in your garden, consider adding some this fall.* **Daffodils** are among the most satisfying of bulbs to grow because they thrive with just a minimum of care once they are established. Knowing the best varieties for our Georgia climate will help ensure your success (see December). Prepare the soil where bulbs will be planted (see September, Planning).

Planting

Plant spring-flowering bulbs. Don't forget to *replant* any spring-flowering bulbs that you dug during the summer. Early-flowering types can be planted under deciduous trees since they will be going dormant by the time trees leaf out fully and create heavy shade.

Most spring-flowering bulbs thrive if they are planted in full sun or part shade, but the flowers will last longer if they are protected from the hot midday sun.

In the middle and northern parts of the state (zone 7 or colder), summer bulbs like **Dahlias, Cannas, Elephant's Ear,** and **Caladiums** should be dug up and stored for the winter. Here are some tips for digging up Dahlia tubers and other summer-blooming bulbs like **Caladiums.**

- Wait until a frost kills back the foliage. Cut back the stem to a height of 12 inches.

- Use a digging fork, and carefully dig around and under the clumps. Lift them out of the ground.

- Follow this technique if you divide the clumps long after you dig them. Use a sharp knife, making sure each tuber has a stalk about 1 inch and an eye (this is where new growth will initiate).

- Dust **Dahlia** tubers with sulfur (see Chemicals, p. 327), and then *cover* them with sawdust, sand, or vermiculite. Store them over the winter in a dry, cool (40- to 50-degree-Fahrenheit) place.

If you decide to store the clumps whole and divide them in the spring, *cover* them with sawdust, sand, perlite, peat moss, or vermiculite, and keep them in a cool, dry place. Separate the tubers two to four weeks before you plant them, using the method described above.

If you have **Elephant's Ear** that you want to save, you can *dig up* the tuberous roots and keep them cool and dry over the winter. The roots can be as big as a softball. If you grow them in containers, *cut back* the foliage after there is a hard frost (to about 12 inches high). Use caution when you cut back the foliage, as the sap contains microscopic crystals of oxalic acid, which can be very dangerous to your eyes. Cover the stems with an old cloth as you prune off the leaves. Keep the container in a cool, dark space, and provide a minimum of moisture to keep the plant alive until spring when you can bring it back outside.

Watering

Water bulbs after you plant them. Apply 2 to 3 inches of mulch on top of newly planted bulb areas.

Fertilizing

Fertilize bulbs when you plant them, with a complete fertilizer like 8-8-8 or 10-10-10 (see Helpful Hints, February for tips on fertilizing **Daffodils**).

Topdress bulbs that you planted last fall (see Helpful Hints, September for tips on how to remember where you planted your bulbs).

Bonemeal is not considered a complete fertilizer, because it does not provide all the nutrients that bulbs need. If you want to use an organic-type fertilizer, look for "Bulb Mate™," which has a 5-10-12 formula. It contains cricket manure, rock phosphate, bonemeal, dolomitic limestone, granite meal, and organic compost.

Pest Control

Clean up any remaining leaf litter. It should be safe to put most leaves on the compost pile even if they were affected by insects or disease, unless the disease is a virus, such as mosaic virus. Any bulbs or plant parts infected with a virus should be disposed of in the garbage.

Pruning

If there are any seeds you want to save, *cut off* the pods while they are still brown and before they turn mushy.

Tips for Drying and Storing Your Bulbs

These tips apply to both spring- and summer-blooming types of bulbs.

DRYING: Find a dry, shady spot in which to spread your tender bulbs as they dry completely. This step is important because the bulbs harden their skin and heal wounds as they slowly dry. This process helps prevent rot later while they are stored inside. Some gardeners wipe their bulbs with a 1:10 solution of bleach and water in order to kill fungi. Others dust the bulbs with sulfur or garden fungicide to protect them. Neither practice is absolutely essential, but each does add a measure of protection. Let the bulbs dry outdoors until the foliage is withered and the stems begin to shrink. Do not let them freeze or get wet.

STORING: Separate the bulbs by variety and color. Small cardboard boxes make good containers. Spread a 1-inch-thick layer of dry peat moss in a box, then place bulbs so they do not touch each other. When one layer is finished, cover it thickly with peat moss, and make another layer.

Label each box clearly. Unlike spring bulbs, which are best stored in cool temperatures, tender bulbs like it warm during the winter. A good storage place is in a closet where temperatures do not fall below 50 degrees Fahrenheit.

When you store your tender bulbs for the winter, you can plant winter annuals like **Pansies, Parsley,** and **Ornamental Cabbage** in their beds. Next spring, in May when the soil is quite warm, you can plant your treasures and enjoy their foliage and flowers once again.

Planning

In coastal areas, there is still time to plant spring-flowering bulbs this month and next month. If you have a large area and you want to grow spring-flowering bulbs, naturalizing or mass planting might be a good technique to try. Prepare the soil ahead of time.

Dig out large areas to the depth required by whatever type bulb you are planting. If you are planting **Crocus** in the lawn, you won't need to dig as deeply as you will if you plant large **Daffodils.** After you dig out an area, set aside the soil. Place the bulbs in the planting space, which can be an irregular shape. This will result in a more natural-looking planting when the bulbs bloom in the spring. If you want a more formal look, plant in rows or a definite geometric shape, and space the bulbs at a regular distance from one another. A cluster of 100 in one spot will make for a more dramatic effect. If you use the same variety, it will also have more of an impact than having a scattering of types blooming at all different times. You can do this easily with **Crocus, Daffodils, Snowdrops,** and **Snowflakes.**

You can also use this technique to create a meadow garden. After you plant the bulbs, add other perennial plants that will bloom at times other than when the spring bulbs are blooming. If you have weeds and want to use a nonselective weed-killer (see Chemicals, p. 327), use a glove (or two gloves, one on top of the other for safety), and wipe the weedkiller on the plants. This way you can control what the chemical touches.

While all **Daffodils** belong to the genus *Narcissus*, not all *Narcissus* are **Daffodils.** The genus *Narcissus* is represented by thirteen different divisions. The divisions are determined by the type of flower such as the Classic Trumpet, Large-cupped, Small-cupped, Double, Jonquilla, and so on. Jonquilla and Tazetta represent two of the divisions of **Daffodils** that do well in Georgia gardens. Below are selections that perennialize well:

- **'Carlton'**, in the Large-cupped Division, offers upfacing two-toned yellow flowers with a vanilla scent; it grows 14 to 16 inches tall.

- **'Erlicheer'**, a vigorous double-flowering Daffodil, produces clusters of fifteen to twenty creamy-white-and-gold fragrant flowers per 12- to 14-inch stem.

- **'February Gold'**, a Cyclamineus hybrid, has gold petals that are recurved (curved back away from the trumpet part of the flower).

- **'Ice Follies'**, in the Large-cupped Division, has flowers with creamy white petals and a yellow cup that turns almost white as it matures.

- **'St. Keverne'**, in the Large-cupped Division, is an heirloom that is all yellow and grows 16 to 18 inches tall. It performs well in coastal gardens, too.

- **'Tete-a-Tete'**, a Cyclamineus hybrid, grows only 6 inches tall and has buttercup-yellow flowers.

- **'Thalia'** is a Triandrus hybrid with two or three white flowers per stem.

In coastal areas, gardeners can grow **Paper-whites** and other **Daffodils** in the Tazetta and Jonquilla division with great success because they don't require a chilling period.

- **'Avalanche'** grows 16 inches tall and produces clusters of flowers (up to twenty) with white petals and a yellow cup.

- **'Chinese Sacred Lily'** is similar to a Paper-white; this Daffodil has white petals with yellow cups, grows 10 to 14 inches tall, and needs staking.

- **'Galilee'** flowers are pure white with a musky fragrance. It grows 12 to 14 inches tall.

Planting

If you haven't planted yet, and the ground is not frozen, get those spring-flowering bulbs in the ground. In coastal areas, this is a great month to plant spring bulbs.

If you want to force **Paper-whites** for the New Year, plant some today. You can plant them in soil and top off the pot with pebbles. Another method that works well is to use a decorative container: Use pebbles to hold the bulbs in place. Fill up the pot with water, but don't cover the top $1/4$ of the bulb. Keep the bulbs in a cool spot with dim light until they put up 3 to 4 inches of stems and leaves. At this point, move them into a bright room; as they grow, move them to the sunniest window you have.

Helpful Hints

If you want to force other spring-flowering bulbs to bloom, there is still time. Below is a list of bulbs that are relatively easy to force. While some bulbs like **Paper-whites** and **Hyacinths** can be forced in water with pebbles, most spring bulbs require oxygen and should be potted up in a pot with soil and drainage holes. You can force these bulbs to enjoy indoors or to bring out into the garden after the danger of frost has passed in early spring.

- Crocus
- Daffodils
- Dwarf Iris
- Glory of the Snow
- Hyacinths
- Siberian Squill
- 'Apricot Beauty' Tulip

Check with your local Cooperative Extension Service for more information on forcing bulbs.

Fertilizing

Topdress any bulb plantings that you plant this fall (see February, Helpful Hints).

Pruning

No pruning is needed at this time.

Watering

Water bulbs you planted this fall for the next two months while they are putting energy into forming roots and before they go into a semi-dormant state for winter. If you are forcing bulbs to get them to bloom earlier, check the pots and make sure they don't dry out completely.

Pest Control

If you haven't cleaned up the garden yet, now is the time to remove leaf litter from summer bulbs and other perennials. A clean garden means fewer places for pest and disease problems to overwinter.

Edibles

Before there were landscapes to beautify, before there were lawns to tend, "gardening" was all about food. It had been a major step for the hunter-gatherers to settle down and build permanent communities. They could make their homes in one spot because they had learned to *cultivate* food rather than *catch* it.

Nowadays, growing food in a garden is not as common as it once was. It is usually cheaper to purchase fresh food at the grocery, and it is a lot less work! Nothing, however, can compare to the taste of a vine-ripened tomato plucked from the vine on a summer morning and consumed in the middle of your garden. Nothing is as juicy as fresh sweet corn that fifteen minutes before being boiled was standing tall in your patch. Few things are as pleasant as sharing the surplus of your garden with neighbors or the local food bank.

Food gardening is not about cost or labor. It is about taste, productivity, and connection to the earth. Georgia is blessed with a long growing period—so long that it is divided into three parts: spring season, summer season, and fall season. This chapter will help you organize your efforts to have food available from your garden in all three seasons. If you want to preserve your food, you can have food from your garden all year long! Maximizing your yield starts with planning.

Planning

Late winter weather plays a big role in determining which vegetables can be planted in the different parts of the state. In general, the south Georgia cool-season vegetable planting period begins in the last week of January. The north Georgia season begins around the first week of March. The Small Garden Plan on p. 339 will give you information on the proper dates to plant your crops.

Where to Plant

Vegetables need full sunshine in order to produce to the fullest. A few hours of light shade is acceptable, but few things will grow where they receive less than four hours of direct sunshine per day. If you have a semi-shaded spot, concentrate on leafy vegetables and **Bean** family members, not **Tomatoes, Watermelons,** and **Corn,** which require lots of sun.

Remember that vegetables can be grown in containers if the sunniest place available is your patio.

A late frost can freeze the blooms on fruit trees, leaving a healthy tree but no fruit for the season. Pick a planting site that gets plenty of sunshine—but not at the bottom or top of a hill, where temperatures are usually colder. Refer to the fruit variety charts on p. 340 for fruit varieties that bloom later and avoid damage.

Organic Gardening

If you are growing food for yourself or your family, you certainly do not want the food to harm you. While researchers and government agencies have stated that synthetic pesticides can be safely used on edibles, some gardeners prefer to use only naturally derived pesticides on their plants. They use beneficial insects, botanical insecticides, and improved varieties so they can avoid using synthetic pesticides. Many organic pesticides are included in the Chemicals section (p. 327). Though organically grown produce may have a few cosmetic flaws, organic growers take pleasure in producing their food in the most natural way possible.

Edibles

Our recommendations for proper soil preparation (see Horticultural Practices, p. 7) will help you produce strong plants that can tolerate insects and diseases but still grow acceptably. For more information, contact Georgia Organics (770-621-GOGA). You will also find much information in *Organic Gardening* magazine (800-666-2206).

If you prefer to use organic fertilizers in your garden, the publication "Converting Soil Test Results to Organic Fertilizer Recommendations" is available from your local Extension Service office (see Resources, p. 353).

Preparing the Soil

A thorough tilling of your vegetable garden is necessary each year to break up soil clumps and old rootballs. See Horticultural Practices, p. 7, for complete instructions on preparing a bed. If the area has not been cultivated for a few years, weeds and insects will have built up in the soil. One way to eliminate them is to solarize the soil.

Soil solarization is a method that uses the sun's warmth to heat the ground and kill weeds and diseases. You can solarize half a planned garden in early summer and repeat the procedure for the other half in late summer. In south Georgia, the best season to solarize is April through August; in north Georgia, June through July.

1 Till the soil in the area to be solarized. Irrigate it thoroughly.

2 Cover the spot with clear (not black) plastic sheeting. Place bricks or stones in the center of the bed to hold the plastic slightly off the ground.

3 Anchor the plastic tightly to the ground on all sides using soil or heavy limbs.

4 On sunny days, sunlight will raise the temperature of the soil to 125 degrees Fahrenheit. Keep the soil covered with plastic for at least six weeks.

Soil Solarization

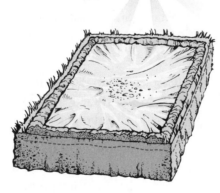

Pollination

In order for a plant to produce vegetables, fruit, or nuts, the flowers must be pollinated. Nature will usually take care of this for you. For tips on vegetable pollination, see the June, August, and September months. If you do not notice many pollinating insects in your garden, see the introduction to the Annuals chapter, and learn how to attract more of them.

Some fruit trees are self-fruitful (pollen from a single plant is sufficient to pollinate the flowers on it). Others are partially self-fruitful or even self-incompatible. Follow these general pollination guidelines when deciding whether you need one or more of each:

- **Apple:** Plant at least two different varieties.

- **Blueberry:** Plant at least two different varieties.

- **Bunch Grapes:** Self-fruitful.

- **Fig:** Self-fruitful.

- **Muscadine Grape:** Plant at least two different varieties; one must be self-fruitful.

- **Peach:** Self-fruitful.

- **Pear:** Most are self-fruitful.

- **Pecan:** Plant at least two different varieties.

- **Plum:** Plant at least two different varieties.

- **Raspberry, Blackberry:** Self-fruitful.

(See fruit variety charts, p. 340.)

Finding Special Seed

Seed packets of the common vegetables can be found at your local garden center. If you want to grow vegetable varieties that are a little less common, catalogs may have what you are looking for. Check the Internet for listings.

Memories of the taste of a particular tomato variety send some gardeners on a fruitless search for that plant at their local nursery. If it is not available there, seed may be available from specialty suppliers. Sources of **Heirloom Tomato Seed** include:

Totally Tomatoes
P.O. Box 1626
Augusta, GA 30903-1626
(803) 663-0016

Tomato Growers Supply
P.O. Box 2237
Fort Myers, FL 33902
(888) 478-7333

Rachel's Tomatoes
SBE Seed Co.
3421 Bream St.
Gautier, MS 39553
(800) 336-2064

Denise Smith is the owner of GardenSmith Greenhouse and Nursery in Jefferson, GA. (706-367-9047). One year she planted 169 tomato varieties—just to see which ones she liked! Here are her favorites:

- 'Banana Legs'—fun name, great yellow color, and "My Absolute Favorite!"

- 'Druzba'—Bulgarian heirloom, name means "friendship," great acid flavor.

- 'Hawaii'—very heat-tolerant, from Valdosta, GA.

- 'Mr. Stripey'—a fun novelty with great tomato flavor; skin and flesh are striped.

- 'Mandarin Joy'—a Japanese hybrid, *very* disease-resistant, great flavor.

- 'Black Krim"—Russian heirloom; good sugar-acid balance.

- 'Garden Peach'—heirloom; a beautiful novelty with terrific flavor.

- 'White Queen'—heirloom; has ivory-white skin and flesh; excellent flavor.

- 'Yellow Stuffer'—looks like a bell pepper, good for stuffing, fun to use.

- 'Caspian Pink'—heirloom; flavor is like Brandywine but seems to take our heat better.

- 'Riesentraube'—heirloom; German name means "giant grapes"; 20 to 40 fruits per cluster, great flavor, takes the heat.

If you are looking for a certain variety of fruit or vegetable that just can't be found through normal channels, the Georgia Farmers and Consumers Market Bulletin is a good source to try. This free weekly newspaper is full of items for sale to farmers and gardeners throughout the state. The pictures of oddly shaped and overlarge vegetables submitted by their owners are consistently entertaining.

Farmers and Consumers Market Bulletin
19 M.L.K. Jr. Drive
Atlanta, GA 30334-4250
Phone: (800) 282-5852

Many gardeners save seed from year to year. If not stored properly, the seed will lose the ability to germinate. You can check their viability by performing the "rag doll" test:

1 Select ten seed from the packet.

2 Arrange the seed in a line down the center of a completely dampened paper towel.

3 Roll the paper towel around the seed to form a tight tube.

4 Place the paper and seed into a resealable plastic bag.

5 Place the bag in a warm spot. Light is not necessary; the top shelf of a kitchen cabinet is a good place to use.

6 Wait ten days. Examine the seed to determine how many have sprouted. If only a few sprout,

Edibles

you are better off buying new seed, if possible. Otherwise, try planting the seed that have sprouted, handling them gently.

When will you know it is time to harvest your vegetables? The following are signs that different vegetables are ready to be harvested:

- **Asparagus:** stem 6 to 8 inches long, has no fiber or strings. (Begin harvesting asparagus only after the plants are well established in their bed.)

- **Broccoli:** bright-green color; head still tightly closed.

- **Cabbage:** head is firm, leaves tight.

- **Cantaloupe:** stem breaks away easily from vine when gently pulled; netting on skin is raised and distinct.

- **Collards:** bright-green color; small midvein on each leaf.

- **Corn, Sweet:** most kernels plump and filled with milky liquid.

- **Cucumber:** skin dark green, seeds soft.

- **Eggplant:** skin glossy; skin springs back when pressed.

- **Lima Beans:** bright-green pod; seeds visibly swollen in the pod, not flat.

- **Okra:** pods 2 to 3 inches long and still tender.

- **Onions:** tops are yellow and three-fourths fallen over.

- **Pea, Southern:** seeds fully developed but still soft.

- **Pole Green Beans:** bean seems full; seed half-grown, not over-mature or dry.

- **Potato, Irish:** tops begin to die back.

- **Potato, Sweet:** most tubers 2 to 3 inches in diameter.

- **Snap Bush Beans:** pods firm when pinched; seeds just visible.

- **Squash, Summer:** skin can be penetrated by thumbnail.

- **Squash, Winter:** skin difficult to penetrate with thumbnail.

- **Tomato,** mature green stage: color changes from green to light green, no pink color on blossom end (these tomatoes can be stored one to two weeks in your refrigerator).

- **Tomato,** pink stage: pink color about the size of a dime on blossom end (these tomatoes will ripen in three days at room temperature).

- **Tomato,** ripe: flesh full red but still firm (may be refrigerated to slow ripening, but these tomatoes should be used immediately).

- **Watermelon:** skin that was lying on the soil turns from light straw color to rich yellow. When slapped, sounds hollow (unripe ones sound as if you're hitting solid wood).

(Courtesy of Dr. McLaurin, "When to Harvest Vegetables," UGA)

Recommended Varieties

Successful gardeners learn from the successes and failures of others. While vegetables grow well in most parts of the country, certain fruits and nuts are not adapted to Georgia conditions. Rather than attempting to grow a fruit that doesn't grow well, make your choices from the following lists as well as the fruit varieties lists in the Appendix.

Bill and Elisa Ford are tireless promoters of the Georgia green industry. They own Johnson-Ford Nursery in Ellijay (888-276-3187). Out of the hundreds of different plants they grow, here are their comments on their Top Ten Georgia Fruits:

1 **Rabbiteye Blueberries** have great-tasting fruit and hardly any pests, and they are heat-tolerant. Try **'Climax'**, **'Woodard'**, **'Tifblue'**, and **'Delite'.**

2 **'Cameo'** apples have striped skin, great taste, and good keeping ability.

Edibles

3 'Honey Crisp' apples ripen before red apple varieties, and have good taste.

4 'Pink Lady' apples ripen in November, have semi-tart taste, and are very pretty.

5 'Yates' apples are small but extra-juicy and sweet.

6 'Cresthaven' Peach blooms late to avoid spring frost damage yet fruit ripens in early July.

7 Asian Pears produce aromatic, crisp, juicy fruit. Try 'Shinko', 'Hosui', and 'Kosui'.

8 'Dormanred' Raspberry is a great ground cover with large red fruit.

9 Figs—give them the right home plus room to grow, and you and the birds will feast on them for years to come.

10 Muscadines are the Georgia grape! They make great eating and a wonderfully disgusting sweet wine. Plant 'Carlos', 'Fry', 'Summit', or 'Triumph'.

Dr. Wayne McLaurin is a University of Georgia Vegetable and Herb Specialist. He and his wife Sylvia are the authors of "Herbs for Southern Gardens," which is available from the University of Georgia Agricultural Business Office (706-542-8999). Here are Wayne McLaurin's favorite herbs:

1 Basil: "I only like the true Basil—don't give me any of the cinnamon- or fruit-scented ones. The regular Basil is by far the best one for Italian cooking. I make wonderful bruschetta (thin slice of Italian bread, thin tomato slice, and a basil leaf, topped with fresh goat cheese)—it's a taste that's hard to beat, even in the finest restaurant."

2 Hot Peppers: "Are Hot Peppers an herb? Sure they are! I have grown all kinds, but I still find the Tabasco types the best for flavor. The others may be hotter, but flavor is what counts!"

3 Lavender: "One of the plants that I truly love. There are lots of kinds, but 'Provence' has proven the best for me."

4 Mint: "Can take a real beating from kids and dogs but keeps on growing. It's not a 'high-class' herb, but when you get that first glass of iced tea on a hot summer day with fresh mint rubbed on the rim of the glass and sit back, and relax—that is worth putting up with the wild growth habit of Mint."

5 Rosemary: "Easy to grow and quite a beautiful plant. There are many different kinds; some grow upright and some have a prostrate growth habit."

6 Thyme: "It is sometimes a challenge to grow, but I *love* to cook with it. The cultivars range from coconut-scented to lemon-scented to plain old thyme-scented—just soooo many kinds to choose from."

Vegetable Garden Fertilization

Run a soil test to determine lime and fertilizer needs (See Horticultural Practices, p. 7). If the pH is low, apply the recommended amount of lime before rototilling the soil so the lime can be mixed with the soil as you till. A pH of 6.0 to 6.5 is recommended for all vegetables except Irish Potatoes, which require a pH of 5.5 to 5.8. Vegetables are classified as Light, Medium, and Heavy feeders, based on their fertilizer needs.

HEAVY FEEDERS

Cabbage	Irish Potatoes	Onions
Celery	Lettuce	Tomatoes

MEDIUM FEEDERS

Artichoke	Corn, Sweet	Okra	Rhubarb
Asparagus	Cucumbers	Peas, English	Squash
Beans, all	Eggplant	Pepper	Sweet Potatoes
Beets	Greens, all	Pumpkin	Swiss Chard
Cantaloupes	Herbs	Radish	Watermelon
Carrots			

LIGHT FEEDERS
Southern Peas

The results of your soil test will detail the exact fertilizer needs of your vegetables. In the absence of a soil test, use the following recommendations:

Before Planting (All Vegetables)

Broadcast 30 pounds of 5-10-10 (or 6-12-12) fertilizer per 1,000 square feet. This can be done just after planting but it is preferable to mix the fertilizer with the soil before the final rows are laid out. Lime and fertilizer can be broadcast and rototilled into the soil at the same time.

During the Growing Season

HEAVY FEEDERS
Side-dress (see June, Fertilizing) with 1 pound of 10-10-10 per 100 feet of row when plants are 6 inches tall. Repeat twice more, at four week intervals.

MEDIUM FEEDERS
Side-dress with 1 pound of 10-10-10 per 100 feet of row when plants are 6 inches tall. Repeat once more six weeks later.

LIGHT FEEDERS
Side-dress with 1 pound of 10-10-10 per 100 feet of row when plants are 6 inches tall.

Organic Fertilizers

Organic fertilizers can be used in your garden instead of synthetic nutrients. Composted hen manure, bloodmeal, steamed bonemeal and Sulfate of Potash magnesia (Sul-Po-Mag) are excellent organic sources of nutrients. As the soil test report you receive will recommend synthetic fertilizers (10-10-10, 33-0-0, 0-46-0, etc.), ask your local Extension Service office (See Resources, p. 353) for a free copy of "How to Convert an Inorganic Fertilizer Recommendation to an Organic One."

Planning

Bare-root fruit trees will soon be available at nurseries. Ask the manager when he or she expects the shipments to arrive. If you want to plant a particular variety, ask if it can be special-ordered for you. If you plan to have dwarf trees, do some research to learn the ultimate size of a mature plant—some semi-dwarf varieties grow larger than you might expect.

Having fruit plants is not a simple matter of planting now, then enjoying fruit for years to come. Most fruit trees, especially **Peaches,** require careful management to control insects and diseases. Smaller fruit plants like **Blueberry, Raspberry, Blackberry,** and **Fig** need much less care. They also take up less room!

Planting

Rototill garden beds where you will plant cool-season vegetables. If the soil is ready, you won't have to tend to this task when the early gardening season begins next month.

Care for Your Plants

Raspberry and **Blackberry** stems (*canes*) are not permanent. On most plants, the canes that bore fruit last season will die during the winter to make room for fresh growth. Now is a good time to remove the brown, dead canes from your plants and tie the green canes to your wire trellis.

Leather gloves are a must when working with brambles. Use jute twine to loosely tie up the canes. It will rot by the end of the year.

Watering

In south Georgia, sandy soil loses water rapidly. Plan to add 1 cubic foot of organic material for each foot of hole diameter before planting a fruit or nut tree. The organic particles will act like a sponge during the summer, storing water when it is available and releasing it when dry weather occurs.

Make a habit of mulching plants with shredded leaves each fall. As the leaves break down, earthworms will mix them with the soil beneath.

Fertilizing

Fruiting plants are deciduous, losing their leaves in winter in most parts of Georgia. Mature plants don't need fertilizer now, since there are no leaves present. New plants, on the other hand, need phosphorus immediately.

Mix 1 tablespoon of 0-46-0 (triple superphosphate) per foot of height into the soil when you plant a fruiting plant. This will give the roots the phosphorus they require when they begin to grow.

Pest Control

Many insects overwinter under the bark of fruit trees.

Spray dormant horticultural oil (see Chemicals, p. 327) on fruit tree branches and trunks to suffocate dormant insects. Thoroughly cover the entire trunk and all branches with the spray.

Pruning

Prune your **Muscadine Grapes** now, removing the long whips that grew last year. Actually, you'll prune back to the first two buds on each long stem, leaving only these to make new growth this year. It is on this new growth that the grapes are produced!

Muscadine Grapevine

After several years of pruning back to two buds, a series of spur clusters (staghorns) will protrude from the main vine arms. If the clusters crowd each other too much, remove a few to give the rest more room to grow.

Pear and **Apple** trees often suffer broken limbs due to an excess of fruit in August.

Shorten long and slender limbs by ¹/₃ to ¹/₂.

Limbs that cross through the branches in the center of a fruit tree rarely bear fruit. They also shade the leaves of more productive limbs.

This is a good time to examine the structure of your trees. Remove crossing limbs, dead limbs, and limbs that deviate from the appropriate form (see February).

Helpful Hints

Most dwarf trees are made to grow that way by grafting a twig from a regular-sized tree onto a "dwarfing rootstock." You can tell you have a grafted tree by noticing the swollen lump near ground level where the two plant parts were joined together.

Sometimes a strongly dwarfing rootstock does not have a brawny root system like a normal tree—this makes it prone to falling over during a forceful windstorm or a severe ice storm. To prevent this, install a deeply-driven post 12 inches from the tree when it is planted. Tie the post loosely to the tree trunk so it is anchored against abnormal wind or weather.

Fig bushes that have become too large for their space can be severely pruned now.

If the space is small to begin with, consider moving the bush to a spot where it can grow at least 8 feet tall and 8 feet wide.

Muscadine Grapevine

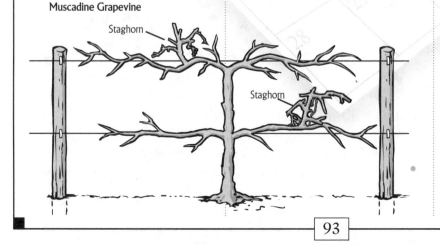

Staghorn

Staghorn

Planning

Asparagus *is easy to grow in a permanent bed.* The key to success is to prepare the soil properly at the beginning, since you won't be able to improve it for several years. Raised beds, deeply dug and amended with copious amounts of organic matter, will give your **Asparagus** a happy home for years.

- Try to find a hybrid **Asparagus** variety like '**Jersey Giant**' or '**Jersey Gem**'. These newer hybrids produce twice as many spears as the old-timers' favorite '**Mary Washington**'.

- Purchase crowns that are more than one year old—two- or three-year-old crowns are best.

- Avoid harvesting spears the first year. The plant needs at least a year to grow vigorous roots.

Planting

Blueberries are among the easiest-to-grow backyard fruit plants. They also make a good hedge, and the leaves are quite colorful in fall. **Blueberry** plants should arrive at your nursery any day now.

- Buy the largest **Blueberry** plant you can find, preferably in a 3-gallon pot. A plant this size has a good chance of bearing lightly in its first growing season.

- **Dig** a 3-foot-wide hole for each **Blueberry** plant, mixing in $1/2$ cubic foot of peat moss for every foot of hole diameter. The peat moss yields the acidic soil that **Blueberries** love.

- Do not fertilize with synthetic fertilizer (10-10-10, etc.) for one year after planting. Use manure or blood meal instead.

Care for Your Plants

It is common to have several days of unusually warm weather in February, followed by a frigid Siberian Express. **Fig** bushes come out of dormancy readily during warm weather, and they can be frozen to the ground if not protected:

1 Make plans to have ready a sheet of black plastic large enough to cover your plant entirely if icy weather threatens.

2 *Anchor* the plastic on all sides with stones or limbs. It is a waste of time to perform this task if you can't cover the entire plant.

3 *Remove* the plastic when the sun comes out the next day. This is especially important if you use clear plastic instead of black plastic. Under clear plastic, temperatures rise rapidly!

Watering

One of the best water-saving investments for a garden is a rubber soaker hose.

- Make a tentative layout of your garden rows and measure the length to determine how much hose to buy.

- A continuous stretch of soaker hose should be no longer than 100 feet.

- You might have to invest in a faucet "splitter valve" so you can send water to each length of soaker hose in its turn.

Fertilizing

Late February is a good time to plant **Strawberries,** if this was not accomplished in the fall (see October).

Once your bed is planted, water it with a high-phosphorus (12-55-6) water-soluble fertil-

izer at ¹/₄ strength (usually 1 tablespoon per 4 gallons of water). This will give the Strawberry *roots the available phosphorus they need without stimulating tender leaf growth.*

Fertilize **Pecan** trees in south Georgia with 1 pound of 10-10-10 per inch of trunk diameter (and again in June).

Helpful Hints

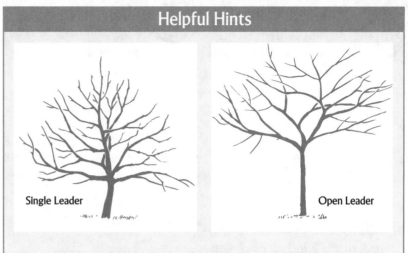

Single Leader   Open Leader

Good pruning shapes a tree to maximize the leaf surface facing the sun. Prune **Apple, Pear,** and **Pecan** trees to a single leader. Prune **Peach, Plum,** and **Cherry** trees to an open leader.

Pest Control

Nematodes are microscopic soil-dwelling worms. Most of them are harmless to plants, but some are parasites of vegetable plant roots. If your **Tomato** or **Okra** roots were swollen and gnarled last year, you may have nematodes in your soil. No nematicides are available for purchase by the homeowner, so you may deter nematodes these ways:

- The best nematode control is to till your garden soil when it is cold and windy. Many nematodes will die due to exposure to wind and cold.

- Soils kept high in organic matter deter nematodes by nurturing competing soil organisms. Add lots of organic material whenever you rototill a garden bed.

- It is best not to plant nematode-susceptible plants in the same spot for three years after discovering this pest. Plant **Corn, Beans,** or **Peas** there instead.

Pruning

Blueberries have a tendency to grow tall sprouts in the center of the bush. Now is a good time to remove them.

Don't prune any branches that are within picking distance. The horizontal branches within 6 feet of the ground will bear most of your fruit.

Apple and **Pear** trees are rarely hurt by winter cold. The story is not the same for **Peach** and **Plum** trees. A week of unseasonably warm weather can force the buds of a **Peach** or **Plum** to swell and come out of dormancy.

For this reason it is better to wait until mid-March to prune these trees, after the threat of a frigid blast is all but gone.

Planning

Start seeds of* Tomatoes *indoors. You'll need six weeks to grow strong plants. They will be ready just in time to plant outdoors when the soil is warm.

- Use peat pots filled with sterile potting soil. *Plant* two or three seeds per pot.

- When the seeds have sprouted and grown 2 inches, pinch out the weakest one(s), leaving the strongest plant to thrive.

Planting

Plant **Beet, Cauliflower, Mustard, Radish,** and **Turnip** seeds outdoors. *Plant* **Strawberries** as soon as they become available at your local nursery.

Care for Your Plants

If you planted a cover crop on your vegetable garden last fall, mow it first, then till the leaves and stems into the soil.

Watering

Water fruit trees you planted in the last six months.

- Apply 1 gallon of water per foot of height per week.

- Keep a 2- to 3-inch-thick layer of mulch over the root system.

- Pull the mulch back 3 inches from the trunk in all directions.

Fertilizing

Plants can't use much fertilizer if they don't have leaves. *Fertilize* established fruit and nut trees when their leaves are expanding. A typical amount is 1 pound of 10-10-10 per inch of tree-trunk thickness. *Repeat* the feeding in May or June.

The feeder roots of a woody plant may extend twice as far as the tips of its branches. Few feeder roots exist close to a plant's trunk. Be sure to *scatter the fertilizer evenly* in a "doughnut" around the plant, applying at least half the fertilizer past the branch tips.

Pest Control

Peach and **Plum** fruit are particularly susceptible to a disease called brown rot. It infects the bloom, waiting until the fruit is nearly ripe to exhibit itself. To treat this problem:

1 *Spray* a fungicide labeled for fruit trees (see Chemicals, p. 327) on the tree when almost all the blooms are open.

2 *Repeat* when 50 percent of the blooms have fallen.

3 Be sure to remove all mummified fruit left on the tree from last season before blooms appear—this will reduce the chances of infection of this year's fruit.

Spray **Apple** and **Pear** tree blooms with bactericide (see Chemicals, p. 327) if you have had problems with fire blight in past years.

Pruning

Peach and **Plum** trees can be pruned when you are reasonably sure severe cold will not come again.

- Remove dead limbs or branch stubs to stem collar, and not flush with the tree trunk. The wound will close faster with less chance of decay.

- Remove limbs that cross through the center or droop too low.

- Remove pencil-sized water sprouts in the center of the tree.

- Try to keep the center of the tree open so sunshine can easily penetrate.

Bunch Grapes are not pruned like **Muscadine Grapes,** because their old canes harbor disease more readily than do those of **Muscadines.** Instead of having permanent fruiting arms, **Bunch Grapes** should be pruned to leave only four healthy canes from last year's growth. The new growth from these canes will produce the fruit.

Bunch Grapes   Cane with 8 to 12 buds

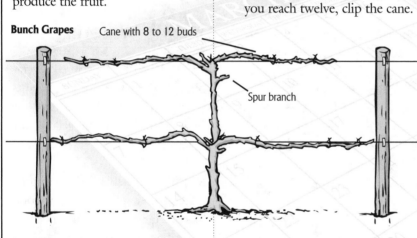

Spur branch

- Select four healthy canes arising from the **Grape** trunk. Two should be growing in one direction, and two should grow in the other along your two-wire trellis.

- Examine the four canes and note the somewhat swollen buds that occur along each one.

- Count the buds on a cane, starting at the trunk, and pro-

ceeding toward the tip. When you reach twelve, clip the cane.

- The result should be *four canes, each having twelve buds.*

- On young vines, or on those that did not fruit strongly last year, leave only *eight buds per cane.*

Finish pruning all grapevines by mid-month (see January). If you wait until later, much bleeding of sap from the cut ends will occur. (Although ominous-looking, bleeding does not harm the vine.)

Finish pruning out dead canes of **Blackberry** and **Raspberry.** Tie green healthy canes to a wire trellis.

Do not delay pruning **Figs** past mid-month. The longer you wait, the more trouble you'll have with rampant, unproductive growth in summer.

It is not necessary in all instances to cut away limbs that are growing too close together. Instead, make a spacer from a 12-inch-long (or longer, if needed) piece of 1×2 wood.

1 Cut a deep notch in each end of the wood.

2 Force the limbs apart and insert the spacer.

3 Leave it in place for at least two years.

Helpful Hints

Digging in your garden will be much easier if your shovel is sharp. To minimize injuries, most shovels are sold with a dull blade. You'll be amazed at the difference a sharp shovel will make:

- Clamp the shovel in a vise, placing the blade upwards.

- Draw a mill file slowly across the edge of the blade, trying to keep the file at a 30-degree angle to the blade.

The blade does not need to be as sharp as a razor, but it should not have a thick or rounded edge.

Planning

If you have never grown vegetables, you might wonder how many you'll have to plant to have fresh produce all summer. The following chart shows the length the planting rows should be for a family of four to have vegetables all summer long. Remember that some of the vegetables should be planted more than once in order to spread the harvest over the summer. Double the amounts if you plan to freeze or can your vegetables.

Vegetable	Row Length (in feet)
Cabbage	25
Collards	25
Corn	40
Cucumbers	5
Eggplant	4
English Peas	20
Irish Potatoes	20
Lima Beans	20
Okra	10
Onions	10
Pepper	3
Snap Beans	40
Southern Peas	30
Summer Squash	5
Sweet Potatoes	12
Tomatoes	12
Turnips/Mustard	12
Winter Squash	5

When **Apples** are in full bloom you can count 150 days forward to determine when to start checking for ripeness.

Planting

Plant warm-season garden crops such as **Tomato, Eggplant, Pepper,** and **Squash** when the soil is quite warm. In south Georgia, this planting time is in late March or early April. Gardeners in the northern half of the state should wait until April 15 to be safe. Of course, some gamblers will plant earlier—but they run the risk of losing everything to a late frost, and even if that doesn't happen, their plants will just sit there, not growing, waiting until the soil is warm.

Fruit trees can be purchased bare-root, balled-and-burlapped, or container-grown. Because the first two types have limited root systems, they are best planted in winter or very early spring. Fruit trees that have been grown in containers have a much more robust root system and can be planted in April and May.

Care for Your Plants

Nematodes (see February) can greatly limit your harvest. These tips will help minimize their damage to susceptible plants if you have nematodes in your small garden:

- Determine where you will place each plant.

- Shovel the soil out of a 1-foot-diameter hole at each spot.

- Fill the hole with bagged topsoil.

- *Plant* seedling plants in the center of the hole.

- By the time nematodes have moved from the contaminated soil into the topsoil, you'll have harvested plenty of produce. *Remove* the entire plant and root system from your property.

Watering

Water newly planted vegetables, herbs, and fruiting plants weekly, providing 1 to 5 cups for small plants, 1 to 2 gallons for shrubs and trees.

Mulching vegetable seedlings immediately after planting is a good practice for three reasons: moisture retention, weed control, and disease control. A thin layer of pine straw or grass clippings works well, or try using newspaper mulch:

1 Unfold a section of the paper, and select a stack of three sheets.

2 Tear the stack halfway down the center, and slip it around the stem of an individual plant.

3 Wet it down to hold in place, then *cover* with straw or leaves.

Fertilizing

You can make a simple starter fertilizer solution at home to use on new vegetable transplants:

1 Add 2 tablespoons of 5-10-15 fertilizer to 5 gallons of water.

2 Mix thoroughly and allow to settle.

3 Pour the solution around new transplants to settle them into the soil.

The jury is still out on the value of commercial root-stimulator solutions for new plants. It is not likely that the products cause harm, so go ahead and use them if you wish.

Fertilize **Pecans** in north Georgia with 1 pound of 10-10-10 per inch of trunk diameter (and again in June).

Do not fertilize **Blueberries** with granular fertilizer during the first year after planting. In later years, *fertilize lightly* in April, June, and September.

Pest Control

Keep a vigilant eye out for chickweed in your garden. Pull it from among your cool-season vegetables, hoe it from the middles of the rows—just DON'T let it go to seed!

Mulch **Tomato** plants right after you plant them, a practice that will help prevent leaf diseases. Early blight is a fungus that splashes onto leaves from the soil during rainstorms or overhead watering. Once the fungus is on the leaves, it will continue to splash up the plant as it grows.

Control with fungicides is difficult; immediate mulching is much more effective.

Pruning

Remove the thin "sucker sprouts" as they arise from the lower trunks of **Apple, Pear,** and **Peach** trees.

Helpful Hint

If you are short on space, **Beans, Cucumbers,** and **Melons** can be grown on a trellis. A wire tomato cage (see June) is a bit small, but serviceable and easy to use. A more permanent trellis can be constructed using two sturdy posts erected at each end of a row:

1 Post tops should be 5 feet from the ground. Stretch heavy wire from post top to post top, anchoring it securely.

2 Stretch another heavy wire between the posts 1 foot from the ground.

3 Weave jute twine (up-down-up-down, etc.) between the wires to form a web on which the vines can crawl.

MAY

Planning

Kiwifruit *is delicious, but the vines are not very cold hardy.* The fruit can be grown in south Georgia, but is not always cold hardy north of Macon. The vine is grown on a double-wire trellis identical to a grape trellis.

- Yearly pruning in March is required because the vine grows so fast. The technique is the same as for **Muscadine Grapevines** (see January).

- A male vine is needed to provide pollen for one to five female vines.

- Don't expect fruit for two years. The vine needs at least this long to establish itself before flowering.

- Make plans to protect the vine with a plastic sheet whenever temperatures fall below 30 degrees Fahrenheit.

Planting

Select **Bush-type** or **Cherry Tomatoes** for patio planting. A huge pot is a must! One plant to five gallons of fast-draining potting soil is a bare minimum. Mix in 1 tablespoon of garden lime per gallon, plus a slow-release fertilizer such as Osmocote® before planting.

Use light-colored pots; otherwise, the pot will absorb sunshine and cause the soil to become too hot.

Plant **Rosemary, Dill, Oregano, Mint,** and **Basil** for savory summer meals.

The soil has to be very warm (above 65 degrees Fahrenheit) to encourage **Corn, Squash, Bean,** and **Field Pea** seed to germinate. Plant by mid-April in south Georgia and mid-May in the northern part of the state. *Make another planting in two weeks to spread out your harvest.*

Care for Your Plants

A weekly inspection of your fruit plants can reveal problems that need attention.

1 *Prune out* any dead limbs or twigs.

2 *Add mulch* if needed. Make sure to keep it pulled back 6 inches from the trunk in all directions.

3 Look for insect or disease damage. Determine if the problem merits control before automatically reaching for a pesticide.

Watering

Georgia summers are famous for prolonged dry periods. The best time to prepare for a drought is before it occurs.

- Lay a soaker hose alongside your **Blueberry, Grape,** or **Raspberry** plants.

- Place a soaker hose on the ground under the branch tips of fruit and nut trees.

- Consider using drip irrigation to water individual plants.

Fertilizing

Fertilize vegetables when they have grown enough to demonstrate that the root system has firmly established itself. This is generally two weeks after planting, or when the plant has grown 3 to 6 inches. (See p. 91.)

Fertilize small fruit trees with 1 cup of 10-10-10 per foot of height; large trees: 1 pound of 10-10-10 per inch of trunk thickness.

Pest Control

Watch for blackened leaves at the ends of **Apple** or **Pear** limbs. This could be the disease *fireblight*.

- *Spray* with streptomycin (see Chemicals, p. 327) before every rain to protect new leaves.

- *Prune out* diseased branches. *Sterilize* your pruner between every cut with a 1:10 mixture of alcohol or bleach in water.

- Mark your calendar to spray again next year when the tree is blooming. Fireblight is spread by honeybees as they travel from flower to flower.

Apply *Bacillus thuringiensis* (see Chemicals, p. 327) to **Cabbage, Broccoli,** and **Cauliflower** to ward off cabbage looper caterpillars.

To prevent leaf diseases, place a newspaper mulch three sheets thick under **Tomato** plants immediately upon planting. Cover the paper with pine straw.

Rabbits are cute, but they can be a real nuisance when they visit your

Rabbit Fence

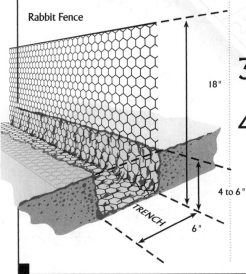

18"

4 to 6"

TRENCH

6"

Helpful Hint

Be sure to throw away the fruit you remove when thinning your fruit trees—don't drop it on the ground.

1 Tie the handle of a small bucket to your belt buckle.

2 Thin fruit with both hands, dropping them into the bucket.

3 When your pants begin to fall down, empty the bucket into a larger container.

---

garden. A short (18 inches tall) fence will keep them at bay while allowing you to easily step over it.

1 Purchase a roll of 1-inch mesh chicken wire 36 inches wide and long enough to encircle your garden. Purchase 24-inch-long sharpened surveyor's stakes onto which you can staple the wire.

2 *Dig* a shallow trench 6 inches deep around the garden. Drive the stakes into the trench at 4-foot intervals around your garden.

3 Use heavy-duty staples to fasten the wire to the wooden stakes.

4 Slip the bottom 6 inches of the wire into the trench and fill with soil. This will prevent the bunnies from digging under your fence.

Pruning

Healthy fruit trees usually produce many more young fruit than the tree can comfortably bear by late summer. Surplus fruit should be thinned out and discarded by mid-May. It may seem wasteful to throw away the green fruit, but the tree will put its energy into ripening properly-sized fruit if you thin properly. **Correct fruit spacing after thinning:**

Peach: adjacent fruit on a limb should be no closer than 8 inches.

Apple: adjacent fruit on a limb should be no closer than 6 inches.

Plum: adjacent fruit on a limb should be no closer than 6 inches.

Pear: adjacent fruit on a limb should be no closer than 8 inches.

Planning

The different varieties of **Sweet Corn** *each require a fixed number of days between planting and harvest.* Unless you want a great deal of **Corn** all at once, plant **Sweet Corn** seed every two weeks. As the different plantings mature, your **Corn** season will be much longer.

- **Corn** can be planted through mid-July.

- Try several different varieties of **Corn.** You might like the new "super-sweet" types (**'Kandy Korn'**, **'Seneca Sweet'**, etc.) better than the old standards (**'Silver Queen'** and **'Truckers Favorite'**).

Though it is not as critical as with **Corn,** it is also beneficial to make successive plantings of other vegetables: **Summer Squash, Lima Beans, Pole Beans,** and **Field Peas** can be planted every three weeks.

Planting

Corn is pollinated by wind currents, not by insects. *Plant* your seeds in several parallel rows side-by-side instead of in one long row.

Vegetable transplants are still available at garden centers, but they might not always be the best quality:

- *Examine* each plant to make sure it does not have leaf disease.

- Short, stocky plants are better than the stretched-out ones that have flopped over each other.

- Try to purchase freshly delivered transplants rather than those that have been on display for several days.

Many vegetable plants can be grown on a trellis to minimize the space they need. Use strips of cloth or jute twine to tie vines to the trellis.

Tomatoes can be *caged* or *staked* to hold the vine off the ground:

- Purchased tomato cages are good for **Bush** and **Patio Tomatoes,** but they are usually too small for other varieties.

- A homemade tomato cage may be made from a 6-foot-high section of heavy-duty fence wire 7 feet long. Join the ends of the fence wire to form a tube 6 feet high and 2 feet in diameter. Slip the tube over a plant. Attach the cage to a sturdy stake driven into the ground to keep it from blowing over.

- To stake the plants, drive a long wooden stake next to each plant; tie the vine loosely to the stake as it grows longer. Pinch the tips of limbs that sprout from the main stem when they have grown 12 inches. Fruit will then be produced close to the stake.

Watermelon, Winter Squash, and **Pumpkin** can also be trellised. Follow these steps to build a structure that will serve one plant:

1 Drive two sturdy posts into the ground 6 feet apart.

2 Stretch a 6-foot-long and 6-foot-wide piece of wire fencing between the posts; nail it to the post securely at both ends.

3 When fruits form, use a large square of cloth to cradle each one; tie the diagonal corners of the cloth to the trellis.

Do not attempt this trellising with large-fruited varieties.

Care for Your Plants

Remove stakes from fruit trees that have been planted for several months. They are now strong enough to stand on their own.

Watering

A drip irrigation system uses *emitters* that slowly drip water wherever you want it to be applied. The emitters are inserted into a plastic pipe that carries water from your faucet throughout your garden.

> *The best way to learn about drip irrigation is to purchase a starter kit that contains the components needed to water a small area. It can be expanded as necessary.*

Soaker hoses laid down the row beside your vegetable plants will water them well without waste.

> *Water Cucumbers regularly to prevent a bitter taste.*

Fertilizing

Side-dressing is the practice of applying fertilizer to the ground beside plants as they grow. If your garden vegetables are growing in a row, it is simple to sprinkle fertilizer on the ground as you walk between rows.

Side-dressing

You may also choose to fertilize in a circle around individual plants or broadcast it over the whole plot.

Fertilizing in a Circle

Broadcasting Fertilizer

It's a common complaint of **Tomato** growers that they have huge vines but few fruit. This condition might be caused by overfeeding with liquid fertilizer.

> *Once your Tomatoes have grown to 2 feet tall, stop fertilizing until blooms appear.*

(See Vegetable Garden Fertilization, p. 91.)

Pest Control

Blossom end rot is a common disorder of **Tomato** fruit. It is caused by a lack of calcium in the fruit when it is small.

- Add 2 tablespoons of lime to the soil when planting individual **Tomatoes.**

- Keep soil moisture levels constant; avoid wide fluctuations of water around the roots. Use mulch under the **Tomatoes.**

- If you notice the fruit has a rotten bottom (the blossom end), *spray* immediately with a product containing calcium chloride (see Chemicals, p. 327).

Pruning

Use garden herbs often in your kitchen, snipping and nipping leaves as you need them. The plants grow best when the branches and leaves are harvested regularly.

Organic Gardening

Organic Gardening Magazine, Emmaus, PA 18098

The Encyclopedia of Organic Gardening, by J.I. Rodale, Rodale Press

Common-Sense Pest Control, by William Olkowski, The Taunton Press

JULY

Planning

Early this month is the time to plant* Pumpkins *for Halloween. Most varieties need at least 100 days of growth to make a suitable Jack-o-Lantern. Varieties that produce "baby" pumpkins are often more successful. Varieties with shorter vines take up less space. If you are still short on space, build a heavy-duty trellis (see June) on which to train the vine.

Planting

You can *root* new **Tomato** plants now to keep your garden productive into October:

1 Put the lower 6 inches of a 12-inch-long **Tomato** branch in a jar of water. Keep it in a shady area outdoors.

2 When roots are 1 inch long, the **Tomato** can be transplanted into a pot.

3 In two weeks the plant will be ready to move to your garden.

If you are conscientious about keeping the soil moist, you can root **Tomatoes** right in the soil. This is how Walter's neighbor Harry does it:

1 *Cut* a 12-inch branch from your **Tomato** plant. *Strip off* all the leaves except the two or three around the tip of the branch.

2 Poke a hole in the garden soil deep enough to insert all but the top 3 inches of the branch.

3 *Water* the soil thoroughly every two days.

4 Make a temporary umbrella for the tender plant using an unneeded branch from a **Holly** or **Aucuba** shrub. *Remove* the umbrella ten days later. Your new plant is rooted in place and ready to grow!

Broad leaf shrub branches

Shading Tender Plants

Care for Your Plants

Don't let fruit tree limbs break: ***prop them up*** with poles, or ***remove some fruit*** to lighten the load.

Pick **Squash, Cucumbers,** and **Okra** regularly. A single fruit left to overmature on the vine will stop bloom production completely.

Watering

It is sometimes said that watering vegetable plants on a hot, sunny afternoon will cause spots to be burned in the leaves because the water droplets focus sunlight on the leaves. This is hogwash.

Quick afternoon showers are common throughout the summer. Neither vegetables, nor trees, nor flowers, nor any other plant are harmed by water on their leaves on a sunny afternoon.

Water weekly your fruit trees and vines that were planted in the last six months. They need approximately 2 gallons of water per foot of plant height.

Fertilizing

Continue to fertilize summer vegetables. (See Vegetable Garden Fertilization, p. 91.)

Don't forget to water the fertilizer into the soil afterwards.

Patio Tomatoes need to be fed regularly because the constant watering rinses fertilizer out of the soil.

You can also mix up a large storage container of water-soluble houseplant fertilizer at $1/4$ strength and simply use it to water the plants each time.

Pest Control

Tomato leaves disappearing overnight? Suspect the tomato hornworm, a big green caterpillar camouflaged among the plant stems. Hornworms are easiest to find in late evening, using a flashlight. Look for black excrement pellets on the ground underneath their feeding site.

Some gardeners prefer not to kill the hornworm caterpillar. After all, it will eventually turn into a sphinx moth.

Tomatoes are susceptible to several diseases, so researchers have bred varieties that are resistant to disease. Look for the letters VFN or VFNT after the variety name. The letters mean the **Tomato** is resistant to:

- Verticillium wilt
- Fusarium wilt
- Nematodes
- Tobacco mosaic virus

Helpful Hint

All members of the **Squash** family (**Watermelon, Pumpkin, Gourd, Cucumber,** and **Squash**) form separate male and female flowers on the same vine. Male flowers are first to arrive. They may regularly appear for weeks before a female flower materializes on the vine. A healthy vine will eventually produce lots of fruit . . . don't worry if at first you have lots of flowers but nothing to eat!

Bees must be present to pollinate the flowers. If you are getting only a few well-shaped fruit, transfer pollen between male and female flowers. Use a cotton swab or camel hair brush, shaking it gently inside the flowers three times each day.

There is no defense against **Tomato** bacterial wilt. The plant seems to wilt markedly during the day but may partially recover overnight. After a week of successive wilts, the plant dies. Bacterial wilt remains in the soil for five years. *Do not plant* **Tomato, Pepper,** or **Eggplant** in a bacterial wilt spot; plant **Beans, Peas,** or **Corn** instead.

If you have no other place to plant **Tomatoes,** *follow the recommendation for thwarting nematodes described in April, Care for Your Plants.*

Pruning

Prune **Figs** lightly now. Remove the tall shoots in the middle of the bush.

Remove the vertical "water sprouts" that emerge from **Apple, Peach,** and **Pear** limbs.

Planning

By now you have likely become tired of harvesting **Beans, Corn, Peppers, Tomatoes,** *and* **Squash.** You can choose to let the whole garden wither for a few weeks . . . but don't forget to plan a fall garden: you can start buying seeds and finding out when transplants will be available at your nursery.

- **Collards, Kale, Mustard, Beets,** and **Turnip** are best planted from seed.

- **Broccoli, Cabbage, Cauliflower,** and **Green Onion** are best grown from transplants.

Planting

If you are not tired of summer vegetables, several can be planted now and still yield a good harvest:

- **Bush Beans** can be grown from seed.

- **Tomato, Bell Pepper, Cucumber,** and **Squash** can be grown from transplants.

Care for Your Plants

Look on the ground around your **Blackberry** and **Raspberry** plants. The canes snaking across the ground should be trained back to their wire arbor.

Watering

Water **Figs** and **Apples** regularly now as they begin to ripen. *Harvest* every morning, before the birds can do their damage.

Water vegetables deeply once each week. (Avoid giving them light sprinkles several days in a row.)

Fertilizing

Fertilize newly planted vegetables with starter solution only. *Do not* fertilize heavily, since this would increase the water needs of your plants.

Do not fertilize established vegetables and fruit. (See Vegetable Garden Fertilization, p. 91.)

Pest Control

Whiteflies are a common pest of **Tomatoes, Pepper,** and **Gardenia.** You can make a trap and catch hundreds of them:

1 Cut out two pieces of cardboard 3 inches by 4 inches in size.

2 Spray-paint the cards bright yellow.

3 Cover the cards with sticky motor oil treatment (STP®, etc.).

4 Nail the cards to stakes driven on both sides of a plant.

5 When trapped whiteflies cover the card, clean it and reapply the sticky stuff.

Deer can devastate a garden overnight. Many repellents have been tried, but few are effective more than a day or two. Repellents that deter deer with their bitter taste are not good choices for something you intend to eat! Wire mesh fencing is effective but expensive. You might want to try a different kind of fence: an electric fence that does not harm deer but gives them a mild electric shock when they touch it. Follow these steps to build a "Peanut Butter Electric Fence":

1 An electric fence consists of a small wire supported above the ground on insulated stakes. A special electric charger is attached to the wire and to a ground rod which has been driven into the ground. You can buy the materials from a hardware store or home improvement center for less than a hundred dollars. After you string the wire around your garden, it's time to train the deer.

2 Turn off the charger and grab a jar of peanut butter and some aluminum foil.

3 Take a tablespoon-sized wad of peanut butter in your fingers and mold it around the wire at some point.

4 Tear off a strip of aluminum foil 3 inches wide and 12 inches long, and center it over the gob of goober-butter. Drape the foil strip on both sides of the wire. Crumple the foil where the foil touches the peanut butter. You should now have a wad of aluminum foil protecting the peanut butter from rain and a narrow flag of shiny foil hanging beneath it.

5 Repeat this procedure at 5-foot intervals along the entire circumference of the wire.

At night, when hungry deer approach your garden, they will smell the peanut butter and investigate with their nose. KA-ZAAAP!!! Those Beans don't look quite as inviting when they are accompanied by a side dish of electricity! When the deer wanders by the next night, they will be reluctant to come close to any shiny, dangling objects—no

matter how good they smell and no matter how inviting the plants inside the wire seem.

6 When you install the electric fence, clear a strip of ground 3 feet wide on either side so you can walk along it every week to keep the wire clear of weeds.

CAUTION: Do not use an electric fence where children or unknowing visitors might come in contact with it. Post signs identifying your fence at intervals around it.

Pruning

Harvest **Squash, Okra,** and **Cucumbers** regularly. If one fruit gets too big, the plant will stop blooming.

Planning

Just because you can find a particular fruit in the grocery store does not mean it will grow in Georgia. Varieties of fruit that *do not grow well* in our Georgia climate are:

- **'Bing'** or any other **Sweet Cherry**—winter temperature swings and late frosts kill **Sweet Cherry** blooms. (Pie cherries such as **'Montmorency'** or **'North Star'** produce moderately well in the northern half of Georgia.)

- **'Bartlett' Pear**—fireblight disease is severe on this variety.

- **'Santa Rosa' Plum**—late frosts kill blooms, and Pierce's disease causes severe leaf drop. It seems to have a limited life span in south Georgia, although it might grow better in north Georgia.

- **Currants, Gooseberry**—high summer temperatures doom these plants.

- The **Pomegranate** is a fruiting shrub familiar to south Georgia gardeners, but it is not as common in the north Georgia; cold winter temperatures can freeze the plant back to its roots or kill it outright. If you would like the juicy fruit and the colorful foliage of a **Pomegranate,** plant it in a spot protected from cold winter winds.

Planting

In north Georgia, it's time to plant cool-season vegetable seeds and seedlings. **Cabbage, Lettuce, Collards,** and **Broccoli** transplants are available at garden centers. **Lettuce, Beets, Turnip, Spinach,** and **Radish** seeds can be planted; **Onion** sets (small bulbs) and **Garlic** can be planted now as well. *Be sure to soak the soil after planting. Rainfall may not occur as often as you'd like.*

Plant **Parsley, Rosemary, Sage,** and **Thyme** from transplants. Examine the small pots before you buy. Sometimes several plants will be growing in one pot; you can gently separate them just before planting and get several plants for the price of one!

Care for Your Plants

Show your kids how to eat a **Muscadine:** pop it in your mouth, suck the pulp out of the skin, enjoy the juice, then spit out the skin and seeds. What a delicious mess!

Wrap cheesecloth around **Sunflower** heads to keep the birds away. The head is ready to harvest when the back has turned from green to brown.

If your late **Tomatoes** aren't setting fruit, the reason could be poor pollination due to heat and humidity.

Use an electric toothbrush to vibrate each flower cluster two to three times a day for three days.

OR

Lightly tap each flower cluster with a pencil four to five times a day for three days.

Watering

This month is typically dry and hot in all parts of Georgia. Late-maturing vegetables need plenty of water for their fruit to ripen. *Water deeply at least once per week.*

Check the soil with a trowel after you water. Make sure the moisture has penetrated 6 inches.

Water **Pecan** trees if rainfall is scant. This is a critical month for the nuts—they will not fill out if water is lacking.

Fertilizing

Fertilize newly planted cool-season vegetables. Since the

soil is quite warm, water-soluble liquid fertilizers will push the plants off to a fast start.

Apply lime to your garden according to the results of your soil test.

Pest Control

Big green caterpillars on **Parsley** and **Fennel** are the precursors of beautiful swallowtail butterflies. Try not to kill them all.

Better yet, plant plenty of **Parsley** *and* **Fennel** *so there is enough for you and the caterpillars.*

Fall webworms construct ugly nests at the end of **Pecan** and other tree branches. The webbing protects the caterpillars from weather and predators.

The best control is the simplest: poke a long, limber branch into the web and pull it from the tree to expose caterpillars to the elements.

Pruning

Remove dead limbs from fruit trees and vines. Remove short stubs that have weak sprouts growing from them.

Helpful Hints

Herbs can be harvested and preserved throughout the summer and early fall. Here are two methods of keeping them for wintertime use:

Freezing

1 Rinse the herbs quickly in cold water, shake off the excess, then chop coarsely.

2 Place large pinches of herbs in an ice cube tray, cover with water, and freeze.

3 Transfer the cubes to plastic bags or airtight plastic containers. Freeze until needed.

Do not refreeze herbs after thawing.

Drying

1 If the herbs are clean, do not wet them. Otherwise, rinse the foliage, shake off excess water, and spread the herbs out to dry on paper towels until all surface moisture has evaporated. Remove any dead or damaged foliage.

2 Tie the stems into small bundles with string, and hang them upside down in a warm, dry place out of the sun. Make small, loose bundles, and allow for good air circulation around each bunch.

3 To air-dry herbs with seeds, tie the herbs in small bundles and suspend inside a paper bag with holes punched in the sides. Suspend the bag in a dark area with good air circulation. Collect the seeds when they are dry, and store in dark containers.

Sage, Thyme, Dill, and Parsley are easy to dry. Basil, Tarragon, and Mint may mold if not dried quickly.

Planning

One of the joys of gardening in Georgia is our long growing season. Gardeners in Minnesota report that their two seasons are "winter and the Fourth of July"! North Georgia gardeners are fortunate to experience 200 to 250 frost-free days per year; south Georgia gardeners may enjoy close to 300 days without freezing temperatures.

- The average date of first frost in Atlanta is November 13. Frost has been recorded as early as October 25 and as late as December 6.

- The average date of first frost in Tifton is November 21. The earliest recorded frost date occurred October 26, while the latest was December 20.

- The most-likely date for a last frost in Atlanta is March 27. The earliest date for a last spring frost was February 16, and the latest frost in spring occurred on April 23.

- The average date for the last frost in Tifton is March 6. The earliest date a final frost occurred was January 27, while the (*surprise!*) date for a late spring frost was April 1.

Planting

Dream of strawberry shortcake for next June! *Plant* **Strawberries** in a well-tilled bed. Good **Strawberry** varieties are **'Florida 90'**, **'Earliglow'**, **'Cardinal'**, and **'Delite'**.

- *Plant* them 12 inches apart, preferably in a raised bed.

- *Cover* plants lightly with pine straw to protect them for the winter.

In south Georgia, all fall vegetables can still be planted. **Cabbage, Lettuce, Collards,** and **Broccoli** transplants are available at garden centers. **Lettuce, Spinach,** and **Radish** seeds can be planted; **Onion** sets (small bulbs) can be planted now as well. *Be sure to soak the soil after planting. October is typically a dry month, and rainfall may not occur as often as you'd like.*

Clip out the woody flower stems of mature **Parsley** at ground level, taking care not to damage new leaves that have emerged there. *Dig* the plants and plant in 6-inch pots to bring indoors to a sunny window.

Although **Parsley** *is usually winter hardy outdoors, you'll have fresh* **Parsley** *handy to use through November if you bring it indoors.*

Care for Your Plants

Prepare your composting area for fall leaves. You can make an inexpensive bin from a piece of wire fence 4 feet wide and 10 feet long:

1. Join the two ends to form a hollow wire barrel.

2. Place a pile of small limbs 6 inches high on the bottom for best air circulation.

3. Pile leaves and other compostables on top of the limbs.

Bring some **Rosemary** inside to dry for winter use.

Dig **Sweet Potatoes,** but let them "cure" in a warm place for five days before you store them in a cool basement or unheated garage.

Harvest **Winter Squash and Pumpkins** before they are damaged by frost. They can be stored in a cool, dry spot for months.

Buy a **Pumpkin** for Halloween. Visit www.Jack-o-Lantern.com for some great carving patterns!

Watering

Though you may need one hose to keep fall vegetables watered, you won't need all the components you used during the heat of summer. *Drain and store* water hoses, sprinklers, and soaker hoses to avoid winter damage.

Fertilizing

If parts of your garden will not be used until next spring, you can improve the soil and prevent erosion by planting a *cover crop* now. Plants can be tilled into the soil just before you plant next spring. Good cover crops are:

Cover Crop	Seeding Rate per 1000 Square Feet
Crimson Clover	3.3 ounces
Winter Wheat	40 ounces
Annual Ryegrass	.5 to 1.0 pounds
Alfalfa	80 ounces

If you decide not to plant a cover crop over your garden for the winter, at least *mulch* the garden with wheat straw to prevent erosion. The straw will be almost completely decomposed by spring.

Pest Control

Use a hoe or rake to remove sprouts of chickweed in your garden. The plants may be small now, but they will cause a *big* problem if left unattended until spring. *Rake out and replace* all the mulch and dead leaves under **Peach, Pear, Apple,** and **Crabapple** trees. You'll prevent diseases on next year's leaves. Clean all the old vines from tomato cages before putting them in storage. Many pests overwinter in plant debris such as vines, stems, and leaves.

Helpful Hints

Cool weather brings a reminder that **Tomato** vines can't bear freezing temperatures. Follow these tips to store green tomatoes:

- Leave fruit on the vines up to the last week before a frost is imminent.

- After picking, remove stems and dry-wipe to remove dirt.

- Sort out fruit that have a bit of pink showing around the stem. These will ripen quickly in a sunny window.

- Select remaining green fruit that have reached mature size and turned whitish-green.

- Wrap individual tomatoes in sheets of newspaper. Place gently in a cardboard box in your basement or a very cool room.

- Green tomatoes will ripen very gradually in storage. Check weekly for rot.

For best flavor, remove from the box and place in a warm window a few days before you need them. If you still have leftover "love apples," look for a good fried green tomato recipe.

Pull out withered plants and put them on your compost pile or rototill them into the soil.

Pruning

Do not prune (except for dead limbs) during this time of year. Pruning causes plants to delay going dormant and can increase their susceptibility to cold damage.

Planning

One of the most important practices of a smart gardener is to keep notes on what happened in the garden during the year. The notes can be kept formally in a journal, or informally in a shirt pocket–sized spiral notepad. Now that the growing season is all but over, take time to jot down anything you'd change for next year.

- Did your **Tomatoes** perform as you expected?

- Was brown rot a problem on your fruit? How (and when) can it be prevented next year?

- Were the rows spaced properly, or should you make adjustments next year?

- Were you able to harvest something almost every month? Were some months heavier than others? Did this overload your ability to use the produce? Should more or less of some items be planted?

- How well did your weed- and insect-control measures work? Should your prevention methods be put into action earlier?

Planting

You can have a winter garden even if you don't own a plot of land. Plant winter container gardens on your sunny patio or porch. Utilize the same large pots that contained your summer annuals.

- Use greens such as **Arugula, Parsley, Mustard, Lettuce,** and **Spinach.** Even **Green Onion** bulbs will grow very well if you have plenty of sunshine.

- Don't be afraid to mix **Pansies** and **Snapdragons** with your edible plants.

- *Fertilize* with houseplant fertilizer according to label directions.

- Move the container(s) to a sheltered spot if frigid or windy weather threatens.

This is a great time to plant bareroot fruit and nut trees—but be sure to plant varieties that grow well in your area! (See the Fruit Varieties charts, p. 340.)

Brambles are highly productive and have few pests. *Plant* **Blackberries** and **Raspberries** now, in the sunniest spot possible. See *Care for Your Plants* for a trellis plan. (See Fruit Varieties charts, p. 340.)

In south Georgia, plant **Carrots** now. They can also be planted in north Georgia, but some winter injury may occur. **'Nantes'**, **'Dan-**vers'**, and **'Chantenay'** are good varieties. *Do not fertilize* **Carrots;** splitting will result. Let them absorb nutrients left over from your summer garden.

Care for Your Plants

Blackberry and **Raspberry** plants should be grown on a wire trellis. You can build a sturdy trellis easily in an afternoon:

1 Set 4×4 pressure-treated posts 10 feet apart. The posts should be 5 feet tall after installing in the ground.

2 *Stretch* three heavy-gauge wires between the posts, at 24, 42, and 60 inches from the ground.

3 *Center* each bramble plant between the posts when you plant them.

4 Tie the canes to the wires as they grow longer.

A cold frame offers the opportunity to enjoy fresh cool-season vegetables for much longer than might be possible with a normal garden. Construct several, using the plans in Annuals, November. To simplify management, you can devote each frame to a different crop: **Lettuce, Spinach, Beets, Turnip Greens.**

NOVEMBER

Watering

Fall is an excellent time to plant fruiting trees, vines, or shrubs, but even though air temperatures are cool, the soil may be dry. Give newly installed plants at least five gallons of water each week unless rain occurs.

At full pressure, most hoses deliver five gallons of water in one minute.

Fertilizing

It is not necessary to fertilize fruits, vegetables, or herbs during the cold season.

Make sure your fertilizers are stored where they will not get wet during the winter.

Helpful Hints

This is a good month to clean tools and pots. Items that might be contaminated with disease spores or pesticides should be thoroughly cleaned. Clean your pesticide sprayers thoroughly with a 1:10 mixture of bleach and water:

1 Disassemble the wand; clean the nozzle.

2 Pressurize the tank and shoot some of the cleaning mixture through the nozzle.

3 Partially fill the tank with clean water and circulate it through the wand and nozzle.

4 Turn the tank upside down to drain. Afterwards, reassemble loosely and store in a covered spot.

Empty any caked potting soil from pots. Dump it on an empty garden bed for rototilling next spring. Rinse out any remaining soil with a hose.

Soak clay and plastic pots, seed trays, and seed-starting items in a bucket filled with a 1:10 mixture of bleach and water.

Allow to dry afterwards, and stack neatly where you can find them when you need them.

Pest Control

When leaves have fallen, thoroughly spray fruit trees with a dormant oil, like Volck™ oil. Dormant oils (see Chemicals, p. 327) are heavier than other horticultural oils; the oil suffocates insects that hide on and under the bark.

Pruning

Remove the foliage of **Asparagus** plants now, before the red berries fall off. Otherwise, seeds will sprout, and the **Asparagus** bed will become too crowded.

Once the leaves fall from fruit and nut trees, examine the trees' form. Make plans to prune them during the winter. (See February for illustrations of correct form.)

Planning

If space is limited, you'll find that several raised beds produce more vegetables than an equivalent amount of flat ground. Choose a warm weekend to construct your beds. Treated or untreated wood, stones, or concrete blocks can be used to line the bed.

- The sides of a bed should be at least 8 inches tall.

- Beds can be any convenient length, but it is easier to weed and maintain beds that are 30 to 40 inches wide.

- *Dig and loosen* the soil inside the bed, rototilling in a 2-inch-thick layer of soil amendment (see Horticultural Practices, p. 7).

- Fill the remainder of the bed completely with topsoil. *Mix it deeply* with the undersoil. Buy extra topsoil—after a few weeks the bed will settle and will need refilling.

Planting

After leaves have been nipped off by frost you can transplant any of your small fruit trees to new sites.

- Don't try to transplant trees larger than 8 feet tall. You'll be more successful buying a new tree rather than waiting for a transplanted tree to start growing again. If the tree is 8 to 12 feet tall, you can reduce its height to 6 to 8 feet by pruning.

- Dig a 6-foot-wide hole into which the tree will be planted.

- No need to fertilize now. Wait until next summer, when the tree has fully leafed out.

Care for Your Plants

If you still have **Beets, Collards, Mustard,** or **Turnip Greens** in your garden, don't be afraid to eat them. Old-timers say they have the best taste when the leaves have endured a frost or two. A thin layer of pine straw will protect them from temperatures below freezing.

Watering

Be sure to turn off the water supply valve and drain your watering system before hard freezes arrive. Wrap outdoor faucets that cannot be drained with insulating foam. Coil up soaker hoses and water hoses, and store them in an out-of-the-way spot so you can work in your garden easily next spring.

Fertilizing

Have a bag of lumpy fertilizer? It doesn't go bad . . . and your plants will appreciate it next year:

1 Spread a sheet of plastic on your garage floor and place the fertilizer in the middle.

2 Use a hammer to break up the lumps into pieces no larger than $1/2$ inch in diameter.

3 Scoop the fertilizer into a lidded 5-gallon plastic bucket. Seal the lid tightly.

4 Use a permanent marker to label the bucket's contents.

Pest Control

Much can be done now to prevent pests and diseases next year in your fruit and vegetable garden. Fruit that didn't get picked during the summer may still be hanging on your trees—these "mummies" should not be left on the tree. *Pick them off* and remove them completely from your garden to prevent potential disease problems. *Rake dead leaves* under fruit trees, vines, and shrubs; replace them with fresh mulch. *Spray* trees with dormant horticultural oil (see Chemicals, p. 327) to kill overwintering insects.

Pruning

A good pair of handpruners and long-handled loppers are essential for maintaining fruit trees and vines. When purchasing pruning tools, the motto "You get what you pay for" is quite true. While inexpensive pruners may cost less than ten dollars, they become dull quickly and are difficult to maintain. Bob Westerfield, Georgia Master Gardener Coordinator, gives these buying, sharpening, and care tips:

- Plan to spend $25 to $40 for good pruners. The best models can be disassembled easily and have a replaceable blade (Felco® #2 is a favorite of many gardeners).

- In general, anvil-type pruners are less versatile than bypass (scissor-type) pruners.

- Brightly colored handles are a plus if you tend to misplace your tools.

Handpruners and loppers can be sharpened after hard use.

1 *Disassemble* the pruner and place the handle in a vise. The blade should be upwards and easily accessible from all sides.

2 Use a whetstone (available at hardware stores) lubricated with oil. Some whetstones have a "fine" side and a "coarse" side for more versatility. Shine a light on the blade so you can see the manufacturer's original bevel.

3 Holding it at the original bevel angle, *slide* the whetstone up the blade from the base to the tip of the blade. Use many light strokes. Strive for a uniformly bright and sharpened edge.

4 Slide the stone against the flat backside of the blade once or twice to break off the tiny metal curls that were formed when the beveled side was sharpened.

5 Use oil or a lubricating spray to *lubricate* your pruners after each use.

6 *Examine* the blade regularly for nicks and chips. Replace if badly damaged.

Never use a pruner to cut wire unless it has a special notch designed for the purpose.

Helpful Hint

Store all your garden tools (shovel, spading fork, trowels, etc.) neatly for the winter—don't pile them in a heap. Spray metal surfaces with a lubricating spray to thwart rust.

- Firmly attach an 8-foot-long 2×4 to the wall of your storage building.

- Hammer twelve-penny (12d) finishing nails into the 2×4 at 12-inch intervals.

- Drill 1/4-inch-diameter holes in the handles of wooden tools and hang them from the nails.

Houseplants

If any class of plants could be described as "pets," it would be houseplants. We talk to them, fuss over them if they are ill, and sometimes give them names. Some gardeners say their plants flower better when they play music for them!

Houseplants give gardening opportunities to anyone, no matter where they live. Whether in a twenty-third floor condo or a poorly lit basement apartment, houseplants can thrive with proper care. Since houseplants are so much a part of the intimate space, problems are magnified if they occur. A spot on an **Azalea** leaf outdoors is barely noticed. The same spot on the **African Violet** passed down from Aunt Louise brings alarm!

Indoor plants bring a feeling of calmness and "homeness" to a space. Visit any shopping mall, and notice how many plants are growing in the common areas. The proprietors know that the plants give shoppers comfort . . . and a comfortable shopper is more likely to return to shop again. In homes, plants bring textural variety to rooms. Real foliage and flowers contrast with flower prints on fabric, floral colors on walls, and finished wood in furniture and flooring. Plants are as important to the dêcor and cheer of a space as are the furnishings and wall coverings.

Houseplant Culture

The two main causes of houseplant problems are not insects and disease but light and water—too much or too little of either. Many houseplants are native to the tropics and they thrive in bright light. They tend to decline in the lower light conditions of a typical interior room. Many other houseplants are conditioned to drenching rain and then a short period of drought. If you keep their soil constantly moist, their roots will quickly deteriorate.

Whether you have a new "baby" of a species you have not yet grown, or a mature plant you've nurtured for years, make sure you know the plant's specific needs for light and water. The lists of houseplants and their light needs that follow plus the description of light levels in March and December will give you pointers on which plants to choose for your situation.

Watering

The water needs of a houseplant are best measured with a "digital" water meter—not the battery-powered gizmo with two steel legs, but the fingers attached to your own hand! Simply put, press a finger 1 inch into the soil of the plant you are monitoring, then bring it out. If your finger is dry, reach for the watering can. If your finger is damp, find another chore to attend to.

Watering "schedules" are unreliable because a plant's water needs vary during the year. When a plant is growing rapidly, in the spring and summer, it needs more water than when it slows down in fall. When the furnace dries the air in your home, plants need more water than when all the windows are open in spring. True, you'll soon "get a feel" for the schedule of watering a plant needs—but be sure to check on your schedule a few times with your handy "digit" during the year.

Houseplants

Recommended Houseplants

The lists that follow will help you decide which houseplants are best for your situation. Our first list comes from our friend Kathy Henderson, who recommends the following plants for the beginner or the expert. Kathy Henderson, a long-time gardening expert in Atlanta, publishes "Kathy Henderson's Garden Gazette", P.O. Box 1161, Stockbridge, GA, 30281, 770-957-4444.

Aglaonema: likes medium light, tolerates a wide range of conditions; some call it "Chinese Evergreen."

Bromeliads: grows in medium light, water both soil and upper vase of leaves.

Christmas Cactus: bloom from Thanksgiving to Christmas for many years.

Dracaena 'Janet Craig': tolerates low light, excellent as a tall feature.

Kalanchoe: colorful flowers on a very sturdy plant.

Kentia Palm: prefers bright light, great for height.

Norfolk Island Pine: needs good light, especially nice at Christmas.

Orchids: be patient, provide good light, and keep moist but do not overwater.

Piggyback Plant: wants medium light, interesting but sturdy.

Rex Begonia: wide range of colorful leaves.

Spathiphyllum: grows great in low light, bold texture, white flowers.

The rest of the lists and descriptions in this chapter (see following pages) were taken from "Indoor Plants" by Dr. Mel Garber, Dr. Paul Thomas, and Dr. Butch Ferree, Extension Horticulturists for The University of Georgia College of Agricultural and Environmental Sciences.

Low-Light Plants	Medium-Light Plants		High-Light Plants
Aglaonema	African Violet	Grape Ivy	Coleus
Cast-iron Plant	Areca Palm	Hawaiian Ti	English Ivy
Chinese	Boston Fern	Holly Fern	False Aralia
Evergreen	Bromeliads	Kentia Palm	Jade Plant
Heart-leaf	Christmas	Ming Aralia	Norfolk Island Pine
Philodendron	Cactus	Nephthytis	Pony Tail Palm
Parlor Palm	Corn Plant	Pleomele	Schefflera
Peperomia	Dracaena	Pteris Fern	Spineless Yucca
Pothos	'Warneckii'	Rex Begonia	Swedish Ivy
Prayer Plant	Dracaena 'Janet	Rubber Plant	Weeping Fig
Snake Plant	Craig'	Sprengeri Fern	**Very High-Light Plants**
Spathiphyllum	Dumb Cane	Spider Plant	Flame Violet
Velvet-leaf	Fern-leaf	Split-leaf	Geranium
Philodendron	Aralia	Philodendron	Hibiscus
	Fiddle-leaf Fig	Wandering Jew	Wax Begonia

Houseplants

Fertilizing

Feeding a houseplant is much less complicated than choosing from among the dozens of available fertilizers. Basically, just choose one and use it according to label directions. Most manufacturers recommend a monthly feeding. If there is a time to vary from this schedule, it is in the winter. With lower light levels, plants can't utilize the amount of fertilizer they used in summer. To take this into account, simply use half the recommended amount when you feed your plants in winter.

Pests

Fortunately, indoor plants have few pests, and those they have are easily controlled if you notice them before they greatly multiply. You'll find descriptions of pests and diseases in the following months:

- March—mealybugs
- June—aphids
- August—spider mites
- October—cultural and environmental problems
- December—root rot and scale

Indoor Plant Reference List

The following plants are listed alphabetically by common name followed by the botanical name and additional common names.

African Violet *Saintpaulia ionantha*. African Violets are among the most popular of flowering indoor plants. Almost all colors are available. Plants range from a few inches to a foot or more in diameter, and leaves grow to form a rosette. Many variegated varieties are available.

Aglaonema *Aglaonema commutatum* (Chinese Evergreen). Many varieties and some hybrids of **Aglaonema** are available, many with highly variegated foliage. Low-growing and compact, it is a tough plant well-suited for many uses in the home or office.

Aralia *Polyscias fruticosa* (Ming Aralia). *P. filicifolia* (Fern-leaf Aralia). *Dizygotheca elegantissima* (False Aralia). These and other species and varieties of **Aralia** are commonly grown. Most are upright and some bonsai-like in appearance. All are highly susceptible to mealybugs and spider mites.

Begonia *Begonia rex* (Rex Begonia). *Begonia* × *semperflorens-cultorum* (Wax Begonia). Many species and varieties of **Begonia** are cultivated. The **Rex Begonias** are grown largely for their large colorful foliage. **Wax Begonia,** commonly grown outdoors as a garden annual, is an excellent indoor plant if there is adequate light.

Bromeliad *Ananas* species. *Vriesia* species. Many **Bromeliads** are cultivated, but light is a limiting factor for many grown indoors. The rosette of most **Bromeliads** forms a vase which holds water. Plants must be of a certain age to flower, often one to two years. When mature, a plant flowers only once, after which the central plant dies. Flowers last from a few weeks to six months. Offshoots form at the base of the parent plant.

Cast-iron Plant *Aspidistra elatior*. This is an often overlooked plant. It is in a class with **Snake Plant** because of its ability to persist under difficult conditions such as extremely low light and sporadic watering. A variegated form with leaves striped green and white is also available.

Continued on following pages

Houseplants

Indoor Plant Reference List

Christmas Cactus *Schlumbergera bridgesii.* Keep **Christmas Cactus** cool at night (50 to 55 degrees Fahrenheit) during October and November to initiate and develop buds for Christmastime flowering. Another method is to place the plant in continuous, uninterrupted darkness for fourteen hours daily at a night temperature of 60 degrees Fahrenheit during October and November. During the daylight hours, make sure the plant receives a minimum of 500 to 1000 foot candles of light (see March).

Coleus *Coleus* × *hybridus.* **Coleus** is commonly grown outdoors in summer for its colorful foliage. It can be grown indoors in adequate light.

Cordyline. (See **Hawaiian Ti.**)

Corn Plant. (See **Dracaena.**)

Croton *Codiaeum variegatum pictum.* There are many varieties of **Croton.** The foliage is among the most colorful in the plant kingdom. High light is required for good growth and good color. **Croton** is highly susceptible to spider mites when grown indoors.

Dracaena *Draceana deremensis. D. surculosa* (Gold-dust Dracaena). *D. fragrans massangeana* (Corn Plant). *D. draco* (Dragon Tree). *D. marginata* (Red-edged Dracaena). *D. reflexa* (Pleomele). *D. sanderiana* (Ribbon Plant). Two common varieties of *D. deremensis* are **'Janet Craig'** (solid green) and **'Warneckii'** (striped). All are good dependable plants, especially where height is needed. **Ribbon Plant** and **Gold-dust Dracaena** are among the smaller of the **Dracaenas,** growing 2 feet tall, while other varieties may reach 10 feet tall.

Dieffenbachia. (See **Dumb Cane.**)

Dumb Cane *Dieffenbachia amoena. D. picta.* These two species are the most common, though there are other species and varieties. The plant is upright in habit and seldom branches. The sap causes dermatitis in sensitive people, thus should be kept out of the reach of children. Lower foliage drop is common.

English Ivy *Hedera helix.* Many varieties of **Ivy** are easily grown as indoor plants. The dwarf varieties are often preferred. There are many different leaf shapes and sizes with widely varying patterns of coloration.

Fern *Nephrolepis exaltata* (Boston Fern). *Cyrtomium falcatum* (Holly Fern). *Rumohra adiantiformis* (Leather-leaf Fern). *Asparagus densiflorus* 'Sprengeri' (Asparagus Fern, Sprengeri Fern). *Pteris quadriaurita* (Pteris Fern). *Adiantum* species (Maidenhair Fern). *Asplenium nidus* (Birdsnest Fern). *Platycerium bifurcatum* (Staghorn Fern). *Davallia fejeensis* (Rabbit's Foot Fern). The Boston-type ferns (there are many varieties) often suffer indoors from low humidity. **Holly Fern** and **Leather-leaf Fern** are often better choices. **Sprengeri Fern** has a high light requirement, and needle drop under low light is common; it is not a true **Fern.**

Ficus *Ficus benjamina* (Weeping Fig). *F. lyrata* (Fiddle-leaf Fig). *F. retusa* (Indian Laurel). *F. elastica* (Rubber Plant). **Weeping Fig** is among the most popular but also most troublesome of indoor plants. The plant is tolerant of a wide range of environmental conditions but sometimes reacts to rapid changes in environment by almost total defoliation. **Fiddle-leaf Fig** can be used where coarse texture is desired. **Rubber Plant** is common and grows stiff and upright;

Houseplants

lower leaf drop is common under low light. All members of the **Ficus** genus contain latex, which can form a sticky residue when leaves or stems are broken or cut.

Flame Violet *Episcia cupreata* and hybrids. **Flame Violets** are beautiful trailing indoor plants with flowers in a variety of colors. Their cultural requirements are similar to those of **African Violets.** They are very intolerant of low temperatures.

Geranium *Pelargonium × hortorum* (Zonal Geranium). *P. peltatum* (Ivy Geranium). **Geraniums** are popular outdoor plants when temperatures are above freezing. They are also good indoor plants and will flower continuously if they are given adequate light.

Jade Plant *Crassula argentea* (Chinese Rubber Plant). **Jade Plant** is a succulent which can grow to more than 10 feet in height. Older specimens take on a bonsai look. **Jade Plant** is very susceptible to overwatering and resultant leaf drop.

Grape Ivy *Cissus rhombifolia.* **Grape Ivy** is easy to grow and well-suited for hanging baskets or where a trailing habit is desired. It climbs easily if given the opportunity.

Hawaiian Ti *Cordyline terminalis* (Hawaiian Good Luck Plant). **Hawaiian Ti** is grown for its colorful foliage, which is streaked with rose to red. It grows upright, similar to some of the **Dracaenas.**

Hibiscus *Hibiscus rosa-sinensis* (Chinese Hibiscus). This is the tropical **Hibiscus** with large showy flowers often seen in garden centers. It is not winter hardy outdoors except in coastal areas. **Hibiscus** requires too much light to flower well under most indoor conditions.

Nephthytis *Syngonium podophyllum* (**Variegated Nephthytis**). Vine-like in habit, **Nephthytis** is easy to grow. It can be used for a variety of purposes from dish gardens to large specimens. Varieties available through tissue culture are compact, non-vining plants for 4-, 6-, and 8-inch pots.

Norfolk Island Pine *Araucaria heterophylla.* **Norfolk Island Pine** is a durable plant where space permits its use. It grows to over 100 feet tall in its native environment and can quickly outgrow its space indoors. Air-layering is useful in renewing overgrown plants. (See Houseplants, May.)

Palm *Chamaedorea elegans* (Parlor Palm). *C. seifrizzi* (Reed Palm). *C. erumpen* (Bamboo Palm). *Chrysalidocurpus lutescens* (Areca Palm). *Howea forsterana* (Kentia Palm). *Caryota mitis* (Fishtail Palm). These and many other **Palms** are grown as indoor plants. Although not the easiest of indoor plants to grow, they are used for their height and graceful character. Watch for scale insects, mealybugs, and spider mites.

Peperomia *Peperomia obtusifolia* (Pepper Face). *P. sandersii* (Watermelon Peperomia). *P. caperata* 'Emerald Ripple'. Many **Peperomias** are grown indoors. Most are small compact plants, but leaf size, shape, texture, and coloration vary widely. **Peperomias** are easily overwatered.

Philodendron *Philodendron scandens oxycardium* (Heart-leaf Philodendron). *P. scandens oxycardium forma* (Velvet-leaf Philodendron). *P. selloum* (Tree Philodendron). *Monstera deliciosa* (Split-leaf Philodendron). There are numerous species and varieties, and

Houseplants

they differ widely in growth habit, leaf size, and ultimate height. **Heart-leaf** and **Velvet-leaf Philodendrons** are useful in hanging baskets or where a trailing or climbing habit is desired. Coarse-leaved or split-leaved varieties are useful as specimens. Some varieties have colorful foliage. Others are upright and non-climbing.

Pothos *Epipremnum aureum* (**Golden Pothos, Devil's Ivy**). Often confused with **Philodendron, Pothos** is one of the easiest of indoor plants to grow. It is well-adapted to hanging baskets or where a trailing habit is desired.

Pony Tail *Beaucarnea recurvata* (**Umbrella Tree**). *Brassaia arboricola* (**Dwarf Schefflera**). **Schefflera** can be grown in tree form or shrub form depending on how it is pruned. It is a handsome plant where space permits, but is very susceptible to scale, mealybugs, and spider mites. The **Dwarf Schefflera** is better suited for many indoor uses.

Snake Plant *Sansevieria trifasciata. S. trifasciata* **'Hahnii'** (**Birdsnest Sansevieria**). **Common Snake Plant** produces leaves up to 4 feet long which originate at the soil line and have bands of gray over deep green. Another variegated type has yellowish-white margins. The Birdsnest types are much shorter and form rosettes only a few inches high. **Snake Plant** is one of the easiest indoor plants to grow.

Spathiphyllum *Spathiphyllum floribundum* (**Peace Lily, White Flay**). One of the most satisfactory plants for low-light situations, **Spathiphyllum** is available in different leaf and plant sizes, depending on the variety. This is one of the few low-light foliage plants that will also flower under low light.

Spider Plant *Chlorophytum comosum.* **Spider Plant** is very easy to grow and is adaptable for hanging baskets. **'Vittatum'** is the common variegated type. All are susceptible to fluoride tip-burn.

Swedish Ivy *Plectranthus australis. P. oertendahlii* **'Variegatus'** (**Variegated Swedish Ivy**). Swedish Ivy is an easily grown, trailing plant suitable for pots or hanging baskets. Tiny flowers appear all year long.

Wandering Jew *Tradescantia fluminensis. T. albiflora. Zebrina pendula.* The **Wandering Jews** are fast-growing, trailing plants. Many have variegated leaves, and the undersides of some are also brightly purple-colored.

Wax Plant *Hoya argentea. H. compacta. H. carnosa.* Several named varieties of **Wax Plant** are available. Some are vigorous vines which climb by means of twining. Many have highly variegated foliage, which is sometimes deeply curled or crinkled. Fragrant star-shaped waxy flowers are produced in clusters.

Weeping Fig. (See **Ficus.**)

Yucca *Yucca elephantipes* (**Spineless Yucca**). Plants grow upright and stiff and may become somewhat grotesque in appearance with age. The plant is often confused with **Dracaena,** but it requires much higher light levels.

Planning

Now that the holidays are over, you may feel the need to clean up and put things back in order, and you may want to give your home a new look. One way to get a new look quickly is to make some changes with your houseplants.

- *Evaluate* the plants you have and your available space. Those that are too large can be pruned. Those that look ratty can be consigned to the compost pile, where they will enrich other plants in the future.

- Decide if you can provide the right conditions for the houseplants you keep. It is better to choose plants that match your conditions than to allow a plant to die a slow death in a poor site. Houseplants tend to do best in bright windows—refer to the Introduction for specific light requirements for many houseplants.

Planting

Blooms and foliage are not the only attributes that a houseplant brings to your home decor. The container in which a plant grows can also be a vibrant accessory.

- Visit home decorating stores to see the wide range of decorative containers that are available. Painted ceramic and metal containers are commonly available, but even an ancient mixing bowl or an antique tin box can be used.

- If the container you admire has no drainage, place a 1-inch layer of rocks in the bottom, and place your nondescript houseplant pot on the rocks. Water will drain normally from the houseplant pot without accumulating around plant roots.

Care for Your Houseplants

If your houseplant leaves have brown edges, this may indicate their environment is too dry.

Mist the leaves twice each day, and/or move them from drafty areas. Try to keep plants at least 5 feet from furnace or air-conditioner vents.

Root rot can also lead to brown leaf edges. Even when plenty of water is available, the water cannot be absorbed if roots are nonexistent. Pull the plant from its pot, and examine the roots. Squeeze a small root between your fingers. It should be firm, not mushy or jelly-like (see December for tips on recovering from root rot).

Brown edges might also mean the leaves are cold. Do not let leaves touch the window glass.

Single-pane windows may have a cold draft moving constantly down the window. Move the plant at least 12 inches away from the window.

Watering

The soil surface may feel dry to the touch, but push your finger into the soil at least 1 inch before deciding if a houseplant needs water. In a typical house, the soil surface in pots dries quickly, while plenty of water is available in soil below. Don't be too quick to water. Roots need a short time of dry soil to "breathe."

Poinsettias are native to Mexico, and they prefer growing in soil that remains on the dry side. Water **Poinsettias** only as needed—when the top inch of the soil feels dry. See September for hints on making a **Poinsettia** change color for the holidays.

On mild winter days, remember to water windowboxes or other outside containers. Give them a good soaking each time, adding water until it runs freely out the drain holes. It is particularly important to water during cold and windy weather. The plants need water around their roots to recover from cold damage.

Fertilizing

Fertilizer acts in concert with light to help a plant grow larger. Due to lower light levels, houseplants do not need much feeding in winter. If your houseplants don't receive much light, do not feed them—or if you do, apply fertilizer at half the rate recommended (see March for more lighting information).

Pest Control

Slow-flying small insects hovering over the soil in a pot indicate a population of fungus gnats. The adults do not cause damage but may be a nuisance. The small white larvae feed on decomposing organic matter (your wet potting soil), and occasionally on plant roots.

Helpful Hint

Poinsettia and **Amaryllis** can be kept for years, but in most of the state it is not practical to preserve **Paper-white Narcissus** bulbs that have been forced to bloom in winter. The main thing that limits their growth is temperature extremes. (In Savannah and other coastal areas, **Paper-whites** can grow successfully outdoors for years.) Most gardeners just pitch the faded plants onto their compost pile, where they can do some good for the rest of the garden.

To control the gnats, move the plant outdoors on a warm day, and drench the soil with a contact insecticide (see Chemicals, p. 327) labeled for use on houseplants. Allow the pot to drain before bringing the plant indoors.

Grooming

Tired of that big **Hibiscus** taking up too much space? You can prune away 1/3 of the total foliage without harming it. Use small clippers to shorten individual branches; make each cut next to where a smaller branch joins the part you are removing.

Faded **Amaryllis** blooms and their stems can be removed now. Treat the **Amaryllis** like a houseplant for the rest of the winter. Plant outdoors in May in a sunny bed. In succeeding years, the bulb will bloom in mid- to late April. In the upper third of the state, dig the bulb each fall and store it in a cool place indoors until you plant it outdoors again in spring. See September for hints on how to force **Amaryllis** to bloom in winter.

Planning

Not all houseplants are equal in the "care needed" department. These tough houseplants require minimal attention:

- **Cast-iron Plant** (*Aspidistra elatior*)

- **Dumb Cane** (*Dieffenbachia* spp.)

- **Peace Lily** (*Spathiphyllum* spp.)

- **Philodendron** (*Philodendron* spp.)

- **Pothos** (*Epipremnum aureum*)

- **Snake Plant** (*Sansevieria trifasciata*)

Planting

Repotting a houseplant is a good indoor chore while it is cold outside. Repotting may be necessary:

- if the rootball is so tight that water penetrates slowly, if at all.

- if the plant seems much too large for its container. Plants may be top-heavy or not proportional to the pot in which they were originally planted. Choose a new pot based on the present size of the plant: a pot diameter 1 to 2 inches larger than the original pot is usually best.

- if you want to move the plant to a more decorative pot.

- if the plant has been regularly fertilized in the same pot for several years. Excess fertilizer and fertilizer salts can accumulate in the soil and cause root damage.

To repot a houseplant:

1. Find a spot where you can make a mess but easily clean it up. Several sheets of newspaper on the dining room table may be adequate for small plants. Your garage or basement, plus a strong helper, may be needed for larger ones.

2. Pull the plant from the pot. Shake as much soil from the roots as possible. Use your fingers to gently *untangle* the roots and loosen more soil.

3. If the soil is hard-packed, *soak* the rootball in a bucket of warm water. Separate the mass of soil and roots with a sharpened stick or a pair of pruners.

4. Scoop fresh potting soil into the new pot. Hold the plant at the correct height to estimate how much soil should be placed at the bottom of the pot. Keeping the plant upright, pack soil around the roots. It is nice to have a helper hold the plant at the proper height in the new pot.

Hold the plant at the correct height.

Pack soil around the roots.

5. *Water* thoroughly, and allow to drain. If the plant has sunk lower than you want, lift it and press soil under the roots to support it correctly. The soil level should be .5 to 1 inch lower than the pot rim.

It is also possible to reduce a plant's size as you repot, keeping it in the same pot but replacing the soil. Instead of preserving the original rootball, you can remove up to $1/3$ of the roots and $1/3$ of the stems and foliage of the plant.

Care for Your Houseplants

Despite your best intentions, some houseplant leaves may turn brown. If the damage affects more than 50 percent of a leaf, *remove* the leaf completely. If the damage is confined to a small area, it can be trimmed away with scissors. Follow the shape of the leaf when cutting to maintain a natural appearance.

Helpful Hint

If the soil in a large pot dries almost completely, it may shrink from the pot sides. When you water, it simply flows around the soilball and exits the bottom of the pot without wetting the soil.

- Wrap a few ice cubes in a paper towel, and place them on the soil surface. The slowly melting ice will gradually wet the soil, and it will re-swell to fill the pot.

- If the pot is small, it might be faster to simply *soak* it in a small bucket of warm water for five minutes.

Trimming a Leaf

Fertilizing

When houseplants are fertilized regularly, fertilizer residues may accumulate in the soil. Yellow, sick-looking leaves that do not improve even when the plant is growing in good light indicate damage from fertilizer salts. You can remove the salts in two ways:

1 *Repot* the plant, replacing all the soil with fresh potting soil.

2 *Leach away* the chemicals. An easy way to accomplish this is to set the plant in your shower and water it heavily several times in one day. As water drains over and over from the pot, fertilizer salts will be removed as well.

Pest Control

Adequate light can be considered part of a pest-prevention program. Plants that are stressed from low light levels are unable to easily fight against and recover from pests (see December for more information).

Grooming

Most plants will naturally lean toward their light source. Unless they are turned once per month, indoor plants acquire an unbalanced look. Small potted plants can be turned by hand. Larger plants in pots can be placed on wheeled plant holders designed for easy turning. Ungainly plants can be pruned back by half to correct asymmetrical growth.

Watering

Potting soil must perform two competing jobs simultaneously: it must *absorb* water but also *release* it readily. Healthy roots require oxygen around them, but they also require an adequate amount of moisture. Watering a houseplant replenishes the moisture held by organic matter particles. As the water drains from the pot, oxygen is brought into the soil. Heavy, poorly drained soils cause root rot because the roots cannot breathe.

Planning

Orchids *have been appreciated as houseplants for hundreds of years.* The **Orchid** family is quite diverse, the largest in the plant kingdom. It includes between 20,000 and 30,000 species. **Orchids** have a reputation for being difficult to care for, but they are very adaptable. They can be quite happy in conditions similar to those required by an **African Violet:** bright, indirect light and temperatures comfortable to humans. The following are the best **Orchids** for growing indoors:

- *Cattleya* plants are known for their use in corsages and for having a flower that can last several weeks. They generally flower only once per year, in spring or fall. They require bright light.

- *Dendrobium* produces long, graceful sprays of flowers that are typically white, lavender, or a combination of the two, during fall and winter.

- *Phalaenopsis*—known as **Moth Orchids,** these are among the most elegant **Orchids** for indoor growing. They have long arching sprays of colorful flowers that remain fresh for several months. Flowering occurs in winter or early spring, and they require less light than **Cattleyas.**

- *Oncidium* plants are referred to as **Dancing Girls** and are very

easy to grow. They produce dainty yellow-and-brown or white-and-brown flowers and flower well even under adverse growing conditions.

- *Paphiopedilum* is one of the best **Orchid** groups to grow under artificial light. There are many hybrids available. They are not fragrant, but they have very interesting and colorful "Lady Slipper"–shaped flowers.

Planting

It can be difficult to remove plants from a pot in which they have grown for several years.

1 *Spread* newspaper under a handy chair or kitchen counter.

2 Flip the pot upside down, and place an edge on the chair seat or counter. Support the plant with one hand.

3 *Strike* the pot bottom sharply with your palm to loosen the plant and lower it from the pot.

Strike the
bottom of
the pot.

Orchids grow slowly compared to houseplants. Most **Orchids** need to be repotted about once every two years. Use osmunda fiber or a commercial orchid potting medium. These substances hold roots in place but drain quickly.

Care for Your Houseplants

Set overwintered houseplants outdoors on warm days, but bring them inside if temperatures go below 50° Fahrenheit. Fertilize and water them more often as light levels increase in spring. *Protect* them from wind and intense sunlight.

Light passing through window glass is reduced in intensity manyfold. Even so, light levels may need to be adjusted, based on the requirements of a specific plant. See the introduction for the light requirements of specific plants.

- East- and north-facing windows, with no drapes or curtains, are generally good for low-light plants.

- South- and west-facing windows, no drapes or fully open drapes, are good only for high-light plants.

- South- and west-facing windows, with sheer curtains *or*

blinds slightly tilted, are good for medium-light plants.

Watering

It is common to place houseplant pots in a saucer to collect water that drains through the pot. Check the saucer an hour after watering, and *discard* any water that has accumulated. Do not allow water to sit continuously in the saucer under the plant—it will wick up into the soil above and cause root rot and poor growth. One way to avoid this problem is to fill the saucer with pea gravel and place the pot on top of the gravel.

There is no correct answer to the question "How often should this plant be watered?"

- The water needs of a particular plant vary according to the temperature, light, and humidity around it. The worst practice is to water plants on a set schedule every week.

- Push a finger an inch into the soil every few days to check its condition.

- Read the care tag before you buy a plant to learn whether a plant prefers moist soil or slightly dry soil, and plan to water accordingly.

Fertilizing

Orchids are adapted to environments where nutritional levels are low, so they do not need heavy fertilization. Use a balanced houseplant fertilizer like 20-20-20, mixed at half the recommended rate, once per month in place of a normal water application.

Pest Control

Mealybugs suck the sap from plant stems and leaves, and they secrete undigested sap as a sticky liquid called *honeydew*. You might notice the sap on leaves and flat surfaces under your plant before you notice the insect. Mealybug-damaged plants look withered and sickly. Look on the underside of leaves and where a leaf joins a main stem. The insects look like small ($1/8$-inch) balls of white fuzz.

- Place the plant in your kitchen sink. A forceful spray of water on the insects will usually wash them off. You may also wipe the leaves with a cloth and sponge.

- If the plant is heavily infested, *spray* with a soap/oil mixture. Mix $1/2$ teaspoon insecticidal soap, $1/4$ teaspoon horticultural oil, and 1 quart of water in a spray bottle. Wet all leaves with the mixture once per week.

- As an alternative, use rubbing alcohol and a cotton swab to dab the alcohol directly onto each mealybug.

- If mealybugs can't be conquered with the methods above, use a contact insecticide product (see Chemicals, p. 327) specifically labeled for use on houseplants. Follow label directions carefully. *Spray outdoors* if possible.

- *Segregate* any infested plants from healthy ones until you are sure the pest is eliminated.

- Sometimes the labor of fighting mealybugs is not worth the results. There is no shame in admitting defeat after a month of effort and putting a heavily infested plant in the garbage.

Orchid Information

For more information about **Orchids,** contact:

American Orchid Society
6000 South Olive Avenue
West Palm Beach, FL 33405

Internet:
www.orchidweb.org

Planning

Not all potting soils are equal. There is a wide array of products available, but some are much better for your plants than others. Fafard™ soil mixtures are favored by many gardeners. Some potting soils also contain fertilizer, which should be taken into account when feeding your plants initially. If a potting soil contains fertilizer, the bag must tell how much the soil contains and how the plant should be fertilized after planting. A good-quality potting soil:

- should not smell "stinky" or "mucky."

- should not be sandy or gritty but should have a mixture of fine and coarse organic particles.

- should contain lots of white beads of perlite, which promotes drainage.

- should fall apart readily after a moist handful has been squeezed.

Planting

Many houseplants can be rooted to increase your supply or to propagate a favorite plant. The best rooting medium is usually a mixture of 2 parts perlite (for good drainage) to 1 part peat moss (for water retention).

A plastic shoebox, filled half-full with the moistened, not soggy medium, makes a good rooting container. **To root stem cuttings:**

1 (a) If rooting **Geranium, Small-leaf Begonia, Kalanchoe, Chrysanthemum,** remove a 3-inch section at the end of a branch. Make a clean cut just below where a leaf joins the stem, and strip all but the top two leaves from the cutting.(b) If rooting **African Violet** or **Gloxinia,** remove an unblemished leaf from the mother plant, leaving approximately $1/2$ inch of stem.

2 Dust Rootone™ on the cut stem end.

3 Insert the stem into the moistened rooting medium in the half-filled box. Several cuttings can be rooted at the same time in the box. Cover the box top with clear plastic kitchen wrap, and place in a moderately sunny window. See March for more on light levels.

4 Since the container is sealed, there is no need to water. Wait three weeks before removing the clear plastic.

5 Keep the potting soil lightly moistened for three more weeks. The cuttings should then be ready to plant into individual pots.

To root a Large-leaf Begonia:

1 Remove an unblemished leaf from the mother plant.

2 Use scissors to cut the leaf into three equal wedge-shaped "pie pieces" with the base of the leaf serving as the center of the "pie." Each wedge should have a leaf vein running down the center.

3 Lay the leaf pieces onto the moist rooting medium in the half-filled box. Place a pebble on the pointed, cut end of each leaf so it touches the soil firmly. Place another pebble in the center of the leaf to hold it in place.

4 Cover the box with clear plastic kitchen wrap, and place in a moderately sunny window.

5 In four to six weeks, leaflets will grow at the edges of each leaf. *Remove* the plastic as soon as you notice them.

6 Allow the leaflets to grow to 2 or 3 inches tall. They should be well-rooted into the soil.

7 Use scissors to cut the "baby" plants away from the "mother" leaf. Take care not to damage the roots. The new **Begonias** can be planted into individual pots and grown to maturity.

Jade Plant, Snake Plant, Aloe, and **Sedum** are best propagated from leaf sections. **To root leaf sections:**

1 Break off a single leaf from your **Jade** or **Sedum** plant. Cut a 3-inch-long tip section from an **Aloe** or **Snake Plant.**

2 Push the leaf part $1/3$ of its length into the rooting medium described above.

3 Cover the box with clear plastic kitchen wrap, and place in a very sunny window. See March for information on light levels.

4 *Remove* the plastic after two weeks.

5 *Mist* the leaf sections daily, but do not allow the rooting medium to become soggy.

6 Tug on each leaf section after four weeks. If it resists the tug, it has rooted successfully and can be transplanted into an individual pot.

Care for Your Houseplants

Repot houseplants that have grown too large for their containers (see February). *Cut back* leggy plants (those that have bare stems at the bottom) by half to encourage compact growth.

Watering

Water houseplants more frequently with the onset of more hours of sunshine from outdoors. The new leaves that are appearing now cause a need for more water.

Fertilizing

Clay pots can be reused if properly cleaned and sanitized. Rinse soil completely from the pot. *Soak* the pot overnight in a mixture of 1 part bleach to 10 parts water. *Scrub away* white deposits of fertilizer salts with a stiff brush.

Pest Control

Moving houseplants outdoors for the summer should be a gradual process, as light levels outdoors are many times more intense than those inside. Nighttime temperatures should be above 65 degrees Fahrenheit before you consider moving out the plants. Move houseplants to a very shady spot at first,

and leave them there for at least a week; two weeks or *even a month* is better. Move them to dappled sunshine for the rest of the summer. It is tempting to put houseplants into full sunshine, but most houseplants cannot adapt to such intense light. Plant leaves can be sunburned and killed by just a few hours in strong sunshine.

Grooming

In order to prolong their blooming, regularly *remove* the withered flowers from **Florist Azaleas** you receive for Easter.

Planning

In addition to offering attractive foliage and flowers, tall houseplants also perform other functions: directing pedestrian traffic, reducing glare through a window, and dividing interior space. Good plants for directing traffic are:

- **Norfolk Island Pine**
- **Palms**
- **Schefflera**
- **Weeping Fig**

Planting

Correct pot size is easy to calculate. In general, the diameter of the pot should be $1/3$ the height of the plant. Shallow-rooted plants, like **Cacti,** need shallow pots. Tree-form plants, like **Schefflera,** need taller containers.

Care for Your Houseplants

Often a **Rubber Plant** (*Ficus* spp.) or a **Corn Plant** (*Dracaena* spp.) will lose all its lower leaves during an extended stay indoors. When it has only a tuft of leaves at the top of a tall stem, the plant is quite unattractive. By "air-layering" the stem, you can produce two attractive

plants from one. May, June, or July are good months for this project.

1 Choose a point on the plant stem where you would like new roots to grow. Use a sharp knife to cut or scrape away the bark in a half-inch band around the trunk.

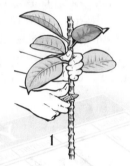

2 *Dust* a rooting hormone like Rootone™ on the cut surface.

3 *Wrap* layers of kitchen plastic wrap around the stem. Use twine or tape to seal the bottom edge of the plastic to the stem.

4 *Insert* a fist-sized mass of well-moistened but not soggy long-grain sphagnum moss into the plastic, around the wound.

5 *Seal* the top of the plastic to the stem with twine or tape. Wrap aluminum foil around the plastic wrap to provide complete darkness. Put your plant outdoors in a semi-shaded location. Water and care for it normally.

6 Wait five months. Unwrap the aluminum foil and plastic. You should see a mass of white roots that have formed around the wounded stem. Cut the stem completely through, 1 inch below the root mass.

7 Now that it has both leaves and new roots, this upper half can be planted in a new pot. The lower half of the plant will

sprout new leaves along the stem within four weeks and will become much more attractive.

7

Are Houseplants Air-Cleaners?

Although houseplants have gained a reputation for cleaning indoor air, the actual scientific research is not so clear.

- Small particles **do** accumulate on leaf surfaces that are numerous or hairy.

- Leaves **do** absorb small quantities of chemical pollutants in a **closed** space.

- The number of plants required to noticeably improve indoor air is more than most people are willing to have in their home.

Watering

One of the most interesting houseplant products to come on the market in the last few years is "water-holding crystals." These chemicals look like grains of salt when they are dry, but they absorb huge amounts of water. When wet, a teaspoon of crystals can fill a quart jar! Manufacturers promise that the crystals, when added to potting soil, will absorb water when a plant is irrigated and release water when the soil is dry.

Research has not completely proven the value of water-holding crystals, as their efficacy seems to be degraded by fertilizers and other soil chemicals. While they do not seem to harm plants, they are not the "miracle substances" their manufacturers pledge. Adding the crystals to the soil in a windowbox

may help the plants in the box survive a missed watering.

Houseplants need more water when they live outside on a deck or patio. Push a finger into the soil regularly to check for dryness, and plan to water more frequently than you did in winter.

Fertilizing

Begin fertilizing houseplants every month during the growing season, when it is sunny outdoors; follow label directions.

Pest Control

Check houseplants growing outside for the summer for pests as you water them. It is easier to control pests outdoors because there is less likelihood of the sprays harming indoor occupants or furniture.

Grooming

Regularly *remove* dead leaves as they occur.

Planning

Bromeliads *are a group of several species of plants known for their stiff, colorful foliage and brilliant flowers.* The **Pineapple** is the best known **Bromeliad**. Most **Bromeliads** have leaves that form a cup (the *tank*), which holds water in the center. In their native habitat, most **Bromeliads** grow in trees, where they get little nutrition and only sporadic rainfall. To care for your **Bromeliads:**

- Keep the tank constantly half-full of water, but allow the soil underneath to dry considerably between waterings.

- Houseplant fertilizer, mixed at ¼ strength, can be put in the tank once each month.

- Every six months, flush the tank by filling it with water, inverting the plant, and then filling it again.

Planting

One of the most common myths about growing houseplants is that one should put a layer of rocks in the bottom of a pot to promote good drainage. In fact, this is not a good practice. After you water a pot, the soil at the top dries out first, while the soil lower in the pot remains moist. The bottom inch of potting soil remains saturated most of the time, and roots do not grow in saturated soil. If you place a layer of rocks in the pot, the amount of saturated soil remains the same but the amount of beneficial, slightly moist soil is reduced, thus giving your plant less soil in which to grow. Instead, place a single pot shard over the drainage hole to prevent soil from sifting out of the pot.

Place a shard over the drainage hole.

A good project for out-of-school children is "garbage gardening," using plant parts that would normally be discarded in the kitchen. Place the planted containers described below in a sunny window or on a shady patio.

Apple, Orange, Lemon. Plant seeds shallowly in a pot filled with potting soil.

Avocado. Stick four toothpicks around the "equator" of the pit, spacing them equidistantly. Use a nail to pierce a starting hole for each. Suspend the pit, pointed side up, over a tumbler of water (the base of the pit should just touch the water surface). When it sprouts a stem and roots, plant into potting soil. *Pinch out* the tip of the stem when it reaches 6 inches long—this will cause it to resprout. When the new sprouts have grown to 6 inches long, pinch out *their* tips. Continue to follow this regimen as the plant grows larger. It will have a compact, densely leaved form.

Carrot. Cut off the top, and place it in a saucer filled with sand or potting soil.

Ginger. Break off a section of the root, and plant it shallowly, on its side, in a pot filled with potting soil.

Peanut. Plant *raw* (not salted or roasted) peanuts in a pot filled with potting soil.

Pineapple. Cut off the top, and place it in a 2-inch-deep clay saucer filled with potting soil.

Sweet Potato. Slice in half lengthwise and place cut side down in a shallow saucer filled with damp sand or a pot filled with potting soil.

Care for Your Houseplants

Plant leaves collect dust just as other household objects do. Now is a good time to give them a spring cleaning. A quick cure for some dusty houseplant leaves is to put the plant in your kitchen sink or shower

and spray the foliage with water for a few seconds.

- **African Violet** and **Gloxinia** have fuzzy leaves. Brush them with a camel hair brush.

Brushing Fuzzy Leaves

- Medium-sized plants without hairy leaves can be washed by immersing them in a sink or bucket of warm, slightly soapy water.

Immersion in Water

- Plants with large leaves benefit from a "two-sided" wipe, sandwiching a leaf between two soft cloths while pulling.

Avoid sprays that claim to make leaves shiny.

Watering

As household air conditioning runs more frequently, indoor air becomes drier. This means your houseplants will need more-frequent watering. Check the dryness of the soil each week by pushing a finger into it 1 inch deep. *Water* as needed.

Fertilizing

Fertilize the indoor plants you've moved out to the patio every two weeks. They will quickly fill out and have more leaves now in the bright light.

Pest Control

Aphids are usually found clustered at the growing tips of houseplant branches. They are easy to control with insecticidal soap or houseplant insecticide (see Chemicals, p. 327).

The Two-Sided Wipe

Make a Bromeliad Bloom

To make a **Bromeliad** bloom, empty the tank, place slices of ripe apple in it, and cover the plant with a plastic bag. Leave the apple in place for three days, then remove the plastic and apple. Refill the tank with water.

The apple releases ethylene gas, a powerful plant hormone. If the plant is healthy, flowering will begin in six to fourteen weeks.

A **Bromeliad** only blooms once. Flowers may last for several weeks, and baby plants will form at the base of the mother plant. They can be gently removed and planted in individual pots.

Aphid

Grooming

Remove faded blooms as you notice them; this will help prevent the spread of disease.

Planning

Several kinds of herbs make good houseplants, although they tend to be short-lived due to the low light indoors. If you have a sunny window for herbs near your kitchen, you can pick leaves and add them fresh to casseroles and soups. The flavor will not be as strong as it would be if the herbs were grown outdoors, but the convenience and freshness make up for this. Good kitchen herbs are:

- **Basil**
- **Oregano**
- **Parsley**
- **Rosemary**
- **Thyme**

Planting

Spider Plant gets it name from the multiple offshoots on springy stems that hang from a mature plant. It is easy to grow more **Spider Plants**—just plant the offshoots into individual pots. The safest method is to plant the offshoots without removing them from the mother plant. After a few weeks in their new home, the stems can be cut away. The small plants will be partially rooted and can grow normally on their own.

Care for Your Houseplants

Despite their sharp spines, **Cacti** can be fascinating and attractive houseplants. Their health depends on adequate sunshine, well-drained soil, and minimal fertilization. A **Cactus** can do well in a bright west- or south-facing window—do not place it more than a few feet from the window. Potting soil that contains organic matter plus a high percentage of sand is best. Do not use "regular" potting soil when you repot a **Cactus**. **Cacti** need fertilizer, but in small amounts. From spring to fall, fertilize every two to three months with a low-nitrogen fertilizer such as 5-10-10. Give a **Cactus** enough water to *soak* the soil thoroughly, but allow the soil to dry slightly between watering; push a finger 1 inch into the soil to determine its dryness. When repotting, gently *wrap* the plant with several layers of newspaper before handling it.

Watering

July is prime vacation time for most families. How will your indoor houseplants fare while you are gone?

- If you'll be gone for only a week, *water* plants just before you leave. They can tend themselves just fine until you return.

- If you'll be gone for two weeks, place an old towel in your bathtub, and *saturate* it with water. Place your houseplants on the towel, and draw the curtain closed, or close the door. The high humidity will keep plant water needs at a minimum.

- If you plan an extended vacation, occasional tending by a friend will be necessary.

The soil in a pot outdoors dries out quickly. Poke holes in it with a pencil to make sure water saturates the soil completely when you water it.

Fertilizing

If you just can't seem to remember when you last fertilized your plants, why not feed them every time you water? Most water-soluble plant foods have instructions for how to dilute the product for this use. If you are unsure, 1/4 tablespoon of fertilizer per gallon of water is a common recommendation. If you mix a quantity of plant food to use over several weeks, be sure to label the container clearly. Most plant food products contain a dye that makes them look like a fruit drink when diluted.

Pest Control

Several insects, including aphids, whiteflies, mealybugs, and scale, suck sap from houseplant leaves and stems. They excrete any sap they cannot digest as a clear sticky liquid (honeydew). The honeydew may coat lower leaves or the nearby floor or tabletop, and a black fungus, sooty mold, may begin to grow on the honeydew. The black coating is easy to wash off, but it is certainly visually objectionable.

If you notice sticky spots or sooty places under your houseplant, examine it thoroughly for insects. See December, June, and March for insect descriptions and control measures. Once the insects are controlled, the honeydew and sooty mold can be washed away.

Grooming

In addition to its attractive foliage, a **Rabbit's Foot Fern** extends furry "feet" (actually rhizomes) that grow over the edge of the pot. If left in a pot for years, the fern will eventually make a ball of feet around the pot. It can be perfectly happy this way as long as the soil is kept slightly moist at all times. When it is so potbound that it requires water every day, the fern can be divided and planted into several new pots.

Use care when pruning houseplants: some have sap that is quite irritating to your skin or eyes. *Wash your hands* after handling cut plant parts. Protect your new puppy and other pets from chewing on these plants. Houseplants known to have irritating sap are:

- **Dieffenbachia**
- **Poinsettia**
- **Philodendron**
- **Pothos**
- **Weeping Fig**

Helpful Hint

Patio plants dry out quickly now. If they wilt each day, it's time to replant them into a bigger pot whose soil holds more moisture—or you can make a drip irrigator from recycled materials. Drill a $1/8$-inch hole in the cap of a 2-liter soft drink bottle. Fill the bottle with water, cap it, and upend it into the soil of the pot to water it slowly during the day.

Helpful Hint

Weeping Fig (*Ficus benjamina*) is known to lose leaves when moved from one light condition to another, whether from room to room or from outdoors to indoors. Although the leaves may fall continuously for weeks after it has been moved, the tree will eventually regain its foliage. Consider carefully if the mess keeps it from being worthwhile to move your plant outdoors in spring and then back indoors each fall. Perhaps it would be happier staying in the same place year 'round.

Planning

The best way to avoid house-plant problems is to avoid bringing a problem home after you buy a plant. While still at the store, examine other plants around the one you've chosen to make sure they do not show signs of insect or disease damage. Even if your plant seems healthy, it could harbor insects. Pull the plant from its pot, if possible, and examine the roots. Squeeze a small root between your fingers. It should be firm, not mushy or jelly-like—most plant roots are white when they are healthy.

Planting

If you have many new outdoor containers to plant in spring or at any time of year, it can be expensive to purchase potting soil for them all. Professionals sometimes mix their own potting soil in order to save money. Here is one recipe.

Ingredients:

- 1 bag (2 cubic feet) finely ground pine bark (Nature's Helper™ Soil Conditioner is one such product)

- 1 cubic foot peat moss (if tightly baled, remove from bag, and fluff with your hands)

- 1 cubic foot perlite

- 2 cups powdered (not pelletized) garden lime

Put on a tightly fitting dust mask before you begin. Pour the materials onto a dry carport floor or onto your driveway. Add the 2 cups of powdered garden lime. Use a clean hoe to thoroughly mix the ingredients. As you mix, spray a fine mist of water onto the mixture to aid in wetting. When everything is mixed, shovel the soil into your containers. Any leftover soil can be stored in a closed plastic garbage can.

Care for Your Houseplants

If you have cared for a houseplant very well for years, don't be surprised if it blooms. Some, like **Jade Plant** and **Snake Plant**, are not known for their flowers, but they will bloom under the right conditions. Pat yourself on the back for your skill at giving a plant exactly what it needs!

Many plants bloom best when they are slightly rootbound, a bit too large for their container. Low light levels are the main reason some plants never bloom.

Watering

African Violets like to grow in soil that is always slightly moist but never soggy or dry. A wick waterer can give them just the moisture they need.

End of wick pushed with tweezers through hole. Must be in contact with potting soil.

Hole cut in lid. Pour water through here

Water

Wick cut from pair of nylon tights

Plastic margarine tub

Wick Waterer

Materials:

- Nylon tights

- Plastic margarine tub

1 Cut the tights into 6-inch-long sections. Each section will make a wick for one plant.

2 Push one end of a wick through the bottom of the pot. Tweezers or a large nail make the job easier.

3 Cut an "X" in the center of the lid of the margarine tub, using scissors or a hobby knife. Cut a dime-sized hole in the lid near the edge.

4 Pull the free end of the wick through the "X" in the plastic lid until it rests against the bottom of the pot.

5 Fill the margarine tub with water. Snap on the lid and the potted plant connected to it.

6 Use a wooden dowel dipped into the tub through the hole to monitor the water height.

Very dilute houseplant fertilizer can be used in the tub to make it automatically water and feed your plant! (Be sure to follow product directions for continuous feeding.)

Helpful Hint

Even the best garden soil is usually too heavy and too moisture-retentive to be a good soil for houseplants, and is possibly contaminated with pests. Commercial potting "soil" contains no real soil at all; it only *looks* like dark earth. This store-bought potting soil contains several ingredients (see facing page for a recipe for making your own potting soil):

- Peat moss holds water and nutrients.

- Ground pine bark provides good drainage and light weight.

- Vermiculite—tiny, shiny, platelike particles of expanded mica—holds air, water, and nutrients.

- Perlite, made from heated volcanic rock, appears as small, white, round balls that crush readily. It is sterile, and provides good drainage.

Fertilizing

Instead of fertilizing your plants with water-soluble plant food, consider using a coated, slow-release product like Osmocote™ or Dynamite™. The granules are sprinkled on top of the soil at the rate specified on the container. The coating allows nutrients to be released whenever you water over several weeks or months. Slow-release products are more expensive but sometimes more convenient than water-soluble fertilizers.

Pest Control

One of the smallest pests of indoor plants is the spider mite. Individuals are smaller than $1/32$ inch long. They might first be recognized by the thin webbing between a leaf stem and an adjacent plant stem. If you suspect spider mites, hold the plant up to a strong light to detect the webbing. Leaves on infested plants look puckered and spotted with tiny yellow dots. Spider mites can come to your home uninvited on gift plants you get from a neighbor, on Christmas trees, and in holiday greenery. People can also spread them accidentally with their hands, tools, and watering cans.

If you discover mites, spray three times at two-week intervals with insecticidal soap (see Chemicals, p. 327). If the infestation is severe on one plant, discard it, and concentrate on protecting other plants that have fewer mites.

Grooming

Prune **Patio Hibiscus** back to two-thirds of its size now if you intend to grow it indoors this winter. Remember that it needs the sunniest spot possible inside.

Planning

Forcing plants to bloom in December is not the mysterious process some believe it is. **Poinsettia,** **Amaryllis,** and **Paper-white Narcissus** all bloom naturally in late spring. With planning, you can fool them into thinking it is spring in December, and they will reward you with color. Here's how:

Poinsettia. Grow the plant as a houseplant after the winter holidays. Prune back the plant to 8 inches tall in April, and place it in the sunniest spot possible indoors, or preferably in a semi-shade spot outdoors. *Fertilize* monthly and *water* as needed. Shorten all branches by half in June, and do a final shaping of the plant in August. The plant should be full of healthy green leaves in September. Beginning the first week of October, use a large cardboard box to give the plant fourteen hours of darkness and ten hours of bright light each day. Continue this regimen, watering and fertilizing as needed, for six weeks. If your efforts have been successful, small yellow flowers will appear at branch ends by mid-November. Once flowers have formed, modified leaves (bracts) below the flowers will grow and change color.

Continue the 14:10 lighting schedule until the plant is ready to be displayed for the holidays.

Amaryllis. After the holidays, *remove* flower stems, but leave foliage intact. Grow as a houseplant until nighttime outdoor temperatures are consistently above 60 degrees Fahrenheit. *Repot* the bulb into a pot three times as wide as the bulb; the neck and shoulders of the bulb should be above soil level. Place it outdoors where it can receive full morning sunshine but only bright afternoon shade. *Fertilize* monthly and *water* as needed during the summer. In mid-September, stop all watering and fertilizing; in early October, cut off leaves just above the bulb neck. Store the bulb in a dry, warm spot until late November. The first week in December, place the pot in a sunny window, and *water* it thoroughly.

If your efforts have been successful, small leaves, followed by a bloom stalk, will appear in mid-December.

Christmas Cactus. Grow as a houseplant until early summer, then move it outdoors to a bright but slightly shaded spot. *Fertilize* monthly and *water* as needed until mid-October. Monitor nighttime temperatures, and bring the plant indoors when temps approach 50 degrees Fahrenheit. Keep it in the coolest but sunniest spot possible indoors (high temperatures and drafts will cause flower buds to drop).

Enjoy the flowers as they appear.

Planting

Root leaves of **African Violet** and **Begonia** plants that you want to give as Christmas gifts (see Housplants, April).

Care for Your Houseplants

Do not water plants with soft drinks, iced tea, or coffee! Sometimes people dump their drink cups into pots during parties, thinking they're doing the plants a favor, but fungus gnats (see January) like to breed in sugar-sweetened soil.

Watering

Puzzled by your plant's water requirements? Why not try a method that allows your plants to water themselves automatically year 'round? All you need is some polyester knitting yarn, a #8 crochet hook, a waterproof saucer for each pot, and a handful of small pebbles. The yarn is inserted into the bottom of each pot and then the pot is supported over water in the saucer.

Polyester yarn wicks water up into the soil automatically, as it dries out. Follow these steps:

1 Cut a length of yarn for each pot. Measure a piece that is twice as long as the pot height (a 6-inch-tall pot needs a length of yarn 12 inches long).

2 Turn the pot on its side, and push the #8 crochet needle up through one of the holes in the bottom. Press it slowly through the soil until the hooked end emerges through the soil surface. Hook the center of the piece of yarn, and pull it back through the soil. Bring the yarn only 1 inch through the bottom of the pot, and allow it to hang free.

3 Place three or four pebbles in the bottom of your waterproof saucer, and set the pot on them. Check to make sure the yarn dangles freely from the pot bottom. Fill the saucer with water just to the level of the pot bottom. The yarn hanging in the water will wick moisture into the soil as it becomes dry.

Helpful Hint

If you intend to bring them indoors for the winter, this is a good month to thin and make smaller the hanging fern baskets you've had outdoors all summer. **Remove** the longer fronds of **Boston Fern,** leaving the vigorous but shorter fronds. Clip back the foliage of **Asparagus Fern** to a length of 10 inches. Shop for a tall pedestal on which to place them before a sunny window. If the only storage spot available is a poorly lit garage, clip ferns back to four inches tall. Water whenever the soil is dry to the touch. Do not fertilize.

4 *Observe* the plant closely for a month afterward to make sure it is getting enough water. Four- to 6-inch-wide pots usually need a single wick. Large potted plants may need three or four yarn wicks per pot, each inserted as described above.

All you have to remember is to keep each saucer filled with water.

Fertilizing

This is the last month for full-strength fertilizer applications. As days get shorter in later months, your houseplants will need much less food (see Introduction).

Pest Control

Examine patio plants for insects if you intend to bring them indoors. Treat with insecticide (see Chemicals, p. 327) now, if necessary, to eliminate pests before the plants come inside.

See March, June, August, and December for descriptions of common houseplant pests.

Grooming

Lightly *trim back* the tropical **Hibiscus** you kept outdoors for the summer. Make plans for where you'll place it indoors in bright light.

OCTOBER

Planning

Fragrant houseplants are not as common as the foliage and flowering types, but there are two plants that do spread a powerful perfume indoors.

- **Gardenia** is best purchased in April or early May, when it is full of buds. **Gardenias** require a sunny south window in a room that's warm during the day but cool at night. These "Hothouse **Gardenias**" can be planted and grown outdoors in the southern half of Georgia.

- **Winter Jasmine** (*Jasminum polyanthum*) blooms in January. Keep in a cool room that has bright but indirect light; east- and north-facing windows are usually fine. All vine tips should be "pinched" (removed with thumb and forefinger) when they've grown 4 inches from their origination point. **Jasmine** has a vining habit, and pinching keeps it compact.

If you want to make spring bulbs bloom indoors early in January, now is the time to get started on *forcing* them. See November for instructions on making bulbs bloom in winter.

Listen to the weather forecast daily. If night temperatures approach 50 degrees Fahrenheit, bring in your patio houseplants.

Mid-October is too late to begin forcing your **Poinsettia** to change color for Christmas (see September for instructions). If you start in late October, the plant will change color just in time for Groundhog Day!

Planting

"Used" potting soil need not be thrown out. It can be reused for other plants as long as it does not contain insects, diseases, or harmful fertilizer residue. This is a good month to "refresh" used soil:

1. *Fill* a large plastic pot ⅔ full with the soil. Pour water into the pot until full. Allow to drain. Repeat once more. This technique will wash away any fertilizer salts remaining in the soil.

2. Place the soggy soil in a baking pan which has 2-inch-high sides. Heat it in your oven at 200 degrees Fahrenheit for 30 minutes. The heat will kill all insects and most diseases that might linger in the soil.

3. *Spread* the soil thinly over newspaper in a covered spot so it will dry completely.

Care for Your Houseplants

If you move a plant inside from the patio, make sure it gets the most light possible indoors (see December).

Watering

You might be tempted by electronic moisture meters which promise to indicate when you should water, but these products vary widely in their accuracy. The presence of fertilizer and the contents of the potting soil affect the reading.

A finger pushed 1 inch into the soil is the most accurate moisture meter for houseplants.

Fertilizing

Organic houseplant fertilizer can be used to feed your plants if you dig it deeply into the soil. Use

Use a fork to make a few holes.

a fork or spoon to make a few holes, and pour the product into them. Beware! Indoor cats and dogs may find the enticing new smell of your pots irresistible and may dig in them to find the fertilizer.

Pest Control

Houseplant cultural problems are sometimes difficult to diagnose. Poor growth can result from a combination of several unfavorable factors. Here is a list of problems and their possible causes to help you sleuth out an answer:

Symptom: Lower leaves turn yellow and drop when touched.

Possible Causes: Usually caused by overwatering; lower leaves may be shaded by upper foliage; may occur when a new plant is moved to a low-light, low-humidity environment.

Symptom: Plant won't bloom.

Possible Cause: Lack of light.

Symptom: There is yellowing and dropping of leaves all over the plant.

Possible Causes: Overwatering; poor drainage; tight soil/root-bound; chilling; fumes from unvented stove or space heater.

Symptom: Tips or edges of leaves seem burned, brown, or both.

Possible Causes: Too much fertilizer; drafts from furnace or air conditioner; plant roots dried out for a short period of time; plant exposed to low temperature for short period; softened water use to irrigate.

Symptom: New leaves of plant are small.

Possible Causes: Soil too dry for long periods; poorly drained soil.

Symptom: New leaves have long spaces between adjacent leaves.

Possible Causes: Not enough light; temperature too high.

Symptom: Leaves are yellow or light green, weak growth.

Possible Causes: Not enough light; lack of fertilizer; poor root system, possibly from poor drainage or overwatering.

Symptom: Water droplets appear on tips of leaves or on floor below—plant appears normal otherwise.

Possible Causes: Some plants, like **Spathiphyllum, Anthurium,** and **Ficus,** are prone to do this *naturally* (if plant seems normal, nothing need be done).

Grooming

Divide your hanging basket of **Boston Fern** into thirds, and plant into three new baskets. Hang in a sunny window, and by spring they'll be big enough to put outside. Do not divide if only low light is available—in that case, it is better to simply *clip back* the fronds as described in September.

Helpful Hints

If you plan to move to another state, can you take your houseplants with you? Some states have laws that govern whether you can bring your houseplants with you when you move into their jurisdiction. If a moving company transports your plants, some states require a certificate of plant health to accompany them. The Georgia Department of Agriculture can send an inspector, for a small fee, to certify your plants. If you transport the plants in your private vehicle, no certificate is necessary. You can call the Georgia Department of Agriculture for a list of different state regulations.

Planning

Indoor light levels during winter are lower than many houseplants can tolerate. The plants become "leggy," stretching toward any light available. A great way to help houseplants thrive in winter is to grow them in a special light stand, keeping them there all winter if possible. Choose dimensions appropriate to your space.

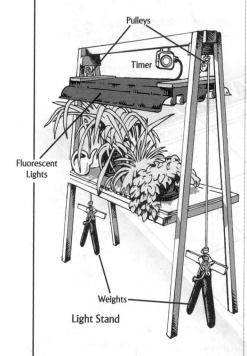

Pulleys
Timer
Fluorescent Lights
Weights
Light Stand

1 Construct the A-frame legs from 2×2 lumber. The top bar and braces are made with 2x4 lumber. (The stand pictured tends to wobble if not tightly constructed—use several coarse-thread gypsum wallboard screws at each joint.)

2 The pulleys, timer, and fluorescent light fixture are available at your home improvement center.

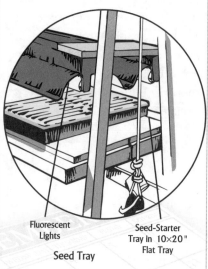

Fluorescent Lights
Seed-Starter Tray in 10×20" Flat Tray
Seed Tray

3 Once constructed, the pulleys allow you to adjust the height of the light source to match plant size.

The same stand can be used to germinate seeds of annual flowers in February.

Planting

It is great fun to "force" into winter bloom those bulbs that normally grow outdoors. With a few bulbs and materials, you can amaze your friends and office mates. **To force a Paper-white Narcissus:**

1 Find an attractive, shallow container (examples: crystal candy bowl, china soup bowl, clay saucer). Fill the container with pebbles, marbles, or smooth river rocks.

2 Pour water into the container until it almost overflows.

3 Gently press several Paperwhite bulbs into the filled container. The base of each bulb should barely touch the surface of the water and should be supported by the marbles or pebbles.

4 Place the container in a sunny window. Within a few weeks leaves will sprout and will be followed by intensely fragrant flowers.

To force a Hyacinth:

1 Twelve weeks before you want blooms, half-fill a clay or plastic pot with potting soil. Place several bulbs, base down, side by side on top of the soil.

2 Cover the bulbs with potting soil. *Water,* and allow to drain.

3 Insert pot in a clear, sealed plastic bag, and place it in the back of your refrigerator.

4 Nine weeks later, remove the pot from the refrigerator and the bag, and place in a warm window. Within three weeks, leaves and flowers will appear.

Potted **Hyacinth**s can be displayed by inserting the pot in a more attractive container, or you can force **Hyacinths** to bloom in a water-filled **Hyacinth** cup instead of soil:

1 Purchase a glass or plastic cup at your local garden center, and fill the cup to the neck with water.

2 Insert a single bulb so that its base barely touches the water surface.

3 Insert the cup and bulb into a plastic bag and into your refrigerator as described above. Roots will grow into the water during the chilling period.

4 Remove the cup from the bag and refrigerator three weeks before you want to enjoy flowers.

Care for Your Houseplants

Put houseplants close to a sunny window, but not too close—the cold draft sweeping down the windowpane can turn leaves brown. Wet your hand and hold it close to the window. If a draft is present, you'll easily feel it.

Give your houseplants a half-turn every month so they don't lean toward the light and become mis-shapen.

Most homes have dry air in winter, but most houseplants prefer higher levels of humidity. Here are some solutions to the problem:

- *Mist* the leaves once every day.

- Install a whole-house humidifier, or place a portable model near your plants.

- *Group* plants close together to maintain humidity around leaves.

Watering

Check the dryness of houseplant soil before you water (press a finger 1 inch into the soil). The watering schedules you were used to in summer will change once the plants are in a heated environment.

Ordinary municipal or well water is satisfactory for most plants. Rainwater or melted snow are excellent. Water run through water softeners, however, should not be used continuously for potted plants because it contains too much sodium.

The chlorine and fluorine that are added to city water do not usually harm plants, but fluoride *can* harm the foliage of your **Dracaena** and **Spider Plants.** The tips of the leaves will turn brown even though the plant has been watered correctly.

If you see symptoms, use only distilled water on these plants. An alternative is to scratch the top of the soil, and scatter over it 2 teaspoons of garden lime per 6-inch pot (larger pots may need more, proportionally).

Fertilizing

Houseplants don't need much fertilizer in the winter. Use a water-soluble fertilizer at half-strength every eight weeks.

Pest Control

Dieffenbachia is a very popular houseplant, but pests often attack it. Check your plant for problems and pests regularly. Spider mites cause leaves to have yellow speckles (see August). Mealybugs make the plant appear to be covered with cotton; they cluster where a leaf base joins the main trunk (see March). Root rot symptoms include droopy foliage even though the soil is moist. *Remove* the plant from its pot, and replace the potting soil (see December).

DECEMBER

Planning

Purchase pots of **Paper-white Narcissus** *for your office and home to bring a touch of perfume to the air.* Instead of a bottle of wine, take a houseplant as a gift to holiday parties. **Amaryllis, Ornamental Pepper, Christmas Cactus,** or **Kalanchoe** will be appreciated for weeks to come.

Planting

One way to increase the decorative potential of a holiday plant is to put it in an ornamental pot:

- Place the original beside the fancy pot to judge if it will fit inside.

- Use a brick or several stones in the fancy pot to support the plant at the right level.

Care for Your Houseplants

Keep holiday plants in the coolest spot possible. Otherwise, the flowers and leaves will drop prematurely.

Keep all houseplants away from drafts and direct heat sources. If you can't move the plant, close the vent.

If you can't close the vent, install inexpensive plastic draft hoods on the vent to divert the air flow.

Watering

Poinsettias do not need fertilizing now, but they do need watering. Check the dryness of the soil daily to keep them looking their brilliant best. Push a finger 1 inch into the soil; *water* when your finger comes back dry. Poke holes, for drainage, in the foil sleeve that surrounds the plastic pot, and place the pot on a waterproof saucer. See March, Watering for further suggestions.

Cold water splashed on the leaves of **African Violet** or **Gloxinia** plants causes ringed spots on the foliage; let water stand overnight before using it to irrigate these plants.

Fertilizing

Continue to fertilize every few weeks, but only at half the rate recommended for summertime. Most products specify the rate to be used during the winter months.

Pest Control

Root rot is a common affliction of houseplants. It is usually caused by an excess of water accumulating around the roots. Pull the plant from its pot to inspect the roots; if you find they are mushy and brown, steps must be taken to help them recover.

- Shake as much soil as possible from the roots. Swirl them in a bucket of warm water to remove the remaining soil.

- Use scissors to remove all roots that look unhealthy. Healthy roots may be any color (most are white), but unhealthy ones are predominantly brown and mushy.

- If more that 50 percent of the roots must be removed, consider tossing the plant on your compost pile and purchasing a new one.

- If more than 50 percent of the roots seem healthy, remove $1/3$ of the leaves to bring the foliage and the root system into better balance.

- *Replant* the houseplant in fresh potting soil (see February), and correct the watering practices that led to root rot in the first place.

Scale insects are tough to control because the females cover themselves with a layer of wax, which makes them less vulnerable to insecticides. Female scale insects look like small (¹/₁₆ inch), oval, legless bumps on stems and the backside of leaves. Scale-damaged plants look withered and sickly and may have sticky sap or a black fungus on the leaves and stems. *Move* an infested plant away from the rest of your houseplants. Scale insects are invasive and will infest other plants. *Remove* scale insects with a twig or your fingernail—the insects will scrape off plant tissue easily. *Spray* heavily-infested plants with horticultural oil or insecticidal soap (see Chemicals, p. 327). A spray containing pyrethrin can also be used.

Be diligent—examine infested plants for evidence of new scale every day. It may take a while to control.

Grooming

Prune your evergreen shrubbery, and bring the cuttings indoors. **Juniper, Holly,** and **Magnolia** foliage is quite decorative when arranged around houseplants. Use **Nandina** berries for a red accent in a table centerpiece.

Indoor Light

One of the main causes of poor houseplant growth is lack of light. Inexperienced gardeners might assume that if they can read a newspaper in a spot, the light must be bright enough there to allow a houseplant to grow. Light that is bright enough to read by might not be bright enough to sustain photosynthesis. Outdoor light intensity on a clear, sunny day may exceed 10,000 foot candles; the light level in a well-lighted interior room may be less than 100 foot candles, which is appropriate only for low-light plants. Refer to Houseplants, March for a comparison of different light levels.

The artificial light in most offices is not intense enough to support flowering plants. Select one of the low-light foliage plants listed in the introduction, or plan to exchange flowering plants with other plants every month.

A quick method to measure light intensity is to spread a piece of white paper in the spot where the plant will be placed. Hold your hand 12 inches above the paper, and notice the shadow on it.

- If the shadow is sharp, dark, and distinct, the light is bright enough to support flowering plants.

- If the shadow is fuzzy or indistinct, the light is bright enough to support foliage plants.

The duration of light is important, too. If bright light is available for only an hour a day, that spot will be best for foliage plants rather than flowering plants. If medium light is supplied for several hours, some of the flowering plants may survive there.

- One way to increase the light level and duration is to place a fluorescent light nearby. The light should be within 12 inches of the plant in order to have any effect.

- It is not necessary to use special grow lights. Cool-white fluorescent bulbs or a combination of cool-white and warm-white bulbs will work just fine.

Lawns

Warren Schultz, author of *A Man's Turf—The Perfect Lawn*, begins his informative book with these words: "The lawn works in mysterious ways." For too many people that is true. Many find lawn maintenance a mysterious process. From selection to planting to fertilizing to pest control, lawn work seems to require more knowledge than do other landscape chores.

Yet grass grows easily beside the highway with no fertilizer, mowing only once a year, and almost no pests beyond lit cigars and errant SUVs. Does having a nice lawn require a college degree, or can just about anyone achieve an attractive turf?

With the information in this chapter, you'll discover that nice lawns are the result of common sense, occasional maintenance, and attention to a few details. In each month you'll see the tasks that need to be done for the various lawn grasses we cultivate in Georgia. If you follow our recommendations, your lawn will look as good as, or better than, your neighbors'—and you will soon find that the "mysteries" of lawn cultivation are quite easy to solve. Following are some lawn basics to get you started.

Which Grass Should You Choose?

Choosing the right grass for a lawn is initially based on how much sunshine the site receives and how much water you are able to apply in the summer. Consider also the amount of labor you are willing to invest in your lawn.

Fescue is classified as a "cool-season" grass, and it stays green all year long. **Bermuda Grass, Zoysia Grass, Centipede Grass,** and **St. Augustine Grass** are all classified as "warm-season" grasses. They are green most of the year, but turn brown (or light green, in the case of **St. Augustine Grass**) and go dormant in winter. The descriptions below will help you decide which grass will grow in your area and which ones match your requirements for appearance and maintenance. The following are our grass choices for Georgia.

Fescue grows best when daytime temperatures do not exceed 80 degrees Fahrenheit—at higher summer temperatures, **Fescue** has all it can manage just to survive. Best for semi-shade sites or lawns that have a mixture of sunny and shady areas, it can be successful in full sunshine *if*

the soil is tilled properly before planting *and* you can irrigate in the summer. It is green year 'round under proper management and adequate irrigation; it's usually best for the northern half of Georgia. Dozens of new varieties of **Fescue** are introduced each year. Proponents of each variety claim theirs is the most shade- and drought-tolerant and the most resistant to disease. Most support these claims by quoting the results of grass-growing trials at research facilities scattered across the country.

- The "turf-type" **Fescue**s are indeed superior to the "pasture-type" **Fescue,** that is commonly called 'Kentucky 31'.

- While there are differences between the "turf-type" **Fescue** varieties, no one variety stands head and shoulders above the rest at all research facility trials.

- The work you do to prepare the soil before planting is much more likely to produce a great-looking lawn than the variety of **Fescue** seed you plant.

Bermuda Grass can be planted by seeding or by sodding. Common **Bermuda Grass** produces fertile seed, which is sold at most garden centers. Hybrid

Lawns

Bermuda Grass does not produce fertile seed; the only way to propagate this, and other sodded grasses, is to grow it from sprigs taken from a "mother" plant. On the flat soil of south Georgia, millions of sprigs are planted each spring to become the sod you purchase during the year.

- **Common Bermuda Grass** is always grown from seed. It is lighter green in color than hybrid **Bermuda Grass,** and its leaves are coarser in texture. Seedheads pop up quickly after mowing, and it invades flower beds rapidly.

- Tifgreen (Tifton 328) **Bermuda Grass** sod is low-growing and spreads rapidly. It has fine texture and soft leaves.

- Tifway (Tifton 419) **Bermuda Grass** sod is darker green than Tifgreen. It is more frost-tolerant, stays green longer in fall, and turns green earlier in spring.

Zoysia Grass is typically installed as sod.

- **'Emerald' Zoysia Grass** has a very fine leaf texture and good shade tolerance. It is less cold-tolerant than other **Zoysia** varieties.

- **'Meyer' Zoysia Grass** has a wider leaf than **'Emerald'.** It has good cold tolerance but less shade tolerance than **'Emerald'.**

- **'El Toro' Zoysia Grass** sod grows rapidly and has a leaf width similar to that of **'Meyer'.**

- **'Zenith' Zoysia Grass** can be planted from seed, grows rapidly, has a dense growth habit, and tolerates light shade.

Centipede Grass may be established from seed or sod. Its appearance is like that of **St. Augustine Grass,** but the leaves are smaller and lighter green in color. It requires less mowing than **Bermuda Grass** or **St. Augustine Grass.** It requires no lime and minimal amounts of nitrogen.

St. Augustine Grass is usually sodded or sprigged for establishment. It is the most shade-tolerant of the warm-season grasses, but the least winter hardy. Injury is likely if the temperature dips below 10 degrees Fahrenheit. Unlike other grasses, **St. Augustine Grass** does not regrow from roots or underground stems that have some degree of cold protection. **St. Augustine** never becomes completely dormant in winter and must begin spring growth from aboveground buds. Named varieties include **'Floratam',** **'Raleigh',** and **'Seville'.**

Too-Good-to-Be-True Grasses

You have probably seen the full-page advertisements in the Sunday paper touting "Amazing Turf!" or "Miracle Grass!" Claims are made that the grass is lush, drought-tolerant, and adapted to much of the United States. While there is a small amount of truth in each advertisement, rest assured that if such a grass did exist, it would be quite an achievement. The best advice regarding miracle grasses is "Buyer Beware!"

Seeding Versus Sodding

As we will point out in April, there are two ways to establish a lawn: by planting seed and waiting for it to sprout, or by laying sod and gaining an instant lawn. Some grasses are better planted from seed, while others can only be planted with sod. See April for a complete comparison of seeding versus sodding.

Planting Grass with Sod

Warm-season grass sod is best planted in early summer; cool-season grass sod grows best if planted in early winter.

Lawns

1 Kill all weeds by spraying the area with a nonselective weed-killer (see Chemicals, p. 327) two weeks before planting.

2 Till the soil thoroughly to a depth of 6 inches, mixing in the recommended amount of lime and fertilizer (see Soil Test, Horticultural Practices, p. 7).

3 Rake the area smooth, removing rocks, clumps, and grassy debris.

4 Roll the area with a water-filled roller to reveal low spots. Fill low spots with soil.

5 Starting along the longest straight edge of the area, lay sod pieces end-to-end. Make sure each piece is tightly placed next to its neighbor. Stagger sod pieces in adjacent rows so seams do not line up. Use a small hatchet or sharp shovel to trim pieces to fit around obstructions.

6 Roll the entire area once more, to ensure good sod-to-soil contact.

7 Water the sod thoroughly (see Watering New Sod, page 149).

Planting Grass from Seed

1 Kill all weeds by spraying the area with a nonselective weed-killer (see Chemicals, p. 327) two weeks before planting.

2 Till the soil thoroughly to a depth of 6 inches, mixing in the recommended amount of lime and fertilizer (see Soil Test, Horticultural Practices, p. 7).

3 Rake the area smooth, removing rocks, clumps, and grassy debris.

4 Roll the area with a water-filled roller to reveal low spots. Fill low spots with soil.

5 Scatter seed according to rates below. Cover *very* thinly with wheat straw ($3/4$ bale per 1000 square feet).

6 Follow the watering guidelines on page 149.

Do not use weed-control products on your lawn for at least six weeks after planting Fescue.

Seeding Rates for New Lawns

- **Bermuda Grass:** 1 to 2 pounds per 1000 square feet

- **Centipede Grass:** .25 to .5 pound per 1000 square feet

- **Zoysia Grass:** 1 to 3 pounds per 1000 square feet

- **Fescue:** 5 to 10 pounds per 1000 square feet

All bags of grass seed are required to have a label that shows the results of various tests on that batch of seed. Always buy seed that has been tested within the past six months for its germination rate. When deciding which seed to buy, compare the germination percentage and the number of weed seed found in each. You may discover that a higher-priced bag of seed is a better value because more of the seed will germinate.

Growing Grass in Shade

All lawn grasses have a difficult time growing in shade. If the shade is too dense for the grass, it will become thin and weed-infested. **Fescue** is the most shade-tolerant cool-season grass. 'Emerald' Zoysia Grass and St. Augustine Grass can sustain themselves in light shade. **Bermuda Grass, Centipede Grass,** and 'Meyer' Zoysia Grass can grow in the shade cast by high **Pine** trees, but no more shade than that.

Even though **Fescue** is the most shade-tolerant grass, it must have at least four hours of direct sunshine per day to remain attractive. There is no substantial difference in the shade tolerance of the various "named" turf-type **Fescue** selections. A thoroughly rototilled seeded lawn (see the process described on p. 148) is the best way to help **Fescue** tolerate shade. To maximize **Fescue's** shade tolerance:

- Apply only $1/2$ the recommended fertilizer rate to shaded lawn areas.

- Raise the mowing height of your mower to 4 inches if possible.

- Irrigate weekly, as weather conditions dictate, but never water after 3:00 p.m.

Watering

The best time to water a lawn is in the morning, preferably before noon. This allows the grass to dry before nightfall, reducing the risk of disease. If the only time you can water is after 5:00 p.m., be sure to water thoroughly only once each week, not every day. Here's how to measure the amount of water applied by irrigation:

1 Place six identical containers randomly in the area wetted by your sprinkler. Plastic cups can be used, but weigh them down with a heavy washer in the bottom of each.

2 Let your sprinkler run for an hour.

3 Measure the amount of water that has accumulated in each cup. Calculate the average of the depths. This gives you the amount (in inches) that has been applied in an hour. Make a mental calculation of how long it will take to apply an inch of water.

Don't be surprised if your sprinkler must run for more than an hour to apply the water your lawn needs.

Watering New Sod

Water newly planted sod deeply and regularly so the roots will explore the soil beneath the original sod. Use a trowel to check how far water soaks into the soil after an irrigation. Heavy clay soil absorbs water slowly. If water runs off before it is absorbed, split the irrigation into two sessions an hour apart. Sandy soil absorbs water rapidly but dries out quickly. Consider splitting the recommended inch of water per week into two irrigations of $1/2$ inch of water three days apart. Here's one example of follow-up watering after sod has been laid:

- Apply $1/8$ inch of water daily for seven days

- followed by $1/4$ inch of water every third day for nine days

- followed by $1/2$ inch of water every five days for ten days

- followed by 1 inch of water per week for the rest of the growing season.

Watering Newly Seeded Fescue, Zoysia, Centipede, or Bermuda Lawns

- Apply $1/8$ inch of water daily until seedlings are 1.5 inches tall

- followed by $1/4$ inch of water every third day for nine days

- followed by $1/2$ inch of water every five days for ten days

- followed by 1 inch of water per week for the rest of the growing season.

Lawns

Watering in Drought

Some grasses have the ability to go dormant when suffering from drought. During dormancy, the grass will turn yellow, but if it is healthy to begin with, it can recover when water becomes available. **Bermuda Grass** can go unwatered without substantial harm for eight weeks; **St. Augustine Grass** can go for six weeks; **Centipede Grass, Fescue,** and **Zoysia Grass** can go for four weeks.

Mowing

Every lawn grass has a height at which it should be mowed. The rule is that only $1/3$ of a grass plant should be removed in one mowing. As an example, if you intend to mow your Fescue lawn at a 3-inch height, you can allow it to grow to 4.5 inches between mowings. If you fertilize moderately, mowing should be needed only once per week.

Mowing Height

Centipede Grass: 1 to 1.5 inches
Fescue: 2 to 3 inches
Ryegrass: 1 to 2 inches
Seeded **Bermuda Grass:** 1 to
  2 inches
Sodded **Bermuda Grass:** .5 to
  1.5 inches
St. Augustine Grass: 2 to 3 inches
Zoysia Grass: .5 to 1.5 inches

Measure the mowing height by stationing the mower on a flat surface and noting the distance between the blade and the ground. Make sure the adjustment levers on all four mower wheels are set to the same height.

If you have a tiny lawn, an unmotorized reel mower may suit your needs. Forget the clanking behemoth your parents shoved across the lawn. Lightweight, easy-to-operate models are now available. You can even store the mower in your hall closet! Sources of reel mowers beyond your local hardware store:

Clean Air Mowing
6014 E Lovers Lane #123
Dallas, Texas 75206
Phone: (888) 423-6100

American Lawn Mower Co.
P. O. Box 369
Shelbyville, IN 46176
Phone: (800) 633-1501

Leveling Your Lawn

Despite your best efforts, your lawn may have spots that are lower than their surroundings. The best time to level lawns is while they are growing rapidly (**Fescue** in the fall, warm-season grasses in early summer). There are two ways to correct low spots:

1 **Topdressing:** Mix a bag of dry topsoil with a bag of fine play sand in a wheelbarrow. If the mixture tends to clump, spread it over a tarp in a covered spot to finish drying. Shovel the mixture, no more than $1/2$ inch deep, into low spots. Use a broom to sweep the soil off the grass blades and sift it down as far as possible. Maintain the lawn normally until the grass has grown over the first layer of topsoil. Repeat the steps above until the low spot is filled.

2 **Fill and Patch:** Use a flat shovel to remove grass from the low spot in large clumps. Set the clumps to the side, and fill the low spot with topsoil. Plant the grass clumps back in place. Water thoroughly, and maintain normally for the rest of the growing season.

Aerating

Aeration is the process of mechanically poking thousands of holes in the soil. This allows water, oxygen, and nutrients to better penetrate to the roots of your grass. Motorized aerator machines can be rented from hardware or tool rental stores. The best aerator is one that has hollow tines (spoons) that pull up plugs of earth as the machine travels along. Solid-tine spike aerators pulled by lawn tractors are of little benefit.

Lawns

- Use a crisscross pattern. First guide the machine over the entire lawn, going back and forth in one direction. Second, direct the machine back and forth at right angles to the first series of trips.

- Examine a square-foot area of the lawn. It, and every other square foot, should have at least twelve holes in it. If not, crank up the machine again!

- If the plugs of soil on the surface are objectionable, let them dry a few days, then drag a 5×5-foot piece of carpet across the lawn to pulverize them.

May and June are good months to aerate warm-season (**Bermuda Grass, Centipede Grass, Zoysia Grass, St. Augustine Grass**) lawns. March and September are the best months to aerate **Fescue.**

Even though aeration damages the grass a bit, it is able to recover rapidly. As the soil plugs disappear from the soil surface, they inoculate the thatch layer with organisms which help it decompose more rapidly. Even if you are not planting seed, plan to aerate lawns growing on clay soil every two years.

Fertilizing

Lawn fertilizer is manufactured by many companies. Each manufac-turer uses a slightly different blend of plant nutrient chemicals to arrive at a final product. Chemicals such as urea, ammonium nitrate, urea formaldehyde, and ammonium phosphate provide a high percentage of the nutrient *nitrogen* (which rapidly growing lawns need more than they need *phosphorus* and *potassium*). Most lawn fertilizer products are granular, but some are designed to be applied after they are dissolved in water. Granular fertilizers tend to last longer (up to three months) in the soil. Slow-release fertilizers are generally better for a lawn than fertilizers that release their nutrients quickly during the first rain.

Liming

Turfgrasses need soil that is only slightly acid in order to thrive. In most parts of the state, the soil is more acid than grass prefers. Garden lime neutralizes acidity and should be applied when needed. It is never the *wrong* time to lime your lawn . . . but how much lime should you apply? Forty pounds per 1000 square feet of lawn area is probably enough, but a soil test (see Horticultural Practices, p. 7) will tell you exactly how much you need. Adding too much or too little lime can harm your lawn in the long run. Don't guess—soil test!

Garden lime can be purchased in bags in one of two forms: powdered or pelletized. Neither form is inherently better. Pelletized lime flows through a lawn spreader more easily, and powdered lime is slightly less expensive.

Selecting a Fertilizer Spreader

Broadcast spreaders are best for large areas. They can apply a lot of material in a short time. For small lawns or lawns that have many corners and tight spaces, a drop spreader is the best choice.

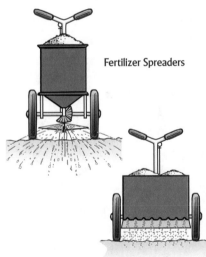

Fertilizer Spreaders

Calibrating a Fertilizer Spreader

It is important to know how much material your spreader is applying when you use it for seeding or fertilizing. Many lawn products list the appropriate spreader setting for several models—but what should you do if your spreader is not listed?

1 Measure an area of 1000 square feet (10 feet by 100 feet, 20 feet by 50 feet, etc.) in your lawn.

2 Set your spreader to one-fourth open.

3 Load the spreader with a weighed amount of seed or fertilizer. (Ten pounds is usually enough.)

4 Operate the spreader over the 1000-square-foot-area.

5 Weigh the amount left in the spreader. Subtract from the amount originally in the spreader. The result is the application rate of the spreader for that particular material per 1000 square feet.

Example: After loading the spreader with 10 pounds of fertilizer and operating it over 1000 square feet, 5 pounds are left. At that setting, and for that material, your spreader dispenses 5 pounds per 1000 square feet.

- Use a permanent marker to write on the spreader the results of your calibration.

- Each different type of seed or fertilizer will require its own spreader calibration.

Hiring a Lawn-Maintenance Company

- Ask friends and neighbors for recommendations of companies they have used.

- Contact the Metro Atlanta Landscape and Turf Association, the Georgia Green Industry Association, and the Georgia Turfgrass Association for a list of companies in your area (see Resources for contact numbers).

- Plan to spend at least an hour meeting with each of your top three choices.

- Ask them to bring copies of their business license and proof of insurance.

- If they will be applying chemicals to your lawn, ask them to provide copies of their pesticide contractor's license and their commercial pesticide applicator's license (both are required by law).

- Give them a printed list of your needs and any lawn problem areas.

- Before their first visit to treat your lawn, take photographs of your lawn in order to document their good work at the end of the year.

Buying Topsoil

If the soil where you intend to grow a lawn is poor, one option is to purchase topsoil and spread it over the existing soil. No standards exist that govern the quality of topsoil. Follow these rules to assure you get what you expect:

- Look in the Yellow Pages™ under "Landscape Supplies—Wholesale."

- Visit the site from which the topsoil will be taken. Some companies offer several grades of topsoil from which to choose.

- Never allow topsoil to be delivered when you are away from home. Inspect and approve each load before it is dumped.

How Much Topsoil to Buy

You'll need a layer at least 3 inches thick to appreciably improve your soil. If your existing soil is extremely poor, cover it with a layer of topsoil 6 inches thick. Remember that covering tree roots with a thick layer (more than 6 inches) of topsoil will harm the tree. A cubic yard of topsoil will cover a 324-square-foot area with soil to a 1-inch depth.

Lawns

Pest Control

It is a common tendency to blame an unsatisfactory lawn on diseases or insects, but lawn problems can usually be traced to improper grass selection for the site and/or improper soil preparation. We have included several tips for identifying and controlling pests in the months that follow. Though they do not attack grass directly, fire ants can make lawn maintenance miserable. Their control is discussed in May. One bit of knowledge to always keep in mind is that soil temperature governs many stages of lawn growth and pest appearance.

Measuring Soil Temperature

Weeds and insect pests emerge based on the warmth of the soil surrounding them. **Crabgrass** requires several days above 55 degrees Fahrenheit in order to sprout. **Fescue** seed sprouts best when the soil temperature is above 50 degrees. **Bermuda Grass** and **Centipede Grass** seed should not be planted if soil temperatures are below 65 degrees. For these reasons, checking the temperature of your soil occasionally will help you time your lawn activities.

Soil temperature can be measured directly by slicing the ground open with a shovel or trowel and insert-ing a household thermometer. If this is too much trouble, you can visit the Georgia Environmental Monitoring Network on the Internet (see Resources, p. 353). Find the site closest to your home and follow the directions to see local soil and air temperatures for the previous thirty days.

Animal Pests

Moles: Mole tunnels seem to appear overnight in spring and fall as the moles search desperately for underground insects. There are two schools of thought on their management:

1 Laissez-faire—Use a lawn roller (or your shoes) to press down the tunnels. The moles will eventually go elsewhere.

2 Trapping—Discover the frequently used tunnels by pressing a portion flat and marking the spot with a golf tee. If the tee is lifted the next day, the tunnel was used overnight. Purchase a lethal mole trap and install it over the tunnel. Remove the pests as they are killed.

There are many folk tales regarding mole control. The following *do not*, repeat DO NOT, work:

- Chewing gum
- Broken glass
- Ultrasonic vibrators

- Noisy windmills
- Moth balls
- Poison peanuts
- Insecticide treatments to the lawn

Geese: If you live near a lake, geese will soon become your nemesis on your lakeside lawn. Their droppings, noise, and occasional aggressive behavior can cause them to wear out their welcome rapidly.

- Try stringing lightweight fishing line back and forth between tall posts near the waterline. The geese avoid anything that disrupts their flight path.

- The chemical methyl anthranilate has been found to make grass distasteful to geese.

Sources of goose repellent:

Goose Chase Repellant
Bird-X, Inc.
300 N. Elizabeth St.
Chicago, IL. 60607
Phone: (800) 662-5021

ReJeX-iT® Repellent
Becker Underwood, Inc.
801 Dayton Avenue
Ames, Iowa 50010
Phone: (515) 232-5907

Armadillos: See Lawns, September.

Planning

Are you spending more time than you would like on taking care of your lawn? Do you really need as much lawn as you now have? Consider these lawn-shrinking tips:

- *Eliminate* the sparsely growing grass in a shady area. Cover the area with mulch, or plant it with a ground cover like **Periwinkle, Mondo Grass,** or **Pachysandra.**

- Grass growing in sharp corners is difficult to mow. *Round* the corners of your lawn with flower beds, shrubs, or mulch.

- A grassy walkway between the front lawn and backyard is likely to have so much traffic in the center that it will never look nice no matter how hard you try. *Install* walking stones to keep footsteps off the grass.

Planting

Fescue sod can theoretically be planted any time the soil is not frozen, but professional growers have the same trouble that you do growing **Fescue** in summer—it's a lot of trouble to get seed to survive in the heat. Because they find it impossible to grow **Fescue** year-round, the growers wait until fall to plant their sod fields. This means that **Fescue** sod is not available during the prime planting time in fall; it becomes available only in December or early January each year.

- Make sure you have rototilled your soil thoroughly to a depth of 8 inches.

- *Rake* the area smooth, and push a heavy roller over it one time before installing the sod.

- *Plant* sod immediately after delivery so it doesn't dry out.

- See Lawns, April for more sodding tips.

Since **Fescue** does not naturally form a mat of roots, sod is often grown on plastic mesh:

- Clip loose ends of plastic with scissors as you work.

- Do not attempt to aerate your newly sodded **Fescue** until next fall—the aerator tines will quickly become entangled in the mesh.

- Once the sod is rooted deeply, the mesh will not be a problem.

Care for Your Lawn

Avoid heavy traffic on dormant lawns in winter; dry grass is easily broken. The living crown of your grass plants may be damaged even though the grass is brown. Since the grass is not growing and able to recover, even a short game of football can cause scars you'll regret in spring.

Watering

Bermuda Grass sod can be successfully laid at any time of year, even if it is brown and dormant. The key to its long-term survival is watering the sod afterwards, even when it looks brown and lifeless. Roots are growing into the soil below—they need moisture. In the absence of rainfall, *apply* $1/2$ inch of water per week (see Lawns, Introduction for more information).

Fescue sod installed in the last six months should also be watered regularly ($1/2$ inch per week). The green leaves transpire a great deal of moisture on sunny, windy days.

Fertilizing

You have probably heard of people who "burn off" their **Bermuda Grass** lawns in winter: they literally set their lawn afire in the mistaken belief that the ashes contain fertilizer that will feed the grass.

JANUARY

- There is a tiny bit of potassium in ashes, but not nearly enough to risk causing a tragedy in your neighborhood. The flames can easily ignite pine straw islands and cedar siding.

- In most municipalities, outdoor burning is illegal.

There is no need to fertilize any warm-season grass at this time.

Pest Control

If you have a **Bermuda Grass** lawn in the northern half of the state, it is easy to spot the green leaves of unwanted **Fescue,** chickweed, or wild onion in your brown turf. If you are *very careful*, you can *spray* the weeds lightly with a nonselective herbicide (see Chemicals, p. 327) now. The weeds will be killed, but if the **Bermuda Grass** is dormant, you won't hurt your lawn. It is important to examine your **Bermuda Grass** closely to make sure it is fully dormant before attempting this task:

- Get down on your hands and knees. Pull back the dead grass foliage and inspect the stems where they come out of the ground. Do you see any green stems? If so, the grass plant is not dormant.

Helpful Hint

On a warm day, chop or mow unwanted kudzu, **English Ivy,** and **Bamboo** to the ground. Spray with glyphosate or triclopyr (see Chemicals, p. 327) on the new leaves in April.

Watch out for poison ivy when working outdoors. Even leafless vines and branches can cause a powerful skin reaction if they are touched accidentally:

- If you see the vine climbing a tree, don disposable gloves and clip the vine at ground level.

- Carefully pull the vine from the tree bark. If it adheres too tightly to pull by hand, use a long-bladed screwdriver to pry it away from the bark. Wash the tool thoroughly afterwards.

- *Repeat* the examination at several spots across the lawn before spraying.

- *Do not* attempt this winter weedkilling trick on **Zoysia Grass, Centipede Grass,** or **St. Augustine Grass** lawns. These turfgrasses can be severely harmed by nonselective weedkillers, as can **Bermuda Grass** if it is not fully dormant. Handweeding is your best option for these turfgrasses.

Mowing

As winter wears on, the tree leaves you failed to rake last fall can blow across your lawn and build up in piles at the edges:

- Don't let leaves pile up and suffocate your grass. Without sunlight, disease will attack grass crowns and roots.

- *Rake up* the leaves and add them to your compost pile, or run over the leafy spots with a lawn mower to shred the leaves into tiny pieces.

Don't store mowers or other motorized lawn equipment near a gas water heater or furnace:

- If the gas tank leaks accidentally, the fumes can ignite and burn down your garage or home.

- Most manufacturers recommend draining the gas tank each winter.

- *Never* store gasoline, even in "spillproof" cans, indoors.

Planning

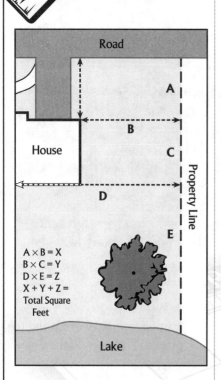

```
Road

                    A

        B
                    C
House
                        Property Line
        D
                    E

A × B = X
B × C = Y
D × E = Z
X + Y + Z =
Total Square
Feet

            Lake
```

When caring for a lawn, there is one basic fact you need to know: how big is it? Application rates for fertilizer and weedkillers are based on applying a certain amount for each 1000 square feet of lawn. Here's how to measure the area—you'll need several soft drink cans, a pencil, and a piece of paper:

- Roughly sketch the lawn and divide it into rectangles.

- Put a can on each corner of each rectangle.

- *Walk* from can to can; count your paces between each can, and mark the figure on the sketch. Assuming your pace is

2.5 feet long, multiply the number of steps by 2.5 to find the length, in feet, of the sides of each rectangle. If you have a longer or shorter stride, adjust your calculation accordingly.

- For each rectangle, multiply the length of the short side by the length of the long side. This tells you the number of square feet in that rectangle.

- Add the area of all rectangles together to find the total square footage of the lawn.

- Note your measurements in your garden journal.

Remember, we're not trying for "exactly"—just "close"!

Planting

If your **Fescue** lawn is thin now, February is a good month to *plant seed*. The soil is cold, so seed will not germinate quickly. However, you need to get started so the seed can take advantage of any warm days that come along:

1 *Aerate* before seeding (see Lawns, Introduction).

2 Scatter 3 to 4 pounds of seed per 1000 square feet if you already have 50-percent grass coverage. Coverage with wheat straw is not needed.

Scatter 6 to 8 pounds per 1000 square feet if planting on newly tilled soil. Cover very thinly with wheat straw (1 bale per 1000 square feet).

3 Plan to water each week between now and August. See following months for watering guidelines.

Do not use weed-preventer products on your lawn for at least six weeks after planting Fescue.

Care for Your Lawn

It is tempting to consider using a "Weed 'n' Feed" product to fertilize your grass and kill weeds simultaneously. Consider these points before making your decision, remembering that there are two kinds of "Weed 'n' Feed" products:

1 A Weed 'n' Feed that promises to *prevent* weeds contains chemicals that will inhibit *all* seeds from germinating. *If you are planning to plant Fescue seed now, this type of product cannot be used.* Weed-preventers vary in the length of time the chemical is active in the soil, affecting how long you must wait before planting any seed. If you used one in a previous season, make sure you read the label—if any of the chemical is still present in the soil, you will not be successful when you plant seed.

2 A Weed 'n' Feed product that promises to *kill* existing weeds can be used *on well-established grass.* Do not use on newly-planted **Fescue** or on other turfgrass that is not yet 50 percent green. Read the label of your Weed 'n' Feed carefully, and follow directions to the letter.

Notice lawn areas where the shade from a tree has caused grass to grow thinly. Now is a good time to *prune out* low limbs to allow more sunshine on the grass. (See Trees, February to learn how to prune properly.) **Southern Magnolia** and other densely leaved trees are notorious for severely limiting grass growth. Consider covering the ground under them with mulch.

Watering

On a rainy day, notice how water flows or stands on your lawn. Frequent flows of water over one spot will cause erosion. Water that stands for more than a half-day in one spot will drown the grass roots.

- Correct the erosion problem by redirecting the water source, slowing it down, or eliminating it.

- Correct the wet spot problem by eliminating the source of water or making the soil level higher so water does not stand. *Plant* new grass on the spot.

Fertilizing

How much fertilizer does your lawn really need? The only way to know for sure is to have a soil test done (see Horticultural Practices, p. 7).

Fertilize **Fescue** *lawns now* (repeat in April, September, and November).

Pest Control

If your weed problem is minor or your lawn is small, hand-digging weeds is effective and permanent. If you choose to use chemical herbicides, here are some options:

- *Spot-spray* chickweed with a broadleaf weedkiller (see Chemicals, p. 327). Don't soak the ground—a light spray is best.

- *Apply* atrazine (see Chemicals, p. 327) to **Centipede Grass** and **St. Augustine** lawns to kill existing broadleaf weeds and to prevent weed seeds from germinating in March.

- On a warm, windless day, *spray* wild onions with a herbicide containing 2, 4-D, and MCPP (see Chemicals, p. 327). Because many concealed bulblets will remain after spraying, hand-digging onions is almost as effective as using a herbicide.

Planning

The calendar is not a very accurate way to determine when to plant grass or apply a weed-preventer. The timing of many lawn tasks is best determined by the temperature of the soil. For example:

- **Fescue** or **Rye** seed germinates when the soil temperature is above 55 degrees Fahrenheit.

- **Bermuda Grass** or **Centipede Grass** seed germinates best when the soil temperature is above 70 degrees.

- **Crabgrass** seed germinates when the soil temperatures are above 55 degrees for seven days in a row.

- **Chickweed** seed germinates when the soil temperature is 70 degrees and declining.

Planting

Aerate **Fescue** lawns and *overseed* them (see Lawns, Introduction) if grass is thin. Wait until soil temperatures are warm, as specified above.

- Listen to the weather forecast to see when a few days of warm weather are predicted. After a couple of days above 50 degrees Fahrenheit, **Fescue** seed can be planted in bare spots.

- The seed will germinate as conditions allow. Even if low temperatures occur for a few days, the seedlings will not be harmed.

- Remember that if you are planting **Fescue** seed, you can't use a weed-preventer herbicide for six weeks after planting.

Lay **Fescue** sod (see Lawns, January).

Care for Your Lawn

Just as the leaves of your **Bermuda Grass, Zoysia Grass,** and **Centipede Grass** grow and wane over the course of a year, the roots of these grass plants do too. Each plant stores a great deal of energy in its central crown in late fall. As grass blades turn brown, roots also die back. When the weather warms in spring, the crown sends out new, green shoots—and roots begin to grow once again. If anything interferes with root growth or a grass's aboveground green-up this month, your lawn will suffer.

- Avoid using weed-*killing* chemicals on warm-season grasses in March (occasional *spot-sprays* are fine). Weed-*preventing* chemicals (pre-emergents) can be used without harm to turfgrass.

- *Do not fertilize* warm-season grasses except in extreme south Georgia.

- Postpone aerating and dethatching until the grass has turned completely green and is growing vigorously.

A late freeze can wreak havoc on warm-season grasses by killing the lush green growth that has begun to appear. To help your lawn recover from an unexpected freeze:

- *Do not fertilize*. Wait until April or May to determine which areas have been killed.

- Irrigate the dead spots lightly with 1/4 inch of water per week, no more.

- If green grass does not emerge by May, *plant* sod or large plugs of grass in each dead area.

- *Fertilize* the lawn on your normal schedule beginning in May.

Watering

Windy days cause grass to dry out.

- *Water* **Bermuda Grass** or **Fescue** sod that was planted within the last six months.

- *Water* **Fescue** lawns that were recently seeded (see Lawns, Introduction).

Fertilizing

Lime raises the pH (the acidity or alkalinity) of soil. This is important because soil pH determines how efficiently plants can absorb fertilizer (see Horticultural Practices, p. 7).

- Most grasses thrive in soil that has a pH of 6.0 to 6.5. If your soil pH is 5.5, only 50 percent of the phosphorus you apply will be used by your lawn.

- Have your soil tested now (see Horticultural Practices, p. 7) to determine the pH.

- If you are unable to have your soil tested, 40 pounds of lime per 1000 square feet of lawn is a typical recommendation.

Lawn grass that is dormant cannot use fertilizer. **Don't fertilize** your **Bermuda Grass, Centipede Grass,** or **Zoysia Grass** lawn now—wait until the whole lawn is at least 50 percent green. Fertilizer that is applied too early may be washed into nearby streams before it is used by your grass. Excess nutrients pollute waterways and the lakes into which they drain.

Pest Control

It's time for the first application of a weed-preventer for all types of lawns. Next application will be in May.

- Remember to *irrigate your lawn* after applying a weed-preventer herbicide. The water dissolves the chemical, making the top $1/2$ inch of soil inhospitable to weed seed germination.

South Georgia gardeners: If you did not do so in February, now is the time to use atrazine on **Centipede Grass** and **St. Augustine Grass** lawns to kill broadleaf weeds that have emerged. This also prevents other weed seeds from sprouting.

On a warm, windless day, kill weeds in your driveway and walks with a nonselective herbicide (see Chemicals, p. 327).

Spot-spray dandelions, curly dock, mugwort, and other perennial weeds with a broadleaf herbicide (see Chemicals, p. 327); you can also dig them out with a dandelion fork.

Mowing

Have your mower blade sharpened now:

- A sharp blade ensures that grass blades are cut rather than torn apart. Clean cut grass is healthier and uses less water.

Dormant lawn grasses can be cut low (scalped) now to speed green-up. Set your mower just low enough to remove only the top of the brown foliage.

If your **Bermuda Grass** was over-seeded with **Ryegrass** last fall, mow it to a height of 1 inch so that the **Bermuda Grass** will begin growing again.

Planning

Not all grasses can be grown from seed. Scientists have hybridized some grass species, particularly **Bermuda Grass,** to develop superior varieties. Hybridization results in seed that will not germinate. Therefore, sod farmers grow hybrid **Bermuda Grass** from sprigs. When the sprigs have grown to cover an area, the grass can be lifted as uniform sod pieces that are shipped to you for planting. Grasses typically installed as sod include the following types:

- **Hybrid Bermuda Grass ('Tifgreen', 'Tifway', 'Tifton 419', 'Tifton 328'**, etc.)

- **Zoysia Grass ('Meyer', 'El Toro', 'Emerald', 'Zenith'**, etc.)

- **Centipede Grass**

- **St. Augustine Grass ('Raleigh', 'Floratam'**, etc.)

- **Turf-type Fescue** (available only in northern half of Georgia)

Sod can be ordered from brokers who arrange for it to be shipped to your site. It can be bought from garden centers in small amounts. Don't wait until the day before sod is delivered to prepare the area. Make sure you have plenty of help to lay the sod. Each sod piece may weigh twenty pounds; carrying hundreds of them in one day can lead to severe back pain.

Some lawn grasses grow readily from seed. The key to establishing a lawn from seed is to control weeds while the seeds are germinating. **Centipede Grass** and **Zoysia Grass** seed do not germinate rapidly. Chemicals that might kill weeds also harm the emerging grass seedlings. Frequent hand-pulling is necessary to keep the weeds at bay. Lawns that can be grown from seed include the following:

- **Fescue**
- **Common Bermuda Grass**
- **Centipede Grass** (somewhat difficult)
- **Zoysia Grass** (somewhat difficult)

Planting

There are two ways to establish a lawn: by planting seed and waiting for it to sprout, or by laying sod and gaining an instant lawn. The following steps ensure a successful sod installation:

1   ***Kill all weeds*** by spraying the area with a nonselective weed-killer (see Chemicals, p. 327) two weeks before planting.

2   ***Till the soil*** thoroughly to a depth of 6 inches, mixing in the recommended amount of lime and fertilizer (see Horticultural Practices, Soil Test, p. 7).

3   Rake the area smooth, removing rocks, clumps, and grassy debris.

4   ***Roll*** the area with a water-filled roller to reveal low spots. Fill low spots with soil.

5   Starting along the longest straight edge of the area, lay sod pieces end to end. Make sure each piece is tightly placed next to its neighbor. ***Stagger*** pieces in adjacent rows so seams do not line up. Use a small hatchet or sharp shovel to trim pieces to fit around obstructions.

6   Roll the entire area once more, to ensure good sod-to-soil contact.

7   ***Water*** the sod thoroughly (see next page).

Sod Replacement

Care for Your Lawn

When you operate a spreader to apply fertilizer or pesticides, **avoid** casting the materials onto your street. Rainfall will wash these chemicals into municipal water-treatment systems or local waterways. The pollution may harm plants and animals that live near water.

Watering

After sod has been laid, the lawn must be watered regularly to keep the sod alive while it establishes new roots. Unlike newly-seeded lawns, the initial watering of sod should be sufficient to moisten the soil under it to a depth of 6 inches.

This will take more than an hour in most cases. Lift a piece of sod and use a trowel to measure the depth of water penetration. See the Lawns introduction for more sod-watering information.

Fertilizing

In late April, most warm-season grasses can receive their first fertilization, while **Fescue** is ready for its last. Any turf fertilizer will suffice unless otherwise noted.

- **Fescue:** Fertilize now, but wait until September to fertilize again.

- **Bermuda Grass:** Fertilize only when the lawn is fifty percent greened-up.

- **Zoysia Grass:** Fertilize only when the lawn is fifty percent greened-up.

- **Centipede Grass:** In south Georgia, fertilize with 6 pounds of 15-0-15 per 1000 square feet of lawn.

- **St. Augustine Grass:** In south Georgia, fertilize if the lawn is fifty percent greened-up.

Pest Control

The presence of big green patches of thin-bladed grass in your **Bermuda Grass** or **Zoysia Grass** lawn is usually a sign of annual bluegrass (*Poa annua*). One way to kill it is to soak a foam paint brush with a non-selective herbicide (see Chemicals, p. 327) and carefully wipe it on the weed but not on your grass. (Be sure to wear plastic gloves on your hands.) Otherwise, make a mental note to use a weed-preventer that is effective on grassy weeds next September; this will prevent the bluegrass seeds from sprouting.

Watch for the bright-green leaves of chickweed in your lawn. *Spot-spray* with broadleaf weedkiller (see Chemicals, p. 327).

Mowing

Two types of mowers are generally available: rotary and reel. Here are the *pros and cons* of each:

Rotary Mower Pros
- Readily available for purchase
- Can be used on all types of grasses
- Easy to repair
- Easy to replace blade
- Mulching models recycle your grass clippings

Rotary Mower Cons
- Wheel may fall into low spots, yielding half-moon shaped scalped areas
- Blade must be kept sharp to achieve best cut

Reel Mower Pros
- Yields an even, manicured cut on **Bermuda Grass** and **Zoysia Grass** lawns
- Less likely to be affected by uneven surface conditions

Reel Mower Cons
- More expensive than rotary mower of comparable width
- Blade must be sharpened by an expert

Planning

It is possible to purchase seed for warm-season grasses like Centipede Grass, Bermuda Grass, *and* Zoysia Grass, *but establishing these lawns from seed is not as easy as establishing a* Fescue *lawn from seed.* Before deciding to plant warm-season grass from seed, consider carefully whether you are willing to spend weeks babying your lawn. These grasses have tiny seed which may take many days to germinate, even under the best conditions; weeds will sprout as the seedlings struggle to grow, and they may overpower the grass seed.

Planting

Warm soil temperatures usher in the very best months for planting all warm-season grasses. Seeding is less expensive, but you must nurture the seed for several weeks before it makes a respectable lawn (see Lawns introduction for seeding rates). Sodding is more expensive, but you will have the satisfaction of an instant lawn (see April for sod planting procedures).

The seeds of **Bermuda Grass, Zoysia Grass,** and **Centipede Grass** are tiny. In order to spread them evenly, they can be mixed with sand:

1 Use very dry, white play sand. A large bucket or a wheelbarrow makes a good container in which to mix.

2 Mix one part (by volume) of seed to ten or twenty parts of sand. In other words, mix 1 cup of seed with 10 to 20 cups of sand.

3 Apply half the recommended rate traveling back and forth in one direction, and the other half traveling at right angles to the first.

Care for Your Lawn

Fescue lawns that were heavily seeded in the past six months may have large patches of straw-brown dead grass. This is caused by too many seedlings growing in a confined space. When dead patches appear, *rake out* the dead grass and sprinkle seed lightly over the spot. Irrigate evenly, and nurture it until the spot matches the rest of your lawn.

Remember when planting in the future to use the correct amount of seed per thousand square feet (see p. 148).

Watering

Lawns need approximately 1 inch of water per week. An inch of water is the amount of rainfall or irrigation it takes to fill a rain gauge or a soup can to a depth of 1 inch (see Lawns introduction for more information).

Fertilizing

Don't apply fertilizer when the grass is wet. The granules will stick to the grass blades and burn them temporarily. Use a drop or a broadcast spreader to apply fertilizer. Hand-casting results in streaks of under- and overfertilization. Try to fertilize just before it rains, or be sure to irrigate the lawn afterwards.

- **Fescue:** If the lawn has not been fed in the past eight weeks, fertilize again, preferably before the middle of the month. Otherwise, wait until September.

- **Bermuda Grass:** *Fertilize now* (and again in June, July, August, and September).

- **Zoysia Grass:** *Fertilize now* (and again in June and August).

- **Centipede Grass** in north Georgia is usually green enough to fertilize by now. Use 6 pounds of 15-0-10 per 1000 square feet of lawn. **Centipede Grass** grows best at a pH of 4.5 to 5.5. Lime is rarely needed.

- **St. Augustine Grass:** *Fertilize now* (and again in June, July, and August).

Pest Control

If you missed the March application of a weed-preventer, crabgrass sprouts will have begun to appear. Use products containing MSMA, CAMA, or DSMA (see Chemicals, p. 327) to control them. Read the herbicide product label carefully, and follow it exactly.

Fire ant mounds are quite visible now. Several months of control can be gained by using the "Georgia Two-Step" method:

Georgia Two-Step Method for Controlling Fire Ants

1

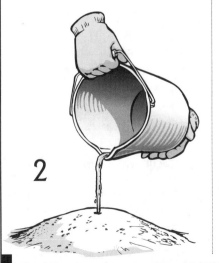

2

1 *Treat the area* with a fire ant bait (see Chemicals, p. 327). The best time to treat is on a warm day, after 10:00 A.M.

2 Apply a powdered or liquid insecticide to individual mounds 48 hours later.

Repeat the procedure in September.

Mowing

As the summer mowing season begins in earnest, check the height of your mower to make sure it is clipping your grass at the correct height (see Lawns introduction for more information).

Mushrooms

After a few days of rain, mushrooms may sprout in your lawn overnight. Mushrooms can be thought of as the "flowers" of a fungus. These "toadstools" are nothing more than the reproductive portion of a fungus that has quietly been consuming organic debris underground. With warm soil and a bit of rain, the fungus decides the time is ripe to reproduce. It is impossible to eliminate fungi from the soil. The best treatment for mushrooms is to simply **pick them and discard them.** They are not edible. Use a five-iron on the largest ones to improve your golf game!

JUNE

Planning

A sharp border on a lawn can make all the difference in its appearance. Whether it is a straight edge next to the sidewalk or a gentle curve next to a flower bed, the observer's eye finds comfort in a neatly defined edge. Make sure the edges of your lawn do not include sharp angles or dead-end corridors—both are difficult to mow. Before constructing a new edge, push your mower along the boundary of your lawn to gain a feel for how easy or difficult it will be to mow. See hints for edging in the Mowing section of this month.

Planting

When the soil has warmed above 65 degrees Fahrenheit, you can *plant sprigs* (small plugs) of **Bermuda Grass, Centipede Grass, Zoysia Grass,** and **St. Augustine Grass.** Sprigging saves money because you can divide a sod piece into hundreds of individual sprigs. On the other hand, sprigging is labor intensive, and you must water and weed your newly-sprigged lawn frequently. Sprigging is best done on a small lawn:

1   *Till the soil* 6 inches deep, adding organic matter, starter fertilizer, and lime as recom-

mended by a soil test.

2   Level the area and *roll it* with a heavy roller to highlight any low spots. Fill low spots with soil before you begin sprigging.

3   Run a motorized core aerator over the lawn twice. This will make hundreds of small holes. The holes should be 3 to 6 inches apart.

4   Soak a piece of sod in a tub of water. Pull apart the sod into as many pieces as possible. Make sure each sprig has roots attached.

5   Keep the sprigs damp in a bucket, and insert them individually into the aerator holes.

6   *Water* thoroughly and regularly (see Lawns introduction for a watering schedule) until sprigs take root. *Remove weeds* by hand.

This is the very best month to plant **Centipede Grass** or **Zoysia Grass** seed (see Lawns introduction for seeding rate). ***Don't go on vacation***—you'll need to water the lawn daily and pull weeds conscientiously for four weeks to ensure success.

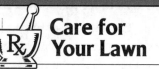

Care for Your Lawn

It may take weeks for the seed of warm-season grasses to sprout and show green leaves. Keep the soil moist and pull any weeds by hand during this time.

Watering

Water hoses will leak if stepped on or driven over too often:

- *Buy* a hose reel to wind up your hose after use.

- *Inspect* the rubber washer and replace if necessary.

Fertilizing

Lawn fertilizers are usually labeled as such. Typically the first number (nitrogen) is the highest among the three fertilizer analysis numbers on the front of the bag. Though the fertilizer numbers differ among brands, any of them can be used successfully if you follow the directions on the bag.

- **Fescue:** *Do not fertilize.*

- **Bermuda Grass:** *Fertilize now* (and again in July, August, and September).

- **Zoysia Grass:** *Fertilize now* (and again in August).

- **Centipede Grass:** *Do not fertilize* unless you skipped the feeding in May

- **St. Augustine Grass:** *Fertilize now* (and again in July and August).

Pest Control

Check your lawn for circular dead spots. It could be "brown patch" (see Lawns, August), but correct your watering and fertilization practices before reaching for a fungicide.

Use a broadleaf weedkiller (see Chemicals, p. 327) to *spot-spray* for violets, wild strawberry, and dandelion in your lawn.

Mowing

Thatch is a layer of undecomposed grass stems and debris that accumulates under grass plants. As the layer of thatch becomes thicker, the grass grows on top of it. During severe cold or drought, grass growing on thatch will be harmed.

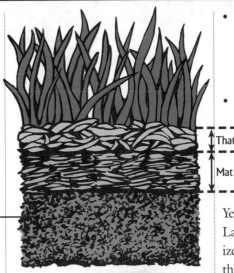

Soil

Thatch
Mat
Thatch
Layer

- Check the thickness of your thatch layer by scratching at the base of a grass plant with your fingers.

- A layer less than $1/2$ inch in depth is not harmful.

- Improper mowing, not grass clippings, causes thatch.

If you have a thick layer of thatch, it can be corrected by using a vertical mower (dethatcher). The height of the blades should be adjusted so they lift up the thatch but don't harm the grass too much.

Vertical Mower

- The best time to dethatch warm-season lawns is when the grass is growing rapidly, typically in May or June.

- *Apply* a light fertilization ($1/4$ the normal rate), a weed-preventer, and $1/2$ inch of water after dethatching.

Yearly aeration of your lawn (see Lawns, Introduction) with a motorized core aerator will also decrease thatch. The cores of soil deposited on the grass surface inoculate it with fungi which consume thatch.

There are a couple of ways to achieve a neatly defined edge for your lawn:

- Use a power edger or string trimmer to slice through grass that grows along the edge of your street, driveway, or flower beds.

  Be sure to wear eye protection when using a powered edger. Warn children to stay away.

- If you have a small lawn, non-motorized edgers are available. They are a bit more work, but they are easy to store.

Planning

Another option for making a defined edge where your lawn borders a flower bed is to dig a trench between grass and bed. This procedure is called trench edging:

- Use a thin shovel to dig a trench 6 inches wide and 2 inches deep along the edge of your grass.

- You can choose whether to leave the trench empty or to mask the bare soil with a shallow layer of pine straw.

- If the trench slants downhill, interrupt the downward flow of water by placing stones or half-bricks in the trench at regular intervals.

Planting

Too hot for the kids outdoors? Now is a good time to lay sod in the bare areas where the kids have been playing ball.

Remember to dig the soil to a depth of 3 to 6 inches, and rake it smooth before laying sod.

It will be hard to keep children off the lawn when you water the thirsty young sod.

Plant sod pieces on half the lawn this month and half next month so the children can at least get some enjoyment from the sprinkler when the first part of the lawn has been repaired.

Can't afford to sod the bare spots in your **St. Augustine Grass, Zoysia Grass,** or **Bermuda Grass** lawn? Buy sod pieces at the nursery, and cut them into dozens of plugs with a hatchet or sharp knife. Some garden centers sell special tools that cut sod plugs to the right size. They can be used to dig matching holes as well.

Plant 3-inch-diameter sod plugs 12 inches apart. They will cover the ground by fall. (Zoysia Grass will be the slowest to spread.)

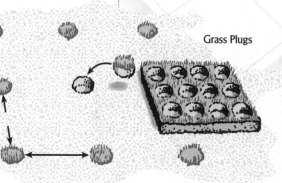

Grass Plugs

Care for Your Lawn

Whether you have sodded or seeded a new lawn, it is important to keep the family and pets off the area until the grass is well established. Compaction from just a few trips across the lawn in one path can prevent good grass growth there for years.

- Sod that is well established cannot be pulled up from the ground. Well-established seeded lawns should appear to be 100 percent covered with grass seedlings.

- Even on a well-established lawn, mowing in the same pattern over and over will result in compaction where the wheels roll. It is best to use a different mowing pattern (vertical, horizontal, or diagonal) each time you mow.

Watering

Turfgrasses have varying degrees of drought tolerance. Ranked from highest drought tolerance to lowest:

First: **Bermuda Grass**
Second: **St. Augustine Grass**
Third: **Centipede Grass, Fescue, 'Emerald' Zoysia Grass,** and **'El Toro' Zoysia Grass**
Fourth: **'Meyer' Zoysia Grass**

It is a shame to discard a perfectly good hose because you accidentally crushed one end with a car tire. Hose repair kits are inexpensive, available at any hardware store, and easy to use. Take the hose with you when you purchase a kit, just to make sure you get the right size. If you can't bring along the hose, look for "universal" kits that work on two or more hose sizes.

Fertilizing

Bermuda Grass: *Fertilize now* (and again in August and September).

Zoysia Grass: *Do not fertilize* unless a previous feeding was missed.

St. Augustine Grass: *Fertilize now.*

Fescue: To avoid disease and drought problems, ***do not fertilize* Fescue** during the summer. If your **Fescue** is more yellow than you prefer, apply a product containing plant-available iron.

Ironite™ is one such product. Apply 1 to 2 pounds per 100 square feet.

Pest Control

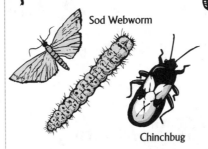

Sod Webworm

Chinchbug

Insect damage to lawn grass is difficult to determine. Symptoms might include numerous dead patches or grass blades that seem to disappear in an area overnight. One way to check if you have harmful insects is to "float" them out:

1 Mix 2 ounces (4 tablespoons) of lemon-scented dish detergent in 2 gallons of water.

2 Pour the mixture over a 2-foot-square area.

Insects such as sod webworms and chinchbugs will come wriggling to the surface of the soapy froth.

3 Collect the insects and have them identified by your local Extension Service (see Resources, p. 353) or garden center.

Mowing

Grasscycling is the practice of leaving grass clippings on the lawn rather than collecting them. Grasscycling saves time and energy, plus it reduces the amount of yard waste that might be taken to the landfill.

- Because clippings contain the nutrient *nitrogen*, grasscycling allows you to reduce the amount of fertilizer you apply by $1/4$.

- Specially-designed mulching lawn mowers do an excellent job of chopping the clippings so fine they cannot be seen.

- Older, side-discharge mowers can also be used if mowing is done often enough that only a third of the grass height is removed in one mowing.

Scorching sunshine can make the soil so hot that grass roots can't grow.

Raise the height of your mower by one notch. It will help the grass withstand hot, dry weather by shading the soil and by raising the humidity at soil level.

Planning

This is an excellent month in which to compare your lawn to others in your neighborhood. The stress of drought, heat, disease, and insects will be evident on lawns whose owners have neglected some facet of their care. If yours is the best on the block, congratulations! If yours is not quite on par with the rest, make notes on what practices you can improve in other parts of the year to make your lawn look its best.

Planting

If your lawn is thinning in dense shade, why not replace the sparse grass with a ground cover like **Mondo Grass, Pachysandra, Liriope,** or **Ajuga?** Even pine straw or wood chip mulch will look better than grass that's struggling along in semi-darkness.

Care for Your Lawn

If there is a secret to having an outstanding lawn, it is regular, leisurely observation of the grass and making time to do a little "problem correction" each week. Weed, insect, and disease problems don't appear out of thin air—they develop over time.

Even though it is hot and sultry outdoors, take time each week to *walk across your lawn,* ice-cold drink in hand, noting small problems and planning your response.

Watering

Water restrictions are common summer occurrences in metropolitan areas of Georgia. Don't fall into the trap of believing that you should water your lawn whenever allowed. *A deep soaking, one per week, is all a lawn needs. (See Lawns introduction for watering information.)*

Fertilizing

- **Fescue:** *Do not fertilize.*

- **Bermuda Grass:** *Fertilize now* (and again in September).

- **Zoysia Grass:** *Fertilize now.*

- **St. Augustine Grass:** *Fertilize now.*

- **Centipede Grass:** *Do not fertilize.* **Centipede Grass** is naturally a lighter green than other grasses. Fertilizing with an iron sulfate product will make **Centipede Grass** greener. Apply 1 to 2 pounds of Ironite per 100 square feet.

Pest Control

White Grub

"Brown patch" and "dollar spot" are two common lawn diseases. Both are best controlled by attention to proper watering and fertilization.

Brown patch symptoms are large circular areas of dead grass, in which the edge and center of each area may be dark green. To control brown patch:

- Keep grass as dry as possible between weekly waterings. *Water* between midnight and noon.

- Follow recommended fertilizer rates. *Do not overfertilize.*

Dollar spot symptoms appear as dozens of small dead spots. To control dollar spot:

- *Water* deeply each week. Do not allow the lawn to become drought-stressed.

- Keep grass healthy with a regular fertilization program.

Both diseases can be controlled, if caught in time, with fungicides (see Chemicals, p. 327). Fungicides are expensive and will not cure an advanced case of either disease.

If you had tremendous numbers of Japanese beetles, you might get some control by poisoning the grubs now. There is no need to use an insecticide if you find only a few grubs when you dig. Eight to ten grubs per square foot is the threshold at which a poison should be considered.

This is the most effective time to apply grub poisons (see Chemicals, p. 327), but remember to water heavily after application, which will wash the chemical down into the soil where the grub lives. Consider using milky spore disease powder (see Chemicals, p. 327) for organic grub control.

If your predominant grass is **Fescue,** now is the time to kill other grasses in preparation for planting **Fescue** in September.

- *Spray* encroaching **Bermuda Grass, Zoysia Grass,** or **Centipede Grass** with a nonselective, systemic weedkiller (see Chemicals, p. 327).

- Seven days after spraying, irrigate thoroughly to encourage sprouts of the invading grass to emerge.

- Seven days after irrigating, *spray* the sprouts of weed grasses with nonselective weedkiller.

Helpful Hint

The biggest reason lawn mower oil goes unchanged and the blade goes unsharpened is the difficulty of working on the machine while it is on the ground. Removing a blade is particularly difficult. If you have an aluminum extension ladder, a cinderblock, and an outdoor flight of steps, you can lift a mower to make it more accessible:

- Place one end of the ladder on the second or third step. Rest the other end on the ground.

- Position the mower at the lower end of the ladder, facing the steps.

- With a great grunt, push the mower up the slanted ladder. As the wheels leave the ground, the underside of the mower frame will scrape along the ladder frame. Shove the mower up the ladder as far as you can.

- Move the upended cinderblock close to the low end of the ladder. Lift the ladder with one hand and place the end rung on top of the cinderblock.

- The mower should now be supported 18 inches off the ground by the ladder frame. You can easily reach under it to loosen the blade attachment bolts or the oil drain plug.

CAUTION: Always disconnect the spark plug when working on a lawn mower.

Now is also a good time to *control broadleaf weeds.* Use a selective weedkiller labeled for use on such pests (see Chemicals, p. 327).

Mowing

How long has it been since your lawn mower blade was sharpened? Cleanly cut grass is healthier and does not look yellow after mowing. The lawn mower blade should be sharpened once each summer to avoid shredding the grass when you mow.

Often **Zoysia Grass** does not appear to need mowing even though it may be growing higher than the recommended .5 to 1.5 inches.

- Mow your **Zoysia Grass** lawn regularly to avoid thatch buildup.

Planning

Whether you're planting seed or spreading fertilizer, an even application of material is important. The best way to accomplish this with a lawn spreader is to use the crisscross method:

1 *Apply* half your material in several passes going in one direction.

2 *Apply* the second half in several passes that are at right angles to the first application.

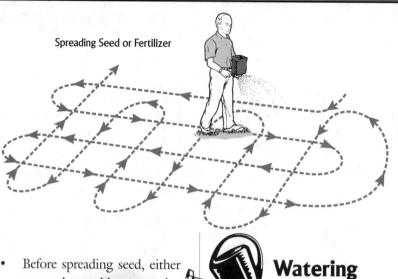
Spreading Seed or Fertilizer

Planting

Fescue is a common lawn grass in the northern half of the state. Fall is the best time to plant it if you are using seed. The planting can be done successfully until mid-October, but the longer you wait, the cooler the soil becomes and the longer it will take for the seed to germinate.

- Planting a new **Fescue** lawn from scratch? Use 6 pounds of seed per 1000 square feet.

- Overseeding an old lawn? Use 3 to 6 pounds of seed per 1000 square feet, depending on how much **Fescue** already exists.

- Before spreading seed, either *aerate* thoroughly or scratch the soil *hard* with a bow rake.

South Georgia lawn-lovers still have time to plant **Common Bermuda Grass** seed and get acceptable growth before winter.

Bermuda Grass sod can still be planted successfully, but it would be better to delay planting **Zoysia Grass, Centipede Grass,** and **St. Augustine Grass** sod until spring.

Care for Your Lawn

After planting **Fescue** seed, it must be mulched with wheat straw to protect it from birds and to hold soil moisture.

Use no more than one bale of straw per 1000 square feet.

Watering

After **Fescue** seed has been planted, it must be watered regularly until the seeds have established a good root system. If you are under watering restrictions, getting good seed-to-soil contact is very important. (See Lawns introduction for watering information).

Fertilizing

Fescue: Fertilize after the middle of the month (and again in November). Use a starter fertilizer (which usually has a high percentage of phosphorus) for the first application if you planted **Fescue** seed. Use any brand of turf fertilizer for subsequent feedings.

Bermuda Grass: Some lawns benefit from a "winterizer" fertilizer application now when growth has slowed but before the grass turns brown. The best date is six weeks before you estimate the first frost will occur in your region. A winterizer fertilizer helps **Bermuda Grass** get off to a strong start in spring—this fertilizer contains a moderate percentage of nitrogen and higher-than-usual percentages of phosphorus and potassium.

Zoysia Grass: *Do not fertilize*.

Centipede Grass: *Do not fertilize*.

St. Augustine Grass: *Do not fertilize* in north Georgia. Fertilize in south Georgia only if the August feeding was missed.

Pest Control

Mole Cricket

The seaport of Brunswick has the honor of being the introduction point of a destructive pest of lawns in south Georgia: the mole cricket. Adult insects tunnel just below the surface of the soil. They feed on grass roots, but the grass suffers great harm just from the drying out of loosened soil. The best first step to mole cricket management is correct watering, fertilizing, and

mowing height. Insecticides (see Chemicals, p. 327) are most effective when applied in June, although cricket damage is most noticeable in September.

After applying sprays or granular poisons (except Orthene), irrigate immediately to dissolve the poison in the soil.

The Georgia Two-Step fire ant control technique (see Lawns, May) is extremely effective when applied now. The combination of a bait and a mound treatment now can bring them to their knees.

Armadillos can be a pest on lawns in south Georgia. They root through the turf looking for grubs to eat. Your lawn will look like a group of small bulldozers visited during the night!

- Use 24-inch-tall fence wire and short wooden stakes to construct a simple funnel trap facing the area from which the animals come each night.

- The mouth of the funnel should be 30 to 50 feet wide.

- The trap sides should taper down to a width of 12 inches—just wide enough to place the opening of a large live trap in the armadillo's path.

- Transport the animals you capture several miles away, and *release* them.

"Winter" weeds germinate in fall but wait to make their appearance the following spring. Chickweed, annual bluegrass, and henbit are common winter weeds.

Mid-September is the best time to put out a pre-emergent winter weed-preventer (see Chemicals, p. 327).

Before planting **Fescue** seed, wipe out weeds with a fast-acting but short-lived weedkiller.

Use a nonselective weedkiller now (see Chemicals, p. 327), and you can plant grass seed in seven days.

Many tough-to-control summer weeds are at their weakest now from summer stress.

Apply a broadleaf weedkiller (see Chemicals, p. 327) to violets, wild strawberry, and wild onion in your lawn.

Mowing

If you raised your mowing height to help your grass during the summer, lower it to the proper height now. See the mowing height list in Lawns, Introduction.

Planning

Before you can move into a new home, it must pass a final inspection and receive a "certificate of occupancy." The county housing inspector won't grant a certificate of occupancy if the lawn has not been planted or sodded. The installation of grass is often the last thing done by the builder before the home sale.

- If you have any input into the decision, make sure the appropriate grass has been chosen for your lawn (see Lawns introduction).

- **Annual Ryegrass** is sometimes allowed, but remember that it must be replaced with a permanent grass in spring.

- Ask the builder how the soil was prepared before seed or sod was planted.

- Test the softness of the soil by pressing a pencil into the earth—if it penetrates more than 2 inches easily, grass can grow readily. If the soil seems rock hard, you will have endless problems with your lawn in the future.

- If you are not satisfied that the lawn will succeed, negotiate appropriate guarantees or concessions at closing.

Planting

Bermuda Grass turns brown and dormant in winter. To avoid this brown look, one can *overseed* the **Bermuda Grass** with **Annual Ryegrass**. The **Ryegrass** will be green in winter but will die out in early summer.

1 Mow the **Bermuda Grass** as low as possible without your mower blade hitting the ground.

2 Spread **Ryegrass** seed evenly at a rate of 5 to 10 pounds per 1000 square feet.

3 Fertilize with starter fertilizer.

4 *Water* thoroughly (see the watering information in Lawns, Introduction).

CAUTION: Overseeding with **Ryegrass** *may weaken the underlying* **Bermuda Grass** *because it competes for available nutrients during the winter. Follow all* **Bermuda Grass** *maintenance recommendations during the year to help it withstand the stress of being overseeded in the winter. Do not overseed thin or weak* **Bermuda Grass** *lawns.*

Fescue seed can still be planted, but don't delay. Cold soil causes the seed to germinate unevenly.

Care for Your Lawn

Moss is a common inhabitant of lawns that are shady or constantly moist. Moss-control chemicals are available, but they are not permanent solutions to the problem. For permanent moss control:

- Dig the soil deeply to make it drain faster.

- Reduce shade by removing low limbs of nearby trees.

- Correct the water-flow problems that cause the soil to be wet.

IMPORTANT: Lime does not eliminate moss. Although moss prefers acid soil, liming will not control the moss unless the environmental conditions mentioned above are corrected.

Watering

Water newly-planted **Fescue** lawns regularly.

Water recently-sodded lawns deeply so the water penetrates 4 inches into the soil below the sod layer.

Drain your lawn irrigation system before winter arrives:

1 Turn off the water valve that supplies your system.

2 Allow the system timer to run through all its cycles in its normal manner. Much of the water in your pipes will run out of the lowest irrigation heads. What water remains will not be under pressure and will not hurt components if it freezes. The system should be fine when you turn it on next year.

An alternative is to purchase a maintenance contract from an irrigation contractor. The workers will check the operation of all of your heads before draining the system in winter. They may also want to shoot compressed air through the pipes to remove all remaining water. They will also check the system again in spring.

Store water hoses where you won't be tempted to move them when they're frozen. A hard-frozen hose is brittle; leaks may result if it is flexed when cold. *A hose reel is very handy for hose storage throughout the year.*

Fertilizing

Fescue: There's still time to give Fescue lawns that first fall feeding. Use any turf fertilizer. Use a starter fertilizer for the first application if you planted seed.

Bermuda Grass: In south Georgia, it may be fertilized with a winterizer product.

Zoysia Grass: *Do not fertilize.*

Centipede Grass: *Do not fertilize.*

St. Augustine Grass: *Do not fertilize.*

Fireplace ashes can be scattered over your lawn rather than disposing of them. They provide a bit of phosphorus and potassium, plus they counteract acidity, just like garden lime. Spread no more than 10 pounds per 1000 square feet per month. *CAUTION: Never store ashes in a flammable container; always place them in a covered metal pail.*

Pest Control

Don't forget to spread a weed-preventer (see Chemicals, p. 327) as soon as possible on established lawns to suppress weeds such as chickweed, *poa annua*, and hairy bittercress next spring.

Remember that weed-control chemicals can harm germinating seed as well as grass that is going dormant:

- Do not apply a weed-preventer to newly seeded **Fescue** lawns.

- Do not use "Weed 'n' Feed" products or a broadcast application of broadleaf weedkiller on any turfgrass at this time.

- *Spot-spray* broadleaf weeds that pop up this fall.

The effectiveness of the Georgia Two-Step fire ant control (see Lawns, May) depends on ants that are actively foraging for food:

- In south Georgia, continue utilizing the Two-Step technique until the weather becomes chilly.

- In north Georgia, treat individual mounds with contact insecticide (see Chemicals, p. 327).

Mowing

Mow warm-season grasses as needed while the weather cools. You can stop mowing after the first frost.

Mow **Fescue** as needed (see Lawns, Introduction for mowing heights).

Planning

On a warm day, walk across your lawn and note any problems that could be cured during the next growing season.

- Does the grass grow evenly in all areas?

- Are particular spots prone to weed and disease problems?

- Was it easy to mow all areas?

- Could the size of your lawn be reduced to save water and maintenance time?

It is a common practice of builders to install **Bermuda Grass** sod in the front lawn and to plant **Fescue** in the back. Remember that if you have two different grasses, they will have two different management schedules:

- **Fescue** is fertilized and mowed in the cool months but not in summer.

- **Bermuda Grass** is fertilized and mowed in summer but not in winter.

If the backyard is sunny, consider converting to **Bermuda Grass.**

Planting

It is very late to be planting Fescue seed in the northern half of Georgia except in the area south of Atlanta and north of Macon. In areas north of Atlanta, you can do it, but germination will take weeks. See the Helpful Hints for a possible solution.

Fescue sod should be available now. It can be installed anytime between now and next summer.

There's still time to plant annual **Ryegrass** for erosion control, or just to use as a green spot in a brown landscape.

Do not plant Zoysia Grass, **Centipede Grass,** or **St. Augustine Grass** sod in the northern half of Georgia now. These grasses do not have enough time to grow good roots before cold weather sets in.

In the southern half of the state, all sods can be planted, but use caution. *Avoid* planting in sunny or windy weather. Remember to *water* new sod regularly until it is well established. (See Lawns introduction for watering schedule).

Bermuda Grass sod can be planted now if you are certain you can water it regularly during the winter to keep the roots moist.

This is an excellent month to plant **Liriope** or **Mondo Grass** in shady spots where grass refuses to grow:

- The easiest way to get plants is to divide a clump already growing in your yard or that of a friend. Ask your neighbors if they have an area where one of these ground covers is growing.

- Dig the clump, wash it off, and divide it into individual plants.

- Replant some of the sprouts where they grew originally. Take the rest to your landscape and install 6 inches apart.

- *Water* twice, at three-day intervals. No further care should be required.

Care for Your Lawn

Are your neighbors raking up pine straw and putting it in bags for the garbage man? If they can't use it in their landscape, ask if you can have some for yours. If you have the space, stockpile bags under a tarp so you'll have plenty of mulch next year.

Keep the leaves raked (or blown) off your newly planted **Fescue** lawn.

174

Watering

Drain your irrigation system (see Lawns, October) and outdoor faucets. If the faucets can't be drained, *cover* them with insulation for the winter. Hardware stores stock foam pipe wrap and faucet covers that are easy to install.

Fertilizing

Lawn fertilizer does not "go bad," even when it becomes lumpy and breaks through the bottom of the bag. If it can be pulverized enough to flow through your spreader, *apply* it to your lawn on the usual schedule. If the lumps are too hard to break, throw them, in moderate amounts (¹/₂ cup per plant), under your woodland trees and shrubs in spring. *Fertilize* Fescue, preferably in the early part of the month. *Do not fertilize* **Bermuda Grass, Zoysia Grass, Centipede Grass,** or **St. Augustine Grass.**

Pest Control

Squirrels may dig holes in your lawn in order to hide acorns. The holes are unsightly, but little can be done to deter the rodents. If the holes bother you greatly, use a live trap, baited with peanut butter, to capture a few of the creatures and give them a nice trip out of town.

Helpful Hints

If you have a **Fescue** lawn spot that simply must be planted in cold weather, there are tricks that can be used to extend the season.

Priming (Pre-germinating)
- Measure the amount of seed you will need and place it in a 5-gallon plastic bucket.
- Cover the seed completely with warm water. Stir gently.
- Let the seed soak overnight in a warm room.
- Strain the water from the seed. Scatter the seed thinly on sheets of newspaper.
- When seeds are dry enough to handle (an hour at most), scatter them over the planting spot.
- Mulch with wheat straw, and **water** immediately.

Greenhousing
- **Rake** the area with a hard-tined garden rake (a bow rake).
- Scatter seed lightly and evenly over the spot. **Water** and cover very thinly with wheat straw.
- Cover the whole area with clear plastic sheeting; anchor it loosely with stones or large limbs.
- Sunshine will warm the soil and encourage the seed to sprout quickly.
- Lift the plastic when the grass is green underneath.

CAUTION: Do not attempt this technique if the weather is unusually warm or sunny. Your seed may overheat and die under the plastic.

Mowing

Fall leaves are much easier to handle when they have been shredded. If you have a bagging mower, simply *rake up* a pile of leaves and *mow through* them until you fill the bag. Shredded leaves can be used as mulch under trees and shrubs or can be added to your compost pile. High-performance mulching mowers can shred leaves so finely they won't be noticed on your lawn; the particles simply add organic material to your soil.

175

Planning

No law says you have to have a lawn (although neighborhood covenants may require one). It is possible to have a very attractive front yard without enduring the work and management details a lawn requires. On a warm December day, walk across your lawn and envision what it would look like if it were filled with beds of flowers or shrubs or tree islands.

Planting

Fescue sod can be planted whenever it is available. In the northern half of the state, **Bermuda Grass** sod can be successfully installed throughout the winter as long as it is kept from drying. *Do not plant* **Zoysia Grass** or **Centipede Grass** sod. In the southern half of the state, all sods can be planted, but use caution. *Avoid* planting in sunny or windy weather. Remember to *water* new sod regularly until it is well established (see Lawns introduction for watering schedule).

Care for Your Lawn

Rake the last of the fall leaves from your lawn. A pile of wet, matted leaves now can lead to big dead spots next spring. Use them for mulch under shrubs and trees.

Fertilizing

Fescue: Fertilize only if the November feeding was missed.

Bermuda Grass: *Do not fertilize.*

Zoysia Grass: *Do not fertilize.*

Centipede Grass: *Do not fertilize.*

St. Augustine Grass: *Do not fertilize.*

Pest Control

Watch for the bright-green leaves of chickweed in your lawn. *Spot-spray* with a broadleaf weedkiller (see Chemicals, p. 327).

Spray for wild onions in your lawn. Do this a second time in February, and another time in April. *If you'd rather not use a herbicide, a stiff dandelion fork can be used to dig out the underground bulbs.*

Fescue lawns that were planted in fall may appear slightly yellow after a December cold snap. *This minor frost damage will disappear in just a few days. It will not reoccur once the grass has become well-established.*

Mowing

Mow **Fescue** and **Ryegrass** regularly, removing only 1/3 of the height each time. Mowers are tough machines, but a little maintenance now will make them much easier to operate:

- Don't leave your lawn mower out in the rain. Water can get in the gas tank and prevent starting next spring. It is best to drain the tank completely, or run the mower until it is out of gas.

- Flip your mower on its side and *clean* the underside of the mower with a sturdy stick. Remove caked grass. Check the mower shaft for string or wire wrapped around it.

- Use a spray lubricant, such as WD-40, to protect and lubricate wheel axles, control cables, and blade height adjusters. A 5-minute task today can save hours of frustration next spring.

- This is a fine time to have the blade sharpened if this was not done earlier in the year.

CAUTION: Always disconnect the spark plug before maintaining a lawn mower.

Perennials and Ornamental Grasses

Perennials and Ornamental Grasses

Perennials, also called *herbaceous plants*, produce fleshy stems that die down each winter, but their roots stay alive and send up new growth in spring. Many perennials will thrive and bloom in the same spot year after year with a minimum of care. Others need to be divided or replaced after two or three years. In the milder parts of Georgia, certain perennials stay evergreen all year long.

Perennials can be grown from seed, but you may have to wait several years before they will bloom. The availability of a wide range of container-grown perennials makes it easy to start a perennial garden and have blooms the same season you plant. Perennials that catalogs describe as "blooming for weeks" may actually be fleeting in our hot, humid climate—because of this, it is best to grow a variety of perennials, including those with striking foliage and distinctive forms as well as those with colorful flowers. This way your garden will not rely solely on flowers to create interest. Plants such as **Hostas** and **Fern**s offer colorful foliage that persists for months, often when little is blooming in the shade garden. In the sunny garden, plants like **Lamb's Ear** and *Artemisia* provide a transition from one group of colors to another, and they, too, look good for months at a time.

While it's true that annuals must be replaced every year, growing perennials is not necessarily more cost-effective. Unless you grow your plants from seed, perennials initially cost more than annuals, and once you get bitten by the perennial bug, you may find you are making lots of trips to the local nursery. Still, when the perennial garden is established, you won't have to replace plants every year the way you do with annuals, and you will have plenty of divisions and cuttings to share with friends and neighbors.

Planning the Perennial Garden

If you're not sure about which perennials will do well in your garden, start with a small area. Examine the environment that your existing trees and shrubs are growing in to help guide you in your choices. Is it a hot, sunny spot, or is it cool and shady? Determine how much sun you get in a particular area. Start by observing the sun at different times of day, beginning in early morning, then at noon, and again in the afternoon. Record how many hours of direct sunlight an area receives. If you want to grow sun-loving plants, four to six hours of direct sunlight is ideal. If you garden in the shade, plants will still need a minimum of light to thrive, perhaps a half-day of bright indirect light. High shade from mature deciduous trees will allow a good bit of light into an otherwise dark area. If there is not enough light and plants are weak and not thriving, you may have to do some selective pruning and open up the canopies of large trees nearby.

Draw a plan on graph paper, indicating which plants you would like to include. While you don't have to have a scale drawing, you can use your house as a reference point to help you locate plants in relationship to one another.

When selecting perennials, consider not only the season of bloom and the flower color, but the color of the foliage, the texture of the plant, and what the plant looks like when it is not in bloom. List the attributes of plants you want to grow: flowers, foliage type, and whether or not

Perennials and Ornamental Grasses

there are decorative seedheads. Note which plants attract bees and butterflies, and which plants die back after they finish blooming (like the **Giant Bleeding Heart,** which seems to disappear soon after its flowers fade). Remember that just one plant of many different varieties will not make an effective display. Think about grouping plants—two or three of the same type will make an impact.

Grouping plants that have flowers with similar colors will also make an effective display. Spring may feature pastel blooms of pink, white, and blue, while summer may be reserved for hot colors like red, orange, and yellow. Remember that green in all its shades is also a color.

Spacing is important, too. Do a little research on the cultural requirements and growth rate of the plants you would like to grow before you purchase them. While you don't want to wait three years for your plants to fill in, you don't want your garden to become overgrown in only one year either.

Ornamental grasses are herbaceous plants that add flair to the garden with their striking forms, foliage, flowers, and seedheads. When planted in masses, they add a sense of drama. When mixed in with your flowers or used as part of a mixed border with shrubs, trees, and perennials, they add a touch of elegance

and grace as they sway in the breeze. Many are long-lived, offering colorful foliage and flowers year after year, beginning in summer and continuing well into winter when their decorative seedheads persist. These plants demand little in the way of care, although division of mature clumps may be required to keep the plants healthy (grasses should be divided in spring). While grasses are often associated with full-sun gardens, there are also types that thrive in shade. Although there are both annual and perennial selections of ornamental grasses, the varieties recommended in this chapter are perennial in most parts of Georgia.

Most importantly, no matter what types of perennials you grow, remember to let the garden tell you what to do. Is the soil well-drained, or does it stay wet and compacted? Knowing the answers to these questions will help you when you make your plant selections. Use your Garden Journal to record what you plant where, including information on sources, the condition of the plant when you plant it, and how many plants you purchased and planted. Photograph your garden before you plant, and then after you plant, at least once a month. This will provide useful information in the future.

On p. 179 is a chart of a few ornamental grasses for Georgia, including varieties that thrive in sun

and some for shade. Certain grasses will also thrive in containers, and can be moved around to add instant interest to the garden.

Soil Preparation

There's an expression that sums up the importance of good soil preparation when growing perennials: Prepare a ten-dollar hole for a one-dollar plant. This means that if you invest in the soil by preparing it before you plant, you can start with smaller plants that will become large and robust in no time.

Eliminate existing weeds before you add soil amendments. If you use a nonselective herbicide like Roundup®, you can spray weeds, wait ten days to two weeks, then begin adding soil amendments.

A slower method that involves no chemicals is to cover weeds with a layer of newspaper, at least one inch thick, and then put two to three inches of mulch over the newspaper. This technique is effective, but it takes six months or longer before the weeds are killed and the newspaper breaks down. You can also place a sheet of black plastic over the weeds, and then put a two-inch layer of mulch over the plastic. Check after six months to see if weeds are dead and gone. Both of these techniques are for patient gardeners.

Ornamental Grasses for Georgia

Botanical Name Common Name	Cultural Requirements	Average Height and Width	Comments
Acorus gramineus 'Ogon' Golden Variegated Sweet Grass	Full sun or shade; moist soil.	6 to 12 inches by 6 inches	Great in containers or to brighten the edge of a woodland pond.
Calamagrostis spp. Feather Reed Grass	Full sun; moist well-drained soil.	2 to 4 feet by 2 to 3 feet	In north Georgia the fall color is orange yellow.
Carex hachioensis 'Evergold' Variegated Japanese Sedge	Full sun in coastal areas, partial shade in other parts of the state; moist, well-drained soil.	2 feet by 2 feet	Effective in rock gardens or when planted in masses.
Chasmanthium latifolium Northern Sea Oats	Tolerates a wide range of growing conditions; full sun and dry soil if kept watered; partial shade and moist soil is best.	2 to 3 feet tall and 2 feet wide	Handsome flowers and foliage. Cut off seedheads in June if you want to prevent this grass from spreading by seed.
Miscanthus sinensis Maiden Grass Japanese Silver Grass	Full sun and moist soil; tolerates drought when established.	5 to 8 feet by 2 to 3 feet	Good for coastal gardens, along the edge of a pond, or at the back of the border.
Pennisetum alopecuroides Fountain Grass	Adapts to a range of soil types; prefers moist soil and full sun.	2 to 3 feet by 2 to 3 feet	Great for the fall garden, attractive flowers and colorful foliage.

Once the site is weed-free and the soil is mostly dry, rototill the area to a depth of twelve to eighteen inches, adding soil amendments as you go. Avoid working soils that are waterlogged. If you have a heavy clay soil, incorporate organic material and coarse sand into the existing soil. A good amended soil recipe calls for one-third organic material, one-third coarse sand (river sand or builder's sand), and one-third existing soil. Make sure the sand you use is coarse sand. Fine sand and too little of it can cause more harm than good by filling in pores and making the soil like concrete. Mix these well and use as backfill. A few examples of organic material are leaf compost, horse or cow manure that has been composted for at least six months, and mushroom compost. These materials are available at local garden centers.

Plan to add more organic material to the soil every season. While mulch will help keep soil temperatures cooler in the summer and warmer in the winter, and will conserve moisture, it does not offer the same benefits that *topdressing* with an organic material does. Once the garden is established, you can topdress with organic material once in spring and once in fall. These materials will break down over time and provide welcome nutrients for the soil.

Perennials and Ornamental Grasses

Fertilizing

If you take the time to prepare your soil before you plant perennials, you should not have to fertilize on a regular basis. Still, some gardeners may want to fertilize new plants with a dilute solution of a liquid fertilizer like Peters® or Miracle-Gro®, at half the recommended rate. Spreading a thin layer (one to two inches) of compost or organic material such as well-composted manure over your perennial beds in spring and then again in fall will help ensure that your soil stays healthy. If you want to fertilize, three times a year is adequate, in spring, summer, and fall. When perennials are dormant, there is no need to fertilize.

Pest Control

Like all plants, perennials are susceptible to their share of insect and disease problems. One of the best ways to keep infestations to a minimum is to maintain healthy plants. Start with vigorous plants, and provide the proper environment like healthy soil, good air circulation, and water on a regular basis.

Monitor your garden by checking plants weekly during the growing season for signs of damage (chewed or discolored leaves). If there is a slight infestation of an insect or disease (less than one-third of the plant), try washing off the affected area with water or using insecticidal soap. If you use chemicals to control a particular pest, take extra caution, and always wear protective clothing and gloves. Treat problems before they get out of control. Whenever possible, consider an organic alternative before resorting to chemicals.

Watering

Too much water can be as harmful as too little. When perennials are newly planted, they will benefit from regular watering if there is not adequate rainfall (one inch per week—measure this by using a tuna fish can).

Here is a method to determine watering time: Dig down 2 inches, and if the soil is dry to the touch, it's time to water. Sandy soils may need watering more frequently than those that have a high clay content. Container gardens may need more frequent watering than perennials that are planted in the ground.

Best Picks
Perennials for Shade

Rick Berry, Nurseryman and Co-Owner of *Goodness Grows,* Lexington, Georgia, has been growing perennials for Georgia gardens for over twenty years. The list below represents some of his top contenders for gardening in the shade.

- *Amsonia hubrectii* **Arkansas Blue Star**
- *Arum italicum* **Arum**
- *Asarum* spp. **Ginger**
- *Begonia grandis* **Hardy Begonia**
- *Dryopteris erythrosora* **Autumn Fern**
- *Epimedium* hybrids **Barrenwort**
- *Heuchera* 'Amethyst Myst' **Alumroot**
- *Polygonatum odoratum* 'Variegatum' **Variegated Fragrant Solomon's Seal**
- *Rohdea japonica* **Sacred Lily**
- *Saxifraga stolonifera* **Strawberry Begonia**
- *Tricyrtis* spp. **Toad-Lily**

Perennials for Georgia

Botanical Name Common Name	Cultural Requirements	Average Height and Width	Comments
Achillea × 'Coronation Gold' Yarrow	Full sun; well-drained soil	2 to 4 feet by 3 feet	Yellow flowers in late spring. Divide in spring or fall. Good for drying.
Alcea rosea cultivars Hollyhock	Full sun; well-drained soil.	4 to 8 feet by 2 feet	Many selections both single and double forms; blooms in late spring or early summer. Easy to grow from seed.
Amsonia hubrectii Arkansas Blue Star	Full sun or partial shade; water during periods of dry weather.	2 to 3 feet by 3 feet	Feathery foliage, pale blue star-like flowers in spring. Plant turns golden yellow in fall.
Anemone × *hybrida* 'Honorine Jobert' Japanese Anemone	Partial shade and a well-drained soil.	2 to 4 feet by 2 feet	White flowers in fall. Not a good choice for coastal gardens.
Aquilegia canadensis Columbine	Shade and a moist soil, although they will tolerate sun.	2 to 3 feet by 1 foot	This native **Columbine** has yellow and red flowers which appear in early spring and last for weeks. A prolific seeder.
Artemesia hybrids and cultivars Wormwood	Sun and well-drained soil.	2 to 4 feet by 4 feet	Silver-gray foliage looks good most of the year. Prune in spring or summer only. Not a good choice for coastal gardens.
Arum italicum Italian Arum	Shade and a moist soil.	12 to 20 inches by 18 inches	New foliage appears in fall and lasts through winter.
Asarum shuttleworthii 'Callaway' Mottled Wild Ginger	Moist, well-drained woodlands.	4 to 9 inches by 8 inches, a very slow grower	Mottled evergreen heart-shaped leaves, this native is an aristocrat.
Asclepias tuberosa Butterfly Weed	Sun, average garden soils.	2 to 3 feet by 2 feet	Flowers in spring for up to six weeks in shades of red, orange, and yellow. Happy in a meadow or the garden.
Aster species and cultivars Aster	Sun, average garden soil.	Range in size from 6 inches to 8 feet tall by 9 inches to 4 feet wide.	No fall garden should be without asters. Cutting them back early in the season will keep plants compact and bushy.
Baptisia australis Wild Indigo	Full sun or partial shade, tolerates poor soil but moist, rich soil is best.	3 to 4 feet by 4 feet	Indigo blue flowers in spring followed by attractive seedpods in summer.
Begonia grandis Hardy Begonia	Shade, moist well-drained soil.	1 to 2 feet by 1 foot	Blooms with pink flowers late summer to early fall. Handsome leaves, reseeds easily.

Perennials for Georgia

Botanical Name / Common Name	Cultural Requirements	Average Height and Width	Comments
Belamcanda chinensis Blackberry Lily	Full sun or partial shade and average garden soil.	3 to 4 feet by 2 feet	Easy to grow; this iris relative produces orange flowers with red spots in summer and lots of shiny black seed in autumn.
Chrysanthemum hybrids Fall-Flowering Mums	Full sun, well-drained soil.	1 to 3 feet by 3 feet	Cut back three times during the growing season (until August 15) for full, more compact plants.
Coreopsis species and cultivars Coreopsis, Tickseed	Full sun, well-drained soil.	12 inches to 3 feet by 3 feet	Yellow flowers in summer, 'Moonbeam' and 'Zagreb' are good selections for Georgia.
Dianthus gratianopolitanus 'Bath's Pink' Cheddar Pinks	Full sun, well-drained soil.	9 to 12 inches by 12 inches	Fragrant pink flowers in spring, gray-green foliage all year-round.
Dryopteris erythrosora Autumn Fern	Shade and an average garden soil.	18 to 30 inches by 2 to 2½ feet	Evergreen in most parts of Georgia, new growth has bronze and pink tinges.
Echinacea purpurea Purple Coneflower	Full sun, well-drained soil.	2 to 3 feet by 2 feet	Purple ray flowers surround a brown cone. Deadheading helps prolong flowering.
Epimedium hybrids Barrenwort	Partial shade, moist, well-drained soil is best.	6 to 15 inches by 15 inches	Good groundcover for shade.
Eupatorium purpureum Joe-Pye Weed	Full sun to partial shade, moist soil.	5 to 7 feet by 3 to 4 feet	Big heads of mauve flowers in fall attract butterflies.
Gaillardia × *grandiflora* Blanket Flower	Full sun, well-drained soil.	2 to 3 feet by 2 feet	A mix of red and yellow, the flowers bloom summer until fall. Great for coastal gardens.
Geranium macrorrhizum Bigroot Geranium	Partial shade, moist, well-drained soil.	15 to 18 inches by 15 inches	Magenta flowers in spring, fragrant foliage.
Helleborus orientalis Lenten Rose	Partial to full shade, moist, well-drained soil.	15 to 18 inches by 15 inches	Evergreen foliage looks good year-round, flowers in late winter to early spring in white, purple, and maroon
Heuchera hybrids Alumroot, Coralbells	Partial shade with a moist, well-drained soil is best; will tolerate full sun with adequate moisture.	12 to 36 inches by 18 inches	Many great selections with colorful foliage, wonderful woodland plant.

Perennials for Georgia

Botanical Name Common Name	Cultural Requirements	Average Height and Width	Comments
Hosta × 'Royal Standard' Fragrant Hosta	Sun or partial shade, moist, well-drained soil.	2 to 3 feet by 3 feet	Tolerates sun more than most **Hostas,** fragrant flowers in late summer.
Iris tectorum Japanese Roof Iris	Full sun or partial shade, moist, well-drained soil.	12 to 18 inches by 18 inches	Blue or white flowers in spring, light green fan-like foliage looks good year-round.
Lantana camara 'Miss Huff' Hardy Lantana	Full sun, well-drained soil.	3 to 6 feet by 3 to 6 feet	Yellow, orange, and pink flowers attract butterflies in summer and fall. Good for coastal gardens.
Liatris spicata, Blazing Star, Gayfeather	Full sun or partial shade, moist, well-drained soil.	3 to 4 feet by 2 feet	Spikes of mauve flowers in summer.
Phlox subulata Moss Phlox	Full sun, well-drained soil.	6 to 9 inches by 12 inches	A carpet of flowers in early spring, found in blue, white, pink, and purple.
Polygonatum odoratum 'Variegatum' Variegated Fragrant Solomon's Seal	Shade, moist soil.	18 to 24 inches by 2 feet	Great foliage plant for the shade garden. Green leaves edged with a broad strip of creamy white.
Polystichum acrostichoides Christmas Fern	Partial shade to shade, moist soil.	12 to 18 inches by 12 inches	Tough evergreen fern, easy to grow.
Rosmarinus officinalis Rosemary	Full sun, moist, well-drained soil.	3 to 6 feet by 3 to 4 feet	Fragrant culinary herb, great for cooking.
Rudbeckia fulgida 'Goldsturm' Black-eyed Susan	Full sun, well-drained soil.	2 to 3 feet by 2 feet	Blooms summer to fall with bright orange-yellow flowers.
Saxifraga stolonifera Strawberry Begonia	Shade, average garden soil.	4 to 6 inches by 12 inches	Stoloniferous habit makes it a good groundcover for shade.
Sedum 'Autumn Joy' Autumn Joy Sedum	Full sun or partial shade, well-drained soil.	12 to 24 inches by 24 inches	Flowers start out green in summer and then turn pink and maroon in fall.
Tricyrtis species Toad-Lily	Full or partial shade, moist, well-drained soil.	1 to 3 feet by 2 feet	Orchid-like flowers in late summer to autumn.
Verbena 'Homestead Purple' Homestead Purple Verbena	Full sun, well-drained soil.	8 to 18 inches by 3 feet	Rich purple flowers in spring and then on and off until frost.

Planning

This is the ideal time to plan your perennial garden.

- Begin by making a wish list of the plants you'd like to include, grouping those that have similar cultural requirements. Include varieties that shine for each season so you can have a progression of blooms and interesting foliage.

- *Sketch* potential designs on graph paper, remembering that once you begin to plant, your plan may change.

- Leave space in your plan to add annual color.

- When you design your garden, remember that several plants of one variety will make more of an impact than single examples of many different varieties.

Siting your perennials against a backdrop of evergreens, a hedge, a fence, or a stone wall will help define your garden and provide structure all year long.

- *Record* weather conditions in your Garden Journal. Keep track of areas in your garden where the soil stays wet all the time. Plan to correct this problem before you plant, or select perennials that will tolerate this environment.

- *Record* what you plant, when you plant it, and the source of your plants.

- Take a photograph of the garden while everything is dormant.

Planting

In south Georgia, perennials can be planted any time they are available.

In north Georgia, it is best to begin planting in late February or early March unless the weather is extremely mild and plants have been grown in containers outdoors for one full growing season ("extremely mild" means the ground isn't frozen and the temperatures have not dropped down to freezing every night). Hardy perennials normally stay outside all year long. This means they are acclimated to the fluctuations that occur with the weather. If they have been grown in a greenhouse, they will not be ready to plant outside until the threat of frost has passed.

If you are uncertain about the frost-free date in your region, check with the Cooperative Extension Service. (See Resources, p. 353.)

Certain unusual varieties of perennials may only be available as seeds. Order seeds now to start indoors under lights. (See February.)

Watering

If temperatures are mild, plants can dry out. Keep them watered and mulched.

Water newly planted perennials (those planted within the past twelve months) once a week if there is not adequate rainfall (1 inch). Use a tuna fish can to measure rainfall.

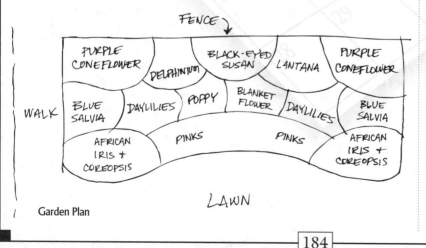

FENCE

PURPLE CONEFLOWER	DELPHINIUM	BLACK-EYED SUSAN	LANTANA	PURPLE CONEFLOWER
BLUE SALVIA	DAYLILIES	POPPY	BLANKET FLOWER	DAYLILIES	BLUE SALVIA
AFRICAN IRIS + COREOPSIS	PINKS	PINKS	AFRICAN IRIS + COREOPSIS

WALK

LAWN

Garden Plan

If you can't tell by a physical inspection whether plants need water, *feel the soil.* If it is dry to the touch when you dig down 2 or more inches, it's time to water. If you don't have many perennials and want to water by hand, 2 gallons of water for a 1-gallon-size plant should be adequate.

Fertilizing

In south Georgia, you can *fertilize* newly planted perennials with a half-strength mix of a liquid like Peters® or Miracle-Gro®.

In north Georgia, there is no need to fertilize your perennials when they are dormant. Now is a good time to amend soil in new beds so you will be ready to plant in the spring. Spread 2 to 4 inches of compost or manure across an area, and mix it in a good 12 inches with the rototiller.

If you have your soil test report on hand, it is good to add the recommended lime, potassium, and phosphorus as you till. These nutrients do not dissolve easily in water or move as freely into the soil as nitrogen does.

Pest Control

Look for infestations of chickweed, a mat-forming winter annual. The leaves are opposite and densely hairy; the white, notched flowers appear in clusters at the ends of the stems. If a crop appears, pull them out before they set seed.

The best time to weed is the day after a gentle rain when plants are easy to pull up, roots and all.

Remove any dead leaves that have accumulated around perennials. This will help eliminate insects that may be overwintering.

Scale can be white or brown and often look crusty. They appear in clusters on the bark, stems, and leaves of plants. *Use horticultural oils to suffocate insects like scale or other pests (see Chemicals, p. 327).*

Grooming

Remove any dead stalks, seedpods, or leaves you missed in the fall. Wait until early spring, just before perennials begin to put out new growth, before you prune plants back hard, to a height of several inches. Some perennials don't need to be pruned back hard, but you can tidy them up by removing dead flower stalks. Perennials that don't require much pruning include:

- *Anemone × hybrida*
- *Asarum shuttleworthii* '*Callaway*'
- *Begonia grandis*
- *Heuchera americana* cvs.
- *Saxifraga stolonifera*
- *Sedum kamtschaticum*
- *Veronica prostrata*

In south Georgia, *cut back* clumps of **Pampas Grass** and other ornamental grasses to a height of 12 to 24 inches.

Planning

Take a soil sample and have it tested by your local Cooperative Extension Service (see Horticultural Practices, p. 7). You will receive a report that describes the nutrients present in your soil, the amounts in which they are present, and specific recommendations for correct fertilizer use. A soil test will also determine the pH of your soil and the amount of lime it needs.

The pH affects the availability of nutrients and whether they are soluble in the soil. A pH of 7 indicates that the soil is neutral. A pH below 7 indicates acidity, and one above 7 indicates alkalinity. Acid-loving plants like **Rhododendrons, Camellias,** and **Azaleas** are happiest in a soil with a pH of less than 5.5. Lime is applied in gardens primarily to raise the pH.

Lime also has a physical effect on soil: in clay soils, it causes particles to form larger units and therefore enables water and air to move more easily through the soil (for information on lime applications refer to Lawns, p. 151). In sandy soils, lime holds particles together so that water is held for a longer time.

As a rule, the rate of application for lime is 4 pounds per 100 square feet. When you apply lime, it is best to make sure that you rototill it in to a depth of 4 to 6 inches. This can be done when you prepare the soil for planting as you add other soil amendments.

Planting and Transplanting

In milder parts of the state you can begin to prepare the soil for planting now, provided it is not too wet (wet soils with a high percentage of clay can turn into large impervious clods). Scoop up a handful of soil and *squeeze* it. If it crumbles easily, the soil should be dry enough to work in.

Rototill to a depth of 12 inches, adding soil amendments as you go. The particular materials you add to the soil will be determined by the type of soil you have. Heavy clay soils will need lots of organic materials (this helps improve drainage, adds microbes, and improves the overall soil structure) and some coarse sand; sandy soils will benefit from incorporating some clay along with organic materials. Organic materials such as mushroom compost, cow manure, horse manure, cottonseed meal, or ground pine bark are all good choices for amendments.

Start perennials from seed indoors under lights. Some seeds require stratification before they will germinate. Referred to as "after-ripening" they may require either a cold-moist or warm-moist treatment. Leaving seeds in a polyethylene bag in the refrigerator for one to four months at 40 degrees Fahrenheit will accomplish this. Other seeds need to be soaked in hot water and then given the cold treatment described above. Some seeds need to have their seed coats broken mechanically before they will germinate. Some need light to germinate and should not be covered with soil.

Read the backs of seed packets to determine what conditions individual perennials require to germinate.

As a general rule, allow six to eight weeks from the time you sow perennial seed indoors until the seedlings will be ready to transplant to the garden.

Certain perennials like **Hollyhocks** are difficult to transplant.

Seeds should be sown in individual peat pots so the roots won't be disturbed when you plant them in the garden.

You can also sow seeds in flats, plastic cell-packs, or individual pots. Whichever type of container you use, make sure to punch holes in the bottom for drainage.

Chain and "S" Hook

Fluorescent
Light

(6) ½" Tee

9⅜"

(8) ½" 45° Elbows

(4) ½" 90° Elbows

1'-6⅝"

1'-0'

1½" Long Blind Plug

1'-5¼"

1'-10"

4'-2"

PVC Portable Light Stand

If you use fluorescent lights to start seedlings, your setup should provide 15 to 20 watts per square foot of growing area.

Watering

Water containers during mild spells. *Water* perennials in the ground if the weather is windy for several days. Check them weekly—if there is not adequate rainfall (1 inch or more per week) and the ground is not frozen, plan to water.

Keep the seedlings you're starting indoors moist; a spray bottle of water is an effective way to water seedlings.

Fertilizing

Once seedlings germinate and are a few weeks old, *fertilize* them with a complete liquid fertilizer at half-strength like Peters® 20-20-20 or another with a similar ratio.

Pest Control

During mild spells (when temperatures are such that working outdoors in a long-sleeved shirt is comfortable—in other words, you don't need a hat and gloves), *reapply* a granular weed preventer. (The best time to apply it is in September in established perennial beds to prevent future crops of chickweed

and other winter weeds from taking over. Read the label carefully before applying (see Chemicals, p. 327).

In extreme South Georgia, *inspect* your perennials for signs of aphids or other insects.

Use a strong blast from the hose or an insecticidal soap to control them. Horticultural oils are also an option; they work by smothering insects (see Chemicals, p. 327).

Helpful Hint

To learn more about growing plants from seed, check course offerings at your local botanical garden. (See Resources, p. 353.)

Planning

If a scoop of soil holds together but crumbles easily, it is dry enough so you can begin planting hardy perennials. Have a list of plants and a plan ready. Local garden centers and nurseries should have a fresh supply of plants for sale now.

Planting and Transplanting

When you purchase perennials, remember that you are investing in a root system. If you start with a weak plant, it will take twice as long as a strong healthy plant before you can expect a big flowering show, as the plant will put all its energy into developing a strong root system. When you ease a rootball out of the pot, you should see fleshy roots covering at least 50 percent of the soil. If they are dried out and brittle, or if there are only a few, this indicates a weak root system.

This is the time to plant bare-root perennials, while temperatures are mild and many plants are still dormant. **Peonies** are often sold bare-root, as are certain varieties of perennials that are available only by mail-order. Before you plant bare-root perennials, *cut off* any broken roots or those that are dried up; *soak* the roots in a bucket of water while you prepare the planting hole.

Tips for dividing perennials:

1 Perennials with lots of fibrous roots can be dug up with a spade or shovel. Get a big clump—more roots are better than fewer roots.

2 Gently pull apart the roots by hand. Cut off any damaged or dead roots.

3 Replant divisions immediately.

4 Water, and apply a 2-inch layer of mulch.

Some perennials should be divided by hand, not with a sharp spade or digging fork, but by digging up a large clump and then teasing apart the roots, making sure shoots are attached to each section:

- *Aquilegia* spp. Columbine
- *Epimedium* hybrids Epimedium (after they flower)
- *Gaillardia* spp. Blanket Flower
- *Geranium* spp. Hardy Geranium
- *Helleborus* spp. Hellebore (after they flower)
- *Heuchera* spp. Coralbell

Other perennials can be divided with the fork or spade technique, in early spring. You can use two pitchforks back to back, or a pitchfork (or digging fork) and a spade to pull

apart the rootballs. Try this method with the following plants:

- *Achillea filipendulina* Yarrow
- *Anemone × hybrida* Japanese Anemone
- *Aster* spp. Aster
- *Boltonia asteroides* Boltonia
- *Chrysanthemum* spp. Chrysanthemum
- *Coreopsis verticillata* Coreopsis
- *Dianthus* spp. Pinks, Carnation
- *Echinacea purpurea* Purple Coneflower
- *Hemerocallis* spp. Daylily
- *Hosta* spp. Hosta
- *Monarda* spp. Beebalm
- *Phlox paniculata* Garden Phlox
- *Rudbeckia* spp. Black-eyed Susan

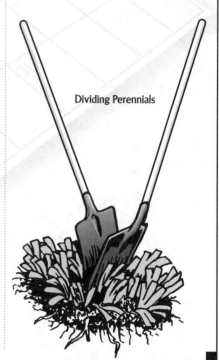

Dividing Perennials

Watering

Water all new plantings and transplants once a week for the first month after they are planted.

Water established plantings once every two weeks if you don't get 1 or more inches of rain.

Fertilizing

If your perennials are in a healthy soil, it is not necessary to use a commercial fertilizer on a regular basis. Instead, consider top-dressing with an organic material such as compost, cow manure, horse manure, or other bagged product. *Spread* the organic material about 1 inch thick, keeping it away from the stems and crown of the plant (the crown is the center of the plant where stems and buds originate). If you do use a chemical fertilizer, apply 1 pound of a complete fertilizer such as 10-10-10 per 10x10-foot square. *Water in* the fertilizer. Too little fertilizer is always better than too much.

Pest Control

Look for yellow or discolored leaves, stippling (dark tiny spots) on leaves, sticky sap, and other signs of insects.

Treat with horticultural oils or insecticidal soaps as needed. Handweed on a weekly basis to help keep weeds at a minimum.

It's not too late to use a granular weed-preventer in your perennial beds if you didn't use one in February (see Chemicals, p. 327).

Read the directions carefully before applying.

Grooming

Cut back your ornamental grasses to a height of about 6 to 12 inches just before or just as new growth is beginning in early spring.

If you have evergreen ornamental grasses such as *Carex*, *pull out* the dead, brown sections. New growth will fill in within a few weeks.

Clean up any remaining leaf litter, dead stalks, or seedpods from the previous season. Now is the time to *cut back* perennials, before new growth begins.

Certain perennials like *Artemisia* 'Powis Castle' and other **Artemisias** can get large and overgrown in one season; it is best to cut them back now, at the beginning of the growing season, rather than in the fall. If they are cut back in the fall, they may not have time to recover before

Double Digging

This labor-intensive method for preparing a planting bed is a favorite of many long-time gardeners.

1 Using a spade, dig up the top 10 inches or more of the soil and set it aside.

2 Dig the subsoil layer, incorporating organic material to a depth of about 10 inches.

3 Amend with organic material the topsoil layer that you set aside, and then place it back on top of the amended subsoil.

The new planting bed will provide a healthy planting bed for years. If you use this method, you can work on one area of the garden each season instead of tackling your entire garden at one time. Amending and tilling the soil this thoroughly is sure to reward you with lush, healthy plants. Continue to feed your soil by topdressing it with organic materials once or twice a year.

the winter, and the plant is sometimes killed back.

Reduce the size of an individual plant by 1/2 or more. Provided you keep it watered, it will fill out within a few weeks.

Planning

If you don't have a plan for your perennial garden, now is the time to create one (see January).

Planting and Transplanting

Divide and transplant perennials.

The best time to divide ornamental grasses is in the spring, just as new growth is beginning. Certain grasses like *Miscanthus* **spp.** and *Pennisetum* **spp.** can develop into large clumps and may require a handsaw to divide them. Make sure each division has roots and shoots before you replant it.

Certain perennials like *Amsonia* **spp.** and *Astilbe* **hybrids** can also be divided with a handsaw in the spring; make sure each division has new shoots and roots.

Harden-off perennial seedlings:

1 Take seedlings outside, and place them in a shaded area, gradually exposing them to more sun each day.

2 Once they are acclimated to the outside environment, you can plant them in the garden. A week to ten days should be long enough for the acclimation.

If seedlings were sown in individual peat pots, you can plant the pot directly into the ground. A few cuts with your pruners into the bottom of the pot will stimulate roots to become established more quickly. Keep peat pots moist while seeds are germinating and when you transplant them to the garden.

If you want to purchase plants, local nurseries and garden centers should have a good selection of perennials from which to choose.

Space plants to allow enough room for growth. Keep in mind that you may have to move or divide plants next year if they get too large.

Watering

For the first few months you may need to *water* every few days if temperatures are high and plants are planted in full sun. After this initial period, check plants once a week for the first growing season. If you do not receive 1 inch of rainfall per week, applying 2 gallons of water per 1-gallon-size perennial should be adequate.

Containers should be checked daily and may need more frequent watering than plants that are planted in the ground. *Water* when the soil 1 to 2 inches deep is dry to the touch.

Fertilizing

If you haven't fertilized yet, you can apply a complete fertilizer like 10-10-10 at a rate of 1 pound per 100 square feet. If you have soil that has been amended with organic amendments, you won't have to fertilize your perennials every month. If you want to fertilize, three times a year (spring, summer, and fall) is plenty.

Pest Control

Check perennials for aphids or other insects; if needed, treat with insecticidal soap or horticultural oils.

If 50 percent or more of the plant is infested, it is advisable that you spray with a contact insecticide (see Chemicals, p. 327).

Look for signs of slugs or slug damage on plants like **Hostas:** the leaves may be chewed, and often there is a silver trail on the leaves or on the ground near the plant.

Use a slug bait to control them. (See Chemicals, p. 327.)

Continue handweeding. *Spot-spray* weeds in perennial beds with a non-selective weedkiller.

Cover perennials with a piece of newspaper to keep any spray from drifting onto desirable plants.

Grooming

Prune back Lantana unless you live in south Georgia where it is evergreen. Even if these plants were overgrown last fall, it is best to prune them now in early spring when they are actively growing. You can cut back $1/3$ to $1/2$ of the total plant, and it will quickly recover.

Helpful Hints

If you have any perennials that need staking, plan ahead. Right about the time the flower buds begin to show color is the best time to stake. You can use a single stake or a series of stakes for multistemmed plants; bamboo stakes work well. For tying, use green or natural-colored jute twine, which will blend in better than white string.

- Certain perennials like **Peonies** or *Phlox paniculata* can be staked now with a circular gridded ring placed on top of three stakes. The stakes should be evenly spaced and adjustable. As the plant grows up through the openings, the ring will keep the plant from flopping over when it is in full flower. This type of stake is called a "grow thru" or a metal hoop support.

- For single-stem plants like **Lilies,** place the stake about an inch from the main stem, and tie jute to the stake, leaving 2- to 4-inch loose ends. Bring the **Lily** stem close to the stake, and tie the loose ends around it.

Staking
Perennials
with a Hoop

- Another method for staking is to use the twiggy prunings from your trees, cut into various 16- to 20-inch lengths. Stick them into the ground all around young plants when plants are about half their expected height, and in no time the plants will cover the stakes. This works well when there are lots of perennials in one area or for plants like **Beebalm** that have many stems.

If you want to keep the amount of staking to a minimum, plant your garden so that one variety of perennial supports another. Early-blooming **Shasta Daisies** make a good mass to plant in front of **Salvias,** which will bloom later.

Staking Perennials with a
Single Stake

Planning

Many perennials are now in bloom or beginning to bloom. Think about the rest of the season and what the garden will look like. Incorporating perennials that have interesting foliage and distinctive forms will help the garden have interest even when there are no flowers. When you plant your perennials, remember to leave space for colorful annuals. And remember that white flowers combine well with most other colors in the garden or help to separate one area of color from another.

Photograph the garden at least once in spring, and write the names of the the spring bloomers in your Garden Journal.

Planting and Transplanting

Continue adding perennials to the garden, including varieties that will bloom in summer and fall like **Salvias, Asters, Chrysanthemums,** and *Helenium autumnale.* Start with healthy plants that have clean foliage and a good root system.

Gently ease the plant out of the pot before you purchase it. If the rootball is covered with roots that are white and fleshy, then the roots are healthy. If there are more roots than soil, the root system may be stressed. If you have purchased a plant that has been grown in the same container for a long period of time it may be "potbound."

If it is potbound, cut the container down one side and ease the plant out. Make two or three clean cuts into the rootball at various points around the ball to loosen the roots. Gently pull them apart, and spread them out in the planting hole. The plant should adjust and begin to grow where you plant it.

The perennials listed below should be divided in spring after they finish blooming:

*   *Dicentra* spp. **Bleeding Heart** (divide by hand)

*   *Iris sibirica* **Japanese Iris** (use a spade or hand saw to divide)

*   *Iris tectorum* **Japanese Roof Iris** (use a spade or handsaw to divide)

Watering

Continue watering new plantings on a weekly schedule. If you have an automatic irrigation system, you will need to adjust its schedule according to the amount of rainfall.

*   It is better for your plants if the system comes on once a week or every few days rather than every day.

*   Keep track of how much water plants receive. Note this in your Garden Journal.

*   Long, slow, thorough watering is best. Allow the soil to dry out between waterings.

Fertilizing

Applying a dilute solution of a liquid fertilizer such as 15-30-15 directly to the foliage of new plantings will give them an added boost. Young leaves absorb the fertilizer quickly. It is best to apply foliar feeds early in the day before the intense heat sets in.

Pest Control

Use insecticidal soap to control insects like aphids, spider mites, thrips, and whiteflies. Apply spray during the early morning before temperatures get too hot (check the label for recommendations).

Spray the plant to the point where the spray is dripping, being sure to cover the undersides of the leaves (see Chemicals, p. 327).

Continue to handweed. Pulling weeds before they flower or set seeds will help reduce future weed infestations.

Spot-spray with a nonselective weedkiller to control weeds, using extreme caution around perennials and other desirable plants (see Chemicals, p. 327).

If the leaves of your **Columbine** are discolored and have a series of silver trails running through them, the problem is leaf miners. The best and easiest treatment is to shear off plants to the ground and destroy the infected foliage after the **Columbine** finishes flowering. A new flush of

growth will quickly replace the old leaves.

Although it is not immune to pests, the native **Columbine, Aquilegia canadensis** *is less susceptible to leaf miners.*

Grooming

Deadheading
Perennials

Depending on the type of plant, deadheading (removing spent blossoms from flowers) can encourage perennials to produce more flowers. Experiment with your favorite plants. Plants that send up more flowers if you deadhead include:

- *Gaillardia* × *grandiflora*
- *Gaura lindheimeri*
- *Scabiosa* 'Butterfly Blue'
- *Verbena bonariensis*
- *Veronica* 'Sunny Border Blue'

Cut or pinch back fall-blooming **Chrysanthemums** and **Asters** by 1/3 and you will have fuller plants in the fall.

Cutting back certain perennials will often delay their flowering by a few weeks and prevent them from flopping over when they finally do bloom. This type of pruning should be done about eight weeks before plants are expected to bloom. Plants that respond to this procedure include *Phlox paniculata* and **Asters.**

Experiment with pruning. If you have a group of one type of plant such as **Beebalm,** *cut back* some of the plants and let the others progress naturally. This method will give you staggered bloom times, which means you will have flowers over a longer period of time.

Planning

Make notes in your Garden Journal about how plants are performing, color combinations that you like, and plants that, based on their performance, may be in the wrong spot. Be sure to list the sources of plants you like so you'll be able to get more of the same. Have you included a variety of perennials to ensure that there is always something of interest in your garden, be it flowers, leaf form, or texture?

Use perennials that complement your existing shrubs and trees. For example, *Robinia pseudoacacia* **'Frisia'** has golden-yellow leaves, and so does *Spiraea* **'Ogon'**; two perennials that complement a planting of these two are the **Variegated Fragrant Solomon's Seal** (green leaves with white edges) and the white-flowered **Fleabane** called *Erigeron karvinskianus* 'Profusion'.

Planting and Transplanting

Continue adding container-grown perennials to your garden. Make sure the soil is prepared before you plant. *Water and mulch* as soon as you get new plants in the ground; this will help keep soil temperatures cooler.

Late spring or early summer is a good time to propagate certain perennials by division, including *Lysimachia nummularia* and *Astilbe*—you may sacrifice a few blooms for one season, but the plants will be robust next year.

Dividing Perennials

Propagate the following perennials by cuttings:

- *Amsonia tabernaemontana*
- *Dianthus plumarius*
- *Monarda didyma*
- *Phlox divaricata*
- *Salvia* × *superba*
- *Sedum kamtschaticum*
- *Sedum spectabile*
- *Verbena tenuisecta*
- *Veronica spicata*

Watering

Water new plantings once a week if there is no rain. As a rule of thumb, apply 2 gallons of water for a 1-gallon-size plant; if plants are smaller, they will need a bit less water. If you use a sprinkler, set out a couple of shallow cans (tuna fish cans work great) to measure the water. You will have applied enough water as soon as the cans contain $3/4$ inch.

Fertilizing

For a quick boost, apply a foliar fertilizer to newly-planted perennials. Use a dilute solution of a water-soluble fertilizer like Peters® 20-20-20 or Miracle-Gro® 15-30-15, following the label directions for half the recommended rate or less. Wait until fall to fertilize established plants.

Pest Control

During hot, humid weather, problems like powdery mildew on **Phlox, Beebalm,** and other perennials may be a problem. To make an organic spray for powdery mildew, combine 1 tablespoon baking soda and 1 tablespoon Sunspray® Ultra-Fine Horticultural Oil in 1 gallon of water. Mix well, and *spray* the plants completely, being sure to wet both tops and undersides of the leaves.

Apply spray early in the day before temperatures get too hot. Avoid spraying when temperatures get above 90 degrees Fahrenheit, as this may burn the plants.

Check for insects, and treat as needed, using insecticidal soaps whenever possible to control problems like aphids, spider mites, and whiteflies.

If you have small infestations of Japanese beetles on **Hollyhocks** or other plants, approach them slowly, *handpick*, and drop them into a jar of soapy water. (See Roses, June.)

Spot-spray weeds in your perennial beds with a nonselective weedkiller (see Chemicals, p. 327).

Handpull weeds that are immediately next to desirable plants that might be harmed by chemical controls.

Grooming

Keep leaf litter at a minimum by pruning off any dead or diseased stems, leaves, or branches.

Continue deadheading perennials to encourage more blooms (refer to Perennials, May; and Horticultural Practices, p. 7).

Helpful Hints

Dry shade is a challenge that many Georgia gardeners face when they have a landscape where tree roots are competing with perennials for moisture. Here is a list of perennials (including a few perennial ornamental grasses) that will thrive in dry shade, even under a large mature tree:

- *Carex* **'Evergold'** (variegated green-and-white foliage lights up the shade garden)

- *Carex* spp. (there are a number of selections of this adaptable ornamental grass)

- *Epimedium* spp. **Barrenwort** (many different selections)

- *Euphorbia robbiae* **Mrs. Robb's Bonnet**

- *Helleborus orientalis* **Lenten Rose** (evergreen foliage, and showy flowers in late winter to early spring)

- *Polygonatum odoratum* **'Variegatum' Variegated Fragrant Solomon's Seal** (grows to 3½ feet tall)

- *Sedum ternatum* **Whorled Stonecrop**

- *Senecio aureus* **Golden Groundsel** (evergreen foliage, yellow daisylike flowers in early spring)

Cut back fall-blooming **Chrysanthemums** now, and you will have bushier plants which won't be as likely to fall over once they begin blooming.

Cut back fall-blooming plants like **Joe-Pye Weed, Swamp Sunflower,** and **Iron Weed** now so that you won't have to stake them in autumn.

Planning

During these hot months, early morning or evening is the coolest time to work in the garden. This is a good time to edge your flower beds and think about planting projects for the fall. It's amazing how edging your flower beds with stone or brick can give your garden a more refined look, setting it off from lawn areas. Here are some ideas for edging flower beds:

- Use a straight-edge shovel to dig into the soil at a slight angle toward the flower bed; be sure to dig down at least 4 inches. *Fill* the trench you have created with the same mulch you use on your flower beds—this will delineate the bed line and separate it from the lawn.

- If you use brick or stone for edging, be sure to start with a level area if the bricks are upright, making sure $1/3$ is buried in the soil; sand is a good filler and will help the bricks settle.

- Other materials to use for edging include treated wood strips, metal, or plastic buried several inches in the soil.

Photograph your garden, and make a list of summer bloomers in your Garden Journal.

Planting and Transplanting

If you add any plants to the garden now, keep in mind that they will probably not put out many roots until soil temperatures cool off. Here are a few tips for planting in the summer:

- Start with healthy plants that already have a robust root system.

- Restrict your planting and transplanting to the shade garden during the hot summer months. Minimize planting in sunny areas since root growth is at a minimum in high temperatures.

- *Water and mulch* immediately after planting.

Watering

Water established perennials during a prolonged dry spell (a month or longer without significant rainfall). About 1 inch per week should be enough.

- Attaching a water wand to your hose can make this chore much easier. Not only is the water more evenly dispersed through the many holes on the end of the breaker, an on/off valve will mean a lot less wasted water.

- Soaker hoses are also an option. Place them in your perennial flower beds, and *cover* them with a light coat of mulch. Be sure to *inspect* them periodically to see how well they are working.

- If you are growing perennials in decorative containers, you can add a granular product designed to absorb and release water in the soil (see Annuals, August). If you do this, be sure to adjust your watering frequency—you will have to experiment, but if you want to be certain you do not overwater, water only when the top 2-inch depth of the soil is dry.

- If you use sprinklers that are set according to timers, you will have to adjust them when there are changes in weather such as rainy days.

Fertilizing

Don't fertilize now. The hot weather makes plants more susceptible to problems, especially if they are encouraged to put on lots of new growth.

Pest Control

Check for aphids, spider mites, and thrips. Sometimes a strong blast of water will get rid of them; insecticidal soaps and horticultural oils can also be effective.

Southern blight is a soilborne fungus that causes stem rot at the soil level and can spread to surrounding plants. If plants are infected, *remove and destroy* them. Leave the area unplanted for six months (if you do plant in the infected area before six months are up, be sure to amend the soil with coarse sand, which will improve drainage). Plants often affected include **Artemisia, Aster, Columbine, Liatris, Phlox, Salvia,** and **Shasta Daisy.** To reduce this problem:

1 Keep mulch away from plant stems.

2 Avoid overwatering.

3 Don't grow the same varieties of plants in the same spot year after year.

4 Good sanitation is also critical. *Collect and destroy* dead and diseased leaves.

Spot-spray weeds in perennial beds with a nonselective weedkiller; use extreme caution around desirable plants (see Chemicals, p. 327). Continue to handpull weeds.

Organic Methods of Controlling Slugs

- Use orange or grapefruit rinds or black plastic cell-packs (six- or eight-packs in which annuals or vegetables are sold). Place the rinds or cell-packs under and near the leaves of susceptible plants. Mostly nocturnal, slugs seek dark, moist areas. In the morning, remove the rinds and cell-packs along with the slugs.

- Use a physical barrier like a 3-inch-wide strip of copper around susceptible plants.

- Slugs avoid areas that are dusty and scratchy. Sprinkle diatomaceous earth, sharp sand, or crushed eggshells around plants that slugs prefer (**Hostas** are a favorite of slugs). Their soft bodies are sensitive to sharp edges, and they can die from dehydration.

- Another popular method for controlling slugs is to place the lid of a large mayonnaise jar next to the plants that may be attacked. Fill the lid with beer, and the slugs will drown.

Grooming

Prune back by ¹⁄₃ to ¹⁄₂ fall-blooming perennials like **Asters, Chrysanthemums,** *Helianthus,* and *Heliopsis*. This will result in fuller plants that shouldn't require staking, although sometimes the flowers will be a bit smaller. Be sure to do this pruning at least eight weeks before the plants would normally bloom.

Fall-blooming perennials begin blooming in September, with other varieties continuing well into October and November.

Continue to *deadhead* repeat bloomers like *Echinacea purpurea,* **Rudbeckia 'Goldsturm',** *Scabiosa,* **Stokesia, Salvias,** and *Verbena*. This will encourage more blooms over a longer period. Plants like **Yarrow** (*Achillea* **spp.**) may or may not bloom again but will be much tidier if you *cut off* the dead flower stalks.

Shear *Coreopsis verticillata* 'Moonbeam' for a second flush of bloom.

Planning

This is a good month to assess the successes and failures in your perennial garden. Make a list of plants you would like to add to the garden in fall once the weather begins to cool off a bit.

Plants for fall blooms or colorful foliage:
(FL = colorful foliage F = flowers)

- *Amsonia hubrectii* . . . . . . FL
- *Anemone × hybrida* 'Honorine Jobert' . . . . F
- *Aster* spp. . . . . F
- *Chrysanthemum* 'Apricot Single' . . . . F
- *Eupatorium purpureum* . . . F
- *Helenium autumnale* . . . . . F
- *Sedum* 'Autumn Joy' . . . . . F

Make a list in your Garden Journal of plants that will need to be divided in fall. If plants are healthy and thriving, you don't have to divide them unless they are getting too large for the space they are growing in.

Planting

You may want to refurbish your decorative container plantings by adding perennials that offer fall blooms or colorful foliage. Another way to brighten up your perennial garden at this time of year is to add some fall and winter annuals.

Plant container-grown ornamental grasses that bloom in fall or that have colorful autumn foliage. After they finish blooming, many of the seedheads provide interest well into winter. Grasses with attractive foliage or persistent seedheads include:

- *Miscanthus sinensis* 'Gracillimus' **Maiden Grass** (5 to 6 feet tall)
- *Miscanthus sinensis* var. *strictus* **Porcupine Grass** (yellow band on green foliage)
- *Panicum virgatum* 'Shenandoah' (a selection of **Switch Grass** with burgundy-red and green foliage)
- *Pennisetum* spp. **Fountain Grass** (flowers are like foxtails and persist into winter)

Watering

Keep perennials watered during the hot dry days, but don't overwater. Feel the soil, and if the top 2-inch depth is dry, it's time to water. A thorough soaking once a week should be adequate if there is no rain. Water plants using a hose at the base of the plant. If you do use a sprinkler, place small cans nearby (tuna fish cans work well), and *water* until there is 3/4 to 1 inch of water in the can.

Avoid overhead-watering plants like *Phlox paniculata* or *Monarda* spp. that are susceptible to powdery mildew. Keeping the foliage dry will minimize this problem.

Fertilizing

Don't fertilize until fall. Fertilizing now will encourage new growth at a time when plants are under stress from heat and drought, making them more susceptible to pest and disease problems.

Scrape away old mulch and add a new 2- to 3-inch layer; this will dress up your garden and help conserve soil moisture.

Pest Control

Continue to *check* perennials for insect and pest problems. Whenever possible, use insecticidal soaps to control infestations of aphids, mites, whiteflies, and other bugs.

Whether you use organic or chemical controls, apply them only as needed.

Perennials with Attractive Seedheads for Fall or Winter Interest

- *Baptisia australis* **Blue False Indigo** (black pods 2 to 3 inches long)

- *Clematis macropetala* and *C. tangutica* (both these species have silky seedheads that persist into winter)

- *Iris foetidissima* **Gladwin Iris** (large seed capsules open in fall to display orange-scarlet seeds)

- *Rudbeckia fulgida* var. *sullivantii* 'Goldsturm' (brown balls of seeds)

- *Sedum* 'Autumn Joy' (flowers start out looking like a head of broccoli, then turn pink, and finally maroon)

If your plants have white powder or black spots on their leaves, they could be suffering from a fungus.

If more than 50 percent of the plant is infected, you may want to throw the plant out and start with a new plant. If only a portion of the plant is infected, there are fungicide sprays you can apply (see Chemicals, p. 327).

Keeping plants groomed will also help reduce problems. Apply any sprays during the coolest part of the day, in early morning or early evening.

This way you will avoid a chemical reaction which can occur when the insecticide reacts with high temperatures and bright sunshine, causing leaf scorch.

Columbines are often affected by leaf miners, which damage the foliage and leave it looking unsightly.

Simply cut off the foliage to within an inch of the base and you should get a flush of new growth that will be pest-free.

Groom plants like **Lamb's Ear** *Stachys* **'Countess Helen von Stein'**. *Remove* leaves that are yellow, brown, or mushy.

This will increase air circulation and encourage the plant to put out new growth.

Continue handweeding.

Removing weeds while they are in flower and before they set seed will help reduce weed infestations next year.

Grooming

- Perennials like **Salvia** will continue to bloom well into fall if you keep them deadheaded: *pinch or snip off* the faded blossoms so that the plant puts its energy into making more flowers and not setting seed.

- *Remove* yellow or diseased leaves of **Iris,** but leave the seedpods for winter interest.

Collect seeds from your favorite perennials as the seedheads dry. Seeds that require no pretreatment, such as cold stratification or scarification, can be stored in the refrigerator until spring when they can be sown outdoors; store them dry in airtight containers or tightly sealed plastic bags. Plants with such seeds are:

- *Aquilegia canadensis* **Columbine**
- *Asclepias tuberosa* **Butterfly Weed**
- *Aster* spp. **Aster**
- *Belamcanda chinensis* **Blackberry Lily**
- *Liatris* spp. **Blazing Star**
- *Scabiosa caucasica* **Pincushion Flower**

Planning

This is a good month to refurbish your perennial garden if it is getting overgrown and tired-looking. Decide which plants to add and which to divide or move to another location. Think about the form and texture of individual plants; include types with attractive foliage as well as those with beautiful flowers. Consider all the seasons. Here is a list of plants that offer three to four seasons of interest:

S = sun lover   SH = shade lover

- *Amsonia hubrectii* **Amsonia** (green feathery foliage in spring, blue flowers, yellow fall color, tawny foliage in winter) S

- *Artemisia* '**Powis Castle**' (feathery gray-green foliage all year) S

- *Asarum shuttleworthii* '**Callaway**' **Ginger** (glossy green mottled foliage all year) SH

- *Carex* '**Evergold**' (green-and-white variegated ornamental evergreen grass) SH

- *Helleborus orientalis* (glossy evergreen foliage and flowers in late winter to early spring) SH

- *Heuchera americana* cultivars and hybrids (colorful evergreen foliage) SH

- *Selaginella uncinata* **Peacock Moss** (evergreen blue-green foliage) SH

- *Stachys* '**Countess Helen von Stein**' **Lamb's Ear** (gray-green foliage all year) S

Planting and Transplanting

If you don't have any perennials that bloom in fall, now is the time to add some—try **Joe-Pye Weed, Asters, Sedums,** and **Chrysanthemums.**

This is also a good season to work on improving the soil by adding organic amendments and rototilling. A soil test before you add amendments will help you determine the *best* amendments to add. Then you will be ready to plant this fall or next spring.

1 Prepare the soil ahead of time. If you are planting a large area, rototill 12 inches deep and add soil amendments to the entire area before you plant.

If you are planting a few plants, just dig individual holes for each plant and loosen surrounding soil. The planting hole should be twice as wide as the rootball, and the depth should be equal to the depth of the container the perennial is growing in.

2 After you plant, water well.

3 *Mulch* new plantings with a 2-inch-thick layer of mulch, keeping it away from the crowns of plants.

Pine straw, shredded pine bark, bark nuggets, leaf compost, or products such as ground pine bark are effective mulches that help keep roots cool and reduce weed infestations.

Once temperatures cool off a bit, it is a good time to *divide and transplant* perennials that have outgrown their spots in the garden or may not be performing as well as they could be. Perennials to divide in the fall include:

- *Amsonia* spp.
- *Asarum europaeum*
- *Astilbe* (can also be done in spring or summer)
- *Baptisia australis*
- *Boltonia asteroides*
- *Chelone lyonii*
- *Coreopsis verticillata* '**Moonbeam**'
- *Epimedium grandiflorum*
- **Ferns** (many different types)
- *Hemerocallis* **spp. and cultivars**
- *Heuchera americana*
- *Lychnis chalcedonica*
- **Irises**
- *Phlox paniculata*
- **Rudbeckias**

Minimize transplant shock by cutting back the foliage by $1/3$ to $1/2$ at the time you transplant. This will help compensate for root loss.

Watering

Even as the weather begins to cool off, it is important to keep plants watered. If there is no rain, *water* perennials about once a week, especially transplants and new plantings. Apply 2 gallons of water for a 1-gallon-size perennial.

Fertilizing

While it is not necessary to fertilize, you can *topdress* your perennial plantings with mushroom compost, horse manure, cow manure, or a similar product. (*To topdress* means to spread a thin layer 1 to 2 inches deep on top of the soil). This will help keep the soil healthy, and plants will respond by developing strong root systems.

Pest Control

Continue to pull weeds before they set seed. This will help reduce weed populations next spring.

This is a good time to use a granular weed-preventer in established perennial beds (see Chemicals, p. 327). It will greatly reduce infestations of winter weeds like chickweed.

Check for slugs, and control as needed (see Chemicals, p. 327).

You can still use insecticidal soaps to control aphids and whiteflies.

Be sure to get good coverage of all the plant surfaces.

Certain poisonous caterpillars and other chewing insects blend in with plant foliage and are difficult to see. Wear gloves that cover you up to your elbows if you are handchecking leaves for pest problems.

The saddleback caterpillar is common now, and the sting is painful like a bee sting. Its name comes from the purplish-brown saddle on its green back.

There are also greenish-yellow caterpillars with black stripes that run horizontally instead of lengthwise. You don't want to kill these caterpillars even though they eat the plant, because eventually they will turn into beautiful monarch butterflies.

This late in the season the monarch larvae won't harm the plant permanently.

You may notice that your *Asclepias tuberosa* **Butterfly Weed** is covered with yellow aphids.

The safest way to get rid of the aphids in this case is to blast them off with the hose.

Grooming

Cut back flowers when they finish blooming, and *remove* any foliage that is diseased or dying. This will reduce the number of places for unwanted pests to overwinter.

Leave attractive seedheads, like those of *Sedum* 'Autumn Joy' or *Baptisia australis*, for winter decorations.

Helpful Hints

Add some fall bloomers to extend the season in your garden. Here are a few to consider:

- *Aster* (many different species and selections)
- *Boltonia asteroides*
- *Ceratostigma plumbaginoides*
- *Chrysanthemum* 'Apricot Single' or 'Hillside Sheffield'
- *Eupatorium purpureum*
- *Helenium autumnale*
- *Helianthus angustifolius*
- *Salvia leucantha* (a tender perennial, it often blooms until frost)
- *Salvia* 'Indigo Spires'
- *Tricyrtis hirta*

Planning

This is an ideal month to add spring-blooming perennials to your garden. Make sure the soil is well prepared and that you have an idea of "what blooms when" before you start adding more plants. Make up a planting list, including information about flower color and the size of the plant and its texture.

Photograph your garden and make notes in your Garden Journal about plants that offer autumn interest.

Planting

Amend planting beds with organic materials and adjust fertility. *Rototill* to a depth of 12 inches if possible; add perennials to your garden.

Now is the time to plant and transplant herbaceous **Peonies**. Follow these steps:

1 *Dig up* the area where they will be planted a few days ahead of time, and let the soil settle.

2 Add lots of compost and some superphosphate (refer to product label for amounts).

3 The **Peony** roots should be planted so the buds (eyes) are 1 to 1½ inches deep. (Deeper planting will prevent **Peonies** from flowering.)

Established clumps of **Peonies** have stopped blooming. The clumps are large and healthy with lots of foliage, they have been fertilized regularly, and are growing in a spot where they receive four to six hours of sun per day. They may need to be divided.

1 *Dig up* the roots (rhizomes).

2 Wash soil off the roots.

3 *Divide* rhizomes into sections.

4 Dig a hole that is 1½ feet wide and about 1 foot deep. Mix in organic matter.

5 *Replant* the sections. Each section should have at least three buds (eyes), and healthy roots. It is important not to plant too deeply.

6 Space plants on about 1- to 2-foot centers.

Herbaceous **Peonies** generally love cold weather, but there are a few varieties that perform well in southern gardens. Tips for growing herbaceous **Peonies** in Georgia:

- Plant single or Japanese forms.

- Plant early-flowering varieties.

- Provide afternoon shade.

- Provide support for heavy flowers. Stake early with rings they can grow through.

- Some varieties for southern gardens are '**Festiva Maxima**', an old-fashioned favorite with double white flowers flecked with red; '**Sarah Bernhardt**', with double pink flowers; '**Imperial Red**', with single red flowers; and '**Seashell**', which has single pink flowers.

Divide plants of *Arum italicum,* **Italian Arum,** after the leaves appear. This shade-lover provides handsome foliage in the fall and winter garden.

Watering

Be sure to keep plants well watered, especially new plantings and recent transplants. If you don't get 1 inch of rain, set out sprinklers, and *water* until there is ³/₄ inch of water in a nearby tuna fish can.

Fertilizing

Topdress perennials with 2 inches of organic materials like composted manures (cow or horse), mushroom compost, or composted leaves. Take care to keep compost away from the stems and crowns.

Fertilize established herbaceous **Peonies** with 8-8-8 and bonemeal. Read the product label for recommended amounts.

Pest Control

Keep beds free of diseased or dead leaves. This helps eliminate conditions that encourage insects to overwinter.

Use insecticidal soap for minor insect problems (see Chemicals, p. 327).

Helpful Hints

If you add new perennials to the garden this fall, draw a rough sketch indicating where they are in relation to existing plants. This will make it easier next spring when plants begin to sprout to separate the flowers from the weeds. Save the labels for any new plants that you add to the garden. This way you can refer to them if you forget the name of a certain variety once it begins to grow and bloom, and you will be able to match descriptions to names.

Some perennials grown for their foliage look good most of the year, even in winter on a frosty morning:

- *Dianthus gratianopolitanus* 'Bath's Pink'

- *Epimedium grandiflorum* Epimedium

- *Heuchera americana* (and many selections of this plant)

- *Phlomis fruticosa* Phlomis

- *Stachys* 'Countess Helen von Stein' (a selection of **Lamb's Ear** with larger leaves)

- *Yucca filamentosa* 'Bright Edge'

Grooming

Cut back spring-blooming perennials now, but wait until early spring to cut back fall-blooming types as well as certain other perennials like **Artemisias,** which overwinter better when you leave them unpruned.

Cut back **Lantana,** but just enough to keep it from blowing around in the winter wind—any hard pruning should be done in early spring.

Planning

In all but the most northern parts of the state, this is a good month to add container-grown perennials to your garden before the ground freezes.

Make notes in your Garden Journal about how your plants performed over the past season. Catalog the photos you took throughout the year.

Planting

Hardy ferns add color and texture to the shade garden. Here is a selection of hardy ferns for Georgia gardens:

- *Athyrium felix-femina* **Lady Fern** (dies back in winter, upright habit, 2 to 3 feet)

- *Athyrium nipponicum* 'Pictum' **Japanese Painted Fern** (deciduous, wonderful variegated grayish-red/silver foliage, grows 1 to 2 feet)

- *Cyrtomium falcatum* **Japanese Holly Fern** (glossy evergreen, 2 to 3 feet tall)

- *Dryopteris erythrosora* **Autumn Fern** (evergreen, new foliage is a coppery color, grows to 3 feet)

- *Osmunda cinnamomea* **Cinnamon Fern** (deciduous, large upright fronds, grows 3 to 5 feet)

- *Osmunda regalis* **Royal Fern** (deciduous, 4 to 6 feet, native to swamps and wet areas)

- *Polystichum acrostichoides* **Christmas Fern** (evergreen, 12 to 18 inches, has a prostrate habit)

- *Thelypteris kunthii* **Southern Shield Fern** (deciduous, 2 to 3 feet, tolerates more sun than most ferns)

Plant **Hellebore**s now for late winter/early spring bloom. Perfect for the shade garden, these evergreen plants look good twelve months of the year.

- *Helleborus foetidus* **Bearsfoot Hellebore** (light-green flowers, blooms from February to June)

- *Helleborus orientalis* **Lenten Rose** (flowers range from white to purple, February to May—the plant tolerates drought and a half-day of full sun, although it will thrive in a moist woodland)

Sow seed of perennial **Poppies**, including the scarlet *Papaver orientale,* which is best grown in the more northern parts of the state:

1 Prepare the soil by adding soil amendments and rototilling. Rake out the area where you will sow seeds.

2 Sow seeds; barely cover them—**Poppy** seeds need light to germinate.

3 *Water* until the soil is wet down 1 inch.

Sow seed of *Asclepias tuberosa* **Butterfly Weed.** These spring bloomers produce a range of flower colors from yellow to orange to scarlet. Germination rate is low, so plant thickly.

Propagate perennials once they are dormant: *Anemone × hybrida* by root cuttings; **Geranium** species and hybrids by division; *Hemerocallis* **Daylilies** by division into plantlets, each with a single fan; and *Heuchera* cultivars and hybrids by division.

Watering

Water new plantings and transplants weekly unless there is adequate rainfall (1 inch per week). If you use a sprinkler, use tuna fish cans to measure the amount of water plants receive. Once the can has 3/4 to 1 inch of water, you have watered long enough.

Once the ground freezes, apply a fresh layer of mulch (about 2 inches, keeping it away from stems and crowns) to perennial beds. This will help conserve moisture and reduce weed infestations.

Fertilizing

There's no need to apply fertilizer now.

Pest Control

Pull weeds when they are young.

Companion Plants for Poppies

When **Poppies** finish blooming by mid- to late summer, they will disappear, leaving a bare spot in the garden. These perennials bloom at different times and can help fill the gaps:

* *Boltonia asteroides* White Boltonia

* *Gypsophila paniculata* Baby's Breath

* *Perovskia atriplicifolia* Russian Sage

Grooming

Once there is a frost, *prune back* dead stalks and leaves of perennials such as **Asters, Chrysanthemums, Salvias,** *Perovskia atriplicifolia*, and other late-blooming plants. Don't cut stems all the way back—leave 3 to 4 inches to help protect the crowns. This will also help you keep track of where perennials are planted so you won't accidentally dig them up when they are dormant.

Prune off the stems and leaves of herbaceous **Peonies** to minimize the chances of fungus spores overwintering.

Planning

It's time to begin think-ing about next year's spring and what you will plant.

Sketch a plan that shows which perennials you want to include in your garden, paying attention to placement, color schemes, time of bloom, and ultimate size. If you're not sure where to begin when designing your perennial garden, try this technique:

- While the perennials are still in their pots, place the pots in the spot where individual plants will grow. Move them around until you are pleased with the design, keeping in mind what plants will look like when they're blooming and during the rest of the year, including the dormant season. Take special note of their blooming time and duration to be sure they offer the display you envision.

- Once you plant your perenni-als, if you think two colors clash or if one variety turns out to be too aggressive for the spot you've planted it in, you can move plants to another loca-tion—perennials are resilient and forgiving.

Planting

In the most southern parts of the state you can add perennials to your garden throughout the year. In areas where the ground freezes, *wait until spring* to add new plants.

Sow seed that requires a cold treat-ment (*Aquilegia* spp. Columbine, *Chelone* spp. Turtlehead, *Echinacea purpurea* Purple Coneflower, and *Phlox paniculata* Garden Phlox). Start them in pots, and leave them outside through the winter, in areas where the temperature stays cool, next to the house in the shade.

Prepare your soil now for spring planting. Wait until a warm, sunny day when the soil is dry. Rent a small rototiller, and till the soil, adding amendments as you go—remember, the better the soil, the better the gardening results. Mix $1/3$ organic material, $1/3$ coarse sand, and $1/3$ existing soil. After you mix all the ingredients together, *mulch* the bed with a good 2 to 3 inches of mulch, and let it sit until spring when you can turn it under and begin to plant.

Watering

Water new plantings and transplants once a week unless there is adequate rainfall (1 inch per week).

Mulch is an insulator and helps reduce weed infestations. If you haven't mulched your perennials this season, apply a fresh layer now, about 2 inches, being sure to keep it away from the stems and crowns of plants.

Fertilizing

You can still *topdress* with composted manure (cow or horse) or mushroom compost. Apply 2 inches of the organic material, then apply a fresh layer of mulch.

Pest Control

Pull any weeds that are left in the garden.

Grooming

If you haven't cleaned up the peren-nial garden yet, do it now. *Prune* dead stalks and leaves—remember to leave 3 to 4 inches of stem as a marker (you will cut down the remaining dead stalks in early spring once new growth begins to emerge). *Discard* any diseased leaves or plants.

Roses

The rose is sometimes called "The Queen of the Garden." The variation in flower color, the heady scent of some (but not all) blooms, and the romantic associations in our culture make it one of the most versatile plants in a landscape. Roses vary in size from miniature to "monster," as anyone who has seen a **'New Dawn'** grow over a garage would agree. Their flowers range in color from purest white to almost black.

Roses have had a reputation for being difficult to grow, but public opinion has begun to change in the last decade. Native roses grow very well in the wilds of North America, China, and Europe. Modern Roses' prickly reputation developed when breeders began growing roses for competition. The flowers on the plants they bred were beautiful, but hybridization left behind the fortitude of the original roses.

Today's breeders have developed (and gardeners have rediscovered) roses that exhibit fortitude *and* beauty. The roses offered by catalogs (see January) and knowledgeable growers provide plenty of choices for your rose garden. Gertrude Stein was correct in literary terms that a "Rose is a rose is a rose," but her advice should be discarded when you select a rose for your garden. The pretty picture on the rose tag may not be possible to match if the plant cannot stand up to Georgia growing conditions. Look for roses described as "hardy in the South," "tolerates heat and humidity," and "little maintenance required" for your first plants. We have scattered lists of recommended roses throughout this chapter.

With roses, it is best to start small and build on your success. In addition to the variety you choose, rose experts agree that the key to success is providing the best environment for your plants from the beginning. Your rose should be planted in well-prepared soil and should receive plenty of sunshine. See January and October for descriptions of the best techniques for preparing a planting site. You'll get years of enjoyment from your roses if you put the right roses in the right spot.

Purchasing

Once you have discovered a rose variety you think will grow well in your garden, be sure to purchase the best plant you can find. If the rose has been grown in a container, do not buy it without checking its root system. Pull the plant from the pot to make sure roots spread throughout the potting medium. Don't be surprised if you find a plant that has vigorous growth above the soil line but few roots below—these roses have been moved too quickly through the production process. Do not buy a rose with weak roots.

You'll find some roses that are promoted as "growing on their own roots." Some producers feel that "own-root" roses are superior because they are less susceptible to stress. Own-root roses also avoid the problem that arises when the lower part of a grafted rose sends forth sprouts that are not like the upper part. If you garden in the north Georgia mountains, own-root roses will sprout back true from the roots even when the upper part of the plant is frozen to the ground.

Rooting rose cuttings, enough to market in sufficient numbers, is a slow process. Many more units of a beautiful rose can be produced if buds are grafted onto the roots of a strong vigorous root stock.

Grafted roses are graded according to their size when they are harvested. A #1 grade rose has larger and more vigorous canes than a #1½ or a #2 grade rose. In general, you get what

Roses

you pay for when buying a rose. Although it might be possible to buy a lower grade rose and wait for it to achieve its potential, this is usually not a good idea. In future years, you will get more pleasure from a single energetic plant than from two that began a bit runty.

Since Georgia has such a favorable climate for rose diseases, do not bring a diseased plant into your garden. Examine all the leaves for the yellow splotches that are symptoms of black spot (see March) or white powder that is a symptom of powdery mildew.

Fertilizing

Any of the commercial rose fertilizers or organic fertilizers will keep your plants happy. Our recommendations in March and the tips in following months will result in strong, vigorous roses. Once you have had several years of experience, you can experiment with the exotic mixtures rosarians sometimes employ.

Watering

Like most other garden plants, roses like to grow in soil that holds water a day or two after irrigation or rain but which dries before a week has passed. The only two times when attention to watering is needed is when a rose is first establishing itself in your garden and during times of extreme drought. Follow our recommendations on soil preparation plus our monthly watering tips and your roses will thrive, even in summer heat.

Pruning

Trees and shrubs might grow for years before they need pruning. Most roses, however, grow and bloom best when pruned properly each year. **Old-fashioned Roses** might need only an occasional touch-up pruning. **Hybrid Tea Roses** require heavier pruning to look their best—this is because they make their blooms on "new wood" (the stems that grew in the past few months). If you want copious blossoms (and what's the point of growing roses if this isn't your goal?), prune your roses properly. The important pruning dates to remember are February (for **Bush Roses**) and June (for **Climbers**). Our calendars for both those months will help you understand how to prune correctly.

Pruning is not limited to February and June, however. Remove dead stems and leaves regularly. Your roses will look neater and will be less susceptible to disease if you follow our monthly tips on what to look for as you wander through your rose garden each week.

Kinds of Roses

Roses are grouped by growth and blooming habit. As you choose the roses you'd like to grow, you'll find the following classifications:

Hybrid Tea. These traditional one-flower-per-stem roses are used mainly as cut flowers. The roses usually have long pointed buds with high centers. Most **Hybrid Teas** have an upright growth habit.

Floribunda. They are similar to **Hybrid Teas** but shorter, bushier, and flower in clusters. They provide an abundance of color to any border, hedge, or containers.

Grandiflora. Basically, **Grandifloras** are tall **Floribundas** with clusters of **Hybrid Tea**–like flowers. This classification can be very confusing, though, because some **Floribundas** grow taller than **Grandifloras**.

Shrub Roses. These are colorful roses that are continuously in bloom from spring to late autumn. They provide beautiful flowers with very little care. **Shrubs** are excellent to use in borders and as hedges, and some do very well in containers.

Climbers. Climbers are tall, upright, and spreading in growth habit, covering large areas. They are excellent for arbors, fences, and hiding an unattractive view.

Roses

Hybrid Tea and Grandiflora
- 'Bride's Dream' (light pink)
- 'Crystalline' (white)
- 'Dainty Bess' (light pink)
- 'Double Delight' (bicolor cream/red)
- 'Dublin' (light red)
- 'Elina' (pastel yellow)
- 'First Prize' (silver-pink)
- 'Gold Medal' (golden-yellow)
- 'Keepsake' (pink)
- 'Marijke Koopman' (pink)
- 'Olympiad' (red)
- 'Peace' (pink/yellow)
- 'Pristine' (white/pink)
- 'Queen Elizabeth' (medium pink)
- 'Secret' (white/pink)
- 'Touch of Class' (coral pink)

Floribunda
- 'Betty Prior' (medium pink)
- 'Brass Band' (apricot peach)
- 'Europeana' (dark crimson)
- 'Iceberg' (white)
- 'Playboy' (scarlet/orange)
- 'Playgirl' (medium pink)
- 'Showbiz' (red)
- 'Sunsprite' (lemon yellow)

Climbers
- 'America' (salmon pink)
- 'Don Juan' (dark red)
- 'Dortmund' (deep red)
- 'Dublin Bay' (red)
- 'New Dawn' (cream pink)
- 'Sombreuil' (white)

Old Garden Roses
- 'Baronne Prévost' (medium pink)
- 'Buff Beauty' (apricot blend)
- 'Celsiana' (light pink)
- 'Charles de Mills' (red blend)
- 'Ispahan' (medium pink)
- 'Madame Hardy' (white)
- 'Marchesa Boccella' (light pink)
- 'Marie Pavié' (white)
- 'Mutabilis' (opens bright yellow, darkens to crimson)
- 'Nastarana' (white)
- 'Rosa Mundi' (pink and white)
- 'Rose de Rescht' (fuchsia or crimson)
- 'Salet' (medium pink)
- 'Souvenir de la Malmaison' (light pink)

Modern Shrub Roses
- 'Abraham Darby' (light pink)
- 'Ballerina' (medium pink)
- 'Bonica' (light pink)
- 'Carefree Beauty' (pink)
- 'Frau Dagmar Hartopp' (medium pink)
- 'Golden Wings' (light yellow)
- 'Graham Thomas' (deep yellow)
- 'Heritage' (light pink)
- 'Lillian Austin' (salmon pink)
- 'Mary Rose' (medium pink)
- 'Penelope' (light pink)
- 'Sally Holmes' (pale pink)
- 'Sparrieshoop' (light pink)
- 'The Fairy' (light pink)

Learning

Growing roses in Georgia is not like growing them in Connecticut or Oregon or Michigan. Gardeners who move to Georgia, bringing their favorite no-care roses with them, quickly find that what works in one part of the country may not be so successful here . . . and the reverse would also be true if you moved out of the South. Rose culture in Georgia has been made more successful by the enthusiastic rose societies that meet throughout the state. If you want to be the "Queen (or King) of Roses" in your neighborhood, find a rose group or garden club (see October), and prepare to learn about and enjoy the exciting culture of roses in Georgia.

Planning

This is a good time to order roses from a rose catalog. Catalog ordering gives you many more choices of color and ultimate plant size than most neighborhood nurseries can offer. Local rose societies and botanical gardens maintain lists of roses that have performed well for their members. If one of their recommendations meets your needs, a catalog from a specialty rose nursery will help you find it.

Rose Catalogs

Antique Rose Emporium
5565 Cavender Creek Rd.
Dahlonega, GA 30533
(706) 864-5884

Roses Unlimited
Rt. 1, Box 587
Laurens, SC 29360
(864) 682-7673

Jackson & Perkins
P.O. Box 1028
Medford, OR 97501
Phone: 800-872-7673 or
(800) 292-4769

Wayside Gardens
1 Garden Lane
Hodges, SC 29695-0001
(800) 845-1124

Planting

How to achieve the best planting bed is a topic of much discussion among rose fanciers. Some prefer amending their native soil and giving their roses a "natural" environment. Others construct raised beds, either mounded or lined. Either way has merit; make your choice and get to work before rose planting season arrives.

- Estimate how many roses you plan to grow in an area.

- The bed should be 4 to 8 feet wide. Plan at first on 6 feet between plants. You can make a closer calculation later, after the plants have been purchased.

- *Remove* all grass from the area. If **Bermuda Grass** was growing there, remove and discard all soil to a depth of 6 inches.

- Shovel up the remaining soil to a depth of 10 inches.

- Pour a 2-inch-thick layer of soil amendment over the bed.

- Add 4 pounds of bonemeal and four pounds of garden lime per 100 square feet.

- *Rototill* the soil and amendments together.

- If the bed is not mounded 8 inches above the surrounding soil, add bagged topsoil to the mound. *Rototill* it completely into the existing bed.

If you choose to line the bed to hold the soil in place, several materials work well:

- Treated lumber (remember to wear gloves when handling)

- Untreated lumber (will last only four to five years)

- Brick (attractive, but mortar joints are beyond the skills of most folks)

- Cinderblock (not very aesthetically appealing; use a cap block to cover the holes)

- Stacked stone (very attractive, but requires a lot of work to build)

 ## Care for Your Your Roses

Existing roses need care during the winter, even during deepest winter.

1 Winter winds can whip **Climbing Rose** canes against their trellis, damaging the bark. Use jute twine to tie the loose canes firmly in place.

2 *Prune out* blackened canes whenever you notice them.

3 Keep a 3-inch-thick layer of pine straw mulch under plants at all times.

Watering

Roses cannot tolerate soggy soil—even in winter. If your rose bed is constantly damp, make a mounded bed.

- *Dig up* the rose after pruning it (see February and March for hints).

- For each rose, pour a bag of topsoil and a bag of gritty "All-Purpose Sand" over the area, and mix it with the existing soil.

- *Plant* your rose(s) in the resulting mound.

- Tamp down the soil around the rose roots with your shoe.

Water any plants you put in last fall. One to 2 gallons of water per plant is sufficient. Remember to *drain the hose* after every use so it does not freeze and crack.

Fertilizing

Roses are dormant in winter and do not need fertilizing.

Pest Control

The pine vole is a rodent about the size of a mouse. Voles live under brushpiles and in hollow logs; they scurry about, hidden under mulch and groundcovers, looking for plant stems to gnaw on. A vole-damaged rose may suddenly break off at ground level and show clear evidence of gnawing at the soil line.

- Pull back mulch 6 inches from the stem(s) of each plant. *Be sure to keep the mulch away from the stems at all times.*

- *Do not* pile brush near your rose garden. Put it at the far edge of your property.

- Keep the weeds at the edge of your property line cut short.

- Voles may be killed with a mousetrap baited with peanut butter. Be sure to cover the trap with an upturned plastic pot so no other animals are harmed. *Some gardeners put a slice of apple under the pot to lure the vole to his last lunch.*

Helpful Hints

Many **Climbing Roses** bloom only at the ends of the canes. This is due to the uneven distribution of plant hormones along the cane.

- You can encourage flowering all along the cane by arching the tip of the canes **outward**–almost horizontally at the end.

- Another technique is to loop back the ends of the canes so they point **toward** the base of the bush.

- Allow horizontal stems to develop along the canes. These will then produce the majority of your flowers.

Pruning

Bright winter days make it easy to see dead branches in the center of a rosebush. Though it is too early to perform your spring pruning, dead limbs can be removed any time you notice them.

Planning

Roses need 4 to 6 hours of full sunshine each day. A location that receives morning sunshine and afternoon shade is best because the leaves dry off faster, offering some protection against black spot and powdery mildew diseases.

Planting

Plant potted and bare-root roses now, a few weeks before the last frost. Before planting, prune away any dead or broken branches.

Bare-root Roses

- *Dig* a hole 12 inches deep and 18 inches wide in your prepared bed.

- Form a cone of earth in the middle. *Spread* the rose roots on all sides of the cone.

- Fill the hole with the soil that has been removed, tamping it firmly as you go.

Bare Root on Cone

Potted Roses

- *Dig* a hole 12 inches deep and 24 inches wide in your prepared bed.

- Gently untangle and *spread* the roots in all directions in the planting hole.

- Fill the hole with soil that has been removed, tamping it firmly as you go.

Care for Your Roses

If you order roses from a catalog, they will be shipped bare-root in order to minimize costs. Bare-root roses are also available at local nurseries; the roots will usually be wrapped in damp wood shavings.

- When your roses arrive home, decide if you can plant immediately or if the plants must be held for awhile.

- If the holding interval will be only twenty-four to forty-eight hours, simply *spray* water on the roots and rewrap them.

- If holding for several days, plant them in potting soil in 2- or 3-gallon pots. Protect them from freezing while you prepare their new home (see January).

Watering

After planting roses, *soak* the soil around them thoroughly. This settles the soil and drives out air pockets.

Fertilizing

Roses bloom best when the soil has a pH of 6.0 to 6.5. For existing rose beds, have your soil tested (see Horticultural Practices, p. 7), and add garden lime and other nutrients to your beds if recommended.

- Phosphorus and lime do not move rapidly down to the plant root zone; it is best to mix them both with your soil when planting a rose.

- In the absence of a soil test, thoroughly mix $1/2$ cup lime and 2 tablespoons 0-46-0 (triple superphosphate) with the soil you pack around the roots of each rose.

Pest Control

Few sights are more heartbreaking than roses chewed to the ground by deer. If deer constantly enter your garden, *spray* valuable roses with a deer-repellent. Many products are available, but their success rate varies. Deer will eat just about anything if they are hungry enough. Plan to *spray* every week, or more often if damage is evident. Year-round spraying is often necessary, switching between products at monthly intervals. Some gardeners fall back on deerproof fencing as their best defense (see Edibles, August). You may wish to consult these catalogs that have deer-control products:

DEERBUSTERS
9735-A Bethel Road
Frederick, Maryland 21702-2017
(888) 422-3337

Deer-Resistant Landscape Nursery
3200 Sunstone Ct.
Claire, MI 48617
(800) 595-3650

Becker Underwood, Inc.
801 Dayton Avenue
Ames, Iowa 50010
(800) 323-339

Pruning

Prune **Bush Roses** severely between now and March 15; the new growth that is produced will bear most of this year's rose blooms. Wait until June to prune **Climbing Roses.**

- *Remove* dead, weak, or damaged canes. Make a flat cut $1/2$ inch below the dead or damaged portion.

Helpful Hints

Roses are the most popular flower given on Valentine's Day. Follow these hints to keep yours looking their best:

- When purchasing cut roses, look for flowers with petals that are just starting to unfurl and buds that are springy to the touch.

- Buy a package of floral preservative. Bleach, aspirin, and soft drinks do not help a rose, but commercial products are specially blended to prolong rose beauty.

- When you arrive home, cut at least 1 inch from the bottom of the stems. Hold the stems completely under water as you do this.

- Place in a vase with lukewarm water to which preservative has been added.

- Every two days, clean the vase, recut the stems, and add warm water and more preservative.

- You can remove one or two outer petals from a bloom if they begin to fade.

- If roses begin to droop, submerge the whole plant in water and let it soak for a few hours.

Pruning Roses

- *Cut away* limbs that rub against another or cross through the center of the plant.

- To shorten a living branch, make a 45-degree-angle cut $1/4$ inch above a bud that points outward from the plant.

- If your rose has been pruned every year, *prune back* the size of the plant by $1/3$.

- If the rosebush is completely overgrown, $1/2$ to $2/3$ of the plant might need to be removed.

Planning

Climbing and trailing roses can surprise you with their appetite for space. Study the label that comes with a new rose and space it accordingly.

- *Plant* roses at least 30 inches from a building. Otherwise, they will lean outward, and the lower branches will become bare.

- *Plant* roses at least 4 feet from other large plants. Roses are heavy feeders and will compete with their neighbors for nourishment.

Planting

If a nearby tree has begun to shade your rose bed, you can either remove the tree or move your roses. *Most gardeners prefer the latter.*

1 *Prune* the rose first so you can work without suffering too many wounds.

2 Use a spading fork to lift and explore the soil 2 feet in all directions from the trunk, looking for shallow main roots.

3 When you have identified the main roots, *lift them completely* from the ground, working from 3 feet away from the plant towards its center. Use handpruners to cut roots that plunge vertically.

4 Thrust a sharp shovel into the soil around the plant, 1 foot from the trunk. Continue in the same manner around the plant, avoiding the previously excavated roots, until you have gone all the way around the plant.

5 With a mighty heave, lever the plant rootball out of the ground. *Mist* the roots with water and *cover* with plastic to keep them moist.

6 Plant in the new, *sunny* bed as soon as possible. (See January, Planting, for tips on making a new bed.)

Care for Your Roses

It is important to coat both the tops and the undersides of leaves when applying pesticides. This is difficult to accomplish with dusts but easier with sprays. *Spray* the underside of leaves first, follow with a light spray over the top.

IMPORTANT: Read and follow all label directions when using a pesticide.

Watering

Newly planted roses, especially bare-root plants, need regular watering. Give each plant at least 3 gallons of water per week. Allow the soil to dry somewhat between waterings.

Fertilizing

Roses need regular fertilization in order to grow the leaves and branches that will support new blooms. Follow these steps to fertilize newly planted roses:

1 In March, *topdress* the soil under each plant with 1 cup bonemeal and 1 cup cottonseed meal. Scratch them into the soil, and water with 1 gallon of water in which $1/4$ cup Epsom salts (magnesium sulfate) has been dissolved.

2 Add 1 cup bloodmeal under each plant in April.

3 When the plant has grown many new leaves and seems healthy, begin using 2 tablespoons of 10-10-10 per foot of plant height each month until September. *Use half the rate* in July and August . . . OR . . . use water-soluble fertilizer (Peter's®, Watch-Us-Grow®,

Miracle-Gro®) at the rate and frequency recommended on the label.

To fertilize established **Bush** and **Climbing Roses,** follow these steps:

1 In March, *topdress* the soil under each plant with 1 cup bonemeal, 1 cup cottonseed meal, ½ cup bloodmeal, and ¼ cup Epsom salts (dissolved in water). Scratch into the soil and *water lightly.*

2 Beginning in April, use 3 tablespoons 10-10-10 per foot of height per plant. *Repeat* monthly until September. *Use half the rate* in July and August . . . OR . . . use water-soluble fertilizer (Peter's®, Watch-Us-Grow®, Miracle-Gro®) at the rate and frequency recommended on the label.

Pest Control

Our heat and humidity make Georgia a prime site for rose black spot, a fungus disease of rose leaves. Old-fashioned roses tolerate the disease by shedding some, but not all leaves. Many of the newer **Hybrid Tea** roses will shed most of their leaves by July if black spot is not controlled. Here are some organic strategies for black spot control:

- Plant only roses that are known to have tolerance or resistance to the disease.

- *Pick off and discard* diseased leaves as soon as you notice them.

- *Spray,* beginning when leaves appear, with a mixture of 1 tablespoon baking soda, 2 tablespoons horticultural oil, and 1 gallon water. *Repeat* every seven days. *This mixture will not completely protect from disease, but it will delay disease onset.*

- Neem oil (see Chemicals, p. 327) has shown some promise as a fungicide and may also be used.

- Replace the mulch under your rose every spring.

Chemical strategies for black spot control:

- *Spray*, beginning when leaves appear, with chlorothalonil, or triforine or myclobutanil (see Chemicals, p. 327). *Repeat* the spray every two weeks.

- Every month, change the chemical you use. This reduces the possibility of the fungus developing resistance to a single chemical.

Annual weeds can be controlled by applying a weed-preventer (see Chemicals, p. 327) to your rose beds now.

Helpful Hints

Sealing cuts is usually not necessary if rose pruning is done during chilly weather. On canes larger than ½ inch, or if you have previously had problems with rose cane borers, smear white glue onto the cut end of the cane. **Cane borers are the immature form of one of several insects. Borers damage a rose by tunneling into the stem or boring around the stem under the bark. Swollen or cracked stems signal their presence.**

Pruning

"Tree" roses have been pruned and trained or grafted to grow into a single straight stem (the standard), topped by a tight head of leaves and blooms. To keep the head compact, *prune it back by half*, leaving as many forks and short branches as possible. After pruning, retie the standard to its support structure if one is present.

Planning

Roses do not serve well as foundation plants near a home. They may be covered with blooms and leaves during the warm season, but they are leafless in winter. There are several ways to use them as part of a landscape:

- Use roses in a mass planting in front of a hedge or in a shrub border.

- Train trailing roses to cover a fence.

- Plant **Climbing Roses** on either side of an arbor.

- Install **Miniature Roses** in a bed of perennial flowers.

Planting

Roses make good container plants outside on your patio. You can enjoy them when blooms are present, and move them back to a less conspicuous spot when the show is over. Select roses that grow medium-sized or smaller.

- To keep the plants upright, use a 24-inch-wide or larger pot, *except* when planting miniature-sized rose plants. Clay pots or wooden containers "breathe" better than do plastic pots.

Good Roses for Containers

'Iceberg'	4 to 6 feet tall, white flowers great for cutting
'Perle d'Or'	3 to 4 feet tall, orange buds, golden-pink flowers
'The Fairy'	3 to 4 feet tall, small double pink blooms
'White Pet'	1 to 3 feet tall, white flowers
'Marie Pavié'	3 to 4 feet tall, pale-pink buds open to white flowers, thornless
'Katharina Zeimet'	3 to 4 feet tall, double white flowers, repeat bloomer

- Purchase a good-quality potting soil. It should be light and fluffy, not heavy and smelly.

- Place the rose in the sunniest spot possible.

- *Check* soil moisture every day. Plan to *water daily* during the heat of summer.

Care for Your Roses

If you want large, exhibition-quality flowers, you can encourage their formation on **Hybrid Tea** roses by *disbudding* several individual stems. Select a stem that has a small but healthy-looking bud at the tip. Cut off any side buds below it.

This directs the plant's energy into producing a large bloom on that stem instead of many small flowers.

Watering

Check on roses that you planted earlier this spring.

- *Pull back* the mulch underneath the plant.

- Make sure the top of the rootball is still at (or slightly below) the surrounding soil surface. If not, pull mulch away completely and add soil to the proper height.

- Replace mulch and *water.*

Fertilizing

Fertilize each plant at midmonth with 10-10-10 or water-soluble fertilizer (see March). It is not necessary to remove the mulch before fertilizing; irrigation and rainfall will take the nutrients to the roots.

Pest Control

Look for aphids clustered at the tips of fast-growing branches.

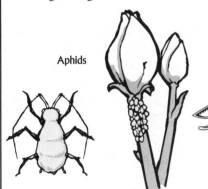

Aphids

- *Blast them off* with a water hose, and give a ground-dwelling spider a hearty meal.

- Examine nearby leaves for ladybugs. *Do not use insecticides* if you see them: ladybugs (and their orange, alligator-like offspring) consume aphids voraciously.

- Tiny, light-brown pods on the backsides of leaves signify you have been joined by another garden friend: tiny, harmless wasps that parasitize and kill aphids. The pods are the parasitized, dying aphids.

- If you are using a fungicide, continue spraying every two weeks (see March).

Were the edges of your rose petals brown when they opened last year? See May Pest Control for a description of thrips.

Now, before buds open, apply a systemic rose insecticide containing disulfoton, dimethoate, or acephate (see Chemicals, p. 327) to control thrips.

Pruning

Many rose plants are produced by grafting a desirable rose onto the stem of a vigorous, but possibly unattractive, rose (the rootstock). The area where the two join is called the *graft union.* It looks like a swollen knob a few inches above ground level. *Don't leave stubs* on the graft union when pruning. A fine-toothed saw blade or sharp knife makes clean cuts and permits you to get close to the graft.

Graft Union

Roses that have been grafted onto a rootstock may produce thin sprouts (suckers) arising from the ground around the trunk, or below the graft union. The flowers produced on these suckers will not be the same as those on the grafted rose above. *Prune away* all suckers back to the root or stem from which they come.

Do not simply cut flush with the ground—follow the sucker back to the origination point on the main plant to make your cut.

If the rose is growing on its own roots, flowers on the suckers will be identical to those on the parent.

You may choose to leave these suckers, in order to have a bigger plant, or to remove them.

"Own-root" roses are those that have been propagated by rooting a cutting rather than grafting.

Some rose fanciers believe that own-root roses are more vigorous, more long-lived, and, if the top is frozen, able to sprout back true to the original variety.

Helpful Hints

Do not allow winter weeds like chickweed or henbit to grow beneath your roses. Pull them out and sprinkle more mulch in their place to inhibit any sprouts you left behind.

Planning

As the first flowers on your **Bush Roses** *fade, remove them regularly.* This will allow new flowers to form.

Rose Cutting

Notice that roses have compound leaves composed of three to seven small leaflets. Whether cutting roses for display indoors or just to remove old flowers, ***make your cut just above a "five-leaflet" leaf.*** Buds growing at the base of "five-leaflet" leaves will produce long stems and healthy flowers. Buds growing at the base of "three-leaflet" leaves are more likely to produce weak stems and flowers. If you prune down to a "seven-leaflet" leaf, you will remove too much of the plant.

Planting

Container-grown roses have been in your local nursery for months by this time. When you remove one from the pot prior to planting, you may find a thick mat of encircling roots.

- Use pruners to ***cut off*** any thick roots on the rootball surface. (You could choose to untangle them instead, but this would be time-consuming.)

- ***Shake the rootball vigorously*** to loosen roots and remove potting soil from the surface. Roots will now be more likely to explore the surrounding soil when you plant.

- ***Spread*** the roots in the planting hole as much as possible before filling with native soil.

- ***Water*** thoroughly. Check back the next day and add soil if the earth has settled too much.

Care for Your Roses

When tying a rose to a supporting structure, the attachment should be strong enough to hold the rose in place but not so tight that the stem is damaged. Many rosarians use a "figure-eight" knot. Use biodegradable jute twine or special green rose tape sold for this purpose.

1 Cut a length sufficient to go around the support once and still have 12 inches left over.

2 Tie the material around the support, using a square knot. Two 6-inch lengths should dangle next to the rose stem.

3 Pull the cane gently to the support, and tie another square knot around it. ***Don't strangle the stem.*** The tie should be loose enough to allow the cane to slip freely within it.

4 Clip off excess tying material.

Watering

Rose ***standards*** (those trained to have a single upright stem topped by foliage and flowers) are sometimes used as potted patio plants. Check the soil's moisture in the pots daily until you have a good feel for how often they need to be watered. When the top inch of soil is dry, ***water*** until the water runs from the bottom of the pot.

If the soil is dry every day, the container is too small. Repot the rose into a container that is double the size of the present one.

Check on roses you planted within the last six months. They will not yet have enough roots to easily survive the summer. ***Water*** them deeply each week. Use a trowel to check how far the water penetrates

(6 inches is a good depth). Two gallons of water are usually sufficient.

Fertilizing

Fertilize each rose plant in mid-month with 10-10-10 or water-soluble fertilizer (see March).

Roses growing in containers need more frequent feeding that those growing outdoors (constant watering leaches fertilizer out of the potting soil). Use a slow-release granular fertilizer that dispenses fertilizer each time the plant is watered, or use a liquid fertilizer: cut the recommended dosage in half, but use it twice as often as the label indicates.

Pest Control

Powdery mildew is a leaf disease whose name perfectly describes its appearance: white powder covering individual leaves and flower buds. It is common in spring and fall when days are warm and humid and nights are cool. Roses that have been planted too close together or where the air remains still are easy victims.

- *Plant* roses where they have plenty of room between adjacent plants.

- *Do not plant* roses close to a wall or solid fence.

- If you have had a powdery mildew problem before, select resistant varieties for planting.

- A fungicide spray can be used to control the disease (see Chemicals, p. 327).

The fungi that cause rose diseases can become resistant to a chemical if it is used over and over. To prevent resistance, change to a different fungicide chemical each month (see March).

Read the product label to make sure you are purchasing a different chemical, not just a different brand.

Rose thrips are tiny yellowish insects that damage rose petals by scraping the cells with their mouth parts in order to suck plant juice. Though they are barely visible to the naked eye, their damage is easy to see: brown edges on rose flower petals. If you suspect thrips are present, cut a damaged rose bloom and slap it against a page of white paper. You'll be able to see the thrips scurrying for cover. Many beneficial insects (lacewings, ladybugs, etc.) feed on thrips. Avoid using contact

insecticide sprays. Besides harming the beneficials, they do a poor job of killing thrips.

Pick off and discard infested blooms. Make a thrips trap by coating a bright-yellow card with sticky oil (see Edibles, August). If the problem is severe, use a systemic insecticide (see Chemicals, p. 327).

Pruning

Do not let faded blossoms remain on your roses. *Remove and discard* them regularly.

Helpful Hints

Fragrance varies widely among roses. The smell will be strongest on a warm and humid afternoon and weakest on a rainy morning. **See November for a list of fragrant roses.**

Planning

There are many kinds of structures onto which **Climbing Roses** *can be trained.* The size of the structure should be in keeping with the eventual size of your rose. Roses do not twine around a support; they must be trained to it. This can be done by tying the canes in place or by resting the canes on supportive parts of the structure. Don't weave the canes in and out of narrow spaces on a trellis. They will be impossible to remove when you prune. When training a rose up a pillar, curve it around the post, barber-pole fashion.

You may notice that your **Climbing Roses** tend to bloom only at the tips. *See January for ideas on how to correct this.*

Planting

Roses that remain unsold at nurseries are often put on sale in June. Use extreme caution when purchasing sale roses.

- Do not buy a plant with light-yellow foliage—it may be weak from lack of fertilizer.

- *Examine* each leaf for black spot disease. If found, do not purchase.

- Pull the rose from its pot and *examine the roots.* If they are brown, smelly, or non-existent, do not bring the plant into your garden.

Care for Your Roses

Perhaps you have a particularly beautiful rose that all your friends admire. Now is a fine time to propagate your rose from cuttings in order to have a nice gift for your friends next spring. Examine stems in mid-June to find those that began growing in April and have now begun to turn from green to brown. A good cutting for rooting is 8 inches long and has brown bark at the base. The stem should not be limber, but should be hard enough to snap when bent.

1 Fill a 6-inch pot with a 50:50 mixture of perlite and peat moss that has been soaked and allowed to completely drain.

2 Dip the severed end of a cutting into a powdered rooting hormone such as Rootone™.

3 Poke a 3-inch-deep hole in the perlite:peat moss mixture with a pencil.

4 Insert the base of the cutting 3 inches into the hole. Firm the soil around it.

5 Insert a pencil or wooden chopstick beside the cutting. The top of the stick should be 2 inches taller than the leaves of the cutting.

6 Slip a clear plastic bag over the pot and cutting. The plastic should touch the leaves minimally. *Adjust the wooden stake to keep the plastic from touching the leaves.*

7 Place the pot, cutting, and bag in a bright but shady spot. Check the soil every three days to make sure it is moist.

The cutting should be well rooted in six weeks. It can be transplanted to a gallon pot for further growth during the summer.

Watering

Regularly water any roses planted in the last nine months. *Avoid wetting the foliage* when you water. A water wand is very handy. It causes a shower of water to cascade over the mulch at the base of the plant without dislodging it.

Check your soaker hoses to make sure they are working properly before the summer heat sets in.

Fertilizing

Follow the fertilization schedule described in March.

Pest Control

Japanese beetles love no plant better than rose leaves and flowers. Nothing is more disheartening than seeing the backsides of a half-dozen beetles merrily feeding on a beautiful blossom. If not controlled, rose leaves will be lace, and the flowers will be disfigured.

Non-Chemical Control

- In early morning, grab an empty soup can and pour an inch of soapy water in the bottom.

- Quietly approach your plants and observe where the cold, slow-moving creatures are resting.

- Gently place the can under a leaf and tap the leaf.

- The beetles will fall off the leaf into the water, and will drown.

- *Repeat* every morning until the population is decreased.

- *Spray* leaves with an anti-feedant containing neem oil (see Chemicals, p. 327). Neem is not 100% effective, but beetles seem to avoid eating leaves where it has been applied.

Make a note to apply milky spore disease powder (see Chemicals, p. 327) to your lawn in spring. The disease is deadly to Japanese beetle grubs but harmless to animals and birds. Remember, though, Japanese beetles can fly in from nearby lawns. Encourage neighbors to treat their lawns as well.

Chemical Control

- *Spray* leaves thoroughly with a contact insecticide every three to four days (see Chemicals, p. 327).

- Do not worry if the insects don't immediately fall from the plant—if they come in contact with the insecticide, they will die in a few hours.

Grub-control insecticide granules for your lawn are rarely effective in reducing beetle numbers. Japanese beetles can fly from neighboring untreated lawns, and the poison will be for naught.

Pruning

In general, **Climbing Roses** produce most of their blooms in early summer, though some may bloom off-and-on during the season. After they bloom is a good time to prune **Climbers** to make them healthier.

- *Cut away* any old, weak, or woody canes.

- Examine the canes that are left. Depending on the size and vigor of your plant, you should leave three to seven strong and vigorous canes.

Helpful Hints

Never put Japanese beetle traps near roses. The scent in the product will attract more beetles than it traps. If you choose to use them, place the traps at the far corners of your property. **Experienced gardeners have found that beetle traps attract more pests than they destroy.**

Planning

Most hybrid roses produce a single flush of blooms in spring or early summer. Some may bloom again in fall. Some species of rose are able to bloom throughout the growing season. Some good repeat bloomers are:

- **'Nearly Wild'**
- **'Old Blush'**
- **'Archduke Charles'**
- **Butterfly Rose** *Rosa chinensis* var. *mutabilis*

Planting

There is no shame in admitting to yourself that a rose has died despite your best efforts. Healthy roses are still available in containers at large nurseries and can be planted now to replace those that fell by the wayside.

- *Take extra care* when digging a new hole for the rose. If the soil is not rich and moist, add plenty of compost or manure.

- Untangle the roots in the container and *spread* them outwards in the hole.

- Fill the hole with soil while keeping the roots spread.

- *Water* deeply, and cancel any long vacations you've planned—this new bloomer will need regular weekly watering between now and October.

Care for Your Roses

Roses that have limber stems can be propagated by soil layering. Like any plant propagated from a cutting, the new plant will be a genetic duplicate of the rose from which it came. Follow these steps for soil layering:

1 Bend a stem down until it touches the earth. Use a dull knife to gently scrape the bark from the stem in a 1-inch-wide area at the point where it touches the soil.

2 Dust the wounded stem with Rootone™.

3 Use a trowel to scoop a shallow depression in the soil under the scraped area.

4 Lay the stem in the depression. Cover it with damp soil and place a brick on top to hold it in place. *In four months, roots will form underground. You can clip the stem that goes back to the mother plant but do not dig up your new plant.*

---

5 *Water* the rooted plant regularly until it loses its leaves.

The new, well-rooted plant can be moved to a new home next spring.

Brown jute twine makes a good material for tying rose canes to an arbor. Unlike nylon, the twine will rot after one season and will not harm plant stems.

Watering

Give roses that were planted last spring at least 2 gallons of water per week.

Check the depth of the mulch under your plants. It should be at least 2 inches thick.

If it is touching the stem, pull it back a few inches from the stem of the rose.

Fertilizing

Halve your fertilization rate during the hot months of summer. Fertilizer will force a rose to produce new leaves, which will demand water that may be scarce (see March).

Pest Control

Spider mites are tiny members of the arthropod family that suck sap from rose leaves. They are not insects, because they have eight legs, like spiders. Most insecticides do not control them; instead, the insecticide kills the beneficial insects which can keep a small mite invasion in check. To identify spider mites, look for creatures that are about the size of a grain of salt and may be red, yellow, or orange. Damage such as bronzed or stippled yellow leaves may be the first indication they are active; tiny webs between the base of a leaf and the stem of a plant may be present. To control spider mites:

- Examine leaves weekly during the hot and dry days of summer. If mites are found early, use a stiff spray of water daily to wash them off.

- *Spray* leaves thoroughly with horticultural oil.

- A miticide (see Chemicals, p. 327) can be used if the population is widespread.

- Avoid planting **Verbena** and **Foxglove** (they're spider mite magnets!) near your roses.

Rose slugs are not true slugs but the larvae of small sawflies. They feed from underneath a leaf, consuming the soft tissue between the veins. The damage appears similar to the damage caused by Japanese beetles feeding, but rose slugs eventually chew large holes in leaves rather than leaving them skeletonized.

Hit the underside of leaves with a stiff spray of water. Insecticidal soap is also very effective on rose slugs.

Pruning

Look for extremely weak or dead limbs every time you walk through your rose garden.

Use a sharp pair of pruners to remove any you find.

The broad blades of common hand-pruners are sometimes too big to fit easily into tight spots on a rosebush. Look for special rose pruners, such as Felco #6, to make pruning easier—its handles are also smaller and more comfortable for female operators.

It is a good idea to occasionally sterilize your pruners, even if you are not aware of any diseases that are present. Sterilize them with 1 part bleach mixed with 9 parts water.

Planning

Some roses have been developed to spread across the ground, becoming a garden ground cover rather than a **Bush** *or a* **Climber.** The blooms may not be huge, but several groundcover roses are very resistant to diseases and insects. Use shears or a lawn mower raised to its highest setting in spring and fall to keep groundcover roses neat and at a uniform height.

Planting

If you move from one home to another in August, you might want to carry your favorite roses with you. Although transplanting in the heat of summer is not recommended, it can be done successfully:

1 *Prune* roses to a manageable size one week before you intend to dig them.

2 Collect a sturdy cardboard box for each plant. Line the inside with a plastic garbage bag. Poke drainage holes in the plastic.

3 *Dig* each rose carefully, remembering that the roots must fit in the box.

4 When the plant is in the box, cover the roots with moist soil. Insert a label with the rose name or description. Place the boxes in the shade near an outdoor faucet at your new home.

5 Inspect the plants daily, water when needed, and plant within two weeks of moving. *Although you might have only bare stems left, healthy roses can usually recover their form in a year or two.*

Care for Your Roses

Part of the enjoyment of roses is to recognize different ones by name. If you grow more than one or two roses, it can be difficult to remember which roses you have. Make it a practice to label each as it is planted, using a permanent label.

- White plastic stakes are inexpensive, but they become brittle, breaking easily after one year.

- Metal labels that stand atop two thick wire legs are durable but can be lost or pulled by accident.

- Thin metal tags that are attached to a rose stem by loose wire aren't likely to be lost but are difficult to read without risking contact with the rose thorns.

See the Helpful Hint to learn how to make your own rose tags.

Watering

Sometimes rose leaves begin to wilt even though you are watering regularly. Wilting can be caused by *too much* water (which causes root rot) as well as *too little*.

- Pull mulch back from the base of the plant before you water. Scrape the soil with a trowel.

- If the soil is moist down to 2 inches deep, no water is needed. Wait until the soil is barely damp at the 2-inch level before watering again.

- If the plant continues to wilt, *dig it up* and examine the roots to determine if they are healthy. Healthy roots feel firm, not mushy, when squeezed between your fingers. The soil should smell "musty" but not "stinky." If the roots do seem rotted, remove them, replant the rose, and correct your watering practices.

Fertilizing

Fertilize roses with 1 to 2 tablespoons of 10-10-10 per foot of height now, accompanied by the pruning noted below.

For a quick pick-me-up, *spray* rose leaves directly with a diluted liquid fertilizer (Peters®, Watch-Us-Grow®, Miracle-Gro®, etc.). Dilute the fertilizer to 1/4 the rate recommended for soil application. A tablespoon of Epsom salts (magnesium sulfate) per gallon of liquid fertilizer adds magnesium to the soil.

Pest Control

If you read much about roses, you may see mentions of fungicide products with which you are not familiar. If the chemical name is mentioned, write it down exactly so you can take it to your local nursery. If they have never heard of it, call your county Extension office for their expertise—it is possible that the fungicide is only available to professional rose growers or that it is so expensive that the average gardener could not afford it.

Helpful Hint

Make your own rose tags:

1 Purchase a package of **thin** aluminum cookie sheets at the grocery store.

2 Use scissors (not your best ones!) to cut rectangular tags 1 inch wide by 3 inches long.

3 Using a ballpoint pen, print the name of the rose on the aluminum. The metal is so thin that it will be embossed by the lettering.

4 Punch a hole near the end of the tag with a hammer and small nail. Thread 6 inches of thin wire (ask the neighborhood handyperson for some) halfway through the hole. Give the two "legs" of wire a twist or two.

5 Attach the tag to a low limb with the wire.

Pruning

Rose blooms are borne on new growth. If you are able to water your roses regularly during this hot season, they can be cut back to stimulate new twigs that will bear flowers in September

- In the southern half of Georgia, cut back **Bush Roses** by $1/2$.

- In the northern half of the state, cut back **Bush Roses** by $1/3$.

- Ever-blooming roses such as 'Nearly Wild' and the 'Butterfly' Rose benefit from a good shearing now, even though they have many flowers.

Planning

If you have an informal garden, you might consider incorporating roses into your perennial flower garden. **Clematis** and roses make happy companions. Vigorous free-flowering **Clematis** vines can be easily trained to grow through a rose plant. Attach the stems to the canes with a natural rope or string. The rose acts as a living trellis. Plant the **Clematis** at least 2 feet away from the rose, and lead the stems of the **Clematis** to the rose with strings or thin bamboo cane.

They can be fertilized together since they are heavy feeders.

Other Rose Companions

- Try some herbs: **Oregano, Rosemary,** and **Thyme.**

- *Erigeron* **'Profusion'** has white to pink small daisy flowers throughout the summer; this spreading plant grows to about 10 inches high.

- *Geranium macrorrhizum* has magenta flowers in spring and good fall color; it is easy to grow.

- *Geranium sanguineum* var. *striatum* has light-pink flowers with crimson veins.

- *Geranium* 'Johnson's Blue' is a hardy **Geranium** that produces a profusion of blue flowers in spring.

Roses need not always be planted in formal beds; they can be used as hedges or as part of a border. Though they aren't dense enough to make an opaque screen, like a **Holly,** they can obstruct rambunctious children and pets without being un-neighborly. Be sure to check plant labels for height, width, and appropriate spacing when buying roses for hedges or privacy. You might want to try **'Cécile Brunner', 'Nearly Wild', 'Archduke Charles',** and **'Carefree Beauty'.**

Planting

You may someday find an old, possibly heirloom, rose that has been completely covered by vines or adjacent shrubbery. It is too weak to move now but could be strong enough by spring if it is uncovered and pampered:

- *Prune away* the vine or shrub covering the rose. Try not to break rose stems or pull off leaves. *Prune* nearby trees and shrubs, if possible, to allow more light to reach the rose.

- *Fertilize* the rose with houseplant fertilizer diluted to half strength.

- Move the rose in early spring to a "nurse bed." Note the flower color when it blooms and observe whether it seems prone to black spot or powdery mildew. If it is not vigorous and healthy after one year, toss it on the compost pile. Don't struggle to grow a loser.

- If the rose performs well, add it to your permanent collection and try to find out its real name from local rosarians!

Care for Your Roses

Continue to *remove faded flowers* from ever-blooming roses. *Prune out* dead stems. *Pull weeds* as they appear. *Edge your beds* using a hand- or motorized edger.

Watering

The usual lawn sprinkler system is fine for your turf but bad for roses; wet leaves lead to diseases that are almost impossible to control. Try a drip system or use black rubber soaker hoses instead.

- Drip systems come in kits containing all the parts to water several plants.

- Soaker hoses can be snaked near each plant under the mulch. The soaker hose is attached directly to your water hose (see Helpful Hint).

Fertilizing

Fertilize each plant in mid-month with 1 to 3 tablespoons of 10-10-10 per foot of plant height, or use a water-soluble fertilizer like Peters® or Miracle-Gro®.

Some rose growers swear by the magical powers of alfalfa pellets (sold at seed and feed stores as animal food). Alfalfa tea is a great fall potion that doesn't interfere with normal rose growth.

1 Add 10 to 12 cups of alfalfa meal or pellets to a 32-gallon plastic garbage can that has a lid.

2 Add water, stir, and steep for four or five days, stirring occasionally; you may also add 2 cups of Epsom salts.

3 The tea will start to smell in about three days, so keep the lid ON. Schedule the opening of the barrel for when the rest of the family is away.

Helpful Hint

Black rubber soaker hoses are sold wrapped in a tight circle that is almost impossible to untangle and lay out without help. You can do it single-handedly by slightly pressurizing the hose with water.

- Choose a hot day; wear old clothes and tennis shoes.

- Lay out the soaker hose near your plants.

- Connect the soaker to your water hose. Turn on the water at full flow for a moment.

- Cut the water flow to a trickle, just enough for a bit of water to weep from the soaker.

- Pull back mulch, put the soaker in place, and re-cover with mulch.

- An inexpensive water timer attached at the faucet makes watering your roses a breeze.

---

4 Use a gallon of brown "tea" on large rosebushes to make strong canes and green leaves late in the growing season.

Pest Control

Caterpillars are not typically a major rose pest, but September is the month you'll notice them, if at all. Caterpillar damage is usually in the form of irregular holes chewed at leaf edges. Small leaves may have more than half of the leaf consumed. The disease spore *Bacillus thuringiensis*, commonly called *B.t.*, is an excellent caterpillar control (see Chemicals, p. 327). *B.t.* is not harmful to birds or humans or other mammals. Apply the spray or dust thoroughly to cover your rose leaves.

B.t. is deactivated within a few days, so repeat applications may be necessary.

Replace all the mulch under your roses. This will prevent diseases on next year's leaves.

Pruning

Prune **Hybrid Tea** and **Grandiflora** roses to remove dead limbs and to shape them for winter.

Planning

One of the best ways to succeed with roses is to grow varieties recommended by experts. When you have proven that roses are easy to grow in your landscape, you can branch out to grow varieties about which you know nothing but that intrigue you. Glen Austin is manager of The Antique Rose Emporium in Dahlonega (see January list). Here are his top ten garden rose choices:

- **'Penelope'** (Hybrid Musk)
- **'Buff Beauty'** (Hybrid Musk)
- **'New Dawn'** (Climber)
- **'Sombreuil'** (Climber)
- **'Dortmund'** (Climber)
- **'Duchesse de Brabant'** (Tea)
- **'Hansa'** (Rugosa)
- **'Belle Poitevine'** (Rugosa)
- *Rosa rugosa* **'Alba'** (Rugosa)
- **'Red Cascade'** (Groundcover)

Planting

This is an excellent time to transplant roses (see March). As plants lose their leaves, less water is demanded from the roots; the soil is still warm, and root growth can occur in the new bed before winter.

Rose growers can be divided into three classes: lackadaisical, committed, and fanatic. Those in the first class dig a small planting hole, shove the rose in place, and hope it survives. Committed rose growers rototill their soil and add organic amendments. Fanatic rose growers develop their very own special rose soil and use it whenever they plant. If you are one of the fanatical rose growers, you can take the advice of Pat Henry, the owner of Roses Unlimited (see January list). She digs a hole 18 inches deep and wide, fills the hole halfway with the following soil mixture, then packs more around her rose roots as she plants it. Pat swears by the results!

Pat Henry's Special Rose Soil

In a wheelbarrow, mix enough of the following ingredients, in the proportions indicated, to fill the hole:

1 part compost
1 part peat moss
1 part good topsoil
1 part red clay

Add and mix thoroughly:

1 cup 0-46-0 (superphosphate)
1 cup dolomitic lime
2 cups alfalfa meal or pellets
1 cup gypsum

Care for Your Roses

- Tip back long canes that are in the way as you walk through the garden.

- Re-tie the canes of **Climbing Roses** to their support structure. It is easier to do this now than when icy winds are howling through your garden.

- Pull weeds from underneath your plants.

Miniature Rose plants are often a temptation when seen at a garden center or on the floral aisle of a grocery store. The plants are small enough to keep indoors and enjoy through the coming winter. Unfortunately, **Miniature Roses** kept indoors never seem to prosper. They are susceptible to spider mites, root rot, leaf diseases, and low humidity. To maximize your chances for success, heed the following tips:

- Place **Miniatures** near a very bright window but never touching the glass. Plan to turn the pot halfway around each week to keep the plant symmetrical.

- If you don't have a well-lit window, build a light stand (see Annuals, February).

- Water only if the soil seems dry to the touch. ***Do not overwater.***

- Keep a sharp eye out for spider mites or mealybugs on the leaves. Control them at once with an insecticide labeled for indoor use (see Chemicals, p. 327).

- Though the blooms are small, a **Miniature Rose** planted outdoors will eventually rival in size the larger-blooming types.

Watering

One way to minimize watering and weeds at the same time is to use landscape fabric under your roses. Landscape fabric is a porous plastic material that allows water and fertilizer to come through but does not allow weeds to grow up through it.

1 *Spread* the fabric over your well-tilled rose bed before planting.

2 Cut an "X" with a razor knife where you wish to plant a rose.

3 *Plant* through the fabric. Tuck the fabric around the stem when finished. (If you decide to use the fabric after your roses are established, cut the fabric into strips that can be placed between and alongside individual plants. Avoid arranging the fabric more than two layers thick.)

4 Cover the landscape fabric with mulch.

5 *Remove* and *renew* the mulch every two years. As it decomposes, weed seeds will sprout in it, which is the situation you're trying to avoid.

Fertilizing

Do not fertilize now. The nitrogen in the fertilizer could cause your roses to be less cold-tolerant.

Pest Control

Rose mosaic virus is a common rose disease that seems to do little harm. It appears as a bright-yellow mottling on individual rose leaves or small branches. The disease is not fatal to plants, but it may reduce flowering and cause early autumn leaf drop. The disease is not spread by insects, by water splash, or by pruning tools, but by grafting a diseased rose onto a healthy one. Amateur rosarians simply prune off the affected leaves.

Professionals seek out roses from reputable growers who can guarantee that their plants are disease-free. These roses will remain healthy unless accidentally infected.

Helpful Hints

Several rose societies meet regularly in Georgia. To find the group nearest you, write the American Rose Society:

The American Rose Society
P.O. Box 30,000
Shreveport, LA 71130

The society's Web site (www.ars.org) offers a huge amount of information on rose culture, expert advice, and rose society contacts.

Pruning

Take time to examine each rose plant individually. *Prune out* any dead branches or weak limbs.

Planning

More than a few gardeners avoid roses because of their thorns. Though most roses have thorns of varying ferocity, some are known to be quite amiable.

Thornless (or nearly so) Roses		
Name	Type	Flower Color
'Lady Banks'	Climber	White and yellow varieties
'Belle de Crécy'	Shrub	Red/lavender
'Reine des Violettes'	Shrub	Red/violet
'Zéphirine Drouhin'	Climber	Pink
'Paul Neyron'	Shrub	Pink
'Heritage'	Shrub	Pink

Planting

Roses can still be planted or transplanted in the southern part of the state.

Care for Your Roses

Here's some good news for gardeners who have grown roses in the colder parts of the United States. *Temperatures in Georgia do not usually drop low enough to permanently harm roses.* While a late frost can eliminate rose blooms for the season, cold rarely kills Georgia roses. You can put away your rose hoops, bales of straw, and snow shelters.

Tie down the canes of **Climbing Roses** *so they can't whip against their arbor in the wind.*

Watering

Roses need at least twelve months to establish or to reestablish a root system.

Water regularly any roses that have been planted or transplanted in the last six months.

Fertilizing

Do not fertilize roses during their dormant season.

Organic fertilizers such as cottonseed meal, bloodmeal, or bonemeal that have been stored for the winter are attractive food for opossums, rats, and raccoons.

Store organic products such as these in a metal trash can that has a tightly fitting lid.

Pest Control

Thoroughly clean your garden sprayer (see Edibles, November), and allow it to dry before storing for the winter.

Pruning

Prune out any dead branches or "in-the-way" limbs.

Helpful Hints

Though your roses have faded, you can still remember their fragrance by making potpourri. Use ingredients you find at a craft shop for your first experiments. Next year you can collect fragrant rose petals and fragrant leaves, blooms, and colorful berries from other plants. A typical potpourri consists of:

- Flower buds, blooms, or petals

- Differing textures added by leaves, peels, or berries

- A fixative to hold the scent of the various components

- Essential oils to add strong scents (such as cinnamon or citrus) to the mix

Once you have gained confidence making potpourri, you can spend next November making personalized mixtures as gifts for your friends during the upcoming holidays.

Fragrant Roses

Name	Flower Color	Type
'Mister Lincoln'	Red	Hybrid Tea
'Rose de Rescht'	Magenta	Portland
'Tamara'	Apricot	David Austin
'Chrysler Imperial'	Velvet Red	Hybrid Tea
'Mme. Ernst Calvat'	Pink	Bourbon
'Alchymist'	Amber	Climber

Suggested Holiday Gifts for the Rose Lover

- Felco #2 or #6 pruners (or #9 for left-handers)

- Medium-handled loppers

- Rose trellis

- Soft and Supple™ water hose

- Jute twine or plastic rose tape

- Blank plant name markers or copper tags

- Rose thorn stripper

Planning

Some gardeners plan their rose beds so they will be as attractive when the blooms are absent as when the plants are covered with blossoms. Rose hips are the fruit (seed container) of a rose bloom. As they age in fall, the hips turn vivid shades of yellow, orange, and red. They are edible and are an excellent source of vitamin C. Do not remove flowers after they fade or the hips will not form. Roses with attractive hips are:

- **'Dortmund'**
- **'Frau Dagmar Hartopp'**
- **'Old Blush'**
- *Rosa rugosa* **'Alba'**
- *Rosa rugosa* **'Rubra'**

Planting

Roses need not always be planted in the ground. They grow quite nicely in containers if given the sunshine, water, and shade they need.

Container Growing Advantages

- You can determine the exact flower color before planting in a permanent location.

- You can evaluate if the rose will grow in a semi-shaded spot.

- The rose does not have to compete with its neighbors for sun, moisture, and nutrients.

- There are no worries about soil problems if you use a premium potting soil.

- Maintenance (pruning, fertilizing, spraying, etc.) is easier.

Container Growing Disadvantages

- Water management is imperative throughout the year.

- Large containers (at least 5-gallon-size or larger) will be needed for large plants.

- A rose plant must grow in a new container for at least a year before it can be moved to a bed.

- Containers may overheat (see Watering).

Care for Your Roses

Roses growing in pots may need protection if winter temperatures threaten to go lower than 20 degrees Fahrenheit. Here's how to keep them safe:

- *Move* the pot close to the house, preferably against a north- or east-facing wall.

- *Wrap* the entire plant and pot with burlap or an old sheet. *Remove* when temperatures warm up.

Watering

Summer sunshine in Georgia can heat the soil in black plastic containers enough to kill plant roots. If you choose plastic pots, use the clay-colored type rather than the dark green or black. Group plants close enough so that each shades the other. Use potted foliage perennials to screen the outermost pots. Place a 1-inch layer of small pine nuggets on top of the soil to insulate it.

Fertilizing

Do not fertilize this month.

Pest Control

Make sure all your pesticides are stored in a relatively inaccessible spot, preferably a locked cabinet.

If you have pesticides that have lost their label, contact the Georgia Department of Natural Resources, Environmental Protection Division at (404-651-5120) for disposal options. While you clean and straighten your pesticide storage area, take time to reread the label on each product. Note the signal word (CAUTION, WARNING, or DANGER), and doublecheck your application practices.

Shrubs

While trees help create the framework for a garden, shrubs act as the middle ground between trees and the herbaceous layer of perennials and annuals. Both native and exotic, shrubs come in all sizes and shapes and perform myriad functions. Depending on the particular selection, a shrub can play many roles. It can provide screening, privacy, or windbreaks; direct foot traffic; create a source of shelter and food for birds; add color and beauty to the landscape with fragrant and showy flowers; and, in winter, can serve as an evergreen anchor or bright accent with showy stems and bark. Evergreen shrubs, including **Anise, Boxwood, Holly,** and **Cherry Laurel,** are ideal plants for creating privacy, defining areas of your lawn, making effective hedges, or serving as a backdrop for your perennial garden. Deciduous shrubs like **Chokeberry, Beautyberry,** and deciduous **Hollies** provide food and shelter for birds, and they make handsome ornamentals with their colorful displays of berries in fall and winter. Some shrubs, such as **Butterfly Bush, Glorybower,** and **Summersweet,** attract butterflies and bloom for weeks during the hot summer months.

When you select a shrub, be sure to choose the right plant for your specific environment. Learn about what cultural conditions it requires, such as full sun, part shade, acid soil, or lots of water. This will help you select a plant that will thrive in your garden. It is also useful to know how large a particular shrub will be at maturity. This knowledge will help you site a shrub. For example, if you choose a large **Holly** as a foundation plant in front of windows, it will require constant pruning to keep it in bounds. Refer to the planting charts for information about the cultural requirements and mature size of individual shrubs.

If you have a garden that receives full sun but the soil stays wet, choose plants like *Itea virginica* that will thrive under these conditions. While many native **Azaleas** will flourish in full sun or part shade, many hybrid **Azaleas** will languish if you plant them in full sun. When choosing shrubs for your foundation planting, think beyond broad-leaved evergreens like **Hollies** or **Camellias.** Consider using a mixture of evergreen and deciduous shrubs, including those with brightly colored spring blooms, colorful fall foliage, and fragrant flowers in winter. With this approach you will be more likely to have a garden that offers year-round beauty. If the spot gets sun in the morning and shade in the afternoon, try combining *Fothergilla gardenii* with **Boxwood** and a few of the smaller **Lace-cap Hydrangeas** like *Hydrangea serrata* 'Blue Billow'.

With shrubs there is a bit more flexibility than with trees. If you plant a shrub and decide next year that it is in the wrong place, you can move it to another location more easily than you can move a large tree. Still, it is best to do some research before you plant so you won't make costly mistakes.

Planting Shrubs

Most shrubs available for purchase are grown in containers. In certain cases, large specimens may be offered balled and burlapped. Shrubs grown in containers can be planted throughout the growing season, provided the ground is not frozen, although early spring and fall are best. Follow these steps when you plant your shrubs.

Shrubs

1 Take a soil test before you plant. The results will determine how much lime and other nutrients you need to add. Add soil amendments and rototill to a depth of 8 to 12 inches. This is also a good time to add any lime to the soil (see February Perennials, Planning). If it is a new planting, amend the whole bed with 4 inches of organic matter.

2 Dig a hole as deep as the container the plant is growing in and twice as wide.

3 Remove the plant from the container. Use a shovel to hit the sides of the container; this will loosen the rootball and make it easier to slide out of the pot.

4 Use a sharp pair of handpruners to make two or three cuts into the bottom of the rootball. This will encourage roots to sprout and establish more quickly.

5 Place the rootball in the hole, and fill in with soil. The top of the rootball should be covered only slightly with soil—piling on lots of extra soil can suffocate surface roots.

6 Water the shrub well (refer to Watering section below for tips on watering). Soak the rootball and the surrounding soil.

7 Apply a 2-inch layer of mulch around newly planted shrubs. Be sure to keep the mulch away from the main trunk or stems. This will reduce the chances of certain disease and insect problems (see Fertilizing section below for fertilizer recommendations).

If you have heavy clay soil, plant your shrub high, so that the top third of the rootball is out of the ground. Mound plenty of soil around the rootball, then apply a good layer of mulch. This technique will ensure that your plant doesn't dry out too quickly, but that the roots won't stand in wet soil.

Watering

Water your shrubs as soon as you plant or transplant them. Place the hose at the base of a shrub and let a slow stream saturate the area. A good rule of thumb is to apply 1 to 2 gallons per foot of plant height. Water once a week for the first six months unless there is a good rain (one or more inches per week is a good rain).

• When watering by hand, apply 5 gallons of water per 10 square feet. This is approximately the amount of water delivered by a garden hose operating one minute at medium pressure.

• Soaker hoses are effective, too. They can water a swath one foot wide on either side of a hose. Depending on the water pressure, a 50-foot-long soaker hose can water 100 square feet of landscape bed in two or more hours.

• Apply 50 gallons of water per 100 square feet when plants show signs of water stress, such as wilting or leaves that turn blue/gray. In coastal areas where soils are sandy, shrubs may need watering more frequently. Dig down 2 to 3 inches. If the soil is dry at that depth, water.

• During periods of extended drought when it doesn't rain for a month or longer, your shrubs will benefit from supplemental watering.

Fertilizing

If your shrubs are vigorous and they put on new growth each season, you probably don't need to fertilize. If fifty percent of the leaves are pale and yellow and the plant lacks overall vigor, you can fertilize three times a year. Fertilize once in early spring, once in early summer, and then once in the fall. If you fertilize with a slow-release granular product like Nursery Special™ in early winter when shrubs are dormant, this will replace the springtime application of fertilizer.

Shrubs

When you plant new shrubs, you can use a starter fertilizer. These products have a high percentage of phosphorus to help establish roots quickly. A fertilizer with a ratio like 5-20-10 is fine. If you don't use a starter fertilizer, you can use a balanced fertilizer like 10-10-10, but you need only to apply one or the other. Read the label carefully before applying any fertilizers. For a new planting, high nitrogren can be detrimental to establishment. Use a ratio with a low first number.

Pruning

Gardeners are often confused about why and when to prune their shrubs. While it's true that your shrubs will grow and bloom even if you don't prune them, a certain amount of pruning, depending on the type of shrub, can help keep a shrub vigorous, increase flower production, and improve overall appearance.

There is no ideal shape or form for shrubs, but there are some useful guidelines for pruning.

- Pruning to remove dead or diseased wood on a regular basis helps to keep shrubs vigorous and can be done during any season.

- Drastic pruning (reducing a shrub by $1/3$ to $1/2$, perhaps to renovate an old shrub that is overgrown and has stopped blooming) should be done in early spring right before the shrub begins to put out new growth (see March for details on renovating overgrown shrubs).

- When deciduous shrubs are dormant, it is easier to see their natural growth habit, which will help guide you when you prune.

- Selecting the right shrub for the right spot can reduce the amount of pruning. For example, **Forsythia** is a large shrub that when left unpruned forms a graceful fountain of foliage. For this reason it is best sited in a spot where it won't have to be hacked back because it covers a window or crowds other plants.

- In general, it is best to prune flowering shrubs as soon as they finish blooming. This way you will avoid the problem of cutting off next year's flowerbuds.

- Become familiar with the growth habit of your shrub. Some **Hydrangeas,** like *Hydrangea macrophylla,* bloom on second-year wood. This means that flowerbuds form on stems that were produced last year or prior to that. In the case of this **Hydrangea** and other shrubs that bloom on old wood, pruning right after they flower keeps you from removing branches that will have blooms next year. *Hydrangea paniculata*, on the other hand, produces bloom on new growth, so you can prune back the old growth in early spring just before the shrub begins actively growing.

Pest Control

The best way to keep pests at a minimum is to start with healthy plants placed in the proper soil. Make sure they get plenty of water, good air circulation, and the proper amount of light. Practice Integrated Pest Management (IPM). Examine your plants on a regular basis for signs of insect or disease problems. If only $1/3$ of the plant is affected by a pest problem, try using an organic control method before you resort to chemicals. If fifty percent or more of a particular shrub is infested with a pest problem, you may need to resort to a chemical control (see Chemicals, p. 327).

Shrubs for Georgia

Variety	Height	Spread	Culture	Comments
Abelia chinensis Chinese Abelia	5 to 7 feet	5 to 7 feet	Full sun to part shade in a well-drained soil.	White flowers tinged with pink from summer to fall.
Aesculus parviflora Bottlebrush Buckeye	8 to 10 feet	8 to 12 feet	Full sun to half shade in a moist, well-drained soil.	White flowers in summer and yellow foliage in fall.
Buddleia davidii Butterfly Bush	5 to 10 feet	5 to 8 feet	Full sun and a well-drained soil.	Fragrant flowers in shades of pink, purple, yellow, and white.
Callicarpa americana American Beautyberry	3 to 8 feet	3 to 8 feet	Full sun or shade with a well-drained soil. Tolerates coastal conditions.	Large clusters of magenta fruits in fall.
Callicarpa dichotoma Purple Beautyberry	3 to 5 feet	3 to 6 feet	Full sun or half shade with a well-drained soil.	Violet-purple fruits in fall.
Calycanthus floridus Carolina Allspice Sweetshrub	5 to 15 feet	5 to 8 feet	Full sun or half shade in a well-drained soil.	Dark-maroon, spicy, pungent flowers in spring.
Camellia spp.	6 to 15 feet	4 to 6 feet	Partial shade with a moist, well-drained soil is best.	Many selections, including those that flower in spring or fall.
Cephalotaxus harringtonia 'Duke Gardens' Spreading Plum Yew	2 to 3 feet	4 to 5 feet	Shade is best, but this plant will tolerate full sun.	Glossy needles look good all year.
Chimonanthus praecox 'Concolor' Fragrant Wintersweet	10 to 15 feet	8 to 12 feet	Full sun or partial shade in a well-drained soil.	Fragrant flowers in winter.
Clethra alnifolia Summersweet	4 to 8 feet	4 to 6 feet	Full sun or shade. Tolerates a range of soil types including wet soils.	Fragrant spikes of flowers in summer attract bees and humans alike.

For more information on planting and care, refer to the *Georgia Gardener's Guide*.

Shrubs for Georgia

Variety	Height	Spread	Culture	Comments
Cotinus coggygria Smokebush	8 to 12 feet	8 to 12 feet	Full sun is best. Adapts to a wide range of soil types.	Purple-leaved selections stand out in the landscape.
Daphne odora Winter Daphne	2 to 4 feet	2 to 4 feet	Partial shade is best. Requires a well-drained soil.	Fragrant flowers in winter make this a winner.
Fothergilla gardenii 'Mt. Airy' Dwarf Fothergilla	3 to 5 feet	3 to 4 feet	Full sun to half shade with a well-drained acid soil.	Tiny bottlebrush-like flowers in spring. Leaf color in fall can be red, orange, or yellow.
Gardenia jasminoides Cape Jasmine	4 to 6 feet	4 to 6 feet	Full sun to half shade with a moist acid soil.	Fragrant flowers in spring and summer.
Hamamelis × intermedia Witchhazel	15 to 20 feet	10 to 15 feet	Full sun to half shade with a moist acid soil.	Fragrant flowers in shades of yellow, orange, and red that look like spiders in late winter.
Hibiscus syriacus Rose of Sharon	8 to 12 feet	6 to 10 feet	Full sun, tolerates most types of soil provided they are well drained.	Flowers from summer to fall. Selections come in shades of pink, lavender, and white.
Hydrangea arborescens 'Annabelle' Hydrangea	4 to 6 feet	4 to 6 feet	Partial shade is best, but will tolerate full sun if there is plenty of moisture.	Flowers in early summer. Large white balls provide a long season of interest.
Hydrangea macrophylla Bigleaf Hydrangea	3 to 8 feet	3 to 10 feet	Full sun to partial shade in a moist, well-drained soil. Acid soils produce the bluest flowers.	Depending on the selection, flowers appear in summer in shades of blue, white, maroon, and purple.
Hydrangea paniculata 'Tardiva' *Panicle Hydrangea*	10 to 15 feet	10 to 20 feet	Tolerates full sun better than most types of **Hydrangeas.** Prefers well-drained soil.	One of the latest of the **Hydrangeas** to flower. Cones of white in early fall.

Shrubs for Georgia

Variety	Height	Spread	Culture	Comments
Hydrangea quercifolia Oakleaf Hydrangea	4 to 8 feet	4 to 10 feet	Sun to half shade with a moist, well-drained soil.	White flowers appear in late spring to early summer and are effective for months.
Ilex cornuta Chinese Holly	8 to 20 feet	8 to 15 feet	Full sun and a well-drained soil. This holly is heat- and drought-tolerant.	The glossy green foliage looks good all year. The cultivar 'Burfordii' is a heavy fruiter.
Ilex crenata Japanese Holly	3 to 15 feet	2 to 10 feet	Grows in full sun or shade but likes a well-drained soil.	Small evergreen foliage.
Ilex glabra Inkberry Holly	4 to 8 feet	8 to 10 feet	Full sun to shade with a moist soil.	The olive green foliage looks good all year. 'Nigra' has purplish foliage.
Ilex verticillata Winterberry Holly	6 to 10 feet	6 to 8 feet	Full sun to partial shade. Tolerates soils that are wet or dry.	The colorful red fruits on bare stems stand out in the winter landscape.
Illicium spp. Anise	6 to 10 feet	5 to 10 feet	Most types prefer partial to full shade with a moist, well-drained soil.	The foliage is evergreen and, depending on the species, ranges from olive to dark green with tinges of red.
Itea virginica 'Henry's Garnet' Virginia Sweetspire	3 to 8 feet	4 to 8 feet	Full sun to half shade. This plant will grow in swampy conditions as well as dry soils.	White pendulous flowers in summer and fall foliage in shades of red, burgundy, and orange.
Loropetalum chinense Loropetalum	6 to 10 feet	6 to 10 feet	Full sun to half shade.	Many selections available. Most have burgundy-colored foliage and pink flowers.

Shrubs for Georgia

Variety	Height	Spread	Culture	Comments
Rhapidophyllum hystrix Needle Palm	6 to 8 feet	6 to 8 feet	Grows in full sun to shade in a wide range of soil types.	Native to the coastal plains, this palm is hardy in most parts of Georgia.
Rhododendron catawbiense Catawba Rhododendron	6 to 10 feet	5 to 8 feet	Partial to half shade in a well-drained soil.	Lilac-purple flowers in spring. There are many selections with a variety of flower colors.
Rhododendron prunifolium Plumleaf Rhododendron	7 to 10 feet	6 to 8 feet	Full sun to half shade. Likes well-drained soils.	Orange to red-orange flowers in late summer.
Rhododendron spp. Spring-Flowering Azaleas	2 to 8 feet	4 to 10 feet	Partial shade with a moist, well-drained soil is best.	Spring-flowering selections come in a wide range of colors.
Trachycarpus fortunei Windmill Palm	20 to 30 feet	10 to 15 feet	Full sun to part shade in a well-drained soil.	A good choice for coastal gardens, this palm is hardy to 10 degrees F.
Spiraea spp. Spirea	2 to 9 feet	2 to 8 feet	Full sun to partial shade in well-drained soil.	Many types of this old-fashioned favorite.
Viburnum dilatatum Linden Viburnum	8 to 10 feet	4 to 8 feet	Will tolerate full sun, but partial shade is best, with a moist soil.	The cultivar 'Iroquois' has large clusters of scarlet fruits in fall.
Viburnum × pragense Prague Viburnum	8 to 12 feet	8 to 10 feet	Full sun to half shade with a well-drained soil.	The glossy evergreen foliage is this plant's main attribute.
Viburnum setigerum Tea Viburnum	8 to 12 feet	4 to 6 feet	Full sun or partial shade with a moist, well-drained soil.	The fall fruits in shades of red to orange are the best reason to grow this **Viburnum.**

Planning

Take a good look at your landscape and think about what you would like to add or change. The best gardens happen not by accident but by careful planning (as well as by a good bit of trial and error!). Come up with an overall plan and you will be able to refer to it as you develop your garden over time. Ask yourself some basic questions before hiring a designer or before you design your own garden.

- How do I like to use my garden? During what seasons is it most important to me?

- Which of my existing plants are thriving and which ones are not performing well?

- How will my garden look in spring, summer, fall, and winter?

- Am I planning to include plants with attractive foliage as well as those with beautiful flowers?

- Which types of plants do I like to feature in my garden? For example, do I like spiky flowers, delicate foliage, pleasing scents, other features . . . ?

Follow these steps if you are drawing your own garden plan:

1 Use a piece of graph paper. Your drawing doesn't have to be exactly to scale, but include a rough sketch of your house to use as a reference when deciding where to locate plants.

2 Indicate the major trees, shrubs, and lawn areas on your plan.

3 Indicate where you have full shade, full sun, or a mixture of shade and sun.

4 Mark areas where there are extreme soil conditions such as soils that stay constantly wet or soils that have a high percentage of sand.

5 A North arrow will help you determine the direction light comes from and how to site future plants.

Once you have your basic visual information you can begin to decide where you want to place additional plants. Start with trees and shrubs—later you will add perennials, annuals, vines, and bulbs. Begin a garden journal so you can keep track of what happens in your garden as it develops. You should note changes to your original plan as well as make comments on the weather and take notes on how your plantings develop. Photograph your garden now so you will be able to compare how it looks in winter with how it looks during other seasons.

Now is the time to take a look at your garden. Some shrubs may have outgrown their allotted space, or they may not be thriving because conditions have changed. Where you once had full sun may be shady now because a large tree has matured. Perhaps a natural disaster turned a shade garden into a virtual desert. Whatever the reason for the changes in your garden, you can take action in response to them:

- In south Georgia, shrubs can be moved to a better spot now.

- Plan to *replace* shrubs that are not thriving with those better suited to your environment.

- Make a list of possible replacement plants with notes on their cultural requirements, ultimate size, and other features. Collect color photographs from catalogs and develop your own reference guide.

- Locate plant sources. When possible, purchase plants from a local or regional nursery—this will help ensure that they will be best adapted to grow in your Georgia garden. Contact the Georgia Green Industry Association (see Resources, p. 355) for a list of nurseries in your area.

Planting

As long as the ground is not frozen or saturated with water, you can *plant* shrubs during mild spells at this time of year.

JANUARY

Watering

Water new plantings.

If there is no rain during mild spells, water evergreen shrubs. Don't let them get to the stage where the leaves or needles begin to look crisp and fall off.

Don't allow large shrubs in containers to dry out. When the top 2 inches of the soil in a container is dry to the touch, *water* until water rushes out the bottom of the container. If the soil has shrunk away from the sides of the pot you may have to apply water several times, allowing it to soak in after each dousing.

Fertilizing

Topdress shrub beds with 1 to 2 inches of organic amendments such as mushroom compost, cottonseed meal, or cow manure. As the organic material continues to break down, it will be a good source of food for your plants when the roots begin to grow in spring. Be sure you don't pile it up around the stems or trunks of plants.

Apply a 2-inch layer of mulch around new plantings. Use pine straw, bark nuggets, shredded bark, leaves, peanut hulls, or cocoa shells.

Helpful Hints for Cut Flowers

Cut branches of **Winter Honeysuckle** *Lonicera fragrantissima* to bring into the house to force into bloom.

Snip a few stems of **Japanese Flowering Apricot** *Prunus mume* when it is in bud. The sweet-scented flowers will perfume a room and lift your spirits.

Cut **Camellias** when they are still in bud but beginning to show color. You will enjoy blooms for a week or more, and the foliage can last for a month if the stems are kept in water.

Pest Control

Remove debris and dead leaves from planting beds to reduce future insect and disease problems.

Depending on the variety, **Camellias** bloom at various times from November through April. *Check* them for signs of petal blight, which is caused by a fungus—the flowers may have brown spots that are irregular in shape, or the buds may turn brown before opening, or the blooms may have a nettled appearance. *Remove and destroy* any flowers or buds that show signs of this blight. The first spots appear on expanding petals; then they spread until the flower is brown and dead. Collecting the fallen flowers will help reduce the spread of this fungus. If more than 50 percent of the flowers appear infected, you may want to use a fungicide to control the problem (see Chemicals, p. 327).

Pruning

Remove any dead or damaged wood from existing shrubs. Dead wood is dry and brittle—if you are not sure if a branch is dead, scratch it with your fingernail. If the inside is green, then there is still hope, and you can wait until spring to see if any buds form.

Renovate overgrown shrubs by removing one-third of the oldest branches from the base of the plant. The oldest branches are usually the thickest. Remember that many spring-flowering shrubs bloom on old wood (branches that grew the previous season), so you will want to wait until after they flower to do any drastic pruning.

Planning

Visit public gardens and make a list of shrubs that provide interest in the winter with blooms, bark, or berries. Note the cultural requirements for these plants. Some shrubs that have fragrant flowers in winter are:

- *Chimonanthus praecox* **Wintersweet**

- *Daphne odora* **Winter Daphne**

- *Hamamelis mollis* **Chinese Witchhazel**

- *Hamamelis* × *intermedia* **Witchhazel** selections

- *Lonicera fragrantissima* **Winter Honeysuckle**

- *Mahonia bealei* **Leatherleaf Mahonia**

- *Prunus mume* **Japanese Flowering Apricot** (a large shrub or small tree)

Make notes in your garden journal about the weather, changes in light, and how your plants perform. Photograph your garden at least once a month to help you keep up with changes.

Plan to add at least one shrub with winter blooms or berries to your garden this spring. Winter wonders include **Winter Honeysuckle,** evergreen **Hollies,** and deciduous **Hollies.** When you select **Hollies** for your garden, keep in mind that you will need a male plant for pollination in order to guarantee the best fruit production. The female selections display fruit in season, while the male does not. For example, the **American Holly,** *Ilex opaca* **'Merry Christmas',** needs one male selection of the same species or hybrid; the same is true of deciduous **Hollies.** Some nurseries sell male selections with the females; one male is sufficient to pollinate a group of females.

Planting

Prepare the soil for spring planting.

1 Add soil amendments and *rototill* to a depth of 8 to 12 inches. You have many choices when it comes to soil amendments for your garden. Although peat moss is an option, it is expensive, breaks down quickly, and causes soil to be more acidic. It is better to use a soil amendment like chicken manure, horse manure, or mushroom compost, or a product like Nature's Helper™ or Clay Cutter™.

2 Test your soil (see Horticultural Practices, p. 7). You can purchase a kit from your local garden center and do it yourself, or send a sample to your local Extension Service (see Resources, p. 353). Contact your Extension Service for information on how to take a soil sample. The Extension Service charges a nominal fee and will send you a detailed analysis of your soil, including information about what you need to add in the way of nutrients and lime.

3 Add lime if recommended by your soil test.

Continue planting shrubs as long as the ground is not frozen. Plant container-grown, bare-root, or balled-and-burlapped shrubs. *Remove* plants from containers.

If you have a balled-and-burlapped shrub and the burlap is a synthetic material, place the plant in the hole and gently *pull out* the material from around the rootball. This will cause the least amount of stress to the roots.

Dig holes as deep as the size of the container the plant is growing in. For bare-root or balled-and-burlapped shrubs, the hole should be as deep as the roots are long. The width of the hole should be at least twice the width of the container.

This is an ideal time to plant a **Winter Daphne** *Daphne odora,* an evergreen that should be in full bloom at nurseries now. One whiff of the powerfully fragrant flowers and you'll be hooked. A hardy evergreen shrub, it grows happily in a large pot, or in the garden if the soil is slightly moist and extremely well drained.

Pruning

Continue to *prune* deciduous shrubs to remove dead wood, rejuvenate them, or keep them from getting too big for the space in which they are growing (as when they block the view from windows or spread out into a pathway). One way to avoid the need to prune constantly is to select the right plant for the right place. Do some research before you plant!

If shrubs have outgrown their original location or have become straggly and spindly in appearance, *prune them back severely* while they are dormant. Prune back **Azaleas, Spiraea, Privet,** and *Abelia ×grandiflora* to a height of about 12 inches.

You may choose to stretch out the pruning over a period of years. Remove 1/3 of the oldest wood in the first year; in the second year, take out 1/2 of the remaining oldest stems and cut back long shoots that grew from the previous season; in the third year, prune out whatever old wood (the oldest wood has the thickest stems) is remaining, and prune new shoots just enough for a pleasing effect.

A Recipe for Amending Clay Soil

1/3 coarse sand (Builders sand, not play sand—almost like a very small gravel); add more sand for soils with more than 50% clay

1/3 organic material (compost, Nature's Helper™, or other bagged products)

1/3 existing topsoil (some clay is beneficial but if you have one hundred percent clay, remove it and replace it with a quality topsoil)

Prune **Camellias** once they finish flowering. Remove faded blooms and snip back the tips of branches for an overall pleasing effect.

A fungal disease that affects the flowers of **Camellia japonica** *and other varieties is spread by spores. Good cultural practices are the best way to control this disease. Refer to the discussion of petal blight in January.*

Prune evergreen shrubs like **Boxwood, Holly, Anise, Leucothoe,** and others before new growth begins. *Remove* dead wood and tip back branches to a desired height.

Watering

Keep new plantings well watered (new plantings are those that have been planted in the last six months). Water once a week if you get no rain.

Pest Control

Reapply weed-preventers (see September) to prevent any future crops of chickweed from being established. A pre-emergent will prevent weed seeds from germinating.

Pull weeds when they are young, before they set seed. This will reduce future populations of weeds.

Use a hand cultivator to scratch out weeds around shrubs. Apply a fresh layer of mulch to help kill weeds and retain moisture in the soil.

To kill insects that overwinter such as scales, lace bugs, and mites, *spray* horticultural oil (see Chemicals, p. 327). Scale insects are particularly difficult to control. Closely related to mealybugs and aphids, they have a waxy shell-like covering, either hard or soft, that protects them from natural enemies and insecticides.

MARCH

Planning

Try not to be an impulsive shopper. Before you head out to the nursery or garden center, make sure you have a list with specific information such as the height, flower color, foliage, cultural requirements, and botanical names of the plants you want. Knowing the botanical names (see Horticultural Practices, p. 7) will help ensure that you get the plants you want. A good example of the confusion that can be caused by plant names is the common name **Wild Honeysuckle.** This name is used for many different types of native **Azaleas.** If you want a specific type of native **Azalea,** it is good to know, for example, that *Rhododendron austrinum* is different from *Rhododendron alabamense.* Have alternatives in mind if you can't find a specific variety.

When you purchase your shrubs, consider which perennials, annuals, and bulbs will make happy companions for them.

Companions for Shade

- **Azalea** and **Woodland Phlox** or **Foam Flower**

- **Camellias** and **Hellebores**

- **Oakleaf Hydrangea** and ferns like the **Autumn Fern**

Companions for Sun

- **Butterfly Bush** and **Lantana**

- **Boxwood** and **Ivy** or **Mondo Grass**

- **Slender Deutzia** and *Scabiosa* 'Butterfly Blue'

Keep up with changes in your garden by recording them in your garden journal.

Planting

This is an ideal time to plant shrubs, provided the ground is not too wet. The soil should hold some moisture. Try the squeeze test:

Take a handful of soil and squeeze it. If it forms a hard ball, than it is probably too wet for planting. If it sticks together momentarily but crumbles easily, it is just right.

Remove plants from the containers. (Refer to February for instructions on how to do this.)

If you have heavy clay soils, plant high so the top third of the rootball is out of the ground. This is especially true for shrubs like evergreen **Rhododendrons,** which resent soils that are not well drained. *Mound* plenty of soil around the rootball and then apply a good layer of mulch, making sure to keep it away from the main trunk. This will ensure that your plant doesn't dry out too quickly, but the roots won't sit in wet soil.

When you plant, fill in with soil around the rootball and *tamp it down* with your shoes or a shovel handle. This will remove air pockets and prevent soil from settling.

Watering

Water new plantings "long and slow"—if you use the hose, a pencil-size trickle is good. Any plants that you have added to your garden within the past six to twelve months will benefit from some extra tender loving care. Depending on the size of the rootball, it may take anywhere from 15 minutes to an hour, with the hose at slow trickle, to water an individual shrub.

Fertilizing

Use a balanced granular fertilizer (10-10-10) around shrubs. Determine amounts according to the size of plants. As a rule of thumb, use 1 tablespoon of 10-10-10 per foot of shrub height. Refer to the product label for specific usage directions.

MARCH

Mulch new plantings 2 to 3 inches deep, being sure to keep mulch away from the trunk or stems.

Pest Control

Inspect Azaleas for signs of lace bugs: the leaves will have tiny yellow speckles. You will treat for these pests in April or May before adults lay eggs.

Use horticultural oil and insecticidal soap (see Chemicals, p. 327) to control insects like aphids, scale, and mites. Read the label carefully. The best time to spray your plants is on a clear day when rain is unlikely for at least six hours—this will give the spray enough time to dry completely. It is best to spray early in the morning when temperatures are coolest. *Avoid* spraying on windy days when the spray can easily drift to other plants.

Pruning

Some evergreen shrubs get overgrown or leggy over time. Now is a good time to renovate **Boxwoods** and other broadleaf evergreens like **Hollies:**

Tips for Growing Boxwood

According to Walt Harrison of Habersham Gardens in Atlanta, the secret to growing **Boxwood** in Georgia is having the right soil pH. **Boxwoods** are happiest in a soil that is neutral to slightly basic, a pH around 7 to 8. This allows for better uptake of iron, which prevents the chlorosis (yellowing of leaves) that **Boxwoods** often exhibit.

Certain plants like **Boxwood** are sensitive to heat and drought stress. To prevent problems, keep the shrubs watered throughout the growing season. Many gardeners have good success with their **Boxwoods** when they mulch with a 1-inch layer of cottonseed meal, keeping it away from the trunk.

- *Prune them back hard*, reducing the overall size of the plant by one third.

- *Prune back* shrubs drastically to a height of 12 inches if they are straggly and have leaves only at the tips of the branches.

Pruning now will give shrubs time to put out new growth that will harden off before hot weather sets in. Pruning tips:

- If you use electric hedge trimmers to prune your evergreens, follow up with a pair of handpruners. Use handpruners to remove stems down to where a branch forks. This will open up the plant and allow light to get in, which will encourage new growth. The result will be fuller, healthier plants.

- In coastal parts of the state, *prune* spring-flowering shrubs like **Azaleas** and **Camellias** after they finish flowering. If your hybrid **Azaleas** (many ornamental **Azaleas** are hybrids) are getting overgrown or leggy, *prune them back* to about 12 inches tall. If you keep them watered and fertilized, they should recover and develop into fully leafed plants.

- Native **Azaleas** require little or no pruning unless they are too large for the space in which you have planted them. They should never be sheared (which means cut back to an even height with electric hedge trimmers or hand shears), but should be pruned to enhance their natural form. It should be noted that some native **Azaleas** can reach heights of 10 feet or more.

Planning

This is a great time to add shrubs to your garden or to transplant existing shrubs. Make sure you have selected varieties that are suited to the growing conditions in your garden. The advantage of purchasing plants in bloom is that you will know the color of the flowers and will be able to give them your own personal sniff test to determine whether or not they are fragrant.

Photograph your garden as it begins to bloom. In your garden journal, keep track of how long your shrubs bloom, noting perennials that bloom at the same time. This will help you plan pleasing combinations like **Beautybush,** *Kolkwitzia amabilis,* underplanted with *Scabiosa* **'Butterfly Blue'.**

Planting and Transplanting

Soak bare-root plants in a bucket of water before planting, and *prune off* any dead or badly damaged roots, such as those that are cracked or broken.

You can plant container-grown shrubs all month long, following these steps:

1 *Dig a hole* that is as deep as the container and twice as wide.

Height of Hole

Width of Hole

2 Use a shovel to hit the sides of the container. This will make it easier to slide out the whole rootball.

Removing Container

3 Use a sharp pair of hand pruners to make two or three cuts into the rootball, spacing the distance between cuts equally. This will encourage new roots to sprout and establish more quickly.

4 *Trim off* any dead topgrowth.

5 Place the rootball in the hole and fill in the soil around it. Don't pile lots of extra soil on top of the top layer of soil—this will suffocate surface roots.

6 *Water* the shrub well.

7 Apply a 2-inch layer of mulch around newly planted shrubs.

When you are transplanting shrubs, dig as large a rootball as possible. The more roots you get, the better success you'll have moving your shrubs. If your shrub is 3 feet across, you should measure 3 feet out from the main stem, all the way around the plant. At this point, take your spade and cut into the roots. Some shrubs, like **Azaleas,** have lots of shallow roots that spread out in every direction, so it is necessary to dig a rootball that is wider than it is deep, looking almost like a thin, wide pancake. Prepare the new location ahead of time. The less time a plant stays out of the ground, the fewer roots will dry out and die. Sometimes a piece of burlap or 4 mil. plastic is a useful tool to help drag the rootball to its new home. Place the rootball on the burlap and pull it to where it will be planted.

After planting, *tamp down* the soil around the roots to remove any air pockets. Fill up the hole halfway with soil, add water, let it settle, and then fill in the remaining soil. Apply a 2-inch layer of mulch, keeping it away from the main trunk. Mulching helps keep the soil cool or warm, depending on the season, and reduces infestations of weeds.

Watering

Water newly planted and transplanted shrubs after you plant them and then once a week (unless there is a good rain) for the first month. Place the hose at the base of the shrub and let a slow stream saturate the area. A good rule of thumb is to apply 1 to 2 gallons per foot of plant height. Soaker hoses also work well.

In coastal areas where soils are sandy, shrubs may need watering more frequently. Dig into the top 2 to 3 inches of the soil to determine if it is dry. Established plantings will also benefit from supplemental watering during periods of drought.

Fertilizing

You can *fertilize* established shrubs in spring. A balanced fertilizer like 10-10-10 is good. Follow label directions for proper application. Too little is better than too much.

As an alternative to chemical fertilizers, you can topdress your shrubs with compost or an organic soil amendment, either store-bought such as bagged cow manure, or homemade compost. Apply a good 1 to 2 inches over the soil surrounding your shrubs. As this material breaks down, it provides welcome nutrients for the soil, resulting in healthier roots and overall increased vigor for the plant.

Pest Control

Check for signs of insect activity or damage. Aphids, scale, or chewing insects may be visible. Try using insecticidal soaps or a strong blast from the hose to control aphids before you resort to using chemical controls. If you notice that **Azalea** leaves are bleached out (silvery and speckled), you may have lace bugs.

Spray with insecticidal soap or an insecticide to treat lace bugs (see Chemicals, p. 327).

Handpull any weeds, or use a cultivator to scratch them out. Once an area is free of weeds, apply a pre-emergent (see Chemicals, p. 327) and a layer of mulch. This practice will greatly reduce weed infestations.

Some gardeners put down weed fabrics to control weed problems, but newspaper will also work. Apply a layer of newspaper at least three sheets thick and then cover it with mulch. (This technique may not be practical for formal gardens.)

Pruning

Prune flowering shrubs like **Forsythia, Flowering Quince,** early-blooming **Spireas** (*Spiraea nipponica* 'Snowmound', *S. thunbergii*), and **Azaleas** as soon as they finish blooming. If shrubs are overgrown and lacking vigor, with very few blooms, pruning can help rejuvenate them. *Remove* one-third of the oldest wood completely, and cut the remaining stems to a height of 12 inches. Follow this practice for the next few years, and you will create a healthy, vigorous plant.

Planning

Now that spring is in full bloom, it is a good time to evaluate individual shrubs and decide if you have the right plants in the right places. Pick a bouquet of flowers from your favorite shrubs. Arrange the flowers in a vase and note the various color combinations. This can help you decide on which colors to add to your garden.

Shrubs for Spring Blooms

* *Deutzia gracilis* (white flowers)

* *Kolkwitzia amabilis* (pink flowers)

* *Philadelphus coronarius* (white flowers)

* *Rhododendron* species and hybrids (many colors)

* *Spiraea* (many species and colors)

* *Viburnum* (many cultivars and hybrids)

Planting

Continue adding shrubs to your garden. Container-grown plants can be planted throughout the year as long as you water properly after planting.

If you transplant a shrub while it is in bloom, thinning it back by one-third will reduce the transplant shock, and the plant will recover more quickly. In the warm coastal parts of the state you will have better success if you transplant shrubs during the cooler months of March or November.

Watering

Water all new plantings once a week unless you have regular long, soaking rains (more than a quick thunderstorm). Keep this practice up until plants are well established, or at least for the first growing season. If you use a sprinkler to water a shrub bed, make sure that all parts of the bed receive good coverage.

One way to measure water application is to use shallow cans like tuna fish cans, placing them in several different areas. When they average ³⁄₄ inch full, you have probably watered a shrub area long enough for that week.

Fertilizing

It's still not too late to *fertilize* your shrubs for the spring if you haven't already done so. Your plants still have time to use fertilizer while they are actively growing. Once it gets hot, growth slows down and plants don't require as much fertilizer. Use a complete balanced fertilizer like 10-10-10. As a general rule, apply 1 tablespoon per foot of plant height. Refer to the product label for detailed information.

Pest Control

Leaves on **Azaleas** or **Camellias** may become distorted and pale green; as they thicken, they turn brown, then white. These are symptoms of leaf gall. While the disease doesn't kill the plant, the symptoms are unsightly. *Handpick* the galls and *destroy* them before they turn white.

Continue to examine shrubs for signs of damage from insects or diseases. Spider mites and aphids will be more active as the weather gets warmer.

If the leaves on your **Crapemyrtle** have a grayish coating, you probably have powdery mildew. Cool nights followed by warm days, poor air circulation, and not enough sun all contribute to an environment that favors powdery mildew. This fungus can affect **Crapemyrtle, Lilac, Hydrangea,** and other plants. For severe infestations, use a fungicide (see Chemicals, p. 327). For an organic alternative to a synthetic fungicide, try spraying a mixture of 4 teaspoons baking soda in 1 gallon of water on the plants. Apply this spray once a week. Be sure to *cover* the tops and bottoms of the leaves with whatever spray you use.

Spot-spray weeds in shrub beds with a nonselective herbicide (see Chemicals, p. 327). *Use extreme caution: do not apply on windy days, since nonselective herbicides kill everything they touch.* You can hold a piece of cardboard in front of a shrub to protect it from damage while you spray the surrounding weeds with the herbicide. If the weeds are close to stems or foliage on shrubs, dip a small paintbrush in the diluted chemical and carefully "paint" the chemical on the weeds. Another, similar method is to don two rubber gloves—to ensure safety—on one hand. Dip that hand in the herbicide and swipe the foliage with the chemical. *Discard the paintbrush or gloves after use.*

Soil Layering

A simple method for propagating **Hydrangeas** and certain other shrubs is by soil-layering, a method that can be used from April through autumn.

1 Choose a limb close to the ground. Press it downward until the stem touches the ground.

2 At the point where the branch touches the ground, scratch the stem (wound it) to expose the inner bark. This is where the roots will develop. You will get even better results if the point of contact also has a node (the part of the stem where shoots, leaves, or buds emerge).

3 Cover the wound (not the entire limb) with soil–the richer the soil, the better results you can expect.

4 Place a brick or rock on top to hold the branch in place. At least 6 inches of branch tip and leaves should be showing beyond the brick.

5 Keep it watered–don't let it dry out.

6 In two months, tug gently to see if roots have formed. If there are substantial roots, cut the new plant from the mother plant. If there are only a few roots, recover with soil and check again in another month.

Pruning

Prune shrubs like **Viburnum, Rhododendron,** and **Mock Orange** after they finish flowering.

Remove spent blossoms before they set seed on evergreen **Rhododendrons** and **Mountain Laurel.** This helps with overall vigor. The plant will be able to put its energy into forming next year's flower buds and new growth instead of seeds.

Planning

Now is a great time to add some summer-blooming shrubs to your garden.

Summer-Blooming Shrubs

- *Aesculus parviflora* **Bottlebrush Buckeye**

- *Buddleia davidii* and selections **Butterfly Bush**

- *Clerodendrum trichotomum* **Harlequin Glorybower**

- *Clethra alnifolia* **Summersweet**

- *Gardenia jasminoides*, many cultivars ('Klein's Hardy' is hardy to 0 degrees Fahrenheit)

- *Hibiscus syriacus* 'Diana' **Rose of Sharon,** white-flowered selection

- *Hydrangea paniculata* 'Tardiva' **Panicle Hydrangea**

- *Hydrangea quercifolia* **Oakleaf Hydrangea**

- *Hypericum frondosum* 'Sunburst' **Golden St. John's Wort**

- *Lantana camara* 'Miss Huff' (really a hardy perennial, it acts like a small shrub in coastal areas and can grow to 6 feet or taller)

- *Vitex agnus-castus* (**Chaste Tree**)

Think about having a variety of shrubs in your garden so it will have something of interest—like flowers, foliage, or fruit—during every season. *Record* your observations in your garden journal, keeping track of what's in bloom, which plants are thriving, and which plants may need to be replaced. Take photos of your garden in summer; they will help you remember what blooms when and the color of different flowers. If you have a videocamera, you can produce a tour of your garden, which may help you decide what to add or subtract in the future.

Planting

Add container-grown plants to your garden as long as the temperatures are not too hot. If temperatures are in the 90-degree-F. range, the plants will be slow to put out roots.

Rototill and *add soil amendments* to areas in which you will plant shrubs in the future.

If you have time, handdigging is another option. You can work on one area at a time, making sure to mix in organic materials to a depth of 12 to 18 inches.

Mulch new plantings with a 2- to 3-inch layer. Keep mulch away from the main stems; when it is piled up around stems, it can create an envi-

ronment that is attractive to insects and pests.

Watering

Summer can arrive quickly. Keep new plantings well watered. Don't wait until plants look wilted before you water; *check* them once a week. If the top 2 to 3 inches of soil is dry to the touch, it is time to water. When you water, do so thoroughly once or twice a week rather than a little every day. This will help your shrubs develop strong, deep roots. If you use a hose, place it near the center of the shrub and let a small stream of water soak in for at least a half hour. If you use a sprinkler, place some shallow tuna fish or cat food cans around the plants, and water until the cans are $3/4$ inch full.

Established shrubs will benefit from supplemental water during periods of drought. Place the hose at soil level near the center of the plant, and saturate the root area.

Fertilizing

If you haven't fertilized shrubs yet, apply some 10-10-10. A granular slow-release fertilizer persists longer than a liquid feed, but both are effective. As a general rule, when using granular fertilizers, apply 1 tablespoon per foot of plant height.

Pest Control

Good cultural practices will help reduce pest and disease problems:

- *Clean up* any leaf litter that accumulates under or around shrubs.

- *Destroy* infected leaves to prevent the spread of diseases.

- Keep shrubs watered and mulched.

- Keep weeds out of shrub beds.

- You can add ground covers under your shrubs and trees to help keep roots cool as well as add interest to the garden.

Examine your shrubs for signs of damage by insects or disease. If you have Japanese beetles in small numbers, try handpicking them and drowning them in soapy water. This is best done in the early morning when they are less active. If infestations are severe, you may want to consider using an insecticide (see Roses, June).

Check shrubs for signs of aphids or spider mites. Use insecticidal soaps to control these pest problems before resorting to chemical controls. Spray early in the day before temperatures are too hot. When you spray, be sure to cover both the tops and undersides of the leaves and the stems; spray to the point where it drips off the plant.

Pruning

Shear hedges when they look untidy and branches are uneven. *Prune* them so they are slightly wider at the bottom than they are at the top. This will result in fuller, healthier plants.

- Conifers like **Hemlocks** should be sheared before midsummer or when dormant in winter.

- **Privet, Barberry,** and other rapid-growing shrubs can be sheared several times during the growing season.

Use electric or hand shears to *prune* the top and the sides of a hedge. Follow up with a pair of handpruners to even out rough spots or clip any stems that were missed. This will result in a more symmetrical hedge over time.

- *Prune Abelia grandiflora* to shape it up. Cut back long shoots. If the shrub is overgrown and straggly, remove onethird of the oldest wood from the base of the plant and then remove another third next year.

Prune spring-blooming shrubs that flower on old wood once they finish flowering. Most shrubs will not require extensive pruning, but if there are long wild shoots or you want to shape the plant, now is a good time to prune so new growth will have time to harden off, and there will be less chance the pruning will affect next year's bloom.

Shrubs to Prune Selectively

- *Kolkwitzia amabilis* **Beautybush**

- *Viburnum × burkwoodii*

- *Viburnum × carlcephalum*

- *Viburnum carlesii*

- *Viburnum macrocephalum*

Prune any late-flowering varieties of **Azaleas** and **Rhododendrons** after they stop blooming. If you wait until later in the season, you'll prune off potential flower buds for next year. *Deadhead* **Rhododendron** blossoms once they finish flowering. This will result in many more blooms next spring.

Helpful Hint

Invest in a good pair of pruning shears. You will have them for years to come, and if you purchase a high-quality type, you'll never have to replace them. Many gardeners swear by their Felco #2 pruners.

Planning

Evaluate the shrubs in your garden. Do they look attractive even when they are not fruiting or in bloom? Do they provide a background or complement for your perennials and annuals? Do you have a mix of evergreen and deciduous shrubs, including those with colorful flowers, foliage, and fruits?

There may be gaps in your garden where shrubs would help fill the void. Think about which shrubs you would like to add or eliminate so you can develop a plan for the fall. Make notes in your garden journal about which plants still look good during the hot summer months.

Planting

This month is generally too hot to add new plants to the garden, as the soil and air temperatures are not ideal for encouraging root growth . . . but if this is the only time you have to plant, get out the shovel! Many of the shrubs that nurseries offer are grown in containers that stay outside all year long. This means that unless the ground is frozen or saturated, plants can be added to your garden throughout the year. This is not true for bareroot plants, which must be dormant when you plant them.

Growing Shrubs in Decorative Containers: Even when the weather is hot, you can add instant color to your garden with containers of shrubs, trees, annuals, and perennials. Mixing colorful perennials with shrubs can create a pleasing effect. Shrubs like **Boxwood** grow happily year-round in containers and can add a touch of formality to the garden. When growing shrubs in containers, make sure you use a soil mix that includes organic amendments, coarse sand, and even a small amount of clay. The clay will help the soil hold moisture.

Soilless mixes dry out quickly and offer little in the way of nutrients. Refer to mix recipe in Houseplants, August.

Watering

This is an important time to *check* shrubs regularly and make sure they are getting enough water. Any shrubs in large containers will probably need watering at least once a day or more. When you water containers, whether shrubs, trees, annuals, or perennials, water until it rushes out the holes in the bottom of the pot. If the soil has shrunk away from the sides of the pot, water, let it soak in, and then water again.

When watering shrubs in the ground, too much water can be as harmful as too little. If you're not sure whether to water or not, *check* the rootball—don't base your watering decisions solely on the time of year.

New plantings should be watered once a week. *Saturate* the rootball. If you use the hose, place it near the center of the shrub and leave it on a slow trickle for 15 minutes or more, depending on the size of the rootball.

If you have a problem spot in your garden where the soil stays moist all or most of the time, it's best not to fight it but to select plants that will not only survive but thrive in such an environment. Shrubs that tolerate soils that are constantly moist include:

- *Clethra alnifolia* **Sweet Pepperbush**

- *Ilex verticillata* **Winterberry Holly**

- *Itea virginica* **Virginia Sweetspire**

Fertilizing

Wait until fall to fertilize any shrubs.

Pest Control

Hot weather seems to encourage pests like spider mites and aphids. *Examine* shrubs regularly for signs of damage; use insecticidal soaps to control these problems before resorting to a chemical pesticide. Sometimes even a blast of cold water from the hose can eradicate a problem like aphids.

Spot-spray weeds around shrubs with a nonselective herbicide (see Chemicals, p. 327). Protect stems and foliage from coming into contact with spray. A piece of newspaper or cardboard makes a good shield against any drift.

If any of your shrubs suffer from powdery mildew, black spot, or insect problems, make sure to *collect and destroy* infected leaves as soon as they hit the ground. This will help reduce the spread of diseases and insects.

A good time to handweed is the day after a long, gentle rain. Scratching the soil with a cultivator around and between shrubs when weeds are small, and before they set seed, is a good practice to prevent serious infestations of weeds. This is also a good time to apply a light layer of mulch around shrubs. Mulch can reduce weeds and help keep the soil cool.

Helpful Hints

- Practice Integrated Pest Management (IPM). This approach to pest control is based on the idea of managing insect populations rather than eliminating them. By choosing the right plants for your growing conditions and using good cultural practices, you can minimize potential pest problems.

- Examine your shrubs and other plants on a regular basis. If less than fifty percent of a plant is affected with a pest, use a physical or biological control before you resort to a chemical control. Physical controls include traps and barriers like copper strips to keep away slugs and snails. Biological controls include the use of beneficial insects like ladybugs that eat aphids and the use of **Bacillus thuringiensis** (see Chemicals, p. 327), a bacterium that kills caterpillars.

Check leaves of **Rhododendrons** and large-leaved **Azaleas** for notches. This symptom is characteristic of the black vine weevil, which feeds at night and hides underneath the shrub by day. Use contact insecticide granules or spray under your shrubs (see Chemicals, p. 327).

You may notice a black mold on the leaves of your **Crapemyrtle.** Called sooty mold, this fungus occurs when insects such as aphids and scale secrete a substance called honeydew—the mold grows on top of the honeydew. Simply *wash off* the leaves and *treat* the insects with insecticidal soap or insecticide (see Chemicals, p. 327).

Pruning

Remove dead branches or blossoms on shrubs once they finish flowering.

Prune hedges of fast-growing species such as **Privet, Glossy Abelia,** *Abelia grandiflora,* **Cherry Laurel,** and even **Holly.** The new growth they put out will still have time to harden off before winter.

Deadheading (removing the dead flower blossoms) your **Butterfly Bushes** will encourage more blooms, and if you are lucky, the shrubs will flower until frost.

Planning

Larger shrubs provide welcome shade for some annuals and perennials, especially during the dog days of summer. Consider underplanting your shrubs with perennial ground covers. Fall is a good time to add plants to the garden. Not only will these ground covers add interest to the garden scene, they will help keep the roots of shrubs cool.

While **Ivy** is a popular ground cover, there are other plants that perform equally well, making good ground covers or companions to plant under shrubs:

- *Acorus gramineus* 'Pusillus' **Dwarf Sweet Flag** is a diminutive grass that makes a good partner for **Virginia Sweetspire.**

- *Ajuga reptans* **Carpet Bugleweed** has numerous cultivars with colorful foliage.

- *Chrysogonum virginianum* **Green and Gold** offers yellow flowers in spring and fall.

- *Helleborus orientalis* **Lenten Rose** is a great companion for **Rhododendrons** and **Azaleas** or **Witchhazels.**

- *Vinca minor* **Common Periwinkle** is another good choice for ground cover.

Hydrangea flowers are great to collect and dry for projects in the fall:

1 Collect blooms when they are dry, or they will rot. A good time of day to collect is after 10 a.m. and before noon.

2 If the bloom feels crisp to the touch, it is ready to cut and dry. If it feels soft to the touch, then it is still too early to harvest for drying.

3 Once you cut the flowers, strip all the leaves and remove any brown or damaged parts of the flower.

4 The best place to store the flowers is in a dark, dry, and warm place (Penny McHenry of the American Hydrangea Society uses the trunk of her car to dry hydrangea flowers). Other methods are to store them in a vase without water or to hang them upside down.

Dried **Hydrangea** *blooms will last for months or years, but the colors will fade over time.*

Planting

It is generally too hot to plant shrubs now, but you can prepare the soil for planting in the fall. If you plant container-grown shrubs, be sure to keep them well watered during the summer.

Watering

Water shrubs planted in the last six months weekly, providing 2 to 3 gallons of water per plant. Water plants growing in pots every day. Water containers until the water rushes out the holes in the bottom and sides of the pot.

Fertilizing

Hold off on any fertilizing until early fall.

Pest Control

Continue examining plants for insect and disease problems. Sometimes a good blast of water will take care of minor insect pest problems.

If needed, *spray* insecticidal soap to control aphids, spider mites, or whiteflies. You can spray insecticidal soap three to four times a week. Always spray in the early part of the day before temperatures get too hot.

Whether you are using an organic or a chemical spray, good coverage is essential. Spray the tops and undersides of leaves as well as the stems, covering completely, until the spray begins to drip off the plant. When you mix your sprays, never use more than the recommended amounts of product, whether organic or synthetic. More is not better. In fact, you can damage or kill plants by using too much chemical in one application.

Spot-spray weeds in shrub beds with a nonselective herbicide. Spray early in the morning when there are no winds and temperatures are coolest (see Chemicals, p. 327).

Use a yellow sticky trap to control whiteflies on **Gardenia.** (See Edibles, August for directions on making a sticky trap.)

Shrubs for Coastal Gardeners

Coastal gardeners must often consider salt tolerance and drought resistance when selecting plants for their gardens. Here is a list of shrubs that tolerate salt spray and coastal conditions:

- *Baccharis halimifolia* Groundsel-Bush
- *Hippophae rhamnoides* Sea Buckthorn
- *Hydrangea macrophylla* Bigleaf Hydrangea
- *Ilex glabra* Inkberry Holly
- *Ilex vomitoria* Yaupon Holly
- *Juniperus conferta* Shore Juniper
- *Myrica cerifera* Wax Myrtle
- *Nerium oleander* Oleander
- *Pittosporum tobira* Japanese Pittosporum (winter hardy only in the most southern parts of the state)
- *Rosa rugosa* Rugosa Rose

Pruning

Finish any pruning or shearing now so there will be enough time for new growth to harden off before winter arrives.

Planning

Fall is an ideal time to plant in the South. Determine now which shrubs you will add to your garden once the temperatures cool off and we get some rain. Make a list before you head out to the nursery. This way you will have an idea of what you want and won't be overwhelmed by all the choices. Plan to include some plants with colorful fall foliage and fruit.

If you haven't taken a soil test in two years, now is the time to do it. Not only will the results provide information about what you need to add to your soil in the way of Nitrogen, Phosphorous, and Potassium (N-P-K), it will give you a reading of the pH. You could have a soil that is rich in nutrients, but if the pH (acidity or alkalinity of the soil) is too low, plants won't absorb the necessary nutrients they require for healthy growth.

Soil pH can range anywhere from 4.0 to 9.0. Most plants are happiest in a soil that has a pH between 6 and 7. Certain plants, however, have particular pH requirements. Knowing what your plants like before you plant will help you determine what to add to your soil.

Fall is a good time to amend your soil, too. Organic soil amendments include mushroom compost, cow manure, chicken manure, and cottonseed meal, to name a few. Make sure you mix in plenty of amendments. Spread a 3- to 4-inch layer over the top of the soil before you rototill. *Till* the soil so that it is mixed in to a depth of 12 to 18 inches. If your soil has a high clay content, mixing in a layer of coarse sand 1 inch thick will help improve drainage.

Record what is happening in the garden in your garden journal. Take photographs of the garden in fall.

If you don't have a compost pile, begin one now. Start with all the leaves that you rake up this fall. Chop up these leaves and other materials—this will lead to compost faster than if you leave the leaves whole. Add your grass clippings and kitchen scraps (minus any meats, bones, or animal fats).

To make compost, you need oxygen and moisture. *Stir* the pile with a garden fork every two weeks and spray it with water. Depending on the weather, you could have black gold in as little as six months.

Planting

Plant container-grown and balled-and-burlapped shrubs.

1 *Dig a hole* that is at least three times as wide as the rootball. When planting balled-and-burlapped plants, it is important to loosen the burlap and any twine that is surrounding the trunk. If the material that surrounds the rootball is artificial burlap, carefully place the plant in the hole and carefully *remove* as much of the material as possible without disturbing the roots.

2 Apply a 2- to 3-inch layer of mulch around all new plantings, making sure to keep it away from the main stems or trunks. This way you won't create a damp, moist environment that is conducive to potential pest and disease problems.

3 *Water* all new plantings once a week unless there is adequate rainfall (1 inch a week). Water thoroughly, making sure the root area is saturated. This could take anywhere from $1/2$ to 1 hour, placing the hose at the center of the plant and allowing a pencil-size trickle.

Look for selections of *Camellia sasanqua*, which bloom early fall into winter. **Camellias** need a well-drained soil that is rich in organic material. Be sure not to plant them too deep (don't pile up soil around the trunk). Apply a 2-inch layer of mulch over an area extending at least 3 feet from the trunk.

Although they will tolerate full sun, partial shade is best.

With its lustrous evergreen foliage and handsome flowers, Camellia sasanqua is popular to train as an espalier, in a hedge, for screening, or in a pot. The flowers—single, double, and semi-double—come in shades of red, white, pink, or rose.

Pest Control

Removing diseased leaves from around shrubs will reduce insect and disease problems next year.

If deer are a problem, the best solution is to build a fence. Often this is not possible and gardeners must resort to other tactics. Deer Off® is an organic product reputed to repel deer and discourage other browsing animals because of its taste and smell.

If you have problems with whiteflies on **Gardenia,** try blasting them with a jet of water from the hose.

Spray with insecticidal soaps to control aphids and spider mites. Be sure to get good coverage—spray until it drips off the plant (see Chemicals, p. 327).

To prevent unwanted crops of chickweed in established shrub beds,

Shrubs with Colorful Fall Foliage or Fruits

F = colorful foliage   FR = colorful fruits

- *Aesculus parviflora* Bottlebrush Buckeye F
- *Aronia arbutifolia* 'Brilliantissima' Chokeberry FR
- *Callicarpa americana* American Beautyberry FR
- *Callicarpa dichotoma* Beautyberry FR
- *Calycanthus floridus* Sweetshrub F
- *Clethra alnifolia* Sweet Pepperbush F
- *Fothergilla gardenii* 'Mt. Airy' Fothergilla F
- *Hydrangea quercifolia* Oakleaf Hydrangea F
- *Ilex serrata* Finetooth Holly FR
- *Ilex verticillata* Winterberry Holly FR
- *Lagerstroemia* many cultivars Crapemyrtle F
- *Viburnum dilatatum* 'Iroquois' FR
- *Viburnum setigerum* 'Aurantiacum' FR

apply a granular weed preventer (see Chemicals, p. 327). *Read labels carefully* before using any pesticide.

If you have a weedy area where you want to plant shrubs in the spring, you can use newspaper to smother the weeds. Put down a layer of newspaper, about three to four sheets thick, and then cover it with mulch. Come spring you can *rototill* the area, *add soil amendments*, and plant.

One of the advantages of not using chemical sprays to control insect and disease problems in your garden is that beneficial insects that can help control pest problems will not be killed. For example, ladybugs are known to feed on aphids, mites, scale, and many insect eggs. Praying mantises feed on a wide range of insects.

Pruning

Prune only dead, damaged, or diseased branches during this season.

Planning

Fall leaf color is usually at its best during this month. Make notes on your favorite shrubs for fall. When you think about what to add to your garden, consider plants with colorful flowers, persistent fruits, and showy bark for fall and winter. Visit public gardens and discover the joys of the fall garden. Keep track of which plants have notable fall color in your garden journal.

Planting

Both soil and air temperatures are cooler now, and with any luck we have had some rain. Plants and people are less stressed now than they were during the hot months of summer when keeping hydrated takes precedence over planting. Now is an ideal time to add new shrubs to your garden or move existing shrubs. *Prepare the new location* ahead of time so that the rootball will stay out of the ground for the least amount of time. The size of the rootball will be determined in part by the size of the shrub. When transplanting shrubs, be sure to dig a rootball large enough to ensure there are plenty of roots. If you can manage lifting a large rootball, remember that bigger is better.

Transplanting

- If your shrub is 2 feet tall and wide, start digging out about 12 to 18 inches from the center of the plant.

- *Dig* at this distance all the way around, loosening the roots as you go.

- Then dig under as far as you can and *cut the roots* so the rootball is free from the hole.

With two people and two spades, you have the advantage of working together on opposite sides.

- Once the rootball is free, take a piece of burlap and slide it under the rootball. This will make it easier to move to its new home.

- When you plant your shrub in its new spot, make the planting area a bit higher than the surrounding soil. Plant the shrub so that the top of the rootball is at the same level as the soil surface in the planting area. This is the best way to provide excellent drainage for the roots.

- Fill in with soil and *water well.*

- Apply a 2- to 3-inch layer of mulch.

If you have an area that you want to plant next spring, you can prepare the soil now. Spreading 2 to 3 inches of composted manure on top of the soil and tilling it in immediately will result in a soil that is rich in nitrogen and ready to plant in spring.

If possible, perform a soil test (see Horticultural Practices, p. 7) before you begin planting this fall. When you plant, you may want to add a cup of garden lime and fertilizer, which can be mixed into the individual planting hole. If you use an organic product like animal manure, make sure it is well composted so it won't burn the roots of plants.

Mulch all new plantings with 2 to 3 inches of mulch.

This is also a good time to *topdress* your shrubs with homemade compost or other materials such as mushroom compost, cottonseed meal, cow manure, or horse manure. Apply 1 or 2 inches of the selected material on top of the soil around the shrub, keeping it away from the main trunk. (Prior to doing this you should have removed old mulch.) Apply a new layer of mulch and water well.

Make sure any homemade compost or manure is well rotted (this usually takes about six months) before you use it in the garden. By following this practice you will avoid burning tender young growth with ammonia. While most shrubs are not likely to put on new growth in the fall, tender growth in the spring can burn if compost is too fresh.

Watering

Keep all new plantings well watered. *Check* them weekly and *water* as needed if there has not been a good rain (1 to 2 inches is a good rain). Don't let the cooler weather fool you. Wind can also cause plants to dry out more quickly.

Fertilizing

You can use a starter fertilizer when planting your new shrubs. Starter fertilizers have a high percentage of phosphorous to help plants establish roots quickly. A ratio where the middle number is high, like 5-20-10, is best. You can also fertilize shrubs with a balanced fertilizer such as 10-10-10. *Read the label* carefully before applying any fertilizers).

Shrubs for Fall and Winter Interest

E = evergreen   D = deciduous

- *Euonymus alatus* Burning Bush D (leaves turn fiery red in fall)
- *Fothergilla gardenii* Fothergilla D (exhibits red, orange, and yellow foliage in fall)
- *Ilex glabra* Inkberry Holly E (olive-green leaves)
- *Kalmia latifolia* Mountain Laurel E (glossy green leaves all year)
- *Leucothoe fontanesiana* Drooping Leucothoe E (dark-green leaves turn purplish-bronze in winter)
- *Nandina domestica* Heavenly Bamboo E (many selections, some with leaves in intense shades of red)
- *Rhododendron catawbiense* Catawba Rhododendron E (large green leaves)
- *Sarcococca hookerana* Sweet Box E (glossy dark-green foliage)
- *Skimmia japonica* Skimmia E (evergreen leaves and brilliant berries)
- *Viburnum × pragense* Prague Viburnum E (glossy green foliage)

Pest Control

There should be fewer insect problems as the weather cools off, but continue to *check* for signs of damage. Use an Integrated Pest Management approach. This includes selecting varieties of plants that are best suited to grow in your environment and eliminating those that have proved to be in constant need of spraying just to keep them healthy. Check **Euonymus** for scale, **Azaleas** for lace bug, and **Rhododendron** for black vine weevil (refer to July for recommended treatment).

Pruning

Prune dead or diseased wood from established shrubs. If there are any wild shoots or suckers, you can also remove them. (Suckers are shoots that arise from roots or underground stems.)

NOVEMBER

Planning

Once leaves fall, examine the structure of your shrubs and determine if they need pruning. Wait until they are dormant in winter or early spring before you do any drastic pruning. If two branches are rubbing or crossing, remove one of them.

Planting

This is an ideal time to plant balled-and-burlapped and container-grown shrubs. The sooner you get them into the ground, the better. This will give them time to acclimate before the weather turns cold. Guidelines for planting shrubs:

1 *Dig a hole* that is at least twice as wide as the container the plant is growing in or the width of the rootball.

2 The depth of the hole should be no deeper than the depth of the container or the rootball.

3 Use the soil you dug out of the hole and fill in around the rootball, tamping it down gently to minimize air pockets.

4 *Water* well and apply a 2- to 3-inch layer of mulch.

Propagate **Azaleas, Hollies,** and other broad-leafed evergreens from cuttings. Here is Walter's preferred method for propagating favorite shrubs:

1 Fill a plastic shoebox halfway (6 to 8 inches deep) with a 50:50 mix of peat moss and perlite. Make sure the mix is barely moist.

2 Take your cuttings. They should be 4 to 6 inches long. Strip off most of the leaves except for the top three or four.

3 Dip the end of the cutting in a rooting hormone like Rootone™, and insert it into the rooting medium.

4 *Label* each variety. Cover the box with clear plastic wrap and place in a sunny window. Check on weekly to make sure the medium has not dried out.

5 In one month, *tug gently* to see if any roots have developed. If the cutting does not resist, press it back into the mix and check again in a few weeks. You should have roots in six to eight weeks.

6 Once you have roots, pot up the cuttings in small pots. *Overwinter* them indoors or in a cold frame until spring, when you can plant them outside.

Watering

Water all new plantings as well as existing plantings so that they are well prepared to go into winter.

Fertilizing

You can apply fertilizer lightly once shrubs are dormant. Use a balanced fertilizer like 10-10-10, applying $1/2$ pound per 100 square feet of shrub bed. The fertilizer will be available to plants in early spring once they start actively growing again. As a general rule when using a granular 10-10-10, apply 1 tablespoon of fertilizer per foot of shrub height.

Pest Control

Remove leaf litter that may harbor overwintering insects or diseases from the ground around shrubs.

Pruning

Limit your pruning to dead or damaged wood. If you want to prune evergreens, wait until they are dormant, usually in December, January, and February.

Here is a list of shrubs that bloom on old wood. Wait until after they flower to prune these shrubs:

- *Chaenomeles japonica*
- *Forsythia* species and cultivars
- *Fothergilla gardenii*
- *Hydrangea macrophylla*
- *Hydrangea quercifolia*
- *Philadelphus coronarius*
- *Rhododendron calendulaceum*
- *Rhododendron catawbiense*
- *Rhododendron maximum*
- *Spiraea prunifolia*
- *Viburnum* (most species and cultivars)

Moles and Voles

Moles may be mistakenly blamed for eating the roots of plants, but it is more likely that voles are the problem. Moles prefer insects. They tunnel through the soil, causing havoc as they go when plants are uprooted. Trapping is the most effective control for moles. Voles burrow under mulch and eat roots and stems as they go. To discourage them, try these techniques:

1 Pull leaves and mulch away from trunks and stems of plants (voles).

2 Put a shovelful of sharp gravel or expanded shale (Permatil™) in the planting hole (moles).

3 Use some castor oil in each planting hole (voles). For small plants a tablespoon should be adequate; for larger plants, use several tablespoons.

Camellias

Camellias are a staple for many Southern gardens. By growing a range of types you can have blooms from early fall through spring. Mulch them with 2 to 3 inches of mulch. The mulch is especially important to conserve moisture and keep the **Camellia** roots cool since they are close to the surface of the soil. Plants do not thrive in soils with a high pH. Water regularly for at least the first two years.

Camellia japonica. This is the **Camellia** that most people think of when they refer to **Camellias.** They grow 10 to 15 feet tall and 6 to 10 feet wide.

Camellia sasanqua. This species is more refined with smaller leaves and flowers. It may grow 6 to 10 feet tall. This species flowers from September into December. Many selections will tolerate full sun and drought but the better the growing conditions, the better the performance of your shrubs in general.

Planning

Make notes in your garden journal about shrubs that look good in the winter. Don't limit yourself to evergreens. Deciduous shrubs with colorful berries, beautiful bark, or fragrant flowers also look good in winter. Plan to add some of these to your garden in the spring, or even now, provided the ground is not frozen.

Evergreen shrubs effective for screening or hedging in the shade:

- *Abelia grandiflora* **Glossy Abelia** (5 to 7 feet)

- *Ilex glabra* **Inkberry Holly** (8 to 10 feet)

- *Illicium* **spp. Anise** (6 to 10 feet, fragrant foliage)

- *Leucothoe populifolia* [*Agarista populifolia*] (8 to 12 feet)

- *Osmanthus heterophyllus* **Holly Tea Olive** (10 to 20 feet)

- *Viburnum × pragense* **Prague Viburnum** (10 feet)

Planting

If the ground is not frozen, continue to *plant* both container-grown and balled-and-burlapped shrubs. Wait until spring to plant bare-root shrubs.

Watering

Unless there is at least 1 inch of rainfall, *water* new plantings weekly and *check* to make sure evergreens don't dry out. If their needles are beginning to drop or to become dry and brittle, the plants may be dried out, a condition that can be avoided by timely watering.

Fertilizing

If you didn't *topdress* your shrub beds earlier in the fall, go ahead and do it now. Apply a 1- to 2-inch layer of organic material such as mushroom compost, cow manure, cottonseed meal, or horse manure around your shrubs. Don't pile it up around branches or stems where insect or disease problems could develop.

Pest Control

Keep removing dead and diseased leaves from shrub beds. This will reduce the chances of insect and disease problems in the spring.

Pruning

You can do a little selective pruning of evergreens like **Hollies,** **Nandinas,** and **Camellias** if you want to use them for holiday decorations, but wait until early spring, just before they begin to actively grow, to do any substantial pruning.

Trees

Trees provide a framework for a garden, acting like a picture frame for the garden scene. They help create scale, and they set the tone for a particular garden type or style.

Whether deciduous, evergreen, weeping, upright, or columnar, trees come in all sizes, shapes, and forms. Depending on the variety, a tree can provide flowers in spring, shade in summer, and colorful foliage in fall. Trees help to define space, create privacy, provide windbreaks, and reduce the amount of energy needed to cool your home. In addition, they add curb appeal and increase property values. Evergreen trees provide screening or a backdrop for shrubs, perennials, and bulbs. Some trees, like **Paperbark Maple** with its glistening cinnamon-colored bark, brighten the winter landscape.

When it comes to choosing a tree for your own garden, be sure you know what the ultimate size of the particular tree will be. This information will help you determine where to site an individual specimen so it won't outgrow its allotted space in a short time or require constant pruning to keep it contained. When you design your garden, site your trees before you choose their companion shrubs and herbaceous plants. Where you locate your trees and the types you select can determine the feel of your landscape. Evergreens are often used in more formal gardens, while deciduous trees can be either formal or informal.

Planting a tree is an investment in the future. Choose your trees carefully, and you will reap the rewards for years to come.

Planting Trees

Trees are sold as balled-and-burlapped, bare-root, or container-grown. Bare-root trees are available for purchase when they are dormant (not actively growing). The best time to plant bare-root trees is as soon as they are dug, or as soon as you receive them.

With balled-and-burlapped and container-grown trees there is more flexibility about what time of year you can plant. Provided the ground is not frozen, container-grown trees can be planted almost anytime, although during the hottest months the trees will sit and wait until soil temperatures cool off before they begin to put out roots.

Balled-and-burlapped trees are dug when trees are dormant, but they may be available from your local nursery throughout the growing season. This means they might have been dug a year ago and have had a chance to recover from any root loss they suffered during the digging process.

When you plant a tree, dig a hole that is wider than it is deep. As a rule of thumb, the planting hole should be at least twice as wide as the rootball. While there may be some controversy about the best way to plant trees, as a general practice it is not necessary to amend the soil in the hole in which the tree will be growing. The sooner the tree adapts to unamended soil, the faster it will become established. If you amend it, you are creating an artificial environment for the tree. It is important, however, that the soil is loose and soft to help root growth.

It is also important to make sure the site where you plant drains easily. If it does not, dig out some of the existing soil and add organic amendments to help improve the texture and drainage.

Trees

After you plant, apply a 2- to 3-inch layer of mulch such as pine bark nuggets or pine straw to help keep tree roots cool and conserve moisture.

Watering

Water your trees as soon as you plant them; for the first six months, apply 1 gallon per foot of tree height per week unless there is one inch or more of rain weekly.

Once they are established, you should have to apply supplemental water only during periods of drought. If there has been no rain for a month or longer, get out the hose. Water is not free, but the money you spend to irrigate a mature tree may save it, which is especially desirable when the tree is a hundred-year old **Oak.**

To supply a tree's minimum needs during times of drought, apply 15 gallons of water per inch of trunk diameter *once* per week. Example: a tree whose trunk is 12 inches thick, 4 feet from the ground, needs 180 gallons of water per week. Attach an inexpensive water timer to your soaker hose and set it to 180 gallons. It will shut off once 180 gallons has soaked out of the hose. Depending on the length of the hose, this could take two to three hours; for this amount of water, the cost will be just a few dollars.

For *optimum* tree health, apply the amount calculated *twice* each week during times of drought.

Fertilizing

A starter fertilizer may be the answer if you want to give a newly planted tree a jump-start. Some starter fertilizers come in a liquid form and can be mixed with water and applied at planting (refer to the product label for detailed information). In general, trees need little in the way of supplemental fertilizer unless you want to accelerate their growth, in which case you should apply fertilizer once in March and once in June. (Extra fertilizer tends to cause problems for mature trees and should be applied only if recommended by a professional arborist.)

Staking

Not all new trees need to be staked. If you have planted your tree in a windy location with very soft soil, staking will help keep the tree upright. To avoid girdling of the trunk or restricting growth, it is important not to pull the cords that attach to the stakes too tight. There should be a little give so the tree can sway naturally and develop a strong trunk. *Remove* stakes from small trees after the first year, and from large trees after the second year.

Pruning

When you plant trees, *prune off* dead or diseased roots or branches. Let the tree get established over a period of one year before you remove any large branches. Limit your pruning for all newly planted trees, including those that are balled-and-burlapped or container-grown; restrict your pruning to removing branches that cross or rub and those that are growing back into the crown of the tree.

Once your trees are established, they should require only a minimum amount of pruning to enhance their natural shape. If you want to train a tree in a formal shape or use it for espalier, more rigorous pruning or shearing may be appropriate.

Using the right tools is one of the keys to proper pruning. Use hand-pruners for branches $1/2$ inch or less in diameter, loppers for branches $1/2$ to 2 inches, and a pruning saw for branches larger than 2 inches. Pole pruners are best for trimming branches high up in a tree. If you need a ladder to reach branches, it's time to call a professional.

Trees

Timing is also important when it comes to pruning. If you're not certain of the best time to prune a particular tree, follow these guidelines: prune spring-flowering trees as soon as they finish blooming, and summer-flowering types in late winter or early spring. Doing so will reduce the chances that you will cut off next year's flower buds. Restrict your pruning in late summer and early autumn to grooming: removing dead twigs, spent blossoms, or seedpods.

Hiring a professional arborist is the best way to care for large trees. As your shade trees mature, you may want to put them on a pruning schedule. You can have a certain number of trees pruned each year, rotating so that mature trees are checked and/or pruned once every three years to remove dead or diseased wood. Regular pruning will help keep your trees vigorous, which makes them better able to ward off pest and disease infestations. If your trees need to be sprayed for any insect or disease problems, the arborist can do this, too.

What to Plant?

Gardeners are often overwhelmed with plant selections. Growers and garden designers who have many years of experience growing plants in our Georgia climate can help. Garden designer Jane Bath is the owner of Land Arts Nursery in Monroe, Georgia, a retail nursery that offers an extensive selection of ornamental plants. Here is a list of small to medium-sized trees that Jane finds outstanding for Georgia gardens:

- *Acer buergeranum* Trident Maple

- *Acer palmatum* Japanese Maple (many selections)

- *Chionanthus retusus* Chinese Fringe Tree

- *Cladrastis kentukea* American Yellowwood

- *Cornus florida* Flowering Dogwood (many selections)

- *Lagerstroemia indica* 'Natchez' Crapemyrtle (white)

- *Magnolia acuminata* × *denudata* 'Elizabeth'

- *Malus* 'Callaway' Callaway Crabapple

- *Oxydendrum arboreum* Sourwood

- *Vitex agnus-castus* Chaste Tree

Trees for Georgia

Name	Height	Width	Culture	Comments
Acer barbatum Florida Maple	25 to 30 feet	10 to 15 feet	Full sun to light shade.	More adaptable than **Sugar Maple** for coastal gardens.
Acer buergeranum Trident Maple	20 to 25 feet	10 to 15 feet	Full sun to light shade.	A good choice for small gardens.
Acer griseum Paperbark Maple	15 to 30 feet	10 to 20 feet	Full sun to half shade, with a moist, well-drained soil.	Outstanding cinnamon bark, leaves often exhibit good fall color.
Acer palmatum Japanese Maple	2 to 25 feet	4 to 20 feet	Morning sun or light shade is best.	Many cultivars with colorful foliage and showy bark.
Cercis canadensis Eastern Redbud	20 to 30 feet	25 to 35 feet	Full sun to half shade, average well-drained soil.	A wonderful native tree. **'Alba'** has white flowers, and **'Forest Pansy'** has purple leaves in spring that turn to green as they mature.
Chionanthus retusus Chinese Fringe Tree	15 to 25 feet	15 to 20 feet	Full sun or part shade; a moist, well-drained soil.	A cousin to the native **Fringe Tree,** this species has glossy foliage and handsome bark.
Cladrastis kentukea American Yellowwood	30 to 40 feet	40 to 50 feet	Full sun or part shade, a moist, well-drained soil.	Smooth gray bark, fragrant white flowers in late spring. Tolerates alkaline soils.
Cornus florida Flowering Dogwood	20 to 30 feet	20 to 30 feet	Full sun to half shade; moist, well-drained soil.	Great tree for four seasons of interest.
Crataegus viridis 'Winter King' Winter King Green Hawthorn	20 to 25 feet	20 to 30 feet	Full sun, well-drained soil.	Outstanding persistent red fruit and handsome peeling bark make this tree a winner.
Cryptomeria japonica Japanese Cryptomeria	40 to 60 feet	20 to 30 feet	Full sun to part shade; moist, well-drained soil.	An elegant conifer for screening or a specimen. Look for the cultivar **'Yoshino'**.

Trees for Georgia

Name	Height	Width	Culture	Comments
Magnolia 'Elizabeth' Elizabeth Magnolia	20 to 30 feet	20 to 30 feet	Full sun to part shade; moist, well-drained soil.	Deciduous **Magnolia** with creamy yellow flowers in early spring.
Magnolia grandiflora Southern Magnolia	40 to 60 feet	30 to 40 feet	Full sun; moist, well-drained soil.	Use as a specimen tree or for evergreen screening.
Magnolia virginiana var. *australis* Sweet Bay Magnolia	40 to 50 feet	15 to 20 feet	Full sun, tolerates wet soils.	Lemon-scented flowers, green leaves with silver undersides. This native is very adaptable.
Malus 'Callaway' Crabapple	20 to 25 feet	20 to 25 feet	Full sun; moist, well-drained soil.	Pink buds open to white flowers.
Oxydendrum arboreum Sourwood	25 to 30 feet	15 to 20 feet	Full sun to part shade; well-drained soil.	White flowers in summer, red fall foliage.
Prunus × *yedoensis* Yoshino Cherry	30 to 40 feet	25 to 40 feet	Full sun to part shade; well-drained soil.	Pink buds open to white flowers in spring; great specimen tree with a graceful habit.
Quercus spp. Oaks	40 to 80 feet	50 to 90 feet	Full sun to part shade, well-drained soil.	Many species are suited for street trees or good for locations where a large specimen is needed.
Tsuga canadensis Canadian Hemlock	40 to 70 feet	25 to 35 feet	A woodland with a well-drained soil is ideal.	Effective as an evergreen screen, hedge, or specimen.
Ulmus parvifolia Lacebark Elm	40 to 50 feet	40 to 50 feet	Full sun, well-drained soil.	Look for selections **'Athena'** and **'Allee'**. A choice tree for both urban and suburban landscapes, it provides interest in every season.

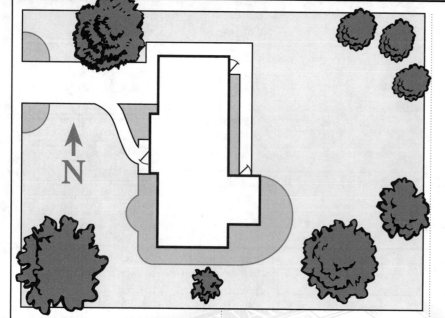

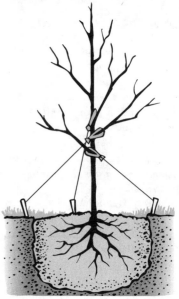

Planting Bare-Root Trees

Planning

Make an inventory of existing trees, and draw a sketch of where they are located in your garden. Use your house as a point of reference, and indicate which direction is North. How do the shadows of the trees fall? Where are the densest shadows? Sketch where the shadows fall and how far they extend. This will help you determine where you have the most sun or shade and where you need to add trees.

Consider the type of soil you have as well as how well it holds moisture. This will help you decide what type of tree to plant.

Plan a mix of evergreen and deciduous trees to create maximum interest in your garden all year long. Evergreens planted in groups make an effective backdrop for deciduous trees. Mixing individual evergreens with a planting of deciduous trees will create interest throughout the year.

Planting

This is a good time to plant trees, especially in the most southern parts of the state where winters are mild and the ground is never frozen. *Plant* balled-and-burlapped, container-grown, or bare-root trees. Before you plant, *remove* all turfgrass and weeds from the soil surface. A flat shovel works well for this.

Bare-root trees are less expensive and easier to handle, and you can order them through the mail. A bare-root tree is usually up to 10 feet tall with a trunk less than 2 inches in diameter. When you purchase a bare-root tree, you are investing in its root system. If the tree has lots of branches but very few roots, it will take a long time to become established.

1 Make sure roots are healthy. *Prune off* any broken or dried-up roots. With clean cuts, the roots will heal quickly and there will be less chance of root-disease problems. This should be done when trees are dormant and temperatures are cold or cool (30 to 40 degrees Fahrenheit is ideal—slightly warmer is acceptable).

2 Keep tree roots moist until you plant. If the roots are dry when you receive the tree, soak them in a bucket of cool water for up to eight hours.

3 If you can't plant within a day or two, dig a temporary pit for the tree roots. *Water* the roots and fill in around them with a mixture of mulch and soil. This will cause the least amount of stress for the tree and help reduce air pockets.

4 When you dig the hole to plant a tree, set the soil aside and use it to fill in around the roots. This way the tree roots will adapt quickly to their soil environment. If needed, adjust the pH by adding lime to your planting hole. It is best to have your soil tested (see Horticultural Practices, p. 7) before you plant.

Do not add fertilizer to the planting hole—it could burn the roots, and it's not necessary until the tree is established. If you use a root stimulator, follow directions carefully.

Although it is not necessary to amend the soil before you plant trees, it is important to be sure the soil is well drained. If the spot stays damp, select varieties that will thrive in wet soils, such as the **Sweet Bay Magnolia** or **Bald Cypress.**

To help improve drainage, add soil amendments like ground pine bark or gritty all-purpose sand, both available at your local home improvement store. If you purchase a product labeled as builder's sand, make sure it contains only sand.

If the existing soil is infertile clay subsoil, you should remove it and replace it with soil that has been amended with organic materials.

Watering

Water trees immediately after you plant them, and then once a week unless the ground is frozen. Apply 1 gallon per foot of tree height per week.

Fertilizing

In a natural forest, trees are the ultimate recyclers. They depend on the breakdown of the leaves that they lose each year for food. In general, trees need little in the way of supplemental fertilizer unless you want to accelerate their growth. Extra fertilizer tends to cause problems for mature trees and should be avoided.

Pest Control

Inspect your trees for pest and disease problems. If you find scale (see Shrubs, March, Pest Control) on the bark or in the crotches (where the branches meet the trunk), *spray* with horticultural oils (see Chemicals, p. 327). Scale is common on **Bradford Pear** trees. Be sure to get good coverage, spraying the branches, trunk, and crotches.

Pruning

Prune bare-root trees when you plant them. *Thin* branches that are closely spaced. This will allow better light and air circulation, resulting in better overall growth. *Prune* any broken roots.

When you prune, make your cut on a slant, just above a bud. On the side branches, make your cut just beyond a bud pointed towards the outside.

Helpful Hint

Choose trees that offer more than one season of interest, like **Dogwoods,** which have flowers in spring and red berries in fall, or **Paperbark Maple,** which has deep-green foliage in summer and peeling cinnamon-colored bark in winter.

Planning

Trees are classed as overstory and understory types. Overstory trees like **Oak, Pine,** and **Hickory** form the upper canopy layer in a forest that has more than one layer. Understory trees like **Redbud, Dogwood,** and **Black Gum** grow beneath the overstory trees. For the most diverse and interesting landscape, *plant a mixture* of these two types of trees, as well as evergreen species for year-round interest.

Planting

In the central and upper parts of the state, *plant* bare-root trees while they are still dormant. In southern and coastal areas, this is a good time to plant balled-and-burlapped or container-grown trees.

Because the soil in the planting hole settles a bit, plant so the top of the rootball is slightly higher than the ground level. This also helps correct a poorly-drained soil situation.

Watering

Water new plantings weekly (new plantings are those that have been in the ground for less than six months). Apply 1 gallon per foot of tree height per week.

Fertilizing

Wait until early spring, just as new growth begins, to fertilize.

Pest Control

As the weather warms, you might notice small holes in the bark of your **Maple, Pecan, Pear,** or **Magnolia** tree. The holes are characteristically $1/4$ inch in diameter and occur in rings around the trunk; often there are several rings in close proximity. The damage is not caused by borers, but by a bird: the yellow-bellied sapsucker. This member of the woodpecker family pecks holes in the bark and licks the sap that oozes out.

Control is nearly impossible. Fortunately, trees are not injured by the annual springtime visit. Hole-pecking will cease for the summer but may briefly reoccur in late fall.

Pruning

This is a good month to prune deciduous trees. Because there are no leaves, you can see the form of the tree and determine where you need to prune. When pruning to remove a large limb, do so in stages so the branch doesn't tear and split back to the tree, peeling off a section of the bark. Do not make a flush cut. Prune back to where the swollen part of the branch comes out from the tree. This is called the *branch collar.*

Limb Removal

Sharp, good-quality tools are best; regular maintenance will ensure they last for a long time.

- Handpruners are ideal for heading and thinning stems up to $1^1/2$ inches in diameter.

- Loppers are ideal for selective pruning of larger branches.

Conifers for the Georgia Garden

Both needled evergreens and broadleaf evergreens like **Hollies** and **Magnolias** take center stage in the winter garden. Needled evergreens come in shades of blue, green, golden, and silver (examples are **Pines, Cedars,** and **Hemlocks**). They range in size from the dwarf to the majestic and are useful as hedges, screening trees, windbreaks, or specimens. It is true that **Leyland Cypress** is fast-growing, but there are many other choices when it comes to conifers for your Georgia garden:

- *Cephalotaxus harringtonia* Japanese Plum Yew tolerates part shade, and deer consume it only as a last resort. There are both upright and prostrate forms. Depending on the cultivar, they range in size from 5 feet to 20 feet at maturity.

- *Chamaecyparis obtusa* Hinoki Falsecypress–there many different cultivars and sizes of this conifer. It prefers a moist, well-drained soil and full sun.

- *Chamaecyparis nootkatensis* Alaska Cedar–growing 20 to 40 feet in the garden, it likes full sun or light shade.

- *Chamaecyparis pisifera* 'Filifera Aurea' is a golden form of the Japanese Falsecypress.

- *Cryptomeria japonica* Japanese Cedar–there are a number of cultivars available, including the popular 'Yoshino', which can reach 50 feet at maturity.

- Saws are useful for branches that are more than 2 inches thick.

  Some saw blades can be sharpened, but others should be replaced periodically. Check the product label for specific information about your blades.

Tips for pruning your newly planted trees:

1 **Remove** dead or diseased branches.

2 **Remove** broken branches below the point of injury back to a healthy branch.

3 **Prune** to remove branches that are crossing or rubbing. Wounds can develop where branches rub, creating an environment conducive to pest and disease problems.

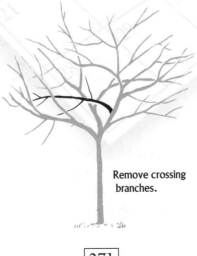

Remove crossing branches.

4 **Remove** branches that form narrow V-shaped crotches with the main trunk. These crotches are weak and may break in the future. To minimize this problem, select improved varieties of trees with strong branching habits.

Planning

Plan to add at least one tree to your garden this spring. Visit your local botanical garden to get an idea of how large a particular variety will be when it matures (see Resources, p. 353).

Sweet Gum trees have distinctive fall foliage, but the seedpods they drop ("**Sweet Gum** balls") can be a tremendous nuisance. There are sprays that cause the flowers to abort so there will be no seedpods, but these are expensive and impractical, as the tree must be sprayed completely every year.

A better solution is to plant the selection known as 'Rotundiloba', which does not form fruit.

Planting

Plant balled-and-burlapped or container-grown trees; refer to February for planting directions.

Watering

Water newly planted trees once a week (unless you get 1 inch of rain) for at least the first six months and up to a year after they are planted. After they are estab-

lished, *check* them monthly, and plan to water if there is a drought.

Winter winds can dry out established conifers. *Check* the soil (feel down several inches), and *water* if it is dry.

Fertilizing

Fertilize trees once they leaf out, with a slow-release fertilizer such as Nursery Special™. Read product label directions carefully before applying any fertilizers. For mature trees, use the following guidelines when applying a granular fertilizer:

1 Estimate the canopy spread of an individual tree in square feet. Apply ³/₄ pound (1¹/₂ cups) of 16-4-8 or 12-4-8 (or a fertilizer with a similar ratio) for each 100 square feet of canopy spread.

Reduce the rate applied by half when fertilizing conifers such as **Pines, Hemlocks,** *and* **Junipers,** *or when trees are growing in a lawn that receives regular applications of fertilizer.*

2 Apply by broadcasting the fertilizer evenly under the tree, as far as the canopy extends and slightly beyond.

3 *Water-in* the fertilizer—this will wash it off any grass blades and help the fertilizer get to the tree roots more quickly.

4 Repeat this fertilizer application in July.

Pest Control

If you see webs in the crotches of your **Crabapple** or ornamental **Cherry** trees, the trees probably have tent caterpillars. The caterpillars leave their nests during the day to feed and can defoliate your tree in no time. Wait until early evening, then *remove* each nest by piercing it with a long stick and winding the web around the end.

For severe infestations, spray inside the web with a product containing B.t. (see Chemicals, p. 327). Remember that even complete defoliation of a limb will not hurt a healthy tree; it will have plenty of time to grow new leaves after the caterpillars disappear in May.

Pruning

Prune to remove dead, broken, or diseased branches, and *prune out* branches that are rubbing or crossing. Both young trees and established mature trees respond to this type of pruning. Pruning large mature trees helps keep them vigorous; such pruning is best done by a professional arborist.

Remove water sprouts (clusters of branches that grow straight up, often from an old pruning wound) on a regular basis. Water sprouts can weaken a tree and can be difficult to get rid of later.

Grafted trees (several weeping forms are grafted) may send out suckers from the underground rootstock. *Prune off* these suckers so your tree can use its energy efficiently to produce the desired healthy leaves, branches, and blooms of the cultivar you selected.

Don't prune **Maples** or **River Birch** now. They *bleed* (produce excess sap) if pruned in late spring.

Although anxiety-producing for the gardener, bleeding does not harm the tree.

Sometimes mature trees create *too much* shade—even shade-loving plants need light to grow. If your shaded **Rhododendrons** and **Azaleas** are not blooming and lack vigor, they may not be getting enough sunlight. *Selectively prune* to remove branches; this will open up your tree and allow more light to reach the plants below.

It will also improve air circulation and reduce the potential for disease problems like powdery mildew.

Prune needled evergreens such as **Pines, Cedars, Hemlocks,** and **Junipers.**

Helpful Hint

Pines send out new growth called "candles." This new growth is soft and pliable and usually a bright, fresh green. To encourage a **Pine** to have denser foliage growth, wait until the candles are 2 to 4 inches long, then pinch or clip off the tips. If you want to prevent the **Pine** from growing larger, wait until the candles are about 1 inch long, then shear them off from both the sides and the top of the tree.

Shearing means that every branch is clipped to an even height at the surface, as with hedges or topiary. The best time to shear needled evergreens is just after they begin to put out new growth in early spring, a time that brings warmer soil and air temperatures.

Pruning now will stimulate dormant buds to begin growing, resulting in a fuller tree.

Planning

When you consider what happened to the American Elm, you can see why you should avoid monoculture, even in your own garden. (Monoculture is planting many plants of only one species in an area.) Years ago, the **American Elm,** *Ulmus americana*, was planted in great numbers throughout the United States; when used as an avenue tree, its graceful vase shape created a dramatic effect. Then the trees were attacked by a fungus known as Dutch Elm disease, a fatal disease carried by Elm bark beetles that bore into elm limbs. The disease spread from tree to tree very quickly, with devastating effects: whole neighborhoods were denuded.

Fortunately for gardeners today, there are a number of disease-resistant selections of the **American Elm.** Look for **'American Liberty' Elms,** a series of six selections introduced by the Elm Research Institute. Other resistant selections are **'Delaware #2', 'New Harmony', 'Valley Forge',** and **'Washington'.** Another **Elm** species that exhibits resistance to the Dutch Elm disease (but not the Elm leaf beetle) is the **Chinese** or **Lacebark Elm,** *Ulmus parvifolia*. The cultivar **Allee®** (**'Emer II'**) has an upright spreading habit and gray to orange-brown peeling bark; **Athena®** (**'Emer I'**) is a broad-

spreading tree with shiny green leaves, some yellow fall color, and colorful bark in shades of gray, green, and orange-brown—both of these are fast- growing and adapt to a range of growing conditions.

Even if you choose these disease-resistant selections, it is still important to plant a diversity of trees in your garden.

Planting

This is a good time to add container-grown or balled-and-burlapped trees to your garden. Be sure to ***water*** them regularly during the first year while they become established.

Watering

Keep watering new plantings. Apply 1 gallon per foot of tree height per week.

Fertilizing

Fertilize trees once they leaf out. Use a slow-release fertilizer such as Nursery Special™.

Palms like a fertilizer that is rich in micronutrients, especially magnesium and manganese. Use a slow-release fertilizer that includes micronutrients (refer to the label). A nutrient ratio of 3:1:2 such as 12-4-8 is best.

Pest Control

Dogwood anthracnose (an-THRAK-nose), a fungus, has been attacking **Dogwoods** throughout forests in the Eastern United States. The symptoms of this disease, also called *discula*, usually show up in lower limbs first and may spread to the whole tree if not controlled. The disease affects **Dogwood** trees whose leaves do not dry off during the day. Leaves will exhibit spots with tan or brown blotches, bordered in purple, and the leaves will become severely distorted. Infected leaves cling to the tree, even after other leaves drop normally in the fall, and cankers form on the main trunk at the junction of each stem. (Cankers are swollen protrusions that can surround a twig or stem, girdling it and causing the branch to die). Trees in a weakened condition are more susceptible to discula—a healthy tree is the best defense against disease and insect problems. Most home landscape **Dogwoods** have plenty of air circulation around them, which protects the leaves from infection. *Discula* is not expected to cause problems for Georgia **Dogwoods,** except those growing in cool mountain valleys. To help prevent **Dogwood** diseases:

- *Plant* **Dogwoods** in a moist, fertile soil, in light shade or full sun.

- *Remove and destroy* any leaves infected with fungus as soon as you notice them. Rake up leaves as soon as they fall, and burn them or dispose of them. Do not add them to your compost pile.

- *Prune out* any dead twigs or branches. Prune only during dry weather. Fungus problems are usually worse during wet weather.

- *Spray* trees that you place a high value on with a fungicide (see Chemicals, p. 327) in early spring.

- Keep trees watered during periods of drought.

- *Plant* disease-resistant **Dogwood** hybrids such as **'Aurora'**, **'Galaxy'**, and **'Constellation'**.

Disease-Resistant Crab Apples

The best way to avoid problems with any plant is to keep it healthy. By choosing varieties that are disease-resistant, you are a step ahead of the game. Many **Crabapple** are susceptible to scab, fireblight, cedar-apple rust, and powdery mildew. Some **Crabapple** selections have been hybridized for disease resistance.

- **'Centurion'** grows to 25 feet high and wide at maturity. Red buds open to rose-red flowers.

- **'Donald Wyman'** grows to 25 feet high, with a large rounded habit. It has white flowers and persistent red fruits in winter.

- **'Harvest Gold'** offers flowers that are pink in bud and white in flower. Its habit is upright and spreading, growing 25 feet high and 25 feet wide. Its golden fruits look good well into December.

- **'Indian Summer'** has rose-red flowers and red fruit. It grows to 18 feet high and 19 feet wide.

- **'Jewelberry'** is a small tree, growing 8 to 12 feet high. Pink buds open to white flowers and are followed by masses of glossy red fruits.

Cornus kousa **Kousa Dogwood** blooms later and is also less susceptible to diseases than *Cornus florida.* Its flowers appear on the tops of the branches above the foliage and are more star-like in appearance. The large, red, strawberrylike fruits hang down and put on a show in late summer to fall. In winter, the colorful peeling bark adds color to the landscape.

Pruning

There is still time to prune or shear candles on evergreens. Restrict your pruning of deciduous trees to removing dead or diseased branches—wait until winter to do any extreme corrective pruning or to remove any large branches.

Planning

Take notes in your Garden Journal on spring-blooming trees. Record the color of their flowers and how long they bloom, the trees' overall appearance, any pest or disease problems, and whether faded blossoms persist or if they drop off and disappear. Use this information to help guide you in your decisions about adding or deleting trees to your garden.

Keep track of varieties that are successful. Knowing the scientific name is the best way to assure that you get the plant you want.

Planting

Plant container-grown trees. Apply 2 to 3 inches of mulch, making sure to keep it away from the trunk. (You can also grow trees in containers on a permanent basis. **Japanese Maples** make lovely specimens when planted in a decorative pot.)

Before you purchase a container-grown tree (or shrub), make sure the plant has healthy roots.

1   One way to check the roots is to lift up the plant by gently tugging on the trunk. If it pulls easily away from the soil, then the plant may have root rot. If it holds firm, it probably has enough healthy roots.

2   Another way to check the health of the whole root system is to gently ease the rootball out of the container. If the upper half of the rootball has lots of healthy roots, you can *remove* any roots on the lower half that look unhealthy, and your tree should thrive.

Watering

Water all new plantings. Thereafter, if there is not adequate rainfall (1 inch per week), apply 1 gallon per foot of tree height per week. *Check* established trees (trees that have been in the ground for a full year or longer) once a month to make sure they are getting enough water.

Fertilizing

When you plant new trees, mix some root stimulator into the existing soil. This will help plants get established more quickly.

If you want to give new trees (those you planted during the past six months) an extra boost, *fertilize* them with a complete slow-release fertilizer that has a ratio like 10-10-10. This should only be done twice a year—March and July are recommended. (See March for more information and application suggestions.)

Generally, established trees don't need to be fertilized.

Pest Control

A bagworm is a wingless moth that forms a protective mass of brown twigs in a cocoon around its body. From a distance the bagworms look almost like tiny cones hanging from a tree. The moths consume great numbers of needles from evergreen plants like **Juniper, Arborvitae,** and **Leyland Cypress.** *Pick off and destroy* the bags whenever you find them. Be sure to *wear gloves* to protect your fingers from the tree needles.

If you choose to use a contact insecticide, April and May are the months when the moths are most susceptible.

If you notice that the leaves on your **Sycamore** tree have irregular brown dead spots and leaf stems are black at the base, you may have **Sycamore** Anthracnose. This leaf blight is caused by several fungi. The fungus first appears on the leaves, then spreads through the veins and down into the stem and branch. The spores that spread the fungus overwinter in the cankers on the branches and in diseased leaves. A lack of overall vigor, heavy rainfall, and low temperatures exacerbate the effects of this disease, which can include total defoliation. Fungicides are effective only if they are applied before the disease appears in the spring. To control the disease:

- *Prune out* any dead or infected leaves, twigs, and branches.

- Rake up and burn infected leaves, to reduce infections in the future.

- *Fertilize* in spring to increase tree vigor.

- *Water* trees during a prolonged dry spell (a month or longer without rain).

You may notice that leaves on your **Red Maple, Oak, Hickory,** or **Pecan** are disfigured and deformed by small growths—bump-like swellings—that cover the leaves. In the worst cases, leaves turn yellow and drop prematurely. This is leaf gall, which is caused when insects like mites, midges, and tiny wasps lay their eggs on tree leaves. This curiosity of nature will not go away even if the larvae in the leaves are killed. There are two approaches to dealing with gall:

Weeping Trees

No matter what the season, trees with a weeping habit make a dramatic statement in the landscape, whether planted in a container or in the ground. The following trees have a weeping growth habit or arching branches.

- *Acer palmatum* var. *dissectum* Japanese Maple
- *Cercidiphyllum magnificum* 'Pendulum' Weeping Katsura
- *Cercis canadensis* 'Covey' (also known as 'Lavender Twist') Weeping Redbud
- *Cercis canadensis* ssp. 'Traveller' Weeping Redbud
- *Cedrus atlantica* 'Glauca Pendula' Weeping Blue Atlas Cedar
- *Cornus florida* 'Pendula' Weeping Florida Dogwood
- *Fagus sylvatica* 'Pendula' Weeping European Beech
- *Malus* 'Red Jade' Weeping Crabapple
- *Prunus subhirtella* 'Pendula' Weeping Higan Cherry
- *Styrax japonicus* 'Pink Cascade' Weeping Japanese Pink Snowbell
- *Ulmus alata* 'Lace Parasol' Weeping Winged Elm

1 Learn to live with this oddity.

2 *Rake and destroy* leaves each fall to reduce insect populations.

Pruning

Remove dead or diseased leaves and limbs on trees. Don't put them in your compost pile or they may introduce problems into your garden in the future.

Prune **Leyland Cypress** to control Seridium canker. The symptoms: older foliage, especially the interior foliage, turns yellow and then

brown; branches and twigs die; sunken reddish, dark brown, or purple areas (the cankers) form on the bark; and sap oozes. The sunken areas are the cankers. Often the infection starts on the lower branches of the tree and moves up.

Prune out diseased limbs, being sure to cut 6 inches below where the infection occurs. This will ensure that you prune where healthy wood is growing. Prune branches that are broken or torn from the main trunk. Sterilize your pruner between each cut with a 1:10 bleach: water mixture.

Planning

If you only have trees that bloom in the spring, now is the time to think about planting some that offer blooms in summer. Many of the southeastern natives offer beautiful blooms and interesting forms. Some consider the **Southern Magnolia** *Magnolia grandiflora* the quintessential Southern landscape plant, with its large, white, deliciously lemon-scented flowers and glossy evergreen leaves. In recent years, a number of meritorious hybrids have been introduced into cultivation.

- **'Bracken's Brown Beauty'** is a selection with a dense, compact habit. It grows to 30 feet high.

- **'Edith Bogue'** is a cultivar that has a pyramidal habit and leaves that are narrower than those of the species, often with wavy margins.

- **'Hasse'** is a selection that offers an upright growth habit and small, very glossy leaves.

- **'Little Gem'** is a cultivar that flowers when it is young, and the undersides of the small leaves are rust-colored. It reaches only 15 to 20 feet at maturity. Great for a container or small garden, it flowers most of the summer.

If you see attractive summer-blooming trees that you like, make notes so you will be ready to purchase and plant them in the fall or next spring.

Planting

Plant container-grown trees, and be sure to keep them watered regularly. Mulch the area around a tree immediately after planting.

Watering

The summer months can be stressful for plants and people. If you don't have an irrigation system, soaker hoses are one way to water your plants thoroughly. Sprinklers are also an option, but make sure you get uniform coverage. *Water* newly planted trees once a week unless you get 1 or more inches of rain.

Japanese Maples with finely divided leaves are quite susceptible to moisture stress during the heat of the summer. The first sign of stress is browning and scorching of the leaves. When planting, consider that **Japanese Maples** prefer a location where they will receive light shade during the hottest part of the day. Spread a 2-inch layer of pine bark mulch under **Japanese Maple** trees

to help conserve moisture. *Water* trees weekly, allowing the soil to dry slightly between waterings.

Fertilizing

Trees do not need to be fertilized until July.

Pest Control

Ornamental **Cherry** trees are affected by a disease called bacterial canker, which causes gum to ooze from the trunk of the tree. It can be distinguished from borer damage because there is no sawdust mixed with the gum. Bacterial canker most often infects weak trees, particularly those that have been planted in heavy clay soil or a place where water stands after a rain.

Transplant the tree if it is small, or redirect the water flow.

Trees are also weakened by a low soil pH. Raise the pH quickly by dissolving 1 pound of hydrated lime in 5 gallons of water. Sprinkle on the soil under the tree branches.

Maintain the pH by scattering 1 pound of garden lime per inch of trunk diameter evenly under the branches of the tree. Wait one year, then have the soil tested to determine if additional lime is needed.

Handpull weeds that are right next to tree trunks. A nonselective weed-killer can be used under and around trees if you make sure not to spray it on foliage, bark, or exposed roots (see Chemicals, p. 327).

Most diseases are detected with your eyes. **Oak** trees, however, sometimes contract a disease that is perceived with your nose. Sap dripping down the trunk of an **Oak,** a few feet from the ground, may indicate a slime flux infection. Also called "wet wood," slime flux is caused by fermentation of the sap under the tree's bark. The oozing sap may smell like vinegar or beer. Wasps, bees, and butterflies are drawn to the smell.

Wash the ooze and slime off the trunk to prevent bark damage. Water the tree regularly during the summer to help it internally fight off the infection.

A silvery sheen on **Dogwood** leaves usually signifies the presence of a fungus called powdery mildew. The fungus sucks moisture from the leaves and causes them to yellow and fall prematurely. It can be prevented by spraying leaves with a fungicide (see Chemicals, p. 327) in early May and continuing through mid-June. Fungicide applied now will not cure the infected leaves.

Summer Blooming Trees

- *Clerodendrum trichotomum* Harlequin Glorybower
- *Franklinia alatamaha* Franklin Tree
- *Koelreuteria paniculata* Goldenrain Tree
- *Lagerstroemia indica* Crapemyrtle
- *Magnolia grandiflora* Southern Magnolia
- *Magnolia virginiana* Sweet Bay
- *Sophora japonica* Scholar Tree
- *Stewartia* spp. Stewartia
- *Vitex agnus-castus* Chaste Tree

Once you see the fungus on the leaves, all that can be done is to protect new leaves.

If the infection is severe, the **Dogwood** *may lose up to half its leaves in July. Water infected trees regularly to help them withstand moisture stress.*

Crapemyrtle leaves may be covered with grayish-white powder, which indicates they are affected by powdery mildew. *Spray* leaves with a synthetic fungicide before plants bloom (see Chemicals, p. 327). Neem oil may be helpful in minimizing symptoms. The National Arboretum developed mildew-resistant hybrid **Crapemyrtles** by crossing *Lagerstroemia indica* with *L. fauriei* (native to Japan, *L. fauriei* has beautiful bark, is cold hardy, and exhibits a high resistance to powdery mildew). The following hybrids are mildew-resistant:

- 'Acoma' (white flowers)
- 'Biloxi' (light pink flowers)

- 'Comanche' (coral pink flowers)
- 'Hopi' (orange-red to dark-red flowers)
- 'Lipan' (medium-lavender flowers)
- 'Miami' (medium-pink flowers)
- 'Muskogee' (light-lavender flowers)
- 'Natchez' (white flowers)
- 'Osage' (clear, light-pink flowers)
- 'Sioux' (bright pink, fragrant flowers)
- 'Tuskegee' (deep-pink to red flowers)
- 'Yuma' (medium-lavender flowers)
- 'Zuni' (medium-lavender flowers)

Pruning

Prune back spring-flowering trees once they finish blooming. *Remove* seedpods.

Planning

It is tempting to transplant small Dogwood or Magnolia trees from the woods into your landscape, but this is usually not a good idea. The roots may be tangled with the larger roots of nearby trees, making transplant shock likely. Only small seedlings can be transplanted successfully—a tree taller than 4 feet is not likely to survive. Because the parentage of the tree isn't known, the seedling may never produce the number of flowers you anticipate. Named, improved selections of trees are more robust, easier to plant, and more likely to bloom regularly.

Make notations in your Garden Journal about how trees are performing. Are there places in your garden where trees can be added? Think about what type of tree would best suit your needs. A medium to large deciduous shade tree can help keep your house cool in the summer and warm in the winter when sunlight is more welcome. When it comes to selecting shade trees, there are many choices. Here is a list of medium to large trees well suited to provide shade:

- *Acer rubrum* (many selections of **Red Maple**)
- *Betula nigra* 'Heritage' **Heritage Birch**
- *Cladrastis kentukea* **Yellowwood**
- *Fagus grandiflora* **American Beech** (there are many selections)
- *Ginkgo biloba* **Ginkgo**
- *Nyssa sylvatica* **Black Tupelo**
- *Prunus × yedoensis* **Yoshino Cherry**
- *Quercus virginiana* **Live Oak**
- *Robinia pseudoacacia* (selections of **Black Locust**)
- *Ulmus parvifolia* **Lacebark Elm**

Planting

Wait until fall to plant trees. If planted now, a time of warm air and soil temperatures, trees won't put out many roots or much branch growth.

Gardeners that live on the coast are challenged to find plants that will tolerate constant winds, salt spray, and sandy soils. Here is a list of trees for coastal gardens.

- *Cryptomeria japonica* **Japanese Cryptomeria**
- *Magnolia grandiflora* **Southern Magnolia**
- *Ilex opaca* **American Holly**
- *Pinus thunbergiana* **Japanese Black Pine**
- *Quercus virginiana* **Live Oak**
- *Thuja occidentalis* **American Arborvitae**
- *Ulmus parvifolia* **Lacebark Elm**

Watering

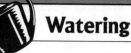

Keep newly planted trees watered. *Water* once a week unless you get 1 or more weekly inches of rain. Drought stress can make your trees more susceptible to insect and disease problems.

Fertilizing

Refer to March for fertilizing guidelines.

Pest Control

Pick off and destroy bagworms whenever you find them (see May). If you choose to use a contact insecticide, April and May are the months when the moths are most susceptible.

Pruning

There is still time to prune trees that bloomed in the spring. Cut off seedpods and *prune lightly* to shape the trees. Prune summer-flowering trees as soon as they finish blooming, if pruning is needed. There are a couple of ways to prune trees.

Heading: Selectively remove the tips of branches at their growing points rather than shearing them back. This selective pruning will leave behind a dormant bud which will eventually grow and fill in empty spaces.

Heading Before

Heading After

Thinning: This type of pruning removes the branch or stem at its origin. Be sure not to make a flush cut—leave a branch collar. When removing large limbs, remove a large section first. A section about a foot long should remain; this will make it easier to finish pruning correctly.

Helpful Hints

Fresh tree stumps are a nuisance in the landscape. Chemical removal is totally ineffective. There are two methods for removing stumps.

1 **Naturally** is the slow, inexpensive method. Eventually, Mother Nature will prevail and the stump will rot away. You can speed up the process by drilling several large, deep holes in the top of the stump. Pack the holes with topsoil gathered from under a nearby tree. Thoroughly soak the soil and stump with water. Cover the stump with clear plastic, and let the sun's heat accelerate the decomposition process.

2 **Mechanically** is the fast method. Rent a stump grinder, or hire a company to grind your stump below the soil surface. Collect the chips, and use them for mulch under shrubs and nearby trees. Avoid mixing the chips into the soil—during decomposition, they will rob nutrients from the grass or plants you use to replace the tree.

1 Cut upward partway through the branch.

2 Cut downward, slightly away from the first cut.

3 Cut off the stub just outside the branch collar (this is the swollen part that comes out from the tree where the branch attaches). The branch collar will gradually close over the wound.

Thinning Before

Thinning After

Planning

Are your existing trees healthy? Begin to make a list of trees to add to your garden this fall. Now is a good time to observe trees and make notes on which ones have survived the summer intact, without any damage from insect or disease problems. Examine the foliage and bark for signs of damage.

* If the bark is cracked and loose around the tree, inspect it for signs of insect problems, and treat as needed.

* If more than 50 percent of the leaves have brown spots or rings around spots, examine them more closely. Your tree may have a fungus that can be identified and treated, if necessary (see Chemicals, p. 327).

* If the edges of the leaves are scorched, make sure your tree is being watered on a regular basis to protect it during periods of drought. Even established trees that have been in the ground for a year or longer benefit from watering if there is no rain for a month.

Planting

Wait until the weather cools off a bit before you plant any trees.

Watering

Keep newly planted trees watered. *Check* them weekly. If you are growing trees in containers, they will need watering more frequently than those planted in the ground.

Trees need watering in summer as do lawns, flowers, and shrubs. A drought-stressed tree is more likely to suffer damage from insects and disease.

* A soaker hose laid under the drip line of the tree and an inexpensive water timer are the best tools.

* Apply 15 gallons of water per inch of trunk diameter *once* per week to supply a tree's minimum needs during drought. Example: a tree whose trunk is 12 inches thick, 4 feet from the ground, needs 180 gallons of water per week. Attach the water timer to the soaker hose and set it to 180 gallons; it will shut off once 180 gallons has soaked out of the hose. Depending on the length of the hose, this could take two to three hours. For this amount of water the cost is just a few dollars.

* Apply the amount calculated *twice* each week for optimum tree health.

Fertilizing

Wait until spring to fertilize trees.

Pest Control

If you have a wooded lot, chances are you have poison ivy. Identifying poison ivy is not always easy, but as a rule, avoid "vines with three leaves." Sometimes **Virginia Creeper,** a desirable vine that has five leaflets, is mistaken for poison ivy. If in doubt, leave it alone! Purchase an inexpensive guide to plants that includes color photographs of poison ivy.

As a young vine, poison ivy crawls along the ground and eventually climbs nearby trees. If left untended, these small vines can climb up the trunks of mature trees and develop into huge vines. As a vine matures, the leaves also get larger and in the fall may turn beautiful shades of red, orange, and yellow. Don't be fooled by its autumnal beauty; this vine causes severe allergic reactions in many people. Do not use burning as a method to control poison ivy. Breathing in the fumes can cause a severe reaction in some people. There are several ways to control it. Whichever way you select, be sure to *wash your clothes, gloves, and body immediately after contact with the plant.*

1 If you decide to be brave and handpull poison ivy, be sure to wear heavy-duty gloves and a long-sleeved shirt.

2 You can also use the plastic newspaper bag method to avoid touching the plant. Slip the bag over your hand and arm. Pull the poison ivy, then carefully pull off the bag so it encloses the plant.

3 *Spray* the mature leaves on the tops, bottoms, and stems with a nonselective weedkiller (see Chemicals, p. 327).

If the foliage on your **Hemlocks, Junipers,** or **Hollies** is speckled with brown or red spots, they may have spider mites, tiny sap-sucking creatures that are kin to the spider. Tap a branch over a piece of white paper, and circle any spots. If they move, you will know mites are present and active. To control, first use the hose to blast these critters off the foliage. If this doesn't work, try using insecticidal soap or a miticide (see Chemicals, p. 327). Wait ten to fourteen days after you spray, then try the white-paper test again.

You may need to repeat applications of miticide for effective control.

You may notice the leaves on your mature **Tulip Poplar** trees turning yellow and dropping prematurely. Premature leaf drop, leaf scorch, and many other dieback problems are often caused by environmental stresses like pollution, or lack of moisture during hot, dry summers. The best control is to keep established trees watered and stress-free during the hot summer months.

Each week, apply at least 15 gallons of water per inch of trunk diameter.

Pruning

After a major thunderstorm, you are probably tempted to get out the saw and clean up! Before you prune, here are some things to think about.

- You may need to hire a professional arborist or tree-removal company if large limbs are hanging or broken and require a chain saw, or if damage to the trees is up so high that an extension ladder is required to reach it.

- *Always follow safety precautions.* Be aware of any power lines that may be hanging in the tree. Don't touch any wires that may be on the ground.

- *Remove* broken branches that are still attached to the tree. Remove hanging branches, and smooth ragged edges with a sharp knife; this will encourage wounds to heal faster and reduce the number of places for insects to hide.

- Damaged smaller branches should be pruned back to where they join a larger branch.

- *Don't top your trees.* Cutting the main trunk back to stubs will reduce the vigor of the tree. New growth from the stubs tends to be spindly and susceptible to future storm damage.

283

Planning

With fall approaching, it's a good time to start shopping for trees. Here is a list of deciduous trees that display flowers or colorful foliage in the autumn.

- *Acer palmatum* (many selections exhibit leaves of red, yellow, and orange)

- *Acer rubrum* (many selections with colorful leaves of red, yellow, and orange)

- *Amelanchier* **spp.** (leaves of red, yellow, and orange)

- *Cornus florida* (red fruits and red to purple leaves)

- *Ginkgo biloba* (yellow leaves)

- *Hamamelis virginiana* (fragrant yellow flowers)

- *Hamamelis × intermedia* **'Diane'** (leaves turn gold)

- *Nyssa sylvatica* (leaves of red, yellow, and orange)

- *Parrotia persica* (leaves in shades of red, yellow, and orange)

- *Stewartia* **spp.** (orange and red leaves)

Planting

Plant container-grown trees this month, but wait until cooler weather to plant balled-and-burlapped trees (refer to February for guidelines on planting).

Watering

Continue to ***check*** newly planted trees on a weekly basis, and ***water*** them if you don't get at least 1 inch of rain per week.

Fertilizing

Wait until spring to fertilize newly planted trees. As long as they are thriving, established or mature trees don't need to be fertilized. However, if you want to topdress your trees with an organic material such as mushroom compost or horse or chicken manure, now is the time to do so. Topdressing breaks down over time and feeds the soil. This is also a good time to apply a fresh layer of mulch around trees. Scrape away old mulch, and apply 1 to 2 inches of topdressing and 2 to 3 inches of fresh mulch.

Pest Control

Fall webworm attacks certain deciduous trees including **Birch, Maple, Cherry, Linden, Willow, Honeylocust,** and **Crabapple.**

- Unlike the eastern tent caterpillar, which build its nests in the spring, the fall webworm is not noticeable until late summer or early fall when the nests appear at the end of the branches.

- Since defoliation is minimal and occurs late in the season, at a time when trees naturally begin to drop their leaves, there is generally no cause for alarm.

- Destroy any nests that can be easily reached by pruning them out (if possible, burn the infested branch once you have removed it from the tree), and don't worry about those you can't reach.

Rake up fallen leaves, and add them to an existing compost pile or use them to start a compost pile. One way to speed up the process of leaf decomposition is to mow with a mulcher mower. The chopped leaves will turn into compost more quickly.

Bamboo is an attractive screening plant, but it is extremely hard to control. It spreads by aboveground rhizomes and belowground roots. A clump can expand more than 20 feet in just a few years. To control **Bamboo** as it is planted:

- *Transplant* small clumps in spring, just before growth begins.

- Identify where you want the plant to grow—and where you don't want it. Dig a trench 18 inches deep around the area. A powered ditching machine is a great help in this endeavor.

- Insert 24-inch-wide aluminum roof flashing edgewise in the trench, leaving 2 inches showing above the soil surface. Lap the ends of the flashing at least 18 inches over each other.

To control **Bamboo** once it has escaped:

- Chop down every cane in the area where you do not wish it to grow.

- **Bamboo** shoots will continue to arise each spring where the canes were chopped down. Inspect the spot weekly, and knock down the shoots as they arise. The **Bamboo** roots will eventually starve if you are diligent about removing the shoots.

Pruning

Remove any dead or diseased branches, but wait until trees are dormant to do any severe pruning. Trees that are pruned now before they are completely dormant could experience cold damage. This damage occurs when new young growth sprouts during mild spells and doesn't have time to harden off before winter sets in (see July).

If the scale-like leaves on your **Cryptomeria** are turning yellow and brown and the plant looks wilted, you may have phytophthora root rot, a problem that occurs in soils that are poorly drained or wet.

The best way to avoid this problem in the future is to select the right plant for the right place. If your soil is poorly drained, select tree species that will thrive in this environment.

You may notice caterpillars with spines and barbed horns chewing on the leaves of your **Oaks, Hickories,** or **Maple** trees. If you do, you are being visited by the Orange striped Oakworm, whose eggs were laid on the branch by a moth in June. These caterpillars are about 2 inches long with eight yellow stripes and a row of large yellow spots. It is disturbing to see an entire branch stripped of its foliage, but the damage done by the caterpillar is not serious (the tree is about to lose its leaves anyway this season). Handpicking is an option; be sure to *wear gloves*. If the tree is small or newly planted, spray the leaves with *Bacillus thuringiensis* (see Chemicals, p. 327).

It is not likely that the caterpillars will return next year, even if you do nothing about them.

If your tree has a long dark line running from the top of a branch all the way to the ground and its bark is split open and peeling back from the trunk and branches, you probably have lightning damage. *Prune back* exploded bark to a healthy strong attachment. *Water* the tree regularly. Do not fertilize.

Only time will tell if the tree will survive.

Planning

This is a great month to plant both evergreen and deciduous trees in Georgia. In the more northern parts of the state they will still have time to establish roots before winter, and in the southern parts of the state, soils will be cooler and less stressful for new plants.

Although it is tempting to transplant small **Dogwood** or **Magnolia** trees from the woods into your landscape, this is usually not a good idea (see July Planning).

Planting

Ginkgo biloba is a handsome large tree whose leaves turn golden in the fall. Its only disadvantage is the messy and offensive-smelling fruit that the female tree produces. To avoid this problem, plant only male cultivars purchased from a reliable source. Male selections grafted or grown from cuttings of other males include **'Autumn Gold', 'Fairmount',** and **'Princeton Sentry'.**

As trees begin to drop their colorful fall foliage and prepare for winter dormancy, nurseries will begin to dig trees for fall planting. These balled-and-burlapped trees should be planted as soon as you purchase them, to ensure the roots acclimate as quickly as possible. Before planting, loosen the burlap around the main trunks of balled-and-burlapped trees, and take container-grown trees from their containers. To plant a balled-and-burlapped tree:

1 Dig a hole that is at least twice as wide as the rootball and no deeper than the rootball.

Hole for Balled-and-Burlapped Tree

2 Cut holes in or remove the burlap that surrounds the rootball. This allows better penetration of water for the roots and helps the tree to become established more quickly.

3 After planting, *water* thoroughly (water the tree weekly for the first year).

4 *Mulch* with a good 2- to 3-inch layer of compost, shredded pine bark, pine straw, or other similar materials, being sure to keep it from direct contact with the main trunk. (When the mulch is thick and comes into contact with tree bark, and we have lots of rain, the tree is bound to have insect and disease problems.)

5 Water the tree weekly for the first year.

Watering

Keep newly planted deciduous trees or conifers well-watered (newly planted trees are those planted within the past six months). Conifers will survive the winter much better if their needles or scales are filled with water when they go into winter dormancy—they will be less likely to dry out from winter winds.

Staking Trees

Wind, humans, and animals can sometimes uproot newly planted trees.

- For small trees, two stakes hammered into the ground near the trunk are adequate. Use a soft rope or cord. Loop a figure eight around the trunk, and tie it to the stake.

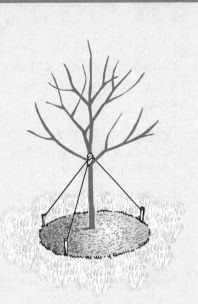

- For larger trees, use three stakes placed at equal distances around the tree, outside the root system. Use cord or wire, covered in rubber hose to protect the trunk. Loop the wire around the trunk, and attach it to the stake. Allow for some slack in the cord or wire. The trunk should be able to move a little as it grows so it will develop strength.

- Stake small trees for one year and larger trees for two years.

  ## Fertilizing

If your trees are growing well, there's no reason to fertilize. If you decide to fertilize, first get a soil test—it will help you determine which nutrients you need to add in the spring.

Pest Control

Rake up any diseased leaves, and dispose of them separately from the compost pile. This will cut down on the possibilities for spreading pest and disease problems in the future.

Pruning

Prune out any dead or diseased wood from newly planted trees.

Planning

This is an ideal month to plant trees in Georgia, provided the ground is not too wet. To determine the ground's wetness, dig up a shovelful of soil. If you can form a loose, crumbly ball that holds together briefly but still breaks apart easily, then the soil is just moist enough for planting. If you can't get the shovel out of the ground easily, then it is too wet.

Evergreen trees provide interest in the landscape all year long, serving as focal points, wind barriers, screening, and hedges, while large deciduous trees provide much welcome shade in the summer. Once you have large key trees sited, it is a good time to think about adding understory trees that will grow happily under the canopy of the larger trees such as **Oak, Hickories,** and **Ash.** Some good understory trees are:

- *Acer barbatum* **Southern Sugar Maple** (25 to 30 feet, good choice for wet coastal areas)

- *Acer buergeranum* **Trident Maple** (20 to 25 feet, colorful fall foliage, handsome bark)

- *Acer leucoderme* **Chalk Maple** (25 to 30 feet)

- *Amelanchier arborea* **June-berry** (20 to 30 feet, flowers in spring, berries in summer)

- *Cercis canadensis* **Eastern Redbud** (20 to 30 feet, pink flowers in spring, flowers appear before leaves)

- *Chionanthus retusus* **Chinese Fringe Tree** (20 feet, white flowers in spring)

- *Chionanthus virginicus* **Grancy Graybeard** (20 to 30 feet, white flowers in spring)

- *Franklinia alatamaha* **Franklin Tree** (20 to 30 feet, white flowers in summer)

- *Halesia carolina* **Carolina Silverbell** (30 to 40 feet, white bell-shaped flowers in spring)

- *Stewartia monodelpha* **Tall Stewartia** (20 to 30 feet, white flowers in summer)

- *Stewartia pseudocamellia* **Japanese Stewartia** (20 to 40 feet, white flowers in summer)

- *Styrax japonicus* **Japanese Snowbell** (20 to 30 feet, white bell-shaped flowers in spring)

- *Styrax obassia* **Fragrant Snowbell** (20 to 30 feet, fragrant white bell-shaped flowers in spring

Planting

If you have cracked and heaved sidewalks, the common culprits are tree roots. The damage occurs when a root grows under the concrete and then swells to a much greater diameter as the years pass.

- Avoid planting trees within 15 feet of a sidewalk or driveway.

- If the cracking has just begun, you might find relief by trenching beside the sidewalk and removing the offending root. Next, install 12-inch-wide aluminum flashing edgewise in the trench to prevent other roots from growing under the concrete.

Tree roots depend on a network of soil organisms, called mycorrhizae, to do much of the work involved to absorb water and nutrients. Research has shown that in poor soils, adding mycorrhizae to the soil when a tree is planted can help it become established faster. You can purchase mycorrhizae from:

Ben Meadows Company
P.O. Box 20200
Canton, GA 30114
770-479-3130

(www.benmeadows.com)

Although any tree can be valuable in some situations, a few seem to have so many problems that they are rarely appropriate for a home landscape.

- **Silver Maples** are prone to weak limbs, which crash down unexpectedly in windstorms. The roots often swell aboveground, making lawn mowing a hazardous experience.

- **Lombardy Poplar** trees are sold for quick screening. They grow tall quickly, but they typically survive only a few years in the Georgia climate.

- **Norway Maple** has invasive roots and is usually short-lived in our summer heat.

Watering

Conifers can dry out quickly in winter winds. Be sure to keep them watered even during the colder months, unless the ground is frozen.

Fertilizing

Fertilize in the spring.

Pest Control

English Ivy is an attractive and hardy ground cover that spreads rapidly, but when the ivy climbs up trees, it is damaging. As it grows into the treetop, the ivy foliage shades lower branches. In addition, the ivy collects additional ice and rain, and the tree may be damaged by the additional weight. **English Ivy** is not a parasite—its aerial roots simply cling to the tree bark for support. Here's how to get rid of it:

- Use a heavy screwdriver to pull the vine from the bark so your pruners can grip the vine enough to clip it in two.

- Pull the vine from the tree trunk as high as you can reach.

- *Remove* the ivy from an area 6 feet from the tree trunk in all directions.

- The ivy in the tree will gradually wither over the following year.

Protect newly planted young trees from damage caused by rodents and lawnmowers.

Build a simple wire cylinder. Use 1/4-inch hardware cloth that is 18 to 24 inches high. Wrap it very loosely around the tree trunk.

Trees purchased from a nursery may have tree wrap covering the lower trunk. Tree wrap makes a great hiding place for boring insects. The string or wire used to attach a stake to the tree will eventually girdle the trunk.

Remove the wrap and any stakes attached to the trunk soon after planting.

Planning

Deciduous trees in the winter landscape become studies in shape and form. Some display striking bark or interesting flowers. Visit botanical gardens and arboreta, and take note of the trees that stand out in the winter garden.

Evergreens serve a multitude of roles as specimen plants, hedges, screens, and windbreaks. **Hemlocks, Pines, Holly,** and **Arborvitae** withstand pruning and can be maintained as large hedges. Pines for Georgia vary in their rate of growth, habit, and ultimate size; they thrive with little or no fertilizer and can survive a good bit of drought. Most **Pines** develop a large taproot; therefore, with the exception of small seedlings, they are best purchased as balled-and-burlapped or container-grown plants. Consider these **Pines:**

- *Pinus rigida* **Pitch Pine** (40 to 60 feet in height by 30 to 50 feet)

- *Pinus strobus* **White Pine**

- *Pinus taeda* **Loblolly Pine** (60 to 90 feet tall)

- *Pinus thunbergiana* **Japanese Black Pine** (20 to 80 feet by 20 to 40 feet; tolerates salt spray)

- *Pinus virginiana* **Virginia Pine** (15 to 40 feet by 10 to 30 feet)

Planting

In the southernmost parts of the state where the ground does not freeze, you can plant container-grown trees.

1 *Remove* the tree from the container. Examine the roots to be sure they are healthy.

Remove tree from container.

2 Use a hand cultivator to loosen the roots. If roots are wrapped around the rootball many times, use a sharp spade or pair of pruners and make four vertical cuts, evenly spaced around the rootball. Gently *tease* the roots at the bottom of the rootball so that they spread out. Make sure there are no large roots at the top of the rootball that could girdle the trunk.

3 Place the tree in the hole on top of a solid mound of soil. Fill in the hole around the tree, about halfway, using your shovel handle or foot to firm the soil and eliminate air pockets. *Water* the tree and add the rest of the soil, being careful not to compact it.

4 *Mulch* the area around the tree with a 2- to 3-inch layer of material, keeping it away from the trunk of the tree (mulch piled up against the trunk of the tree can cause it to rot).

5 Once it is planted, *water* the tree thoroughly. Thereafter, water the tree regularly, weekly for the first six months or so, and then once a month for the next year, if there is not adequate rainfall.

Watering

Keep new plantings watered.

Fertilizing

Hold off on fertilizing until early spring.

Pest Control

Rake up any leaf litter that you missed in the autumn; this will reduce the number of places for insects to overwinter.

Pruning

Prune out any dead, diseased, or broken branches from trees planted in the past six months.

If you have deciduous trees that require major pruning, schedule the work to be done in the next few months while trees are still dormant. Be sure you hire or consult with an arborist if you are not sure which branches are alive and which are dead.

Helpful Hints

CHOOSING A "CUT-YOUR-OWN" CHRISTMAS TREE

- Call the Georgia Farmers and Consumers Market Bulletin (404-656-3682) in early November and ask for their yearly Christmas tree farm issue.

- To investigate other farms, visit the Georgia Christmas Tree Growers Association (www.gachristmastree.com).

- Plan to bring the whole family on the outing. Many farms have wagon rides, a petting zoo, or other activities.

- Bring a big piece of plastic to use to cover the tree on the way back. Otherwise, the tree needles will be as dry as toast after a frigid and windy ride on top of your car.

CHOOSING A CUT CHRISTMAS TREE FROM A LOT

- Good varieties are **Fraser Fir, Scots Pine, Noble Fir, White Pine, Virginia Pine,** and **Leyland Cypress.**

- Shake the tree or pull your fingers lightly down a branch–few needles should drop out.

- Remember to cut at least $\frac{1}{2}$ inch off the base of the tree before standing it in water.

CARING FOR A LIVE CHRISTMAS TREE

- Good varieties are **Cryptomeria, Hemlock, Hinoki Cypress, Umbrella Pine, Arborvitae, Leyland Cypress,** and **Virginia Pine.** Not recommended: **Colorado Blue Spruce, Alberta Spruce,** and **White Pine.**

- Plan to have the tree indoors for no more than seven days so it will have a better chance of surviving when you plant it outside.

- Keep the rootball moist. Ice cubes wrapped in a cloth and placed on top of the ball will slowly trickle water to the roots.

- If you cannot plant the tree on your property, offer to plant the tree at a local school, church, or synagogue.

Vines and Ground Covers

Much as rooms are more complete with window treatments and floor coverings, gardens have a more finished look when they are enhanced with vines and ground covers. Both groups of plants play important roles in the landscape and extend the possibilities for adding color and interest to your garden all year long. Vines add verticality and help make maximum use of your growing space; ground covers provide a carpet beneath shrubs and trees, offer an alternative to lawns, and help conserve soil moisture.

Vines and How to Use Them

There are many selections of vines for Georgia gardeners, both annual and perennial, including types grown for brightly colored flowers, attractive seedpods, dramatic foliage, and distinctive bark. Whether you train them to grow up a masonry wall, fence, or arbor, vines require a structure or surface to grab, cling to, twine around, or drape over. The types and styles of available supports are as diverse as the many varieties of vines that grow and thrive in Georgia. The size and durability of the structure you use to support your vines should be determined by the characteristics of the particular vine you are growing. Large woody ornamental vines such as **Wisteria** require substantial support, perhaps a large solid arbor. Other vines, such as **Carolina Jessamine,** can be trained to cover a fence.

What makes a plant as a vine? This depends on the individual plant. Some plants, like certain types of **Cotoneaster** or old-fashioned **Shrub Roses,** are not true climbing plants but simply have a lax habit—you can train them to grow up a structure or against a wall by tying branches and stems in place. Certain other roses require little or no encouragement before they threaten to take down a building. To keep them in check you must prune them two or three times a year. Still other plants bloom in the same spot year after year without requiring constant care.

Vines enhance the garden scene and complement other blooms: **Roses** and **Clematis** are a classic combination, often blooming at the same time. Some vines, like **Carolina Jessamine** and **English Ivy,** can be left to sprawl on the ground, making effective ground covers. Vines come in all forms, from the cultivated climbing **'New Dawn' Rose** to the **Crossvine** *Bignonia capreolata,* a native vine in our woods.

Vines and shrubs can live as happy companions in the garden. There are vines with fantastic foliage, colorful flowers, and interesting fruits, helping to provide year-round interest. When you use a shrub as a living trellis for a **Clematis,** you can have blooms in more than one season. For example, if you train a summer-blooming hybrid **Clematis** to grow up through an **Azalea** that blooms in spring, you will have flowers in the same spot at two different times of year. To maintain this combination, simply *cut back* the **Clematis** after it flowers (see March for more information about pruning **Clematis**).

How Vines Climb

The popular **English Ivy** attaches itself to trees, walls, and other surfaces with short, *clinging* adventitious roots. In a similar fashion, **Climbing Hydrangea** and **Boston Ivy,** also true clinging vines, attach themselves with rootlike holdfasts. **Honeysuckle, Akebia, Wisteria,** and **Star Jasmine** *twine* their stems around supports. **Porcelain Berry** and climbing types of **Clematis**

Vines and Ground Covers

attach themselves by *twisting,* using a leaf petiole as a tendril to cling to a support. There are also vines like **Climbing Roses,** which have no means of attachment and require *tying* to hold them to a support.

Ground Covers and How to Use Them

Any plant that effectively covers the ground might be considered a ground cover. Turf or lawn is perhaps the most popular ground cover, but in this chapter we will focus on alternatives to turf. Ground covers serve a number of functions. As a living mulch, they not only help conserve soil moisture, but they keep roots of trees and shrubs cool in the summer and warm in the winter. Some ground covers, like **Periwinkle,** offer handsome evergreen foliage. Others, like **Green and Gold,** display attractive flowers in spring, and handsome foliage throughout the growing season. On a steep bank where turf is impractical, ground covers like **Monkey Grass** can be invaluable for controlling erosion.

Area Covered by 100 Ground Cover Plants

The following chart (reprinted with permission) comes from the publication "Spacing Plant Material: Groundcovers" produced by The University of Georgia Cooperative Extension Service. It predicts the area that will be covered if you use 100 plants at various planting distances.

Planting Distance (inches)	Area Covered (sq. ft.)
6	25
12	100
18	225

This information is especially useful when you are trying to figure out how many plants you will need for covering large areas with ground covers. Remember that starting with small, well-rooted plants is not only easier but more cost-efficient. The chart is intended as a guide, not absolute instructions. In certain places where you want an immediate effect, such as on a steep bank where erosion is a problem, you may want to space plants closer together. Or you may be planting a fast-growing spreader like **English Ivy,** and you can space plants farther apart if you have time before you need the spot to look filled in.

Planning

Before you purchase vines and ground covers to add to your garden, take stock of where you will use these plants. If you are planting a vine like **Wisteria,** make sure you provide a structure that is strong enough to support this tenacious climber. It twists its stems around a support and can get very large, both in height and in the diameter of its woody stem (4 inches in no time)—the bigger the arbor, trellis, or gazebo, the better. Other vines, like many of the hybrid **Clematis,** will be happy to twine around a piece of clear nylon line and won't threaten to take down your two-car garage.

When it comes to ground covers, some, like **Mondo Grass,** are well suited as a substitute for lawns while others, like **Green and Gold,** are better for creating a patch of color in a woodland garden. It pays to do some research before you begin to plant. Choose the right plant for the right place, and you will have greater success.

Vines and Ground Covers

Soil Preparation

Whether you are planting vines or ground covers, soil preparation is important. If you are trying to cover a large area of ground, there are two methods you can use for preparing the soil.

1 Prepare the entire area before you plant.

2 Prepare individual holes, mixing a shovelful of organic material with the existing soil in the hole.

The second technique may be faster and is all that is needed for certain plants that have many stoloniferous roots, or for plants that root easily from their stems and leaf nodes (**Ornamental Raspberry** puts out roots wherever it touches the soil). Another approach for covering a large area with a ground cover is to prepare the planting area, put down 1 to 2 inches of mulch, and then plant through the mulch.

Fertilizing

Vines and ground covers can be treated like perennials and shrubs when fertilizing. If you mix a slow-release granular fertilizer into the soil when you plant, you will not need to fertilize as often as you would if you use 10-10-10 or 8-8-8. As a general rule, you can apply fertilizer twice a year, once in March and once in June. If you have a large area of ground covers in place of a lawn, you can broadcast the fertilizer. If you plant vines in combination with shrubs or trees, they won't need to be fertilized separately but will get enough fertilizer when you fertilize their companions.

Pest Control

Vines and ground covers are subject to many of the same pest and disease problems that affect other ornamental plants, like aphids, spider mites, scale, and fungus. To help keep damage to a minimum, select varieties that are suited for the environment in which you will plant them. Practice Integrated Pest Management, or IPM (see Trees, June). Keeping plants watered and mulched will help them ward off problems, too.

Pruning

Once established, most ground covers require only a minimum of pruning. **English Ivy** and **Periwinkle** can be pruned if they are getting out of bounds or if you want them to fill in and become more bushy in growth. Other ground covers, like **Green and Gold, Bugleweed,** and **Mazus,** do not require regular pruning but may need to be divided if clumps get too large and begin to lose vigor. **Monkey Grass** will benefit from annual pruning or shearing in early spring to a height of 2 to 3 inches. This can be easily accomplished with a lawn mower. Within weeks new growth will cover any sign of pruning.

Perennial vines should be pruned selectively, depending on when they flower. To avoid cutting off flower-buds, it is important to learn whether a particular vine blooms on old or new growth. Certain perennial vines like **Carolina Jessamine** can be pruned back to a height of 1 foot if they are straggly and lack vigor. Annual vines don't require pruning; they can be left until they are killed by a frost. At this point you can easily clean up and remove the dead vines.

Perennial Vines for Georgia

Name	Size and Habit	Culture	Comments
Akebia quinata **Five-leaf Akebia** **Raisin Vine**	Grows 20 to 40 feet long. An evergreen climber, the leaves emerge with purple tinges and turn blue-green as they mature.	This tough vine tolerates a wide range of soil types and grows in sun or part shade.	There are curious chocolate-purple flowers and showy dark-purple fruits.
Ampelopsis brevipedunculata **Porcelain Berry**	A deciduous climber with twining tendrils. Grows to 20 feet or higher and needs a strong support.	Plant this vine in full sun or part shade in a well-drained soil.	Grow this vine for its colorful fruits, which appear in late summer in shades of lavender-blue and purple.
Bignonia capreolata **Crossvine**	Grows to 30 feet or higher. Produces 2-inch brownish-orange, trumpet-shaped flowers in spring.	Plant this semi-evergreen (except in the most southern and coastal areas, where it is evergreen) vine in full sun or part shade in a soil that is moist, but well-drained.	'Tangerine Beauty' has bright apricot-orange flowers that last for weeks.
Clematis spp. and cvs. **Clematis**	Depending on the type, **Clematis** vary greatly in height from less than 1 foot to over 40 feet high. The flowers on the species are often tiny, but the hybrids can have flowers up to 10 inches across.	**Clematis** like sun and a soil that is moist, but well-drained. Mulching is especially helpful to retain moisture.	The climbing types are not self-clinging, but twist for support, clinging with a petiole. If you don't provide a structure (even string will do), **Clematis** will sprawl on the ground.
Decumaria barbara **Climbing Hydrangea**	Grows to 30 feet high or higher with glossy green leaves that are 2 to 4 inches long and 1 to 2 inches wide.	A native vine that likes shady woodland situations with a moist soil, it will also tolerate dry soils.	This deciduous vine bears clusters of fragrant white flowers in May or June.
Gelsemium sempervirens **Carolina Jessamine**	This hardy evergreen vine grows 10 to 20 feet high and spreads out with equal vigor if given a support to grow on.	Grows best in full sun, but tolerates shade. Plant in a moist, well-drained soil.	Fragrant yellow flowers appear any time from February to April.
Hydrangea anomala petiolaris **Climbing Hydrangea**	A true clinging vine that attaches itself with rootlike holdfasts. Grows 60 to 80 feet.	Plant this woody vine in full sun or shade in a moist, well-drained soil.	Slow to get established—once it does, this is a four-season plant. White flowers in midsummer, fresh green leaves all summer. Foliage turns buttercup yellow in autumn.

Perennial Vines for Georgia

Name	Size and Habit	Culture	Comments
Lonicera × heckrottii Goldflame Honeysuckle	Grows 10 to 20 feet high but is not invasive like many **Honeysuckles.** From spring until frost, produces flowers that are carmine in bud with yellow insides.	Grows in full sun or half shade. Plant this vine in a soil that is moist, but well-drained.	A deciduous vine except in the lower and coastal parts of Georgia, where it is semi-evergreen.
Parthenocissus quinquefolia Virginia Creeper	This vigorous vine grows 30 to 50 feet high and clings to the ground, fences, and walls.	Grow this deciduous vine in full sun or shade, in most soil types.	In the autumn the leaves turn shades of purple, red, and crimson.
Passiflora spp. and cvs. Passionflower	These vines climb by tendrils, reaching 20 to 30 feet or higher. There are evergreen, semi-evergreen, and deciduous types.	Plant this vine in full sun in a well-drained soil. Has beautiful flowers; some have edible fruit.	A favorite larval food of the Gulf fritillary butterfly.
Polygonum aubertii Silver Lace Vine	A fast-growing deciduous vine, it can cover 100 square feet in a season. It becomes a mass of creamy-white flowers in spring.	Great for quick cover on a fence, arbor, or hillside. Plant in full sun. This aggressive grower is drought-tolerant.	To delay flowering, cut this vine back to the ground in early spring. A good candidate for seashore gardens.
Schizophragma hydrangeoides Japanese Hydrangea Vine	This woody vine climbs by holdfasts to 30 feet or higher.	Train this vine to cover masonry walls or trees, in a shade garden.	The selection '**Moonlight**' has blue-green foliage that has a silvery cast.
Trachelospermum jasminoides Confederate Jasmine	With support, this evergreen vine will grow to 20 feet high. Fragrant white flowers, shaped like pinwheels, appear in spring and summer.	Plant in sun or shade in moist, well-drained soil.	Foliage starts out a glossy light green and turns darker as it matures. Great for training on walls, pergolas, and arbors.
Wisteria floribunda Japanese Wisteria	The leaves are 12 to 16 inches long, divided into fifteen to nineteen leaflets. Clusters of violet flowers are $1^1/2$ feet long. This vine will grow to heights of 40 feet or more.	Plant this aggressive vine in a well-drained soil in full sun.	Prune after it stops flowering and then again in summer. Stop pruning by the end of June so that you won't prune off next year's flowerbuds.
Wisteria frutescens American Wisteria	The leaflets are 7 to 12 inches long, and the compressed clusters of flowers are 4 to 6 inches long.	Plant in full sun in a well-drained soil.	Overall, the **American Wisteria** is less aggressive than the Asiatic types.

Ground Covers for Georgia

Name	Size and Habit	Culture	Comments
Ajuga reptans Bugleweed	Depending on the cultivar, it can grow 4 to 10 inches tall and spread 18 inches or more.	Grow in moist, well-drained soil in part shade.	There are many selections with dark-purple foliage. This ground cover can be invasive.
Chrysogonum virginianum Green and Gold	Grows 6 to 9 inches tall and 12 inches wide. There are 1-inch-wide yellow daisy flowers in spring, followed by sporadic flowers in autumn.	Plants thrive in shade in a moist, well-drained soil. If planted in full sun, they must have soil that is constantly moist.	A great woodland ground cover. **'Eco Lacquered Spider'** has gray-green foliage and long stolons. It spreads much more rapidly than the species.
Fragaria 'Pink Panda'	Each plant grows 4 to 6 inches tall and spreads out 12 to 18 inches in one season.	Plants are happiest in full sun to partial shade in a soil that is well-drained.	This ground cover has beautiful foliage and pink flowers in early spring.
Juniperus conferta Shore Juniper	Grows 1 to 2 feet high and 6 to 8 feet wide.	Plant in full sun in a well-drained soil. Great for coastal gardens.	There are numerous prostrate selections of **Juniper** that make good ground covers for full-sun situations.
Lamium maculatum Spotted Nettle	Grows 8 to 12 inches high and 18 inches wide. Stoloniferous and creeping, this plant makes a good variegated ground cover.	Part shade is ideal for this ground cover. A moist well-drained soil is best.	There are many improved selections with handsome foliage.
Liriope muscari Monkey Grass	Grows 12 to 18 inches tall and 12 inches wide. Forms large clumps but does not spread by underground stems. Produces spikes of lilac-purple flowers in August.	Grows in heavy shade or full sun. This tough evergreen will tolerate heat and drought better than most.	**Monkey Grass** can be used as a substitute for turf. Mow clumps to the ground in late winter, and plants will put out a flush of new growth as spring arrives.
Liriope spicata Creeping Liriope	Spreads by underground stems to form large clumps. Grows 8 to 9 inches high.	Grows in sun or shade.	Can be very invasive. Effective for holding soil on banks.
Mazus reptans Mazus	Grows 2 to 4 inches tall and 12 inches wide. This mat-forming ground cover is useful between stepping stones, in a woodland, or in a rock garden. In the spring it produces purplish-blue or white flowers.	Plant this aggressive spreader in a moist but well-drained soil in partial shade or full sun. Protect it from hot afternoon sun.	The tiny flowers, purple and yellow, look like miniature Snapdragon blooms. There is also a white-flowered form.

Ground Covers for Georgia

Name	Size and Habit	Culture	Comments
Ophiopogon japonicus **Mondo Grass**	Grows 3 to 12 inches tall and spreads 9 to 12 inches wide. The pale-lilac flowers that appear in summer are often hidden by the leaves.	Grow in a moist, well-drained soil in part shade, although it will tolerate full sun.	Great for an evergreen ground cover or edging plant. **Black Mondo Grass** grows to 6 inches high and has almost black foliage.
Pachysandra terminalis **Pachysandra**	Grows 9 to 12 inches tall and 18 inches across. A rapid spreader, plants colonize an area quickly.	Plant this evergreen under trees or in other shady locations. Prefers a moist, well-drained soil.	There is also a variegated selection, **'Silver Edge'**, with creamy-edged foliage.
Rubus calycinoides **Ornamental Creeping Raspberry**	Grows 6 to 12 inces tall. A rapid spreader, it roots wherever its stems touch soil.	Plant this tough creeper in full sun or partial shade in a well-drained soil.	Fast-growing and evergreen, this ground cover adapts to a wide range of landscape situations.
Saxifraga stolonifera **Strawberry Begonia**	Grows 4 to 6 inches tall and 12 inches across. Spreads to cover an area with long stoloniferous runners. Produces white flowers in summer.	Plant this handsome ground cover in the shade in well-drained soil.	The **Strawberry Begonia** is also used for hanging baskets and in pots.
Vinca minor **Periwinkle**	Grows 6 to 12 inches high and spreads out in every direction. The glossy evergreen foliage looks good all year.	This species prefers shade and moist areas.	**Vinca** can be used for erosion control on banks.

Flowering and Fruiting Ground Covers

Ceratostigma plumbaginoides Dwarf Plumbago 6 to 12 inches high

This hardy perennial may be semi-evergreen in the mildest parts of the state but even where it is deciduous, the indigo-blue phlox-like flowers in late summer to early autumn are reason enough to grow this plant. The foliage is bronzy to dark green and then in autumn it gets tinges of red. Plant this bloomer in full sun or part shade.

Cotoneaster spp. and cvs. Cotoneaster

Many different types exist from the very low-growing ground huggers to those with long trailing branches. Many are effective for bank plantings with colorful fruit in shades of red and orange. Some begin to color in summer and provide interest through the winter. Cotoneasters prefer full sun or part shade.

Galax urceolata Galax 6 to 9 inches high

The foliage is 6 to 9 inches high with spikes of white flowers 2$\frac{1}{2}$ feet tall. This native perennial grows in tufts and is a slow grower, but in a woodland garden it makes an elegant evergreen ground cover. Up to 5 inches across, the shiny heart-shaped leaves take on shades of bronze in the autumn.

Galium odoratum Sweet Woodruff 6 to 12 inches high

Long grown for the fragrant flowers and foliage used to make May wine. Great for the shade or part shade, this perennial likes a moist, well-drained soil. Be warned: this plant is an aggressive spreader. Give this plant full shade in the most southern part of the state.

Hemerocallis spp. and cvs. Daylily 1 to 6 feet tall

Daylilies make a trouble-free flowering ground cover on a bank, or as part of a mixed planting. The dwarf varieties are well suited for mass plantings. Plant **Daylilies** in full sun or part shade.

Hypericum calycinum Creeping St. Johnswort 1 foot tall

This evergreen to semi-evergreen plant is a survivor that can grow and compete with tree roots, tolerate poor soil, or help control erosion on a steep bank. Bright yellow flowers, 3 inches across, occur throughout the summer. If the plant gets overgrown, use the lawn mower or prune it back hard when it is dormant. **Hypericum** prefers full sun or part shade.

Mitchella repens Partridgeberry 3 to 6 inches tall

This creeping native is perfect for the woodland garden with ferns, mosses and other shade loving plants. The roundish evergreen leaves are less than 1 inch long. Tiny white flowers appear in late spring to early summer and are followed by bright red berries, less than $\frac{1}{4}$ inch wide.

Sarcococca hookerana humilis Himalayan Sweet Box 1 to 2 feet high

This ground cover spreads very slowly by underground runners. The glossy evergreen leaves, 1 to 3 inches long, hide the tiny but powerfully fragrant flowers when they perfume the air in early spring. The flowers are followed by small black fruits. A great ground cover for the shade garden.

Planning

This is a good month to begin planning what you will add or take away from your garden. Identify areas where you want to add vines or ground covers. If your garden looks flat or one-dimensional, vines might be the answer, as they provide instant verticality. If you are running out of space to grow plants, remember that vines grow upwards, and some require only a wall or fence to grab onto and a narrow space to put down some roots. Many vines will also grow happily in large containers, trailing over the edge or climbing up onto a trellis.

Add a structure like an arbor, trellis, pergola, or gazebo. Gather information and ideas about the best structure for your garden; it should be functional and attractive. Peruse garden magazines and books for ideas, or consult with a garden designer about which type of structure will work best for your garden style. In addition to providing a place for your vines to climb, cling to, or twine on, arbors and other garden structures can serve as key elements in the design of your garden. Placement of the structure is *very* important. An arbor can lead a visitor from one point to another, invite you to approach, or direct your attention toward a particular view. Positioning an arbor at the end of a path, with a bench placed beneath the arbor, makes a stronger statement than placing one in the middle of your garden.

If you are growing perennial ornamental vines, think about what they will look like throughout the year. What does the foliage look like in autumn? If there are flowers, are they fragrant? Does a particular vine offer attractive bark in winter?

Hire a professional to draw up landscape design plans, or refer to plans in a book. Take time to make sure the scale of whatever structure you build or have built fits into your garden and relates to your house and garden. As a rule of thumb, bigger is usually better. What looks like a massive structure on paper is often just right once it is constructed and standing in the garden. If you don't feel confident about getting the proportions right, and hiring a professional is too expensive, invest in some bamboo poles and construct a temporary arbor. Observe it for a week to determine if the size is appropriate. This is an inexpensive way to learn about scale before you build a permanent structure.

If you have an area of lawn that is thin and patchy because it is beneath large mature shade trees, think about replacing the lawn with ground covers. *Measure* the area so you will know how many plants to purchase in the spring (see p. 293, Area Covered by 100 Groundcover Plants). **Mondo Grass** or **Liriope** are alternatives to turf, and both thrive in the shade.

Visit your local botanical garden or arboretum, and make notes about ground covers or vines that offer interesting foliage and flowers.

Planting

Unless you live in the most southern part of the state, wait until the weather is a bit milder and the ground is not frozen or soggy before you begin to plant.

Watering

If you have areas of ground covers that have been planted in the past six months, they should be watered weekly (at least 1 inch per week) if there is no rain and if the ground is not frozen. Use a sprinkler, and set out small cans, such as tuna fish cans, to measure how much water the plants receive. Water until the tuna fish can is approximately 3/4 full, which should equal about an inch of water.

Fertilizing

Wait until early spring to fertilize vines or ground covers.

Pest Control

In South Georgia, *check* evergreen ground covers like **Vinca** and **Euonymus** for insect infestations such as scale or spider mites. Scale looks like white and brown specks firmly attached to stems and leaves. The scale, sucking insects that cause leaves to turn yellow and drop, also causes branches to die back. *Spray* with horticultural oil to control. Read and follow label instructions (see Chemicals, p. 327).

Pruning

If you have annual vines that are still clinging to walls, fences, arbors, or other supports, it should be easy to *pull or prune* them off and clean up the surfaces now that they have died. Save any seeds that you missed collecting in the fall. They make easy and inexpensive presents for your gardening friends. Once they drop their leaves, it is easier to see where you want to prune your vines, especially if you want to train them as an espalier (see May).

Helpful Hints

If you love **Wisteria** and have planted one but still have no blooms after many years, here are a few things to consider:

- Budded, grafted, or cutting-grown plants bloom much sooner than seed-grown plants. If you have grafted plants, be sure to remove any suckers that sprout below the graft so they won't overpower the upper part of the vine. If you purchase a named selection of **Wisteria,** chances are it is a grafted plant. Look for a swollen area, almost like a collar, that surrounds the main trunk. This is a good indicator of a grafted plant.

- **Wisteria** does not need fertilizer on a regular basis. If your vine is healthy and producing lots of vegetative growth but not blooming, withhold all nitrogen fertilizer for an entire growing season. If it still doesn't flower, try pruning the roots in spring, after the time when it would normally bloom. Make vertical cuts through the roots with a spade, 1 foot from the main trunk.

- *Prune* to remove dead or damaged stems and twigs from woody vines.

- *Prune* **Wisteria** vines to reduce or thin side shoots from the main stems. These shoots produce flower-producing spurs. For the best blooms, shorten these shoots back to two or three buds. Because it is such an aggressive grower, **Wisteria** needs to be pruned on a regular basis, sometimes two or three times a year.

If you have large areas of evergreen ground covers like **English Ivy** or **Vinca,** wait until early spring to prune them back close to the ground, and do so only if they need it. Established beds of **English Ivy** or **Vinca** can go for years without being pruned, but if they become overgrown and straggly or start to spread beyond where you want them to, prune away.

Planning

This month it's time to peruse catalogs and think about which annual vines you might like to add to the garden in spring. Many are easy to grow from seed that can be started indoors in March (see Annuals, February). Think about adding some with colorful flowers or interesting fruits. Below is a list of annual vines with a brief description of each. All of these vines are happiest if they receive full sun and are planted in well-drained soil.

- *Clitoria* spp. **Butterfly Pea Vine** produces striking blue flowers.

- *Cobaea scandens* **Cup-and-saucer Vine** is a vigorous grower to 25 feet with bell-shaped flowers that open yellow-green and then turn to purple. There is also a white form.

- *Cucurbita* spp. **Gourd Vines** come in many different sizes and shapes.

- *Dolichos lablab* **Hyacinth Bean** has purple flowers followed by purple pealike pods; it is a perennial in the Coastal South.

- *Ipomoea alba* **Moon Vine** is known for its fragrant white flowers. Measuring 6 inches across or larger, the flowers open in late afternoon and wither the following morning.

- *Ipomoea batatas* **Ornamental Sweet Potato Vine** is grown for its colorful foliage. There are selections with nearly-black foliage and others with leaves that are chartreuse.

- *Ipomoea purpurea* **Common Morning Glory** is a twining climber with heart-shaped leaves. The funnel-shaped flowers range in color from deep purple to bluish-purple or reddish flowers with white throats.

- *Ipomoea quamoclit* **Cypress Vine** is a twining vine with delicate ferny foliage and striking scarlet flowers. It's a hummingbird magnet.

- *Mandevilla* 'Alice du Pont' is a tropical vine that may be root-hardy in the Coastal South but should be grown as an annual farther North. This vine is best purchased as a small plant.

- *Mina lobata* **Firecracker Vine** has flowers that are scarlet, yellow, and orange. A vigorous climbing vine, it blooms in fall.

- *Podranea ricasolina* **Pink Trumpet Vine** is really for coastal gardeners but can be treated as an annual in other parts of the state. It has glossy green foliage and 2- to 3-inch-wide flowers shaped like pink trumpets marked with red veins. You may want to purchase a plant instead of growing it from seed, since it is a slow grower.

- *Thunbergia alata* **Black-eyed Susan Vine** may survive as a perennial in the coastal parts of Georgia but is an annual in the rest of the state. A twining plant, the flowers are orange, yellow, or white with a purple-black throat.

- *Tropaeolum* spp. **Climbing Nasturtium** has flowers that range from orange to yellow to cream. Slightly fragrant, the flowers are also edible.

Ground Covers:

If you have a bank where grass won't grow, plant ground covers to control erosion. One way to get started is to use erosion-control burlap. Put down a layer of pine straw, then put down the burlap. You can use metal stakes to hold it in place. Plant the ground covers in the open areas of the burlap netting. Small, 4-inch pots or plugs are easy to plant, and if the plants are well rooted, they should establish quickly. The burlap will decompose as the ground covers grow. Some people put down the mulch before they plant and then dig small holes into the mulch for each plant. Whether you mulch before or after you plant, be sure to water afterwards. See the facing page for a list of ground covers to use for erosion control.

Planting

In the southern parts of the state, this is a good time to plant ground covers and perennial vines. Wait until soil and air temperatures warm up to plant annual vines.

Watering

Water new plantings of ground covers (areas that have been planted within the past six months). A sprinkler is a good way to cover a large area of ground covers. Place several small cans around the area (tuna fish or cat food cans work well). When the cans are about ¾ full, the ground covers are probably watered well enough for the week.

Fertilizing

Wait until March to fertilize vines and ground covers.

Plants that Help Control Erosion

Evergreen ground covers can help control erosion. The following list of erosion-control plants includes vines that are also effective ground covers.

- **Carolina Jessamine** (a vine)
- **Creeping Liriope**
- **English Ivy** (a vine)
- **Monkey Grass**

- **Ornamental Raspberry**
- **Pachysandra**
- **Periwinkle**
- **Shore Juniper**

Pest Control

English Ivy is a popular ground cover for shade, and with good reason. Mostly undemanding, it is only occasionally affected by a bacterial leaf spot that causes leaves and stems to blacken and shrivel. Such leaves have brown or black spots that are surrounded by yellow halos. Environmental conditions like overhead watering and frequent rain contribute to the spread of this disease. The best control is to *remove and destroy* infected leaves and stems. It is also good to avoid using sprinklers at night when the foliage will stay wet for a long period of time. *Spray* diseased foliage with Mancozeb (see Chemicals, p. 327).

Periwinkle (*Vinca minor*) can develop a root fungus if it is planted in soils that are not well drained. Leaves and stems wilt and die, making it easy to pull them out of the ground. This soilborne fungus enters through the roots, especially in soils that are poorly drained. The best solution is to *remove and destroy* infected plants, and to improve soil drainage or eliminate water flowing through the area.

Pruning

This is a good month to get out the lawn mower and *cut back* your tattered or winter-damaged **Monkey Grass.** By cutting it back now there will be a reduced chance of cutting off new growth. Set the mower at the highest setting and mow down the foliage. The grass should be about 3 inches high when you finish. If you have only a small patch of **Monkey Grass,** you can cut it back with a pair of sharp shears. Once spring arrives, fresh dark-green leaves will quickly cover up the ragged edges.

Planning

Start annual vine seeds indoors under lights (see Annuals, March). Read seed packages carefully to determine how long it will take until they are ready to plant outdoors. Some require a cold treatment before they will germinate, and others require mechanical abrasion such as nicking the seed coat.

If you have an area of turf that you want to change to ground covers, be sure to prepare the soil before you plant. If there is any grass left, *spray* it with a nonselective weed-killer (see Chemicals, p. 327). After the grass is dead, *rototill* to a depth of 8 to 12 inches, adding soil amendments as you go.

Planting

Plant perennial vines and ground covers that have been grown in containers and are now available at garden centers.

This is a good time to *divide* over-grown plantings of **Monkey Grass, Creeping Liriope,** or **English Ivy.** Use a large spading fork and dig up clumps. If you have a large bare area you want to cover, you can divide the clumps into small sections and plant them 12 to 18 inches apart. Make sure each division has an equal ratio of roots

to foliage or shoots. *Replant* the divisions, apply a 2-inch layer of mulch, and water.

Transplant **Clematis** vines before new growth begins. Dig as large a rootball as possible—the more roots, the better. Prepare the new site ahead of time so that the roots are out of the ground for the shortest amount of time. This way fewer will dry out. It is often said that **Clematis** like a hot top (foliage) and cold feet (roots). It is more accurate to say that **Clematis** prefer full sun and plenty of soil moisture. Mulching is very important to help conserve soil moisture.

Watering

Water any new plantings of vines and ground covers as well as existing plantings if there has not been rain (at least 1 inch a week is best).

Fertilizing

If ground covers are planted under trees that are on a regular fertilizing program, they will get plenty of nutrients when the trees are fed. It is not absolutely necessary that you fertilize your ground covers, but if you think they need it,

apply 1 pound (2 cups) of 8-8-8 or 10-10-10 per 100 square feet. Use a broadcast-type spreader to get even distribution over the area. Wash any fertilizer off the foliage when you finish. If you do fertilize, twice a year is adequate, once in March and once in June.

Pest Control

If your **Pachysandra** has leaves that are light brown or tan on top, it has leaf scorch. *Transplant* your **Pachysandra** to a shadier location.

Use a granular weed-preventer twice each year, once now and once in September. An application this month will help cut down on infestations of summer annual weeds. Look for products formulated specifically for ground covers (see Chemicals, p. 327).

English Ivy can be a blessing or a curse . . . it can become a pest. A rapid spreader, sometimes it leaps from the planting bed and climbs up into the trees. Shading lower branches and collecting litter, rain, or ice, **Ivy** can cause damage to tree limbs. For information on controlling **English Ivy,** see Trees, November.

Pruning

Prune back vines that are overgrown, including **Wisteria, Ivy, Trumpet Creeper,** and **Climbing Hydrangea.** *Wait* to prune spring-flowering vines like **Carolina Jessamine** until after they bloom.

Prune back late-flowering **Clematis** to a height of about 2 to 3 feet. Such **Clematis** flower on current-season's growth, which is the last 2 to 3 feet. Plants in this group include *Clematis viticella, C. flammula, C. tangutica, C. × jackmanii, C. maximowicziana, C.* 'Perle d'Azur', *C.* 'Duchess of Albany', and others.

Prune back large-flowered hybrid **Clematis** such as 'Nelly Moser', 'Duchess of Edinburgh', and 'Marie Boisselot'. These hybrids bloom in mid-June on short stems from the previous season's growth. Prune to remove dead or weak stems, and *cut back* remaining stems to the first pair of healthy green buds. You can plant other plants under the **Clematis** in this group to conceal the bare stems that develop at the base of the plant as it matures. Perennials like **Hardy Geraniums** or small evergreen shrubs make happy companions for **Clematis.**

Helpful Hints

The main reason to prune **Clematis** is to encourage plants to produce a maximum amount of blooms. The question of when to prune is determined by whether the particular **Clematis** blooms on second-year wood (growth from the previous season) or on new growth, and if it blooms early or late. Even without pruning, your **Clematis** will grow and bloom, but perhaps not as profusely. Try to purchase named varieties; this will make it easier to determine what the plant requires in terms of its environment and pruning. Here are some simple tips to guide you when pruning your **Clematis.**

- If you are growing early-blooming **Clematis,** both the large-flowered types and the small-flowered types, prune lightly in early spring so as not to destroy the growth that has the flowerbuds.

- Late-blooming **Clematis,** large-flowered and small-flowered types, should be pruned hard in early spring so the plant can produce strong growth on which blooms will later develop.

- If early-blooming large-flowered types develop into a tangled mess, cut them down below the tangle. Close to the ground is fine, but don't cut into the larger woody stems. Your **Clematis** should recover by the end of the growing season and produce good blooms the following season.

- If you want early-blooming large-flowered types to bloom later, prune them back hard in the spring, and they will bloom in the summer.

Wait until after they flower before pruning early-flowering **Clematis** such as *Clematis alpina, C. macropetala, C. armandii, C. montana*, and *C. chrysocoma.*

Planning

Now that spring is here, **Daffodils** *are in bloom.* Think about adding some ground covers to help mask **Daffodil** foliage once the bulbs finish blooming. Remember that you should always leave foliage on **Daffodils,** as it is storing energy for next year's flowers. **Hellebores** and **Hosta** are both well suited as ground covers for **Daffodils, Hyacinth, Dutch Iris,** and **Summer Snowflake.**

Clematis vines make great companions for roses. You can choose **Clematis** that bloom around the same time that a rose does so that the two flowers will complement each other, or select a **Clematis** that will bloom after the rose is finished. For a winning combination, train *Clematis viticella* **'Etoile Violette',** which has purple blooms with yellow stamens, to grow up and through *Rosa* **'New Dawn'.** Vigorous and free-flowering, this **Clematis** blooms from midsummer to early autumn, so that even when the rose has finished blooming, you will still have flowers. When you choose a **Clematis** to grow with a rose, select species or hybrids that bloom on current-season's growth so that if you need to prune back the vine early in the spring you will still get blooms that season.

If you have an infestation of **Japanese Honeysuckle** or **English Ivy** that you want to eradicate, this is a good time to get started. Digging out plants, especially the roots, will be easier if you recognize the plants early. Learn to identify the foliage. You can also cut **Ivy** and honeysuckle back to the ground, let them put out new growth, and then *spray* with a nonselective weed-killer (see Chemicals, p. 327). It may take this twofold approach to get rid of **Ivy** or **Honeysuckle,** as both are tenacious plants.

Planting

Direct-sow seeds of annual vines in spots where you want them to grow. Some vines like the **Moonflower** are easier to establish if you start the seed in peat pots and then, once the seed has germinated, *transplant* the peat pot directly into the garden.

Plant ground covers and perennial vines in your garden.

Transplant annual vine seedlings you started indoors under lights to small pots outside. Place the pots in an area that gets lots of bright light but no hot sun. Keep them in this location for a week to ten days before moving them to a spot where they receive full sun.

If there is a threat of frost, move the plants to a garage or a protected area. Wait until the frost-free date arrives before planting your new vines in the garden. Check with your local Extension Service about the date of the last frost in your region.

Watering

Water newly planted vines or ground covers, and water the areas where you sow annual seed. Use a sprinkler to get gentle, even coverage. Keep vines in containers watered, too. Let the soil get dry to the touch, then water thoroughly, letting the water run out of the bottom of the pot.

Fertilizing

To help them get established, *fertilize* ground covers that were planted within the last six months. Use 1/2 pound or 1 cup of 8-8-8 or 10-10-10 per 100 square feet (this is half the recommended rate for established ground covers).

Fertilize vines only if they need it. If they are healthy and robust, there is no need to fertilize.

Applying a fresh layer of well-composted manure around the base of your vines will provide them with nutrients over a long period of time. Use caution to keep the manure from touching the main stem.

Pest Control

Beware of the vine with "leaves of three." Many people are allergic to the toxic oil from poison ivy leaves and vines (for control, see Trees, August).

Handweed ground cover areas. Scrape away old mulch, and apply a fresh layer of mulch approximately 2 to 3 inches deep. This will cut down on weed problems and help conserve moisture.

Aphids are tiny, soft-bodied, pear-shaped, and mostly wingless insects, coming in many colors, including green, yellow, tan, and black. They can attack the new growth of **Clematis** and other vines, sucking plant juices and disfiguring the buds and leaves. Try using a strong blast of water from the hose to get rid of them.

Helpful Hints

Clematis wilt is caused by a fungus. Present in the soil and on the plant, the spores become active when a specific combination of temperature and humidity occurs. The stems appear to wilt suddenly, often just when the flowers are beginning to open, and the leaves and stems are discolored. The fungus works itself around the stem of the **Clematis,** cutting off the flow of sap. As soon as you notice that a stem is wilted, prune it off until you reach healthy tissue. Sometimes this means you will have to prune a stem to below ground level. Discard all prunings and dead material. Do not add them to your compost pile.

- **Clematis** are usually more susceptible to attacks by fungus during the first two years of growth. Once they develop woody stems the fungus has a harder time penetrating the bark.

- **Pinch back** your **Clematis** to encourage side shoots on a regular basis during the first two years. This reduces foliage and therefore the stress on the roots.

- Plant **Clematis** deeply. If a shoot is killed to ground level, new shoots may appear from a node below the soil surface.

Pruning

If they need to be tidied up or are getting too rampant for the space they are growing in, *prune* spring-flowering vines like **Carolina Jessamine** as soon as they finish blooming.

Planning

Ground covers can help you solve problems in the garden. For example, the area between stepping-stones is the perfect place to use ground covers instead of turf. If the site is sunny, try some of the **Creeping Thymes** or *Laurentia*, which has beautiful tiny blue flowers. For shade, **Dwarf Mondo Grass, Ajuga,** or *Vinca minor* provide evergreen foliage all year long and require a minimum of upkeep.

In addition to training vines to grow on arbors and pergolas, you may find they are great for covering concrete walls and chain-link fences or framing doors, windows, or garages. Selecting the right vine for the right location will help ensure success.

Self-clinging vines such as **English Ivy, Virginia Creeper, Crossvine,** and **Trumpet Creeper** are ideal for a concrete wall. You may have to help them get started by tying up a few vines and attaching them to the wall until they take hold.

Planting

Plant ground covers and vines throughout the month.

There is still time to *direct-sow* seeds of annual vines like **Purple Hya-** cinth Bean, **Moon Vine,** and others in spots where you want them to grow. Check seed packages for more information about how long specific varieties of vines take to germinate.

Watering

Water new plantings of ground covers and vines.

Fertilizing

Fertilize annual vines with half the recommended rate (on the label) of a complete liquid fertilizer with a ratio like 20-20-20.

Fertilize newly planted (planted within the last six months) ground covers to help them get established at a rate of ¹/₂ pound or 1 cup of 8-8-8 or 10-10-10 per 100 square feet. This is half the recommended rate for established ground covers. Remember, you need only fertilize your ground covers twice a year. The recommended times are March and June.

If you add organic material to the soil when you plant, you won't have to fertilize your vines, but topdressing with composted manure will give them extra nutrients.

Pest Control

New growth on some of your vines may look puckered and may be covered with tiny lime green bugs. Aphids voraciously feed on new growth of vines like **Clematis** and **Honeysuckles.** Try blasting them off with a jet of cold water from the hose. If this doesn't do the trick, use an insecticidal soap (see Chemicals, p. 327).

Pruning

Make sure vines are tied in place, firmly but not tightly, where you want them to be. If they are woody vines like **Akebia,** make sure the stems are not girdled by the wire or cord you used to tie them to a trellis, arbor, or fence. **Wisteria** is an aggressive vine. After it blooms, *cut back* long twining new growth before it forms a tangled mess with the main vine. Save those stems that you want to use to extend the height or width of the vine. Tie them to supports. Use plastic tape so you won't girdle the stems. Many **Wisteria** are grafted and have a swollen area, the graft union. *Prune* to remove any suckers that occur below this union, as they will not produce the strong growth that the grafted plant does.

Espalier

Developed by gardeners in Europe during the 16th and 17th centuries, the term espalier was applied to fruit trees that were trained in the open, either as a permanent feature or in preparation for placing them on walls or against a trellis. Although they were trained in many shapes, the most common was a tier of horizontal branches on either side of the main stem. When trained on posts and wires, they were not only productive in a small space, they screened views and acted as walls between one section of garden and another. Today, espalier is also practiced to train plants for pure ornament, in both traditional and irregular patterns, depending on the growth habit of the individual plant.

When you grow vines on a wall, there are several approaches. You can attach panels of lattice to an existing wall and then train the vines on the lattice. This forms a flat trellis. To give the trellis more depth, attach the lattice to the wall on top of 2×4 spacers. Use 1×4 boards to cover up where two sections of lattice join. Plantings at the base of the lattice will help cover up the fact that the trellis is not attached at ground level.

On wooden fences or walls, you can create a framework using screw eyes threaded with galvanized wire (12 to 14 gauge). The wires should be about $1^1/_2$ feet apart.

For masonry walls, use anchors with screws or lag screws, threaded rod, nuts, and washers.

The goal is to provide firm support, good air circulation for the plants, and an appealing design. Be patient—it will take a few years of pruning and training to achieve a desired design. For formal designs, any branches that obscure the design can be pruned away. For informal designs, let the natural growth habit of the plant determine where you prune. Here is a list of perennial vines for espalier that produce showy flowers and/or fruit:

- *Akebia quinata* has clusters of purple flowers in spring that are often followed by 2- to 4-inch-long, purple, sausage-type fruits in summer to fall.

- *Bougainvillea* cultivars offer a long season of bright color for coastal gardens. The colorful parts that surrounds the tiny flowers are actually bracts.

- *Clematis armandii* is an evergreen species that has masses of tiny white fragrant flowers in early spring.

- *Pyracantha* hybrids produce red, orange, or red-orange fruit in late summer. The fruit last well into winter.

- *Rosa banksiae* is an evergreen climber that produces masses of yellow or white flowers in early spring.

- *Wisteria* spp. is an aggressive vine that has beautiful clusters of violet to violet-blue flowers in April to May.

Planning

Make notes in your garden journal about the performance of vines and ground covers in your landscape. Which ones are thriving, and which ones have pest or disease problems? If an area of ground cover is not successful, think about which plants you will use to replace them. Visit your local botanical garden and see what's blooming.

If you have an area that's infested with poison ivy or **English Ivy** that you want to eradicate, *spray* with a nonselective weedkiller (see Chemicals, p. 327), and then come back in two to four weeks and spray again, or dig out the roots. (Use extreme caution when working around poison ivy if you are allergic to it.) When fall arrives, you can amend the soil and plant something new!

Planting

You can still add vines and ground covers to your garden. Annual vines like the **Cypress Vine, Mandevilla,** and **Passionflower** add a tropical flair to the summer garden. They can be trained on a structure or a trellis, or combined with lots of colorful annuals in a large decorative pot. When you add a **Clematis** to your garden, apply 2 inches of mulch over the soil, keeping it away from the main stem. This will help retain soil moisture. As an alternative, you can plant ground covers or herbaceous perennials over the root area of the **Clematis** and then lightly mulch the ground covers. *Vinca minor* plants or some of the **Hardy Geraniums** make good ground covers for **Clematis.**

Watering

With the arrival of warmer weather, plants dry out more quickly. Be sure to check new plantings of vines and ground covers weekly to see if they need water. If the soil feels dry to the touch when you push your finger into it 2 inches, it's time to water. **Clematis** vines like plenty of moisture, so be sure to check them on a regular basis. Plants growing in pots will need to be checked on a daily basis.

Fertilizing

To help them get established, *fertilize* new plantings of vines and ground covers that have been planted in the last six months.

If ground covers are not planted under trees or shrubs that are fertilized on a regular basis, apply 1 pound (2 cups) of 8-8-8 or 10-10-10 per 100 square feet. Use a broadcast-type spreader to get even distribution over the area. Wash any fertilizer off the foliage when you finish.

During the growing season, **Clematis** vines will benefit from monthly feeding with a complete liquid fertilizer (a ratio like 20-20-20) at half the recommended rate on the label.

Pest Control

Pull weeds in ground cover beds.

If leaves and buds on your **Clematis** vines are disfigured and have a dusty grayish-white coating and the flowerbuds don't open, your vine has a fungal disease called powdery mildew. Poor air circulation can contribute to this problem. If possible, *move* the vine to a more favorable location. You can try to improve air circulation in the area where your **Clematis** is growing by removing or pruning nearby shrubs that are crowding your vine, but it may be more practical to relocate the vine. As soon as you notice signs of this disease, *spray* with a fungicide (see Chemicals, p. 327).

Look for signs of spider mites. Infested leaves will be spotted with yellow or black specks. Pests like aphids typically cluster around the new growth; where they feed, buds and shoots look distorted. If less than 50 percent of a plant or group of plants is affected with a particular insect pest, then use insecticidal soap to try to eradicate the problem. If more than 50 percent of the plant is affected, you may want to use a synthetic contact insecticide (see Chemicals, p. 327).

If the lower leaves on your **Bugleweed** are yellow and the plants are mushy and die (they pull up easily and have no roots), the problem is crown rot. Fortunately, the problem is environmental—usually poorly draining soil. Once you improve soil drainage by adding coarse sand or small coarse gravel, you will eliminate the problem, and the area can be replanted.

The problem is scale if clusters of hard white and brown specks cover the stems and leaves of your **Euonymus** ground cover, and the leaves turn yellow and branches die. *Spray* with horticultural oil or a systemic insecticide (see Chemicals, p. 327).

Helpful Hints

Clematis can be propagated by stem cuttings.

1 Take cuttings in May or June from the semi-hard shoots produced in the current season. This means that they will probably be taken from the middle of a long stem.

2 Find a section of stem that has a node (a joint on a stem, the point of origin for a leaf or a bud; sometimes swollen or with a distinctive scar) with leaves.

3 Cut between this node and the node below. You should end up with a section that has only a node at the top end of the cutting. The cutting should be 1 to 2 inches in length.

4 Dip the cutting in water and then in rooting hormone like Rootone™.

5 Stick the cutting in a mix of two parts sand or perlite and one part peat moss.

6 Supply high humidity, warmth, and bright light. The cuttings should root in four to six weeks.

7 If the cuttings root by early August, plant them in your garden. If rooting occurs in late August or September, overwinter the plants in pots in a protected spot, and plant them out in the spring.

Pruning

Prune any wild suckers or shoots of your **Wisteria** for one last time this season. Next year's flowerbuds will begin to form in midsummer.

There is still time (wait no later than July) to *prune* spring-flowering **Clematis,** including *Clematis alpina, C. macropetala, C. armandii, C. montana*, and **C. chrysocoma.** Prune to reduce their size or train them to fit a certain framework or trellis.

Planning

Monkey Grass, English Ivy, *and* Mondo Grass *are familiar evergreen ground covers for shade. There are even some ground covers that bloom in shade.* Below is a list of those that bloom in shade. Think about adding some of these to your garden this fall. They will brighten up the woodland and add interest under a shrub. You can also plant these ground covers as a carpet for spring bulbs, like some of the early-blooming miniature **Daffodils** or **Giant Crocus.** Plant the ground covers in fall at the same time you plant your bulbs. This way you'll know where your bulbs are, even when they're not blooming.

- **Bugleweed** has 4- to 5-inch spikes of blue flowers in spring to early summer.

- **Green and Gold** has yellow flowers in spring, some in summer, and then a few in fall.

- **Mazus** has purplish-blue **Snapdragon**-like flowers with yellow markings in spring and early summer

- **Partridgeberry,** *Mitchella repens*, has tiny white flowers in late spring or early summer followed by bright-red berries less than 1/4 inch wide. It is not a good choice for coastal gardens.

- **Periwinkle** has five-petaled lavender-blue, purple, or white flowers in spring.

Planting

You can plant ground covers or vines now, but don't expect much growth while the air and soil temperatures are hot. The roots will wait until soil temperatures begin to cool off in the fall before they put on any significant growth.

Watering

Keep new plantings well watered. *Check* containers daily and plants in the ground weekly (see June for more details on watering). Apply 1 to 2 inches of mulch to new plantings. This will help reduce weed infestations, keep soil temperatures cool, and conserve moisture.

Fertilizing

Fertilize annual vines with half the recommended rate of a complete liquid fertilizer with a ratio like 20-20-20. With any luck, many of your vines will bloom until frost. There's no need to fertilize perennial vines or ground covers now.

Pest Control

Look for signs of aphids, spider mites, or other insects. Try washing them off with a blast of water from the hose or using an insecticidal soap before you resort to using a stronger pesticide (see Chemicals, p. 327).

Pull weeds in ground cover beds.

You may see young branch tips on your ground cover **Junipers** turn red or brown, then gray. Once they die, tiny black spots, which are the fruiting bodies of the fungus, may appear on the dead needles and stems. These symptoms mean your **Juniper** suffers from twig blight, a fungus that can enter the plant through both healthy and wounded tissue. Young plants are more susceptible than mature plants. *Prune out and destroy* infected twigs and branches as soon as you notice them. *Spray* plants with a fungicide (see Chemicals, p. 327) at two-week intervals in the spring, when plants begin to put out new growth. Here are some prevention tips:

1 Plant **Junipers** in sites where they will get plenty of sunlight and good air circulation.

2 *Avoid* overhead watering or watering at night when foliage will stay wet for several hours.

3 *Don't overfertilize*, and avoid wounding the plant; prune during winter if possible.

Pruning

If you have **English Ivy** or **Virginia Creeper** growing on a wall around doors or windows and it threatens to cover the windows, *cut it back* now. You can root the **Ivy** clippings by sticking them in a soilless mix or wet sand. In four to five weeks you should have rooted cuttings that you can plant directly in the ground.

Helpful Hints

You may inherit a garden that has been neglected for a long period of time, and has aggressive vines like **Wisteria** may be running rampantly through it. Here are some suggestions for controlling or eliminating **Wisteria:**

1 Spray the vine when it has lots of foliage with a nonselective weedkiller like glyphosate (see Chemicals, p. 327). Spray the foliage on the top and undersides until it drips off the plant.

2 Wait ten days to two weeks. Cut off any remaining green foliage.

3 Wait another two weeks, and when a new batch of foliage flushes out, spray it with the weedkiller again. Repeat this until the **Wisteria** goes dormant in winter.

Another method is to cut the **Wisteria** vine down to the ground, and paint the cut surface with a weedkiller containing triclopyr (see Chemicals, p. 327). These techniques can also be used to eliminate **English Ivy, Bittersweet,** and **Grapevines.**

Planning

It's too hot to do much in the garden this month, so plan ahead for fall. If you have areas of ground covers that need renovating, you can spray with a nonselective weedkiller (see Chemicals, p. 327), and then wait until fall to amend the soil and plant.

Planting

Wait until fall to add vines and ground covers to your garden.

Watering

Keep new plantings watered. *Check* them on a weekly basis. *Water* if the soil is dry when you dig down 2 inches with your finger.

Fertilizing

Wait until spring to fertilize your vines and ground covers.

Pest Control

Your **Junipers** may have spider mites if tiny yellow spots appear on the needles and some needles are brown and covered with tiny webs. To test for mites, hold a blank sheet of white paper under a branch and tap lightly. Circle some of the specks (no bigger than a pinhead) that fall onto the paper. If the specks move, you have spider mites, which are most active during hot, dry weather. Inspect plants on a regular basis. To control the mites, *spray* your **Junipers** with a blast of cold water from the hose. For severe infestations (when **50** percent or more of the needles are damaged), *spray* with insecticidal soap, horticultural oil, or a synthetic miticide (see Chemicals, p. 327). You may have to use two or three applications, spaced at weekly intervals, to eradicate the problem.

Bougainvillea normally blooms in the spring and fall, and it is hardy for coastal gardeners. For gardeners in the rest of the state, it can be grown in a container and kept in a greenhouse or sun porch over the winter. Sometimes **Bougainvillea** doesn't bloom in spring, and there may be no indication that it will bloom in fall. The "no bloom" syndrome is the result of not enough sunshine. Follow these steps to a remedy:

1 **Bougainvillea** should be planted in a spot where it gets full sun—this means four to six hours of direct sun each day.

2 **Bougainvillea** produces more blooms when potbound, so plant it in a confined pot or planting bed.

3 Apply a water-soluble fertilizer such as 20-20-20 every three to four weeks in the spring or summer.

4 Let the soil get slightly dry between thorough waterings. Plants will go dormant in the winter. Begin to reduce watering in November to once every three to four weeks. Wait until spring to resume regular watering and feeding.

Pruning

Remove any dead or diseased stems or twigs of vines and ground covers, and dispose of them. It is best to discard diseased plant material away from your compost pile.

Check vines on your arbor or pergola to make sure they are not being girdled, which means the tie cuts into the stem, restricting the flow of water and nutrients. Tie up shoots that you want to train as part of an espalier (see May).

Helpful Hints

Kudzu, although not native to the South, spreads as if it has always lived here. This woody vine is native to China and Japan. Here in Georgia, an established vine can grow to reach 60 feet in one season, with leaves up to 12 inches wide and long. This hardy pest climbs and covers buildings and trees, shades their leaves, and strangles them until they die. If left untended, it keeps growing. Here are some tips for control:

- The key to success is to attack the entire area covered in kudzu at one time. Kudzu plants put out roots all along the vine, and when one section of the vine is killed, this tough plant has the ability to segment itself so that the rest of the vine can keep growing. By the end of August, kudzu plants are exhausted from vigorous summer growth and have expended most of their reserves.

- One approach to eradication is to mow all the foliage before the plant goes dormant each winter. Repeat the mowing in spring and summer.

- Another approach is to **spray** the entire plant with a broadleaf herbicide containing triclopyr or glyphosate (see Chemicals, p. 327). Apply the spray until it drips off the leaves. Since the plants have no reserves, they will not have the energy to sprout many new leaves in spring.

- Watch for signs of growth in early spring. An established kudzu vine can send up sprouts for years before it is substantially weakened. **Spray** new growth when leaves have expanded but before the plant has a chance to harden-off and spread.

- Kudzu is also vulnerable when it flowers, usually in September. The long pendulous purple flowers are fragrant and attractive for such a pesky vine. **Spray** the flowers and the foliage with triclopyr or glyphosate. It is quickly translocated to the roots where it kills the plant.

- Some people take advantage of these woody vines to make baskets. Collect the vines in winter, and you will have less kudzu to kill in the spring!

Planning

Fall is a great season to add vines and ground covers to your garden. Plan to plant as soon as the weather cools off a bit. Make notes in your garden journal on how annual vines performed this year and which ones you'd like to add to the garden next year. Think about combinations of vines, both annual and perennial. Take a soil test (see Horticultural Practices, p. 7). The results will tell you the quantities of nutrients and lime you need to add to the soil. Prepare the soil (see Horticultural Practices), add soil amendments, and rototill the areas where you will add ground covers later this fall or next spring.

Planting

Add container-grown ground covers and vines to your garden. This is a good time to add **Clematis.** Whether you are planting or transplanting **Clematis,** experts recommend that you dig a hole 18 inches wide and 24 inches deep, mixing in 1 part good topsoil and 1 part composted manure. **Clematis** is known to put out roots to a depth of 18 to 24 inches—this is the reason for preparing such a deep hole.

Divide established ground covers if they are crowded, or you want to move some to another area.

- Dig up large clumps of **Liriope** or **Mondo Grass** with a digging fork or shovel.

- Use a digging spade or straightedge shovel, and chop straight through the clump to break off sections. Shake off loose soil, but remember, the more roots, the better. Make sure each division has roots and shoots.

- Dig up individual pieces or small sections of **Ornamental Raspberry** and **English Ivy.** They put out roots all along their stems, just about anywhere they touch soil. With these particular vines there is no need to dig a deep bed, as the roots are close to the soil surface.

- Have the new planting area prepared ahead of time so that roots won't dry out.

- *Water and mulch* transplants.

Watering

Even as the weather starts to cool off a bit, don't forget to water new plantings. Any ground covers or vines that have been planted in the last six months should be checked on a weekly basis to see if they need water.

Fertilizing

Wait until spring to fertilize perennial vines and ground covers. If you want to topdress areas where you have vines planted, use mushroom compost or well-rotted horse or cow manures. This will provide good organic material, which will provide nutrients as it breaks down over the winter and next spring.

Pest Control

Check vines and ground covers for signs of dieback or root rot, such as black stems or a group of leaves that are partially black and wilted. If a section of ground cover is suffering because of poor drainage, dig up the plants and add a generous amount of coarse sand (builder's sand or small crushed stone) to the soil. Replant only the healthy portions, and discard those with unhealthy roots or foliage. Sometimes starting over completely with new plants is the most cost-effective control.

Check for insect problems like aphids or mites The more insects you eradicate this fall, the fewer will overwinter and cause problems next spring. If you notice only a few pests, use a blast of cold water from the hose to control them. If there is a severe infestation, use an insecticidal soap or a synthetic pesticide (see Chemicals, p. 327).

Use a granular weed-preventer in established ground cover beds to prevent winter weeds like chickweed and hairy bittercress (see Chemicals, p. 327).

Pruning

Limit your pruning to dead or diseased leaves, stems, and twigs on vines.

Prune off dead or diseased leaves on ground covers, but don't cut them back severely now—wait until they are dormant.

Helpful Hints

For gardeners who like edible ornamentals beyond grapes, there are a number of uncommon ornamental vines that also produce tasty fruits.

- *Actinidia arguta* **Hardy Kiwi** is a heavy bearer of greenish-purple edible skinned fruits the size of grapes.

- *Momordica charantia* **Bitter Melon** or **Balsam Pear** has light-green lobed and puckered leaves and bright-orange fruits that split open to reveal red interiors.

- *Passiflora incarnata* **Maypop** or **Passionflower** fruit is prized for its juice.

- *Passiflora* **'Incense' Passionflower** has sweet egg-shaped fruits.

- *Rubus laciniatus* **Fern-leaved Blackberry** produces slightly tart berries.

- *Schisandra chinensis* has fragrant white flowers and bright-red edible fruits.

Cut off seedpods as they ripen from annual vines like the **Purple Hyacinth Bean, Moon Vine,** and others. Do this on a cool, dry day. *Remove* the seeds from the pods as soon as possible, carefully cutting away the seedpod. Keep seeds cool and dry until you sow them next spring (see Annuals, September). If you store them in plastic baggies, like sandwich bags, be sure to include a label with the name of the seed in the bag. Seeds from your garden make great gifts for the holidays.

Planning

Looking at plant combinations in nature is often the best teacher of what can work in your own garden. Deciduous trees provide the perfect living trellis for many vines. The key is selecting those vines that will make good companions for particular trees. A chosen vine should never be so vigorous that it suffocates the tree, and the tree should not be so strong as to overshade the vine.

When planting, keep in mind that the soil near the tree roots may be on the dry side. For this reason it is best to apply a good 2 inches of mulch around the roots of the vine, using caution to keep it away from the main stems. If you start with a small vine, in a 1-gallon pot, it will be easier to dig a hole large enough to accommodate the vine. Self-clinging vines like *Hydrangea anomala petiolaris* and **Virginia Creeper** are well-suited for training on trees, but those that climb by tendrils also make happy companions for many trees. Train vines like **English Ivy, Wisteria, Trumpet Creeper,** and **Akebia** to grow up dead but sturdy small trees. In this way their aggressive nature becomes an asset.

Because the soil near tree roots is often exhausted and shady, certain vines like **Clematis** should be planted a good distance from a mature tree (4 feet).

1 Plant on the sunny side of the tree so the **Clematis** will get a good start.

2 Use bamboo canes or strings to guide the vine into the tree.

3 Once the **Clematis** reaches the tree, it will decide where it wants to grow.

Here is a list of vine-and-tree combinations to consider:

- *Bignonia capreolata* / **Oak** trees, **Black Gum, Maple** trees

- *Clematis* 'Jackmanii' / *Robinia pseudoacacia* 'Frisia'

- *Hydrangea anomala petiolaris* / **Oak** trees or **Loblolly Pine**

- *Lonicera* × *heckrottii* / **Oak, Maple,** or **Pine** trees

- *Schizophragma hydrangeoides* 'Moonlight' / **Oak** trees, Loblolly Pine, Black Gum

Harvesting and Curing Gourds:

L.H. Bailey, the famous botanist, wrote the following definition of gourds: "hard-shelled durable fruit grown for ornament, utensils, and general interest." Gourds grow on vines. Here are some tips for harvesting and curing ornamental gourds:

- Gourds must reach maturity on the vine.

- Once stems turn brown and dry, it is safe to cut and remove gourds.

- To preserve their colors, store gourds in a cool, dry place.

- The American Gourd Society recommends the following recipe to preserve gourds:

Mix 1 cup of Twenty Mule® Team Borax into 3 cups of hot water. Stir until dissolved. Let the mixture cool to lukewarm. Bring another pot of water to boil. Dip the gourd into the boiling water briefly, then soak it in the borax solution for 15 minutes. Do not rinse. Hang gourds in a cool place to dry for several weeks. Provide the best air circulation possible. Gourds can be waxed with a good-quality floor wax when dry.

Planting

Plant container-grown vines and ground covers this month. When planting **Clematis,** a 2-foot-deep planting hole is recommended, filled with equal parts of soil and compost. Set the crown at least 1 inch deep (some experts suggest 3 to 4 inches deep). *Water* generously, and apply 2 inches of an organic mulch. To encourage better branching as well as an abundance of larger flowers, cut the **Clematis** back by half at the time of planting.

If you are growing **Ornamental Sweet Potato** vines (*Ipomoea batatas*), you can dig the tubers and overwinter them now. They are also edible, but stringy. Some have handsome foliage, like **'Blackie',** which has leaves of dark purple brown; **'Margarita',** which has chartreuse foliage; and **'Tricolor',** which has leaves of pink, white, and green.

Watering

Water plants that have been planted within the last six months, unless they receive at least 1 inch per week of rainwater. *Check* weekly to see if they need water.

Fertilizing

There is no need to fertilize ground covers or vines now, but it is a good idea to *prepare* the soil in new beds, adding organic material before you plant, whether you will plant later this fall or next spring.

Helpful Hints

There are a number of vines that exhibit colorful leaves or leaves with interesting textures. Below is a list of both annual and perennial types that are noted for their foliage.

A = Annual   P = Perennial

- *Humulus japonicus* **'Variegatus', Variegated Japanese Hop** vine, has handsome variegated leaves that brighten the garden all summer until frost. A

- *Hydrangea anomala petiolaris* **Climbing Hydrangea** has leaves that turn buttercup yellow in fall. P

- *Lygodium japonicum* **Climbing Fern** has delicate lacy foliage until frost. P

- *Parthenocissus quinquefolia* **Virginia Creeper** has leaves that turn shades of purple, red, and crimson in autumn. P

- *Wisteria frutescens* **American Wisteria** leaves turn yellow in autumn. P

Pest Control

During mild weather, certain insects may still be active. *Check* for evidence of aphids or scale. Signs may include distorted leaves or shoots, or brown hard spots on the undersides of leaves. If there is a mild infestation, *spray* with insecticidal soap or horticultural oil (see Chemicals, p. 327).

Rake up leaves that cover your ground covers. The better the light and air circulation, the happier they will be. Add these leaves to your compost pile, or use the lawn mower to chop them up. Finely chopped leaves can be put back on your flower beds as mulch.

Pruning

Limit your pruning to removing dead or diseased wood of vines.

Planning

This is a good month to look at the garden and see where you can use vines and ground covers to help solve problems. If you have a chain-link fence in an area that is mostly shady and want to cover it quickly, vines like **Carolina Jessamine** or **English Ivy** are ideal. Both are evergreen and easy to train. You can tuck new growth up and through the links of the fence. The yellow flowers of **Carolina Jessamine** in spring are an added bonus. If you want to have late-season color in the garden with vines, the **Climbing Aster** *Aster carolinianus* produces masses of lavender daisies in November. It has a lax habit, and the long stems must be tied up. An open brick wall is ideal, because you can weave the stems in and out of the openings.

Sometimes an area where a patch of lawn is required is simply too shady to grow turf with any success. In all but the northern parts of the state, there is an alternative: **Dwarf Mondo Grass** can make a rich green carpet that looks good all year long and requires only a minimum of care. It will thrive even with a moderate amount of foot traffic. The ultimate height of **Dwarf Mondo Grass** is 3 to 4 inches. When planting, you will probably want to space individual plants 6 to 8 inches apart to get a thick covering in a short amount of time. Once your new lawn is established you can use a broom to sweep off leaves that accumulate. The more air, light, and moisture your **Mondo Grass** lawn receives, the happier it will be.

Planting

Plant container-grown vines and ground covers as long as the ground is not frozen.

Watering

Keep up with watering new plantings on a weekly basis if there is no regular rainfall, at least 1 inch per week. Fall weather may be cooler, but it can also be dry.

Fertilizing

There is no need to fertilize established vines and ground covers now. If you plant a large area of ground covers and use small rooted plugs, prepare the soil before you plant, being sure to incorporate generous amounts of organic material. When the soil is friable and rich in organic materials, it will be easier for roots to establish.

Pest Control

Once there has been a hard freeze, pull down annual vines and *dispose* of them. This will help reduce the number of places in which insects can overwinter. Rake up leaves in ground cover beds, and add them to the compost pile.

Weed ground cover beds. Whenever possible, pull weeds before they flower and set seed. This will reduce future infestations of weeds.

Check vines and ground covers for insects like scale, aphids, or spider mites. *Spray* with horticultural oils (see Chemicals, p. 327).

Pruning

Before or when you pull up annual vines that were killed by frost, collect any remaining seedpods, and save the seed for next year. *Prune* to remove any dead, diseased, or broken branches of vines. Cut away and dispose of any leaves or stems on ground covers that are damaged by insects or fungus. You can usually recognize fungus because the leaves and stems are black and look rotten.

Helpful Hints

The ancient art of topiary is defined as the practice of training shrubs and small trees into ornamental or fantastic shapes such as animals, letters, and geometric forms. One way to create topiary is to train vines on forms. Usually metal, these forms can be placed in the ground or in a large decorative pot. Many types of **English Ivy** and **Asian Star Jasmine** are easy to train on topiary forms.

1 Start with many small plants (in 2- to 4-inch pots) that have long trailing stems.

2 Tuck the stems up and through the form, covering as much area as possible.

3 Clip new growth on a regular basis to encourage stems to branch.

4 Tuck stems as they develop, and clip as needed to define the shape of the topiary. (This can be as often as once every two weeks during the growing season.)

Planning

As winter approaches, take time to review the gardening year and examine your successes and failures. If you tried certain vines for the first time, did you grow them in the best manner? While many vines make good garden companions for roses, shrubs, or trees, some are best grown alone. Take, for example, the **Moon Vine.** This aggressive vine will quickly cover a structure or plant. If paired with another aggressive grower like the **'New Dawn' Rose,** it can create a maintenance headache. When the **Moon Vine** dies at the end of the growing season, it is nearly impossible to extricate it from amongst the canes of a rose without incurring bodily harm. For this reason, **Moon Vine** and other aggressive annual vines like **Morning Glories** are best grown on their own structures where they won't damage other plants.

Planting

Plant container vines and ground covers before the ground freezes.

Watering

Keep new plantings well watered. *Check* them once a week.

Fertilizing

There's no need to fertilize vines or ground covers this month. Their growth is slowing down, as they enter the dormant season.

Pest Control

Pull weeds out of ground cover beds and from the base of vines. If you see signs of scale or spider mites, treat plants with horticultural oil (see Chemicals, p. 327).

Pruning

Once vines are dormant, you can *prune* to shape them, but be sure not to prune off flowerbuds for next spring.

If your **Luffa Gourds** have turned brown on the stem, you may think it is too late to harvest them—but it's not. **Luffa Gourds** should be left on the vine until the stem is completely dry and the gourd is beginning to turn brown at both ends or the gourd is completely dry. Once they are harvested, they can be peeled. If the shell has dried completely, you can peel it away bit by bit. You can also soak the gourd for 15 minutes to 2 hours, softening the shell and making it easier to peel. The interior sponge will have 40 to 80 seeds.

- Soak the sponge in warm water, and then hang to dry. Adding a small amount of bleach to the water will make for a bright **Luffa** sponge.

- Save any seeds from desirable **Luffa** sponges for next year's crop.

- **Luffa** sponges make great gifts.

Helpful Hints

Color in the winter garden comes from foliage, fruits, flowers, and bark. Below is a list of ground covers and vines that hold their own in the winter garden.

VINES

Gelsemium sempervirens
Hedera colchia 'Sulphur Heart'
Hedera helix cultivars (vine or ground cover)

GROUND COVERS

Acorus gramineus 'Ogon'
Asarum shuttleworthii 'Callaway'
Cyclamen hederifolium
Helleborus hybrids and cultivars
Juniperus species and cultivars
Liriope muscari
Ophiopogon japonicus
Rubus calycinoides
Vinca minor

Garden Words You Should Know

As an aid to better gardening communication, here is a list of garden words you might hear—plus a sentence in which you can use each one. (Thanks to Pike Family Nurseries® for allowing the use of this list.)

aerate: to poke holes in a lawn so oxygen and water can better penetrate

"If it rains on Friday, the ground will be soft enough for my rented aerator to make really deep holes on Saturday."

aggressive: fast-growing, invasive; describes a plant to be avoided unless you give some thought to how you will control it

"They told me Bamboo was aggressive, but I didn't realize it would send up sprouts 20 feet away from where I planted it!"

annual: a plant that survives only one growing season: a **Marigold** is a summer annual, a **Pansy** is a winter annual

"I know I have to buy them every year, but annuals sure bloom vigorously while they're growing!"

balanced fertilizer: a fertilizer that has identical N-P-K numbers

"My bulbs have finished blooming. I guess they need a bit of balanced fertilizer to make them strong for next year."

balled-and-burlapped: describes a large tree whose roots have been wrapped tightly in burlap after the tree is dug

"It took three people to lift the rootball of a ten-foot-tall balled-and-burlapped Maple!"

bed: a tended spot for growing plants

"That bed of Daylilies sure is pretty in the sunshine!"

blossom end rot: a rotten spot at the blossom end of tomato fruit, caused by lack of calcium

"The time to prevent blossom end rot is when the baby tomatoes are the size of marbles."

broadcast spreader: a spreader designed to "whirl" its contents over a large area

"Sometimes we borrow a neighbor's broadcast spreader for our big lawn."

broadleaf weed: a weed that has a round or broad leaf—dandelion, chickweed, clover, etc.

"These wild onions in my lawn don't look like broadleaf weeds, but that's how they're classified."

chlorotic: yellowish and sickly due to a lack of nutrients

"My Azalea leaves are chlorotic. Is that caused by water standing around the roots or by the soil not having enough acid?"

compost: rotted plant material

"These leaves have been piled back here for years. I think I'll put the compost at the bottom of the heap onto my vegetable garden and dig it in."

cool-season grass: a grass that grows best in cool weather and stays green year-round

"I heard that Atlanta is in the zone in which cool-season grasses really take a beating from the summer heat."

core aerator: a machine having hollow tubes that plunge into the soil and bring up cores of earth

"I used to have a spike aerator—but it never loosened my soil as well as a core aerator does."

crotch: the angle where a limb and a larger limb or a trunk meet

"No wonder that Bradford Pear split apart—it's full of narrow crotches!"

Garden Words You Should Know

cutting: a 6- to 12-inch-long twig that can be forced to grow new roots after being pruned from a plant

"My grandmother used to root rose cuttings by sticking them in the dirt and covering each one with a quart jar."

desiccated: dried out

"I know I shouldn't have planted that Japanese Maple in full sunshine. Now the leaves are desiccated around the edges."

dethatcher: a powered machine (also called a vertical mower) that slices into the thatch layer in order to reduce it

"I'm glad I waited until May to use a dethatcher. I could have really hurt my Zoysia Grass if I'd dethatched while it was brown."

dormant: describes a plant that is "sleeping" for the winter

"Centipede Grass never goes completely dormant. That's why you can't spray Roundup® on it to kill winter weeds."

drip line: the imaginary line under the farthest extension of a tree's limbs

"More than 50 percent of a tree's roots are outside the drip line!"

drop spreader: a spreader designed to drop its contents through evenly-spaced holes

"I have a lot of curves and nooks in my yard, and a drop spreader lets me fertilize evenly."

focal point: a landscape feature that draws the eye toward itself

"A bench in front of a hedge makes a nice focal point."

fungicide: a chemical that inhibits or kills fungi

"My neighbor was really surprised when I told him a fungicide wouldn't help a bit if he wanted to kill aphids."

grassy weed: a weed that has leaves similar to those of lawn grass—crabgrass, annual bluegrass, nutgrass, etc.

"Nutgrass is rated the hardest-to-control grassy weed."

green-up: the process by which a plant comes out of dormancy and puts on new leaves

"It is a good idea to wait to fertilize Zoysia lawns until they have achieved 50 percent green-up."

herbicide: a chemical that will kill plants

"I've tried digging and I've tried mowing; this year I'm using a herbicide on my kudzu!"

honeydew: the sticky liquid secreted by sucking insects

"My car was covered with honeydew from aphids after I parked under a Maple tree."

horticultural oil: a thin oil designed to be sprayed on insects to suffocate them

"Horticultural oil is about the only thing you can use to control scale on Euonymus shrubs."

inch of water: a measurement of how much water falls into a container; plants need approximately one inch of water per week

"Ronnie, put out a couple of soup cans in the lawn to make sure the sprinkler applies an inch of water before you shut it off."

lime: a chemical added to the soil to raise its pH (a measure of soil acidity)

"I know that pelletized lime is the same as the powdered stuff, but the pellets sure go through my spreader better."

mulch: to spread materials under a plant in order to decrease water loss and inhibit weed growth

"Mulching my Rhododendrons with chopped leaves helped them get through the drought easily."

mulching blade: a lawnmower blade that has been specially designed to chop grass blades thoroughly before they fall

"That mulching blade made a big difference in reducing the amount of clippings I could see on my lawn."

N-P-K: Nitrogen-Phosphorus-Potassium—the most important nutrients needed by plants

"I remember what the N-P-K numbers on a fertilizer bag mean by saying to myself 'Up-Down-All Around'."

organic matter: rotted leaves, composted pine bark, mushroom compost, aged manure, etc.; usually mixed with existing soil to make it less heavy and compacted

"I'll dig a two-inch layer of organic matter deep into my flower bed before I plant my seed."

perennial: a plant that grows for several seasons in your area

"My Lantanas were perennial when we lived in Savannah, but they're only annuals up here in Suwanee."

pH: a measurement of the acidity of your soil

"It's remarkable how much lime it has taken to raise my garden's pH from 5.0 to 6.0!"

pinch: to remove the growing tip of a limb, in order to make it branch

"I pinched my Redtip Photinia in early summer. Now it has many more leaves."

Poa annua: annual bluegrass; a bright green weedy grass that makes prolific white seedheads in May

"I used to try to pull out 'Po Anner' by hand in the spring. Then I got smart and started using a pre-emergent weed chemical on my lawn in the fall."

pollen: the fine, yellowish powder produced by the male part of a flower; when united with the female part of the plant, seeds are produced

"Pine tree pollen covered my car so thickly I could write my name in it!"

post-emergent: a chemical that kills plants after they have emerged from the soil

"I was on vacation in March; I'll use a post-emergent on the crabgrass that's already sprouted."

pre-emergent: a chemical that prevents seeds from sprouting or growing

"It is best to apply a pre-emergent by mid-March to prevent crabgrass seeds from sprouting."

prepare: to thoroughly till or spade the soil to a depth of eight inches or more

"Preparing this bed is harder than I thought it would be; maybe I should rent a tiller."

prune: to remove a limb or branch

"Let me show you how to prune that rose back to a limb that's growing in the right direction."

rhizome: a fleshy root that extends from a plant, allowing it to spread and make new plants

"We must have dug up a ton of rhizomes around that Bamboo clump before we could install an underground plastic barrier to keep it under control."

rootball: the root system of a plant before it is planted

"I used my fingers and a stick to untangle the rootball before I planted that holly."

root zone: the entire area in which a plant's roots grow

"We used two bales of pine straw to mulch the whole root zone of the Dogwood I planted last year."

scalp: to mow off the top inch of dormant Bermuda Grass in order to accelerate green-up

"I'll scalp my lawn when average daytime temperatures approach 50 degrees Fahrenheit."

Garden Words You Should Know

slow-release fertilizer: a fertilizer whose granules have been manufactured to release nutrients over several weeks rather than all at once

"Those little white balls on top of the soil under a potted Azalea aren't insect eggs—they're just granules of slow-release fertilizer."

soilless mix: a mixture of peat moss and other materials that does not include mineral soil

"Why in the world do they call soilless mix potting soil when it is not soil and has no soil in it?"

soil test: a chemical test that measures the nutrients in your soil and its acidity

"I need to have a soil test done by the Extension Service so I'll know how much lime to spread on my lawn."

stolon: a thin aboveground plant part that grows from the main plant to adjoining areas

"If my neighbor's Bermuda Grass stolons didn't grow into my Fescue lawn, it might look pretty nice in the winter."

stoloniferous: describes a plant that spreads by stolons

"If I had known Bermuda Grass was so stoloniferous I wouldn't have planted it near the flower bed."

sucker: a small sprout that emerges at the base of vigorously growing trees

"Those suckers I pruned off my Crapemyrtle made excellent stakes to prop up my Peonies."

systemic pesticide: a chemical that is absorbed by roots or leaves and then travels throughout the plant

"Lots of rose growers use a systemic pesticide on their plants to control aphids."

tap root: a central root that extends downward in the soil under the trunk of a tree

"When I saw the big trees that fell after the storm, I realized that trees growing in clay soil don't have a tap root."

thatch: a layer of undecomposed grass stem pieces on which turfgrass may attempt to grow

"Landscapers say that unless the thatch layer is more than one-half inch thick, a lawn won't be harmed."

till: to thoroughly mix soil; often done with a shovel or a motorized tiller

"Bill tilled until the toil got to him."

topdress: to spread a thin layer over the ground

"Golf courses use sand to topdress their tees, but topsoil is a better choice to fill low spots in most homeowner lawns."

warm-season grass: a grass that grows best in summer and turns brown in winter (ex. **Bermuda, Zoysia, Centipede**)

"Even though it's a warm-season grass, if you keep the weeds out of it, a tan Bermuda lawn looks really attractive in the winter."

weed and feed: a product that combines fertilizer and a weed-control chemical in the same bag

"This weed and feed label says to avoid application to newly seeded Fescue until it's been mowed four times."

well-drained soil: soil through which water passes rapidly

"I thought the soil on my red clay slope was well-drained because water never stands there. Unfortunately, it is poorly drained, because the water can't penetrate the clay. No wonder everything I plant there dies!"

zone: an area of the country that is distinguished from other areas by its winter low-temperature readings

"I know palms are hardy down in Florida's zone 9, but I'm trying to find some that are hardy in Atlanta's zones 7 and 8."

—Courtesy of Pike Family Nursery

Using Chemicals in Your Garden

In a perfect world, insects and diseases might attack other people's gardens . . . but *never* yours! In a perfect world, diseases and insects would be easy to control with little forethought. Unfortunately, Georgia gardeners do not live in a perfect world. Not even close!

Our long, hot, humid summers provide an excellent breeding ground for insects and diseases. Although these pests serve nature's overall purpose, that is little consolation when we find disfigured flowers and vanishing leaves.

Some gardeners avoid using chemical pesticides in their garden. Some prefer to use chemicals only sparingly. Others use chemicals, where appropriate, to solve many of their garden pest problems.

We do not take sides in the organic versus synthetic pesticide debate. We realize that some pesticides that are considered to be organic can still be dangerous if used improperly, and we know that some synthetic chemicals have a very good environmental safety record when used according to label directions.

Our preference is that landscape and vegetable garden plants be grown in the healthiest manner possible. Healthy plants are better prepared to fight against pests and usually thrive in spite of them, without the use of pesticides of any kind.

Even healthy plants, though, may suffer so much damage that they become unsightly, and diseases or insects can cause a weak plant to die. In such situations, gardeners may want to resort to using pesticides.

What Is a Pesticide?

A pesticide is a chemical that is used to kill or control a pest. The chemical can come from organic sources and be called an organic pesticide, or it can come from a chemical manufacturer and be called a synthetic pesticide. In either case, it is still a pesticide.

Pesticides can be classified according to the pests they affect. An insecticide kills insects. A fungicide kills fungi. A herbicide kills plants. Miticides, bactericides, and molluscicides are also used in the garden or landscape, to control mites, bacteria, and slugs and snails.

Organic Pesticides

Organic pesticides usually come from plant, animal, or mineral sources. *Pyrethrin* is an insecticide that comes from Chrysanthemum flowers—*pyrethroids* are insecticides similar to pyrethrin that have been synthesized in a laboratory. *Bacillus thuringiensis* (*Bt*) is a disease spore that is an excellent control for caterpillars. Diatomaceous earth is a mineral that kills crawling insects by drying out their protective body coating. Many organic pesticides are used by commercial farmers and landscapers because they offer superior efficacy or safety.

Synthetic Pesticides

A synthetic pesticide is manufactured in a laboratory or chemical plant. Synthetic chemistry allows great amounts of a chemical to be manufactured at low cost.

Which One Is Safer?

Most of the synthetic and organic pesticides available to gardeners have been tested and studied at length by scientists to make sure they do not present a great risk to the user or to the environment.

Neither organic nor synthetic pesticides can be considered safe in all circumstances. Just because it comes from a laboratory does not mean a synthetic pesticide is more dangerous than an organic one. Before any product may be sold as a pesticide, it must pass extensive tests devised by researchers and the government. The tests help make sure the pesticide is effective and, when used properly, is unlikely to harm humans, animals, other organisms, or unintended targets.

Using Chemicals in Your Garden

It is important to treat *all* pesticides with caution and to use them properly.

How Do Pesticides Work?

Whether synthetic or organic, most pesticides work by interfering with a chemical process in the pest. The synthetic insecticide *chlorpyrifos* interferes with nerve transmission in an insect. Organic insecticidal soap dissolves pest cell walls so they dry out. If you want to know more about how a pesticide works, visit ExToxNet (http://ace.orst.edu/info/extoxnet/) on the Internet.

Some pesticides are *systemic* and some are *contact* pesticides. A systemic insecticide, like the chemical *acephate*, is drawn into a plant's leaves and is spread throughout the plant's tissue. An insect feeding on any part of the plant is affected by the chemical. A contact insecticide, like horticultural oil, must touch the insect directly in order to affect it.

Read the Label!

The best way to learn how to use a pesticide safely is to read its label. Government rules mandate that specific information must be included on the label. Signal words such as WARNING, CAUTION, and DANGER must be clearly visible. Usage instructions must be plainly written. The active ingredients must be listed (although the tongue-tangling names of some chemicals are intimidating to all but scientists!). Do not use a pesticide until you have read the label completely and understand how to use the product.

Pesticide Safety

Any chemical, whether vinegar from the kitchen, bleach from the laundry, or soap from the bath, can be harmful if it touches the wrong part of your body. Garden chemicals can harm your body as well. When applying pesticides, take special note of whether you are required to wear long pants, gloves, or eye protection. Follow the recommendations exactly each time . . . even if you have used the chemical dozens of times before. Wash your hands after using garden chemicals. If a pesticide is sprayed on your sleeve or pants leg, wash the clothing separately from the rest of your family's clothing.

Storing Pesticides

In general, dry fertilizers and pesticides need to be kept dry, and liquid fertilizers and pesticides should be kept from freezing. Dry chemicals need to be protected from humidity as well as rain. A lockable cabinet is the safest place to store pesticides. Failing that, store yours in a large plastic sealable tub. Label the tub and place it where children and pets cannot get to it.

Labels on pesticide containers tend to become tattered over time. Use a rubber band around the bottle to keep the accordion-style directions neat. If the label comes off a container completely, dispose of the chemical according to the directions below.

Disposing of Pesticides

It is hard to estimate how much of a pesticide you'll need for some jobs. When spraying dormant oil on an **Apple** tree, will it take a quart or a gallon? When spot-spraying weeds, should you mix a pint or a sprayerful? Sometimes you'll have pesticide left over when you are finished with a job, and what should be done with the excess?

Most often the best answer is to save the mixture for a few days and use up what's left. Most pesticides do not deteriorate rapidly and will remain effective for at least a week. If the job at hand doesn't need another application, look for another site. Does a neighbor need the pesticide on his or her lawn? It is not a good idea to simply dump the surplus in one spot; that could lead to surface water contamination.

Using Chemicals in Your Garden

Most homeowner pesticide products are not manufactured in such a concentrated form that a single accident would pose great harm to the environment. Call your county government for specific directions. Small containers of pesticide concentrate can be disposed of by pouring the liquid into a gallon container of kitty litter, wrapping the container several times with newspaper, and putting it out with your garbage. Municipal landfills are designed to keep chemical contaminants out of the environment.

Beneficial Insects

Most gardeners use insecticides with reluctance, knowing that beneficial or harmless insects perish alongside harmful ones. You can minimize the need for insecticides by encouraging beneficial insects to make their home in your garden.

Remember that it takes a few days or weeks for beneficial insects to build their populations enough to control pest insects. One reason we consistently recommend using water to wash aphids from plants is that water does not harm the tiny beneficial wasps that parasitize aphids naturally. Initially allowing a bit of damage to your plants often permits natural controls to strengthen. Common beneficial insects include the following:

- Ladybug: both adults and larvae are voracious aphid eaters.

Ladybug and Nymph

- Green lacewing has larvae that eat spider mites, aphids, and other small insects.

- Ground beetles consume many insects that hide in mulch at night.

- Garden spiders catch whiteflies, ants, beetles, and leafhoppers in their webs.

- Hornets, paper wasps, and yellow jackets may be pests at times, but these insects love to eat leaf-feeding caterpillars.

- Parasitic wasps are tiny insects that are non-threatening to humans. They lay their eggs on aphids and caterpillars, parasitizing and killing them.

The following are some ways to encourage beneficial insects:

- In out-of-the-way corners, plant **Bronze Fennel, Queen Anne's Lace, Dill, Lemon Balm,** and **Parsley.** Do not remove their flowers, since these provide nectar for adult beneficial insects.

- Plant attractive annual flowers such as **Alyssum, Candytuft, Marigolds,** and **Salvias,** which are also alluring to beneficial insects.

- Learn to identify beneficial insects and their immature life stages. A lady beetle larva looks like an orange-and-black alligator. You might think it a pest unless you have learned to recognize it.

- Emphasize ant control in your garden or landscape. Ants tend aphids, scales, and mealybugs, and they interfere with the natural enemies of these pests.

- Use low-impact insecticides such as insecticidal soap, horticultural oil, and **Bt** before reaching for synthetic contact insecticides.

Some gardeners feel they can achieve control of pests by releasing purchased beneficial insects in their landscapes. Researchers caution that it probably doesn't pay to make a mass release. Most will disperse and fly to other yards some distance away. It is usually best to *attract* beneficials rather than *import* them.

Garden and Landscape Chemicals

The following list contains many of the common garden and landscape pesticides available when this book was published. Some may become unavailable in the future, and newer ones may become available. This list is a guide for the reader who wishes to know some of the products from which gardeners can choose. The inclusion or exclusion of a product should *not* be taken as an implication that it is suitable or unsuitable for your use. It is the reader's responsibility to read the label of any product thoroughly to determine if it can be appropriately used to solve a garden problem. Read and follow all label directions.

The use of pest controls is the choice of the individual gardener. In fact, it may not always be necessary to use pesticides to control insects since insects may not cause significant damage to individual plants. In certain cases, you should consider the use of organic pest controls. If you choose to use nonorganic pest controls, it is recommended that you consult your local garden center or Extension Service for correct pest identification and control recommendations. Once you have decided to use a specific pest control product, you must read and follow label directions carefully.

Chemicals

Contact Insecticides (Kill insects by direct contact)

Product Name	Chemical / Active Ingredient
Bayer Advanced™ Azalea, Camellia, Rhododendron Care	disulfoton + 16-8-8 fertilizer
Bayer Advanced™ Grub Control	imidacloprid
Bayer Advanced™ Lawn & Garden	cyfluthrin
Bayer Advanced™ Rose & Flower Insect Killer	imidacloprid + cyfluthrin
Bonide® Cygon	dimethoate
Bonide® Eight	permethrin
Bonide® Lindane	lindane
Bonide® Sevin	carbaryl
Bonide® Systemic Rose and Flower Care	disulfoton (Disyston)
Dexol® Cygon	dimethoate
Diazinon	diazinon
Dursban®	chlorpyrifos
Ferti-Lome® Systemic Rose Food	disulfoton
Green Light Conquest®	permethrin
Malathion	malathion
Ortho Bug-B-Gon Ready Spray®	diazinon
Ortho Bug-B-Gon® Insect Killer	esfenvalerate
Ortho Bug-B-Gon® Multi-purpose Garden Dust	permethrin
Ortho Isotox® Insect Killer Formula I	Acephate + fenbutatin-oxide (hexakis)
Ortho Orthene®	acephate
Ortho Volck® oil	refined horticultural oil, usually used during dormant season
Ortho® Home Defense	bifenthrin
Ortho® Houseplant and Garden Insect Killer	bifenthrin
Ortho-Klor®	chlorpyrifos
Schultz® Houseplant and Garden	pyrethrin
Sevin®	carbaryl
SunSpray® Ultra-Fine Horticultural Oil	refined horticultural oil, usually safe to use in summer

Using Chemicals in Your Garden

Chemicals

Systemic Insecticides (are absorbed by plant tissue; insects are killed when they ingest the tissue or sap)

Product Name	Chemical/Active Ingredient
Bayer Advanced™ Rose & Flower Insect Killer	imidacloprid + cyfluthrin
Bonide® Systemic Rose and Flower Care	disulfoton (Disyston)
Ferti-Lome® Systemic Rose Food	disulfoton
Ortho Isotox® Insect Killer Formula IV	acephate + fenbutatin-oxide (hexakis)
Ortho Orthene®	acephate
Dexol® Cygon	dimethoate

Combination Insecticide and Fungicide Products

Product Name	Chemical/Active Ingredient
Bonide® Bulb Dust	methoxychlor + thiram
Bonide® Insecticide, Miticide, Fungicide	captan + malathion + methoxychlor
Ortho® Home Orchard Spray	captan + malathion + methoxychlor
Ortho® RosePride Orthenex Insect & Disease Control	acephate + triforine + hexakis
Spectracide Immunox® Plus	permethrin + myclobutanil

Contact Miticides (kill mites by direct contact; some are also systemic and kill mites when they ingest sap)

Product Name	Chemical/Active Ingredient
Bonide® Kelthane	dicofol
Green Light® Red Spider Mite Spray	dicofol (Kelthane)
Ortho Isotox® Insect Killer Formula I	acephate + fenbutatin-oxide (hexakis)
Safer® Insecticidal soap	potassium salts of fatty acids
SunSpray® Ultra-Fine Horticultural Oil	refined horticultural oil, usually safe to use in summer
Vendex®	hexakis

Bait Insecticides (are absorbed onto common ant foods; ants are killed when they ingest the bait)

Product Name	Chemical/Active Ingredient
Amdro® Fire Ant Bait	hydramethylnone
Logic®	fenoxycarb
Pennington® Fire Ant Killer Bait	spinosad
Spectracide® Fire Ant Bait	pyriproxyfen
Terro® Ant Killer	borax

Chemicals

Fungicides (inhibit the growth or establishment of fungi on plant tissue)

Product Name	Chemical / Active Ingredient
Armicarb® 100	potassium bicarbonate
Bonide® Captan	captan
Bonide® Fung-onil	chlorothalonil
Captan®	captan
Daconil®	chlorothalonil
FirstStep®	potassium bicarbonate
Green Light Fung-Away®	Bayleton (labeled for lawns)
Green Light® Mancozeb	mancozeb
Green Light® Powdery Mildew Killer	neem oil
Green Light® Systemic Fungicide	Cleary's 3336, Topsin-M
Kaligreen®	potassium bicarbonate
Ortho Funginex®	triforine
Remedy®	potassium bicarbonate
Spectracide Immunox®	myclobutanil

Herbicides (affect the growth of plants)
PRE-EMERGENTS (prevent seed from growing)

Product Name	Chemical / Active Ingredient
Balan®	benefin
Gallery®	isoxaben (selective pre-emergent broadleaf weed control)
Green Light Portrait®	isoxaben
Green Light® Amaze	benefin + oryzalin
Green Light® Betasan	betasan
LESCO™ Pre-M Plus	pendimethalin
Preen® for Groundcovers	EPTC (Eptam)
Preen®	trifluralin
Scotts Halts® Crabgrass Preventer	pendimethalin
Security Purge®	atrazine
Snapshot®	treflan + isoxaben
StaGreen CrabEx™	dithiopyr
StaGreen® Crabgrass Preventer & Fertilizer	treflan + benefin
StaGreen® Crabgrass Preventer	prodiamine
Surflan®	oryzalin
Team®	benefin + trifluralin
Vigoro® Crabgrass Preventer	dithiopyr
XL®	benefin + oryzalin

Using Chemicals in Your Garden

Herbicides (affect the growth of plants)
SELECTIVE POST-EMERGENTS (kill certain plants but not others)

Product Name	Chemical/Active Ingredient
Ace Hardware® Lawn Weed Killer	2,4-D, MCPP, dicamba
BASF Vantage®	sethoxydim
Cyanamide Image®	imazaquin
Dexol® Grass Out	fluazifop
Enforcer Weed Shot®	2,4-D, MCPP, dicamba
Enforcer® Brush Killer	triclopyr
Green Light Wipe-Out®	2,4-D, MCPP, dicamba
Green Light® Bermudagrass Killer	fluazifop
Green Light® Spot Weed Killer	MCPA, MCPP, dicamba
Hi-Yield Basagran®	bentazon (controls broadleaf weeds in a limited number of ornamentals)
Hi-Yield® Post-emergence Weed Killer	sethoxydim
Monsanto Manage®	halosulfuron
Ortho Brush-B-Gon®	triclopyr
Ortho Grass-B-Gon®	fluazifop
Ortho Weed-B-Gon® Chickweed, Clover, & Oxalis Killer	triclopyr
Ortho Weed-B-Gon® Crabgrass Killer	MSMA, CAMA
Ortho Weed-B-Gon® Lawn Weed Killer	2,4-D, MCPP, dicamba
Ortho® Crabgrass Killer Formula II	calcium acid methanearsonate
Safer® Weed Away	2,4-D, MCPP, dicamba
Security Purge®	atrazine
Spectracide Weed Stop®	2,4-D, MCPP, dicamba
Spectracide® Brush Killer	2,4-D, MCPP, dicamba
Vigoro® Lawn Weed Control	2,4-D, MCPP, dicamba

Nonselective Weedkillers (kill all plants but chemicals are soon inactivated in the soil)

Product Name	Chemical/Active Ingredient
Ace Hardware® Grass and Weed Killer	diquat
AgrEvo Finale™	glufosinate
Bonide® KleenUp	glyphosate + acifluorfen
Enforcer Next Day® Fence & Grass Edger	diquat (or cacodylic acid, read label)
Enforcer Next Day® Weed & Grass Killer	diquat (or cacodylic acid, read label)
Enforcer Roots & All™	pelargonic acid, fluazifop, MCPP and 2,4-D
Green Light® Grass & Weed Killer	sodium cacodylate, dimethylarsinic acid

Using Chemicals in Your Garden

Nonselective Weedkillers (continued)

Product Name	Chemical / Active Ingredient
Monsanto RoundUp®	glyphosate
Nature's Glory™ Weed & Grass Killer	acetic acid
Ortho KleerAway®	glyphosate
Safer® SureFire	glyphosate
Spectracide® Grass & Weed Killer	diquat + fluazifop

SOIL STERILANTS (kill all plants in an area for months or years)

Product Name	Chemical / Active Ingredient
Enforcer Next Day® Edger	cacodylic acid
Green Light Com-Pleet®	prometon
Ortho Triox®	glyphosate + imazapyr
Spectracide® Total Vegetation Killer	prometon

Bactericides (inhibit the growth or establishment of bacteria on plant tissue)

Product Name	Chemical / Active Ingredient
Agri-mycin®	streptomycin sulfate
Bonide® Fire Blight Spray	streptomycin sulfate
Bonide® Mancozeb	mancozeb
Lime-sulfur	calcium polysulfide

Molluscicides (kill slugs and snails)

Product Name	Chemical / Active Ingredient
Bonide® Slug, Snail & Sowbug Bait	carbaryl + metaldehyde
Deadline®	metaldehyde
Green Light® Bug + Snail Bait	carbaryl + metaldehyde
Ortho Bug-Geta® Snail & Slug Killer	metaldehyde
Sluggo®	iron phosphate

Growth Regulator

Product Name	Chemical / Active Ingredient
Monterey Florel®	ethepon (prevents fruit, seed formation on trees)

Using Chemicals in Your Garden

Chemicals

Blossom End Rot Spray

Product Name	Chemical/Active Ingredient
Blossom End Rot spray	calcium chloride
Security® Stop-Rot	calcium chloride

Organic Insecticides

Product Name	Chemical/Active Ingredient
Azadirachtin	leaf extracts from the neem tree
Caterpillar Attack®	***Bacillus thuringiensis*** var. ***kurstaki:*** a naturally occurring soil bacteria that is lethal to caterpillars but harmless to mammals and birds.
Diatomaceous earth	fossilized bodies of diatoms (primitive ocean creatures). The fine powder cuts and dries the waxy coating on an insect's body.
Doom®, Milky Spore Disease	***Bacillus popillae:*** a naturally occurring soil bacteria that affects Japanese beetle grubs in the soil.
Green Light Rose Defense®	neem oil
Green Light® BT Worm Killer	***Bacillus thuringiensis*** that has been micro-encapsulated to make it more long-lasting
Green Light® Roach Powder	boric acid
Green Light® Rotenone	rotenone
M-One®	***Bacillus thuringiensis*** var. ***san diego:*** a naturally occurring soil bacteria that is lethal to Colorado potato beetles but harmless to mammals and birds.
Mosquito Dunks®, Mosquito Bits™	***Bacillus thuringiensis*** var. ***israelensis:*** a naturally occurring soil bacteria that is lethal to mosquito larvae but harmless to mammals and birds.
Neem	oil extracted from neem tree nuts
Nematodes	Nematodes are microscopic soil worms. Some types feed on plants and are harmful. Some feed on insects and are helpful to gardeners.
Pyrethrin products	pyrethrin: a chemical contained in chrysanthemum flowers
Rotenone	rotenone: a chemical extracted from the root of the derris plant
Safer® Caterpillar Killer	***Bacillus thuringiensis*** var. ***kurstaki***
Safer® Crawling Insect & Ant Killer	diatomaceous earth
Safer® Insecticidal soap	potassium salts of fatty acids (insecticidal soap)
Safer® Tomato & Vegetable	insecticidal soap + pyrethrin
Security Dipel®	***Bacillus thuringiensis*** var. ***berliner:*** a naturally occurring soil bacteria which is lethal to caterpillars but harmless to mammals and birds
SunSpray® Ultra-Fine Horticultural Oil	a refined petroleum oil that is safe for use on plants

Using Chemicals in Your Garden

Chemicals

Organic Nonselective Herbicides

Product Name	Chemical/Active Ingredient
Nature's Glory™ Weed & Grass Killer	acetic acid

Organic Pre-emergent Herbicides

Product Name	Chemical/Active Ingredient
WOW!®	corn gluten meal

Organic Fungicides

Product Name	Chemical/Active Ingredient
Armicarb® 100	potassium bicarbonate
Copper	copper salts
Dexol® Bordeaux mixture	copper sulfate/hydrated lime mixture (quite poisonous)
FirstStep®	potassium bicarbonate
Garden sulfur	sulfur
Kaligreen®	potassium bicarbonate
Lime-sulfur	calcium polysulfide
Remedy®	potassium bicarbonate
Safer® Powdery Mildew Killer	neem oil

Organic Molluscicides

Product Name	Chemical/Active Ingredient
Slug-Out™	fatty acids of potassium salts (insecticidal soap)

For more information on Organic Pesticides, contact Georgia Organics (770-621-GOGA) or www.georgiaorganics.org.

Other Gardening Products

PermaTill® (expanded shale)
Carolina Stalite
Salisbury, NC
(877)-PERMATILL

Concentrated Landscaper Mix (CLM)
ItSaulNatural Garden Products
Atlanta, GA
(770) 535-1511

Rubber Mulch
Hobo's Rubber Products
Acworth, GA
(770) 974-2985

Shredded rubber in a variety of colors.

Rubber Wholesalers
Cartersville, GA
(706) 334-2331

Recycled rubber for a wide variety of uses.

(Need 1.5 pounds of rubber for every square foot covered 1 inch thick. Prices range from $.40 to $.50 per pound.)

Company Contacts

Bayer™ products
Bayer-Pursell, LLC
(877) 229-3724
http://www.bayeradvanced.com/

Bonide® products
Bonide Products, Inc.
Yorkville, NY
(315) 736-8231
http://www.bonideproducts.com/

Enforcer® products
Enforcer Products, Inc.
Cartersville, GA
(770) 386-0801
http://www.enforcer.com/

Green Light® Company
San Antonio, TX
(210) 494-3481
http://www.greenlightco.com/

Hi-Yield® and Fertilome products
Voluntary Purchasing Group, Inc.
Bonham, TX
(903) 583-5501

Monterey® products
Monterey Chemical Co.
Fresno, CA
(559) 499-2100
http://www.montereychemical.com/

Ortho® products
The Scotts Company,
Columbus, OH
(888) 295-0671
http://www.ortho.com/

Miracle-Gro®
The Scotts Company
Marysville (888) 270-3714
http://www.scottscompany.com/
scottshome.htm

Roundup®
The Scotts Company
Columbus, OH
(888)-295-4120
http://www.roundup.com/

Safer® & Dexol® products
Verdant Brands, Inc.
Bloomington, MN
(612) 703-3300
http://www.verdantbrands.com/

Spectracide® products
Spectrum Brands, Inc.
St. Louis, MO
(800) 332-5553
http://www.spectracide.com/

Armicarb®
Helena Chemicals
Memphis, TN
(901) 748-3200
http://www.helenachemical.com/
sales.htm

FirstStep®
W. A. Cleary Chemical Co.
Somerset, NJ
(800) 524-1662
http://www.clearychemical.com

Remedy®
Gardener's Supply Co.
Burlington, VT
(800) 863-1700
http://www.gardeners.com

Fruit Zone Map

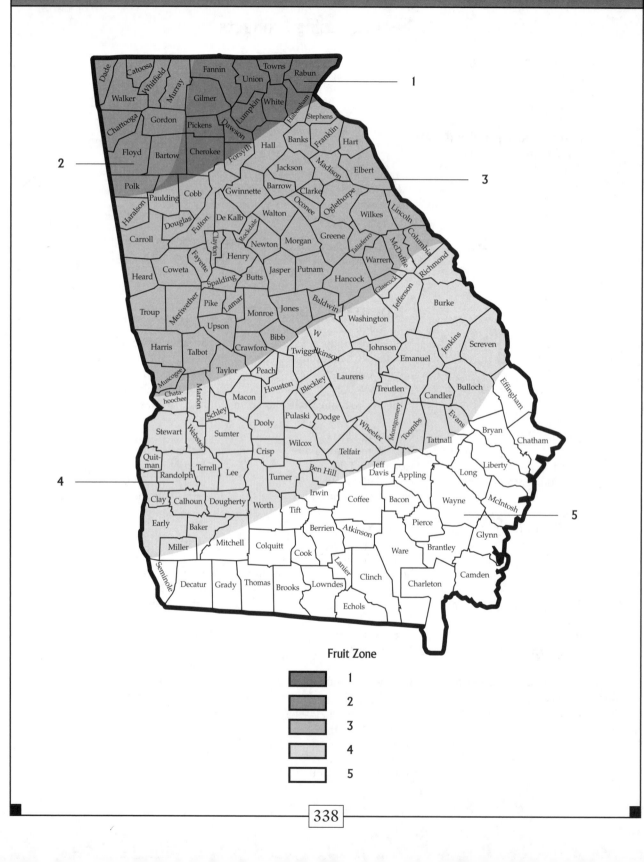

Fruit Zone

- 1
- 2
- 3
- 4
- 5

Small Garden Plan

Small Garden Plan for Georgia
Garden Size: 25 feet wide, 50 feet long

2'	Asparagus [1]
2½'	Cabbage + Lettuce [2]
2½'	Onion Sets [3]
2½'	Parsley or Turnips + Radishes + Carrots + Beets [4]
2½'	Garden Peas + Cabbage [5]
2½'	Bush Green Beans + Broccoli [6]
2½'	Southern Peas + Cauliflower [7]
2½'	Staked Tomatoes + Bell Peppers + Eggplant [8]
3½'	Staked Cucumbers + Pole Beans [9]
2'	Potatoes [10]

Planting dates are for middle Georgia. South Georgia can plant 10 to 14 days earlier in spring. North Georgia should plant two weeks later in spring.

[1] Set crowns in March. Buy one-year-old crowns. Do not harvest the first year.
[2] Set **Cabbage** and **Lettuce** March 1. Set **Leaf Lettuce** between cabbage plants.
[3] Set March 10–20. Set thick; then thin and eat as needed.
[4] Around March 20. Set **Parsley** or **Turnips** thick; mix **Radish** seed sparingly with **Carrots.**
[5] Early and late February for **Peas.** Sow **Peas** as early as the ground can be prepared. **Cabbage** plants will need to be grown, because they will not be available from commercial sources at this time of year.
[6] **Beans** April 1; **Broccoli** July 10.
[7] **Peas** April 1; **Cauliflower** July 10. **Cauliflower** plants will need to be grown from seed.
[8] After frost danger. Prune **Tomatoes** to one stem.
[9] After frost danger. Stake and prune **Cucumbers** and train to climb string or stakes.
[10] Late February.

Vegetable	Recommended Cultivar	Vegetable	Recommended Cultivar
Asparagus	'Jersey Gem'	**Lettuce**	'Bibb'
Bush Green Bean	'Tendergreen'	**Onion Set**	'Granex 33'
Pole Bean	'Kentucky Wonder 191'	**Parsley**	'Extra Curled Dwarf'
Beets	'Detroit Dark Red'	**Garden Pea**	'Little Marvel'
Broccoli	'Green Comet'	**Southern Pea**	'Pinkeye Purple Hull'
Cabbage	'Early Round Dutch'	**Bell Pepper**	'Yolo Wonder L'
Carrots	'Scarlet Nantes'	**Radish**	'Cherry Belle'
Cauliflower	'Snowball Y Improved'	**Staked Tomato**	'Better Boy'
Staked Cucumber	'Dasher II'	**Turnip**	'Purple Top'
Eggplant	'Black Beauty'	**Potato**	'Red Pontiac', 'Kennebec'

Courtesy of Wayne J. McLaurin, Extension Horticulturist, University of Georgia College of Agricultural and Environmental Sciences Cooperative Extension Service.

Fruit Varieties

The following lists were compiled by Dr. Wayne McLaurin, Dr. Butch Feree, Dr. Gerard Krewer, Dr. Stephen Myers, Dr. Scott Nesmith, and Dr. Tom Crocker. All are horticulturists for The University of Georgia College of Agriculture and Environmental Sciences.

Apple Varieties Recommended for Home Use for the Different Zones in Georgia

Variety[1]	Zone[2]	Characteristics[3]	Pollination Code[4]
'Anna'	5	Excellent shaped fruit with blush of red. Ripens mid-June to early July. Very early crisp yellow apple of excellent quality.	A
'Ginger Gold'	1-2-3	Good for fresh eating, sauce, and pies. Ripens late July to early August. Excellent-quality apple.	B
'Gala'	1-2-3	Good for fresh eating or salads. Ripens early August.	B
'Mollie's Delicious'	1-2-3-4	A versatile apple. Good for fresh eating, pies, and sauce. Ripens late July to early August.	B
'Ozark Gold'	1-2-3	Matures in early August. Yellow, russet-free apple of excellent quality.	B
'Red Delicious'	1-2-3-4	Early fall variety ripening in late August to early September. Large, firm, crisp, sweet. Good for fresh eating or salads.	B
'Jonagold'	1-2-3	Ripens early September. Very large, yellow apple with red blush. Very high-quality, sweet, juicy apple.	C
'Golden Delicious'	1-2-3-4	Ripens one or two weeks after 'Red Delicious'. Good producer. Fruit good for sauce, fresh eating, and pies.	C

Apple Varieties Recommended for Home Use
for the Different Zones in Georgia

Variety[1]	Zone[2]	Characteristics[3]	Pollination Code[4]
'Fuji'	1-2-3	Fall variety ripening in early October. Does not color well, but quality is superb. Good for cooking, eating, and baking.	B
'Mutzu'	1-2-3	Ripens early October. Yellow apple of exceptional quality. Crisp and juicy. Slightly tart. All-purpose.	B
'Rome Beauty'	1-2	Ripens early October. Red apple that is primarily grown for baking.	C
'Stayman'	1-2	Ripens early October. Rusty red finish. Superb-quality all-purpose apple that is tart. Fruit cracking a problem when dry period followed by rainy period.	C
'Yates'	1-2-3-4	Late fall variety ripening in late October. Small, dark red. Juicy, mellow, sub-acid. Best keeper.	B
'Granny Smith'	1-2-3-4	Matures in late October to early November. Yellow-green apple of excellent quality. Good all-purpose variety.	B

[1] Listed in order of ripening.

[2] See Fruit Zone Map, p. 338.

[3] Ripening dates for all varieties except 'Anna' are based on averages from Athens, Georgia. Ripening dates for 'Anna' are based on averages from Monticello, Florida.

[4] Varieties followed by a common letter bloom at approximately the same time. Since most apple varieties are self-unfruitful (require pollen from another variety to set fruit), plant two or more varieties that have the same letter so fruit set will result. 'Stayman', 'Mutzu', and 'Jonagold' have sterile pollen and should not be used as a pollen source for other varieties; therefore, plant at least two other varieties with any or all of these varieties.

Fruit Varieties

Pear Varieties Recommended for Home Use for the Different Zones in Georgia

Variety / Hybrids	Zone[1]	Characteristics	Pollination Code[2]
'Orient'	1-2-3-4-5	An excellent pear for most of the state. Resistant to blight. Flesh white; a good keeper. Very large fruit.	B,C
'Carrick'	1-2-3	Excellent for preserving. Trees resistant to blight.	B
'Waite'	1-2-3	An excellent pear for the northern half of the state. Resistant to blight. Pollen sterile. Plant with **'Orient'.**	C
'Kieffer'	1-2-3	Large; skin yellow. Poor quality. Subject to blight in wet years. Good for preserves.	A,B
'Baldwin'	4-5	An excellent pear for the southern half of the state. Resistant to blight.	A
'Magness'	1-2-3-4	Pollen sterile. Plant with **'Orient'.** Fruit excellent quality but not very productive.	C
'Moonglow'	1-2-3-4	Vigorous tree that produces fair to good-quality fruit. Nearly free of grit cells.	C
'Starking Delicious'[3]	1-2-3-4	An excellent pear for the northern half of the state. Fruit excellent quality. Moderately vigorous.	C
'Dawn'	1-2-3-4	Good-quality fruit. Almost entirely free of grit cells. Moderately vigorous tree.	C
'Warren'	3-4-5	Very high-quality fruit. Resistant to blight.	B,C

[1] See Fruit Zone Map, p. 338.

[2] Plant two or more varieties followed by a common letter. Multiple letters by some varieties indicate that they will pollinate other varieties followed by either letter.

[3] **'Starking Delicious'** is considered by many experts to be the same as **'Maxine'.**

Fruit Varieties

Peach Varieties Recommended for Home Use
for the Different Zones in Georgia

Variety	Zone[1]	Flesh Color	Stone Freeness	Harvest[2]
'Junegold'	4,5	Yellow	Cling	47
'Surecrop'	1,2,3	Yellow	Semi-free	43
'Juneprince'	4,5	Yellow	Semi-free	35
'Gala'	3,4	Yellow	Semi-free	33
'Redhaven'	1,2,3	Yellow	Semi-free	28
'Suwanee'	4,5	Yellow	Free	22
'Nectar'	1,2,3	White	Free	22
'Harvester'	3,4	Yellow	Free	21
'Redglobe'	1,2,3,4	Yellow	Free	13
'Georgia Belle'	1,2,3	White	Free	3
'Cresthaven'	1,2,3	Yellow	Free	3
'Redskin'	1,2,3,4,5	Yellow	Free	2
'Jefferson'	1,2,3	Yellow	Free	-3

[1] See Fruit Zone Map, p. 338.

[2] Days ripening before or after (-) **'Elberta'** at Byron, Georgia. The average ripening date for **'Elberta'** at Byron is July 20, but the actual date will vary slightly from season to season. North Georgia (Zones 1, 2, and upper part of 3) is 7 to 10 days later, while Zone 5 to 7 is 7 to 10 days earlier.

Fruit Varieties

Plum Varieties Recommended for Home Use
for the Different Areas in Georgia

Variety	Zone[1]	Characteristics	Peak Harvest[2]
'A.U. Amber'	1-2-3-4-5	Medium size, excellent flavor for season. Red-purple skin with yellow flesh. Partially self-fruitful.	May 31
'Methley'	1-2-3-4-5	Medium size, excellent quality. Dark purple skin; deep red flesh. One of the best varieties. Partially self-fruitful.	June 3
'Rubysweet'	1-2-3-4	Large firm red-fleshed fruit with greenish-red skin; excellent flavor.	June 12
'A.U. Rubrum'	1-2-3-4-5	Red flesh. Fruit medium to large. Maroon skin color.	June 15
'Morris'	1-2-3-4	Fruit medium to large. Reddish-black skin and red flesh. Firm and crisp with good flavor.	June 16
'A.U. Homeside'	1-2-3-4-5	Red skin, amber flesh. Large size. Soft.	June 18
'A.U. Roadside'	1-2-3-4-5	Red flesh. Medium to large fruit size. Very good quality.	June 19
'A.U. Producer'	1-2-3-4-5	Dark red skin with red flesh. Good quality.	June 20
'Byrongold'	1-2-3-4	Medium to large round fruit. Mild to slightly tart flavor. Yellow skin with occasional blush. Firm and keeps well. Good quality.	June 29
'Black Ruby'	1-2-3-4-5	Purple-black with yellow flesh. Upright tree. Good quality.	June 29

[1] See Fruit Zone Map, p. 338.

[2] Average date at Byron, Georgia. (Courtesy Jim Thompson, USDA)

Fruit Varieties

Bunch Grape Varieties Suggested for Backyard Trials in Areas 1 and 2 in Georgia

Varieties for the Upper Piedmont and Mountains in Approximate Order of Ripening

Variety	Area of Georgia	Red Wine	White Wine	Juice, Jelly	Fresh Eating	Comments
'Aurora'	1		X		X	Good wine and fresh eating
'Cascade'	1 and 2	X			X	Performed well in Georgia test
'Ontario'	1				X	Green to amber
'Fredonia'[1]	1 and 2			X	X	Blue fruit
'Delaware'[1]	1 and 2	X		X	X	Reddish fruit, small but sweet, good red wine[2]
'Venus'	1 and 2			X	X	Seedless, blue-black fruit
'Mars'	1 and 2				X	Seedless, blue fruit
'Reliance'[1]	1 and 2				X	Seedless, red fruit
'Buffalo'	1 and 2			X	X	Good yields
'Niagara'	1 and 2			X	X	Golden fruit[2]
'Cayuga White'	1 and 2	X				Vigorous vine
'Concord'	1	X		X	X	Blue fruit ripens unevenly, not recommended

[1] Most outstanding varieties.

[2] Should be grafted on 'Dog Ridge' or similar rootstock for best results.

Bunch Grape Varieties Suggested for Backyard Trials in Area 3 in Georgia

Several hybrid bunch grape varieties have recently been developed which are worthy of trial plantings in middle and south Georgia. All of these have good resistance to Pierce's Disease, the primary limiting factor to bunch grape culture in the middle and southern portion of Georgia. The following table lists suggested varieties for home plantings.

Bunch Grape Varieties for Middle and South Georgia in Approximate Order of Ripening

Variety	Red Wine	White Wine	Juice Jelly	Fresh Eating	Comments
'Blanc Dubois'		X		X	Good white wine
'Orlando Seedless'				X	Small, greenish-yellow fruit
'Suwanee'[1]		X		X	Good fresh and as wine
'Blue Lake'			X		Purple fruit
'Conquistador'[1]	X		X	X	Very good, similar to Concord[2]
'Lake Emerald'		X		X	Greenish fruit
'Black Spanish' ('Lenoir')	X				Dark purple fruit
'Daytona'				X	Low yield but good eating, pink fruit[2]

[1] Most outstanding varieties.

[2] Graft on **'Tampa'**, **'Lake Emerald'**, **'Florilush'**, or **'Dog Ridge'** rootstock.

Fruit Varieties

Muscadine Varieties Recommended for Home Use for the Different Zones in Georgia

Variety	Flower Type[2]	Size	Color	Main Uses	Comments
'Carlos'[1]	P.F.	Medium	Bronze	Juice, wine	Productive
'Cowart'	P.F.	Large	Black	Fresh eating	Good flavor
'Dixie'	P.F.	Medium	Bronze	Juice, wine	Good cold tolerance
'Fry'[1]	F.	V. large	Bronze	Fresh eating	Fruit rot and winter injury a problem; excellent flavor
'Higgins'	F.	Large	Bronze-pink	Fresh eating	Mild flavor; late season
'Jumbo'	F.	V. large	Black	Fresh eating	Low sugar content
'Loomis'[1]	F.	Med-large	Black	Fresh eating	Excellent flavor
'Magnolia'	P.F.	Medium	Bronze	Juice, wine	Good flavor; good winter hardiness
'Nesbitt'[1]	P.F.	V. large	Black	Fresh eating	Good cold tolerance
'Noble'[1]	P.F.	Small	Black	Juice, wine	Productive
'Scuppernong'	F.	Medium	Bronze	Wine, fresh eating	Very old variety; low yields
'Summit'[1]	F.	Large	Bronze-pink	Fresh eating	Good winter hardiness; more disease-resistant than 'Fry'
'Tara'[1]	P.F.	Large	Bronze	Fresh eating	Fairly good flavor
'Triumph'[1]	P.F.	Med-large	Bronze-pink	Fresh eating	Early season

[1] Most outstanding varieties

[2] P.F. = Perfect flowered (produces pollen and fruit)   F. = Female flowered (produces fruit only)

Fruit Varieties

Rabbiteye Blueberries

The most important things to remember about starting **Rabbiteye Blueberries** is to plant more than one variety for cross-pollination. Cross-pollination is necessary for fruit set.

Early Season	Mid-Season	Late Season
'Austin'	'Bluebelle'	'Baldwin'
'Brightwell'	'Briteblue'	'Centurion'
'Climax'	'Chaucer'	'Choice'
'Premier'	'Powderblue'	'Delite'
'Woodard'	'Tifblue'	

'Climax', 'Chaucer', 'Choice', and **'Woodard'** are not suggested for mountain areas because they bloom early. **'Austin', 'Climax',** and **'Premier'** are the earliest ripening rabbiteye varieties. To lengthen your harvest season, select one or more of these varieties, and one or more of the other varieties. **'Baldwin', 'Centurion',** and **'Delite'** are the latest maturing Rabbiteye varieties. With early, mid-season, and late varieties, you should enjoy fresh blueberries for six weeks.

'Woodard' is a good berry for fresh eating but develops a tough skin when frozen. **'Brightwell', 'Centurion', 'Tifblue',** and **'Powderblue'** are generally the most resistant to spring freeze.

Fig Varieties for Georgia

Variety	Color of Fruit	Size	Quality of Fruit	
			For Fresh Use	For Preserving
'Brown Turkey'	Bronze	Medium	Good	Excellent
'Celeste'	Lt. brown to violet	Small	Very good	Excellent
'Hunt'	Dull bronze with white specks	Small to medium	Good	Excellent
'Kadota'	Bright greenish yellow	Small to medium	Fair	Excellent
'LSU Purple'	Reddish to dark purple	Medium	Good	New variety– unknown
'Magnolia'	Bronze with white flecks	Medium	Fair	Excellent

Fruit Varieties

Strawberry Varieties by Season and Areas of Adaptability

Variety	Early	Mid-Season	Late
'Florida 90'	S[1]		
'Sunrise'	M,N		
'Earliglow'	M,N		
'Cardinal'		M,N	
'Surecrop'		M,N	
'Tioga'		M	
'Apollo'[2]		M,N	
'Albritton'			M
'Delite'			M,N

[1] S = South Georgia, M = Middle Georgia, N = Piedmont and North Georgia.

[2] 'Apollo' should be planted with another variety to ensure fruit set. Other varieties can be planted alone.

Fruit Varieties

Pecan Varieties for Homegrowers

Variety	Size	Kernel Quality	Scab Resistance	Productivity
'Stuart'	Large	Excellent	Resistant	Very good
'Elliott'	Small	Good	Very resistant	Very good
'Curtis'	Small	Excellent	Very resistant	Very good
'Gloria Grande'	Large	Excellent	Resistant	Very good
'Sumner'	Large	Excellent	Resistant	Very good

Recommended Raspberry Varieties:

- 'Heritage' (for northern third of Georgia)
- 'Redwing' (for northern third of Georgia)
- 'Dormanred' (a trailing variety; good for entire state)

Recommended Blackberry Varieties:

- 'Navaho' (erect)
- 'Cherokee' (erect)
- 'Cheyenne' (erect)
- 'Gem' (trailing)
- 'Black Satin' (trailing)
- 'Kiowa' (trailing)

Bibliography

Annuals, Perennials, Vines, Grasses, and Ground Covers

Armitage, Allan. *Armitage's Garden Perennials.* Portland, OR: Timber Press, 2000.

Armitage, Allan. *Herbaceous Perennial Plants.* 2nd edition. Champaign, IL: Stipes Publishing, 1997.

Cutler, Karan, ed. *Starting from Seed.* Brooklyn, NY: Brooklyn Botanic Garden, 1998.

Greenlee, John. *The Encyclopedia of Ornamental Grasses.* Emmaus, PA: Rodale Press, 1992.

Grey-Wilson, Christopher, and Victoria Matthews. *Gardening on Walls.* London: Collins Publishers, 1983.

Harper, Pamela. *Perennials: How to Select, Grow, and Enjoy.* Scottdale, PA: H P Books, 1985.

Hastings, Don. *Gardening in the South: Flowers, Vines, and Houseplants.* Dallas, TX: Taylor Publishing, 1991.

Howells, John. *A Guide to Clematis.* London: Bookmark Ltd., 1990.

Jones, Samuel, and Leonard Foote. *Gardening with Native Wild Flowers.* Portland, OR: Timber Press, 1997.

Loewer, Peter. *Tough Plants for Tough Places.* Emmaus, PA: Rodale Press, 1996.

Mickel, John. *Ferns for American Gardens.* New York, NY: Macmillan Publishing, 1997.

Still, Steven. *Manual of Herbaceous Ornamental Plants.* Champaign, IL: Stipes Publishing, 1993.

Summit, Ginger. *Gourds in Your Garden.* Los Altos, CA: Hillway Press, 1998.

Vengris, Jonas, and William A. **Torello.** *Lawns.* Fresno, CA: Thomson Publications, 1982.

Welch, William C., and Greg Grant. *The Southern Heirloom Garden.* Dallas, TX: Taylor Publishing, 1995.

Wilson, Jim, *Bulletproof Flowers for the South.* Dallas, TX: Taylor Publishing, 1999.

Winterrowd, Wayne. *Annuals for Connoisseurs.* New York, NY: Prentice Hall, 1992.

Bulbs

Heath, Brent, and Becky Heath. *Daffodils for American Gardens.* Washington, DC: Elliott & Clark Publishing, 1995.

Ogden, **Scott.** *Garden Bulbs for the South.* Dallas, TX: Taylor Publishing, 1994.

Edibles

Chambers, David, and Lucinda Mays. *Vegetable Gardening.* New York, NY: Pantheon Books, Knopf Publishing Group, 1994.

Hastings, Don. *Gardening in the South with Don Hastings: Vegetables and Fruits.* Dallas, TX: Taylor Publishing, 1987.

McLaurin, Wayne, and Sylvia McLaurin. *Herbs for Southern Gardens.* Available from the University of Georgia Agricultural Business office (706-542-8999), 1999.

Swenson, Allan. *Fruit Trees for the Home Gardener.* New York, NY: Lyons & Burford, 1994.

Weaver, William. *Heirloom Vegetable Gardening.* New York, NY: Henry Holt & Co., 1997.

Bibliography

Lawns

Murphy, Tim, et al. *Weeds of Southern Turfgrasses.* Available from the University of Georgia Agricultural Business office (706-542-8999), 1993.

Schultz, Warren. *A Man's Turf: The Perfect Lawn.* New York: Clarkson Potter Publishers, 1999.

Trees, Shrubs, and Roses

Brown, Claude, and L. Katherine Kirkman. *Trees of Georgia and Adjacent States.* Portland, OR: Timber Press, 2000.

Dirr, Michael. *Dirr's Hardy Trees and Shrubs.* Portland, OR: Timber Press, 1997.

Dirr, Michael. *Manual of Woody Landscape Plants.* Champaign, IL: Stipes Publishing, 1998.

Gardiner, J.M. *Magnolias.* Chester, CT: Globe Pequot Press, 1989.

Gates, Galen, et al. *Shrubs and Vines.* New York: Pantheon Books, 1994.

Halfacre, R. Gordon, and Anne R. Shawcroft. *Landscape Plants of the Southeast.* Raleigh, NC: Sparks Press, 1979.

Hastings, Don. *Gardening in the South: Trees, Shrubs and Lawns.* Dallas, TX: Taylor Publishing, 1987.

Tripp, Kim, and J.C. Raulston. *The Year in Trees.* Portland, OR: Timber Press, 1995.

Vertrees, J.D. *Japanese Maples.* Portland, OR: Timber Press, 2001.

Welch, William C. *Antique Roses for the South.* Dallas, TX: Taylor Publishing, 1990.

General Bibliography

Ajilvsgi, Geyata. *Butterfly Gardening for the South.* Dallas, TX: Taylor Publishing, 1991.

Aronovits, Avis, and Brencie Werner. *Gardening 'Round Atlanta.* Atlanta, GA: Eldorado Publishing, 1996.

Bender, Steve, and Felder Rushing. *Passalong Plants.* Chapel Hill, NC: The University of North Carolina Press, 1993.

Bender, Steve, et al. *The Southern Living Garden Book.* Birmingham, AL: Oxmoor House, 1998.

Harper, Pamela. *Time-Tested Plants.* Portland, OR: Timber Press, 2000.

Hipps, Carol Bishop. *In a Southern Garden.* New York, NY: Macmillan Publishing, 1995.

Lawrence, Elizabeth. *A Southern Garden.* Chapel Hill, NC: University of North Carolina Press, 1991.

Lawson-Hall, Toni, and Brian Rothera. *Hydrangeas.* Portland, OR: Timber Press, 1995.

McDonald, Elvin. *100 Orchids for the American Gardener.* New York, NY: Workman Publishing, 1998.

Olkowski, William, and Sheila Daar. *Common Sense Pest Control.* Newtown, CT: Taunton Press, 1991.

Overy, Angela. *Sex in Your Garden.* Golden, CO: Fulcrum Publishing, 1997.

Tekulsky, Matthew. *The Butterfly Garden.* Boston, MA: Harvard Common Press, 1986.

Wasowski, Sally. *Gardening with Native Plants of the South.* Dallas, TX: Taylor Publishing, 1994.

Botanical Gardens

Atlanta Botanical Garden
Piedmont Park at The Prado
Atlanta, Georgia 30357
(404) 876-5859
http://www.atlantabotanicalgarden.org

The Atlanta Botanical Garden is a lush oasis in the heart of Midtown Atlanta. The ABG features fifteen acres of landscaped gardens, a conservatory that houses endangered tropical and desert plants from around the world, and a fifteen-acre hardwood forest with walking trails. This is an easily accessible gardening resource in the midst of urban Atlanta.

Atlanta History Center
130 West Paces Ferry Road, NW
Atlanta, Georgia 30305
(404) 814-4000
http://www.atlhist.org

On the grounds of the Atlanta History Center, visitors can experience thirty-two acres of gardens, woodlands, and nature trails that show the horticultural history of the Atlanta region. Seven distinct gardens feature a variety of gardening styles from native plantings to formal landscaping with boxwoods and classical statuary. A Garden for Peace has been installed as part of an international effort to promote world peace.

Callaway Gardens
P.O. Box 2000
Pine Mountain, Georgia 31822-2000
(800) 225-5292
http://www.callawaygardens.com

Located seventy miles southwest of Atlanta and thirty miles north of Columbus, Callaway Gardens is a manmade landscape in a unique natural setting. It was conceived by its creators Cason Callaway and his wife Virginia as a place for visitors to discover natural beauty. Today, Callaway Gardens features the largest glass-enclosed butterfly conservatory in North America, and Mr. Cason's Vegetable Garden showcases Southern vegetables and annual flower trial gardens. In addition, the Sibley Horticulture Center showcases a year-round floral display that integrates indoor and outdoor plant settings. More than a million people visit the 1500 acres of Callaway Gardens each year.

Fernbank Museum of Natural History
767 Clifton Road, NE
Atlanta, Georgia 30307
(404) 929-6300
http://www.fernbank.edu/museum

Fernbank Science Center
156 Heaton Park Drive, NE
Atlanta, Georgia 30307-1398
(404) 378-4311
http://fsc.fernbank.edu

The grounds of the Fernbank Museum of Natural History and Fernbank Science Center feature two distinct garden areas. Adjacent to the Fernbank Science Center is the Fernbank Forest. For many years visitors have walked through the sixty-five-acre woodland, a primeval Piedmont forest containing one-and-a-half miles of paved trail lined with signs identifying various specimens. The grounds of the Fernbank Museum of Natural History feature the Stanton Rose Garden. Visitors there will see 1300 roses, including All-America Rose Selections test plants.

Georgia Southern Botanical Garden

Georgia Southern University
1211 Fair Road (State Highway 67)
Statesboro, Georgia 30460
(912) 871-1114
http://www2.gasou.edu/garden

The Georgia Southern Botanical Garden is a ten-acre site located two blocks from the campus of Georgia Southern University. The garden features native plants of Georgia, particularly those of the Coastal Plain. Various gardens include a Magnolia/ Holly allee, a butterfly border, and an arboretum. Also within the botanical garden are a children's vegetable garden, nature trails, and seven original farm structures.

Massee Lane Gardens

One Massee Lane
Fort Valley, Georgia 31030
(912) 967-2358
http://www.peach.public.lib.ga.us/ACS

Beginning with the planting of one Camellia plant in 1936, Massee Lane Gardens now serves as the headquarters for the American Camellia Society. Located on the site of a former peach farm dating from the early 1900s, the garden also features an education museum, a rose garden, and a Japanese garden.

Perimeter College Botanical Garden

3251 Panthersville Road
Decatur, Georgia 30034
(404) 244-5090
http://www.gpc.peachnet.edu/~ddonald/botgard/george3.htm

The Perimeter College Botanical Garden focuses exclusively on Georgia native plants, and includes the largest collection of native plants in the state. Dozens of native ferns are featured along a shaded forest path. Approximately 1500 sun- and shade-loving native plants can be seen at the Perimeter College South Campus.

Southeastern Flower Show

(404) 888-5638
http://www.flowershow.org

The Southeastern Flower Show benefits the Atlanta Botanical Garden as well as amateur and expert gardeners throughout the South. Held in the later part of February every year, the show features dozens of gardens presented by top garden designers, judged horticultural classes, and an extensive vendors market. Seminars and workshops by gardening experts make this a must-go event for Georgia gardeners.

State Botanical Garden of Georgia

2450 South Milledge Avenue
Athens, Georgia 30602
(706) 542-1244
http://www.uga.edu/~botgarden

The State Botanical Garden of Georgia is a 313-acre preserve under the direction of The University of Georgia. The garden has five miles of nature trails, an International Garden, and a three-story tropical conservatory. The State Botanical Garden holds educational programs all year long and has a growing and active patrons organization.

Educational and Professional Organizations

Extension Service
http://www.ces.uga.edu

Local phone numbers can be found under your county government phone listings. The University of Georgia Cooperative Extension Service is an educational organization sponsored by the University of Georgia and local county governments. All Extension Service offices have staff members who specialize in agriculture/horticulture, home environment, and youth development. Offices offer free educational pamphlets and advice, and many publications are available for download at the Extension Service Web site.

The Garden Club of Georgia
(706) 227-5369
http://www.uga.edu/gardenclub

A statewide organization of gardeners dedicated to inspiring beautification, conservation, and gardening education in Georgia.

Georgia Environmental Monitoring Network
http://www.georgiaweather.net

This unit of The University of Georgia maintains dozens of weather monitoring sites scattered throughout the state. Data from each site is uploaded daily to the Internet, where visitors can track historical and current rainfall amounts, soil temperatures, air temperatures, and other climatic conditions. Very handy for settling arguments about how "bad" the weather was in the past.

Georgia Forestry Commission
(800) GA-TREES
http://www.gfc.state.ga.us

Educates citizens about the importance of Georgia timber and forests. Supplies tree seedlings in bulk at low cost to citizens.

Georgia Green Industry Association
(888) GET-GGIA
http://www.ggia.org

A statewide organization of landscape and nursery companies that promotes professionalism in the industry. Sponsor of the Georgia Certified Landscape Professional and Georgia Certified Nursery Professional programs.

Georgia Native Plant Society
(770) 343-6000
http://www.gnps.org

An organization of gardeners interested in learning more about the care and culture of native plants. Monthly meetings are free and open to the public.

Georgia Organics
770-621-GOGA
http://www.georgiaorganics.org

An organization of gardeners interested in learning more about gardening organically.

Georgia Perennial Plant Association
(404) 237-8071
http://www.georgiaperennial.org

An organization of gardeners interested in learning more about the care and culture of perennial plants. Monthly meetings are free and open to the public.

Metro Atlanta Landscape & Turf Association
(770) 732-9832
http://www.malta-inc.org

An organization of Atlanta landscape companies and associated professionals. Publishes "The Landscape Source," a free booklet listing members and their areas of expertise.

Plant Index

Plant Index

Plant Index

Plant Index

Plant Index

Plant Index

Plant Index

Plant Index

Plant Index

Plant Index

Gardening Index

About the Authors

Walter Reeves and Erica Glasener

Erica Glasener is a horticulturist and garden designer living in Atlanta, Georgia. She is the award-winning host of "A Gardener's Diary" on HGTV. Glasener is the former director of education for the Scott Arboretum of Swarthmore College in Swarthmore, Pennsylvania. In addition, she serves as a contributing editor to *Fine Gardening Magazine* and writes a bi-weekly column on garden design for *The Atlanta Journal-Constitution*. She has written numerous articles for *The New York Times*, *The Farmer's Almanac*, and *Atlanta* magazine. Erica is the co-author of the *Georgia Gardener's Guide* and *My Georgia Garden: A Gardener's Journal*, both published by Cool Springs Press.

Walter Reeves is a former DeKalb County Extension Agent living in Atlanta, Georgia. Best known to Atlanta-area listeners as the radio host of "The Lawn and Garden Show with Walter Reeves," he also reaches gardeners through his weekly columns in *The Atlanta Journal-Constitution*. Walter helps gardeners throughout the state as the host of "Gardening in Georgia," shown weekly on Georgia Public Television. When answering gardeners' questions, the Fayette County native often draws upon his years of gardening experience acquired while growing up on his family's farm. Walter is the co-author of the *Georgia Gardener's Guide* and *My Georgia Garden: A Gardener's Journal*, both published by Cool Springs Press.